Managing Innovation, Design and Creativity

Bettina von Stamm
London Business School

WILEY

Copyright © 2003 John Wiley & Sons Ltd, The Atrium, Southern Gate, Chichester,
West Sussex PO19 8SQ, England

Telephone   (+44) 1243 779777

Email (for orders and customer service enquiries): cs-books@wiley.co.uk
Visit our Home Page on www.wileyeurope.com or www.wiley.com

Reprinted May 2004, January 2005, June 2005

This publication is designed to provide accurate and authoritative information in regard to the subject matter
covered. It is sold on the understanding that the Publisher is not engaged in rendering professional services. If
professional advice or other expert assistance is required, the services of a competent professional should be sought.

Other Wiley Editorial Offices

John Wiley & Sons Inc., 111 River Street, Hoboken, NJ 07030, USA

Jossey-Bass, 989 Market Street, San Francisco, CA 94103-1741, USA

Wiley-VCH Verlag GmbH, Boschstr. 12, D-69469 Weinheim, Germany

John Wiley & Sons Australia Ltd, 33 Park Road, Milton, Queensland 4064, Australia

John Wiley & Sons (Asia) Pte Ltd, 2 Clementi Loop #02-01, Jin Xing Distripark, Singapore 129809

John Wiley & Sons Canada Ltd, 22 Worcester Road, Etobicoke, Ontario, Canada M9W 1L1

Wiley also publishes its books in a variety of electronic formats. Some content that
appears in print may not be available in electronic books.

Library of Congress Cataloging-in-Publication Data

Von Stamm, Bettina.
     Managing innovation / by Bettina von Stamm.
          p. cm.
     Includes bibliographical references and index.
     ISBN 0-470-84708-5 (pbk. : alk. paper)
       1. Technological innovations. 2. Creative ability in business. 3.Technological
     innovations – Management. 4. Creative ability in business – Case studies. I. Title.

HD45.V65 2003
658'.514 – dc21

                                                   2003043292

British Library Cataloguing in Publication Data

A catalogue record for this book is available from the British Library

ISBN 10: 0-470-84708-5 (P/B)
ISBN 13: 978-0-470-84708-4 (P/B)

Typeset in 9.5/13 pt Gill Sans Light by Laserwords Private Limited, Chennai, India.
Printed and bound in Great Britain by Antony Rowe Ltd, Chippenham, Wiltshire.
This book is printed on acid-free paper responsibly manufactured from sustainable forestry
in which at least two trees are planted for each one used for paper production.

Contents

Introduction

If you say 'innovation and creativity are vital to growth', nine out of ten people agree with the statement. But when you ask if people know how to practice and inspire creativity in their day to day life, nine out of ten people say no.

Kris Murrin, co-founder ?WhatIf!

'Innovation', 'creativity' and 'design' are surely amongst the most frequently used words in business today, not least because excelling in these areas is widely acknowledged to be associated with business success. But while most managers agree that innovation and creativity are essential to assuring long-term success, many struggle with realizing it in their businesses, and translating it into everyday reality.

This is partly due to the variety of meanings associated with these terms, and partly due to a gap in current business education where subjects are generally taught in clearly defined and distinctive disciplines. However, if innovation, design and creativity are to play to their full potential, they cannot be taught in such a segregated way. Innovation, design and creativity are disciplines that span boundaries, and need to be understood in an integrated manner. Creating an innovative organization requires more than understanding the design of an efficient new product development process, more than how to write innovation into a company's strategy document, and more than maintaining an active research and development department. Innovation, design and creativity need to permeate every aspect of an organization. It is of the uttermost important to be aware that creating a more innovative organization is much more about changing one's frame of mind than it is about a changing the company's processes or vision statement. Innovation, design and creativity have to do with curiosity, a taste for experimentation, a dissatisfaction with the status quo, and the desire to continuously improve things.

To help understand the various components that make for an innovative organization, and the mindset that is required to facilitate it, this book combines a set of ten case studies with chapters on issues relevant to innovation such as cultural issues, teams, knowledge management and branding. The aim of this book is to provide managers and students with insights that help them create sustainably innovative organizations – rather than understand how to create a 'one-off' innovative product or service. The insights will help the reader to appreciate and understand how their organization can gain most from innovation,

> **Preconceptions...**
> - Innovation is about technology
> - Innovation is something our R&D people do
> - Innovation cannot be managed
> - Design is just about styling
> - Nicely designed things don't work
> - Design is expensive
> - Creativity cannot be taught
> - Creative people are weird and disorganized
> - Creative ideas come out of the blue

design and creativity, and more importantly how to translate these buzzwords into action and fill them with life.

The ten case studies are:

1. The BBC's *Walking with Dinosaurs* – selling and delivering an innovative television series

2. ihavemoved.com – financing and strategy development for an internet company

3. Black & Decker's 'Quattro' – design selection and development of a multi-purpose power tool

4.   The Lotus Elise – innovating through prototypes and collaboration

5.   'Saquinavir' by Roche – understanding industry context

6.   Dumfries Recycling's 'Plaswood' – understanding context and constraints for developing 'green' products

7.   GKN's Light Composite Joint Disc – radical innovation in large organizations

8.   The Bank of Scotland's 'Shared Appreciation Mortgage' – defining meaning of success and failure and dealing with multiple audiences

9.   John McAslan & Partner – how to use the built environment to support company culture

10.   The TTP Group – the example of a company with an innovation culture

Supplementary chapters explore a number of subject areas that are pertinent to understanding innovation, creativity and design:

- What are innovation, creativity and design?
- How to organize for the development of new products?
- What are the implications of globalization?
- Strategy – emergent or planned?
- What role do brands play in innovation?
- How to approach market research?
- What is it about teams?
- What role do prototypes play?
- Why and how to collaborate for innovation?
- What are the effects of industry and cultural context?
- What role do knowledge management and internal networks play?
- Green design – clean environment or clean conscience?
- What to do about intellectual property?
- What is the role of venture capitalists and business angels?
- How to infuse innovation?
- How to innovate in the service industry?
- Success or failure – a question of definition?
- What is architecture's contribution to a company's culture?
- How and when to use external consultants?
- What are the characteristics of an innovative organization?

The book can be used as a reader by managers who are interested in getting a better grasp of innovation as well as a core text for business education in innovation. Matrices that set out how and in what context the cases can be used are shown in Appendix I.

Acknowledgements

I would like to thank the Design Council in general for sponsoring the writing of the case studies, and Lesley Morris in particular for her ongoing support and involvement. I would also like to thank participants from the case study companies who have generously given their time, and without whom this book would not have been possible.

As, in my view, the understanding of innovation requires insights into a great many subject areas – and I would never claim to be an expert in all of them – I have solicited friends and colleagues on particular chapters. I would like to thank, in particular, Mario Gagliardi for his insights on design-related issues, and his comments in general and the patience to read (almost) the entire book; Lance Batchelor for making me rethink the structure for Chapter 6; Wendy Batchelor for providing some feedback on the chapter on intellectual property; Beatrice K. Otto for comments on the sustainability chapter; and finally, Tim Ambler on his comments and input on the chapters on branding and market research.

And finally, I would like to say a *big* thank you to the good spirits that ensure that my domestic life does not descend into chaos while I enjoy myself writing and working: Sally (Girling), Kathleen and Dick (Mallows), Janet (Parker) and Mike (Horn). What would I do without you?

1 What are Innovation, Creativity and Design?

This chapter provides an introduction to innovation, design and creativity. It sets out the meaning of these words in the context of this book, how they fit together, and introduces some useful frameworks for the subjects.

INNOVATION

New opinions are always suspected and usually opposed, without any other reason but because they are not already common.

John Locke

Innovation, just as many other things in management and life, means different things to different people. What does innovation mean in the context of this book?

Often 'creativity' and 'innovation' are used interchangeably. However, there are fundamental differences. In fact, creativity is an essential building block for innovation. This is reflected in the now widely accepted definition of innovation equalling creativity plus (successful) implementation. Creativity alone, to come up with ideas, is not enough. To reap the benefits one needs to do something with it – history tells many tales of great inventors who were not able to reap the benefits of their labour, think of the x-ray scanner, invented by EMI but made a commercial success by General Electric, or VCRs invented by Ampex/Sony but successfully commercialized by Matsushita. Why might that be? Let's take a closer look at the two components of innovation: creativity and implementation.

Implementation – putting ideas into practice – is made up of three aspects: idea selection, development, and

> ### Xerox's Palo Alto Research Center (PARC)
>
> In the flagship research division of the Xerox Corporation, set up in 1970, many aspects of modern computing were invented, including the Graphical User Interface (GUI), the mouse, the laser printer and the desk top computer. Invented but not commercialized. For example, both the GUI and the mouse were commercialized first by Apple then by Microsoft. It seems that senior management's narrow focus on Xerox's core business – photocopiers – prevented them from having the vision to pursue anything that was not directly related to copiers, leaving it to others to commercialize the great inventions coming out of PARC, and gain the benefits.

commercialization, and of course creativity is needed here too. What do organizations need to achieve implementation? They need processes, procedures and structures that allow the timely and effective execution of projects; implementation is about team effort. But even companies that have all the right processes, procedures and structures in place are often unable to be innovative.

Taking a closer look at creativity might help to explain why that might be. If implementation is putting an idea into practice, creativity is coming up with the idea in the first place. Creativity is an essential part of innovation, it is the point of departure. One of the big concerns for many companies is therefore how to generate more and better ideas – how to become more creative. Consider a few things about creativity:

- As opposed to commonly held opinion, creativity, the act of coming up with an idea, is an inherently individual act – it is the development of an idea and the implementation where the team is needed.

- Creativity has little to do with the 'flash of inspiration out of the blue'. To quote John Hunt, Visiting Professor for Organizational Behaviour at London Business School, 'Creativity is not something where someone who has never worked in that field suddenly gets this marvellous idea. Creativity is relating a concept to a particular body of knowledge. The existing body of knowledge is as vital as the novel idea and really creative people spend years and years acquiring and refining their knowledge base – be it music, mathematics, arts, sculpture or design.'[1]

- While there is generally some debate as to whether creativity is for the selected few or everyone, while certain people are more creative on their own accord than others, creativity can be stimulated and supported through training, and by creating the right work environment and atmosphere. In her research Harvard Business School Professor Teresa Amabile has identified certain characteristics that support creativity in the workplace (see Figure 1.1).

- However, creativity cannot be ordered, it relies much more on intrinsic motivation, on people being enthusiastic, inspired and knowledgeable.

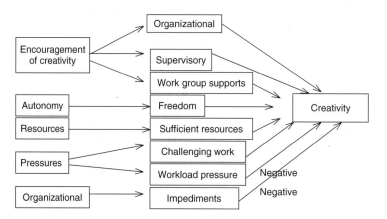

In her model Amabile has identified five environmental components that affect creativity:

- Encouragement of creativity (which encompasses open information flow and support for new ideas at all levels of the organization, from top management, through immediate supervisors, to work groups);
- Autonomy or freedom (autonomy in the day-to-day conduct of work; a sense of individual ownership of and control over work);
- Resources (the materials, information, and general resources available for work);
- Pressures (including both positive challenge and negative workload pressure);
- Organizational impediments to creativity (including conservatism and internal strife).

The components fall into two categories, they are either stimulants to creativity (tapped by scales assessing organizational and supervisory encouragement, work group support, sufficient resources, and challenging work), or obstacles to creativity (tapped by scales assessing organizational impediments and workload pressure).

Figure 1.1   Model for Assessing the Climate for Creativity (KEYS) (Amabile *et al.* 1996) (reproduced by permission of Academy of Management Journal)

- Finally, companies tend to require hard facts but creativity and innovation are often based on intuition. And by the way, as early as the mid-80s authors such as Peters and Waterman (*In Search of Excellence*) suggested that the modern American manager's over-dependence on analytic thought and quantitative analysis was a principal cause for the loss of its worldwide pre-eminence (as reflected in stagnating productivity, ageing and obsolete machinery, and inferior but more expensive products).

So implementation is about being organized and about using the methodological and systematic approach of a 'hare brain' (see Box 1.1). It needs to be structured and cannot be left to chance. Time is of the essence – you need to be fast. Creativity is less straightforward than implementation, it is not about a new process or establishing a new structure. To be creative people have to think differently. To be innovative people have to behave differently. And to be successful organizations have to employ people that think and behave differently. This is why I often define innovation as 'a frame of mind'. Creativity is about being different, thinking laterally, making new connections. It is about allowing the 'tortoise mind' to work. Creativity can be encouraged, not forced. Time is of the essence too, but in as much as creativity cannot be rushed, you need to allow it. Organizations that want to embrace innovation therefore need to find ways of reconciling the tension that lies in the juxtaposition of creativity and implementation.

BOX 1.1   Summary extracts from Claxton's *Hare Brain, Tortoise Mind*

In his book *Hare Brain, Tortoise Mind*, Guy Claxton makes some interesting observations about the way we think that are relevant to understanding creativity and innovation. The first concerns different modes of responding to a situation. Whereas most of the other models aim to put people in boxes, Claxton goes a step back and suggests that we all are capable of two different ways of responding to a situation. The second explains how people's unconscious exerts an influence in the classification of a new situation.

Modes of response

Claxton describes three different modes of how people respond to a situation. The first is spontaneous and immediate. The person does not think consciously about the situation and a possible response. Claxton classifies such a response as 'instinct'. An example would be removing your hand when it is put accidentally on a hot hob. No one would think whether the sensation is pleasant or not, the hand would be removed as quickly as possible. Instinctive reactions can generally be observed when reacting to a threat where there might not be sufficient time to assess the situation if it is to be survived.

The second mode is based on 'conscious, deliberate, purposeful thinking'. Claxton calls this the 'd-mode' or the 'hare mode'.[1] The following is an extract from the traits he has identified for the d-mode:

- D-mode is much more interested in finding answers and solutions than in examining the question.
- D-mode treats perception as unproblematic.
- D-mode values explanation over observation.
- D-mode seeks and prefers clarity, and neither likes nor values confusion.
- D-mode relies on language that appears to be literal and explicit.
- D-mode works with concepts and generalizations.

It seems that one could replace 'd-mode' with 'management'...

---

[1]'D' stands for default because he feels that that is the mode we use normally.

▶

However, traits of the d-mode are important and necessary for completing a task: a preference for structure, the ability to plan and organize, to be in control. Structuring and planning help within keeping to a set time frame. Hence, the d-mode is efficient and effective when the problem is clear-cut and when there is one possible, straightforward solution. The d-mode is less appropriate when the situation is intricate, ill defined or complex – and it seems that most product development tasks fall into the last category, rather than into the first.

If a task is complex and fuzzy Claxton suggests that a third mode of response, the 'tortoise mode', is more likely to yield satisfactory results. This mode of responding is slower, less conscious and less 'provable'. Here a person is more concerned with understanding the questions than with providing an answer fast. This might just be exactly what I suggest organizations need to do to improve their new product development. The process of processing the information is less conscious and people often feel that the answer has come 'out of the blue' and Claxton argues that there is a significant advantage in allowing the process of 'slow thinking' when assessing a situation. However, today people are often not 'allowed' to let 'things sink in'. The emphasis, particularly in new product development, is on speed. Claxton remarks on this particular aspect by pointing out that 'time pressure increases the likelihood to rely on existing habits and knowledge'.

This first insight from Claxton's book provided a better understanding of different modes of thinking. It helps to appreciate different approaches – and speeds – of finding solutions. The second insight from Claxton's book I would like to refer to here concerns how we classify new situations as it might help to shed some light on what feeds our habits and assumptions.

Assessing situations

Claxton's work provides insight into how we come to rely on habits and assumptions. Assessments are often based on familiar seeming patterns the accuracy of which was not questioned. New patterns are fitted to match known patterns rather than being acknowledged as different. With the benefit of hindsight, it seems obvious that people have been relying on past experience, on the seemingly obvious. This is related to the issue of prior knowledge. An established mindset, or a dominant logic, can prevent us from seeing things as they are but make us see them as we think they should be.

According to Claxton this is because our mind tends to recognize patterns without us being consciously aware of it. This can lead to something being identified as a familiar pattern while, upon closer investigation, it is not.[2] Therefore, one has to be aware of the 'pattern recognition process' which happens in what Claxton calls the 'undermind'. An awareness of this process can help to keep an open mind when approaching a new problem. Once an initial assessment of the problem has been made, it should then be asked whether it actually can be taken at face value or whether there are hidden layers of complexity which need to be understood and acknowledged.

However, again human nature does not seem in favour of revising a once made assessment, as Claxton points out, 'What seems to happen is that we build up an intuitive picture of the situation as we go along, and it takes work to "dismantle" the picture and start again.' So if later information seems to be at odds with the picture so far, we may unconsciously decide to reinterpret the dissonant information, rather than radically reorganize the picture. And the more we feel under pressure, the less likely we are to make the investment of 'starting from scratch'.

The last observation is particularly relevant in new product development. To illustrate how our mind responds to seemingly similar tasks I would like to cite from Claxton's book where he relates an experiment, undertaken by Abraham and Edith Luchins in the 1950s.

---

[2]Please refer to Claxton's book for examples and research supporting his proposition.

▶

They [the Luchins] set puzzles of the following sort. 'Imagine that you are standing beside a lake, and that you are given three empty jars of different sizes. The first jar holds 17 pints of water; the second holds 37 pints; and the third jar holds 6 pints. Your job is to see whether, using these three jars, you can measure out exactly 8 pints.' After some thought (which may, to start with, be quite logical), most people are able to end up with 8 pints in the largest jar. Then they are set another problem of the same type, except this time the jars hold respectively 31, 61 and 4 pints, and the target is to get 22 pints. And then another, with jar holding 10, 39 and 4 pints where the target is 21 pints. You will find that the same strategy will work for all three problems. But now comes the critical shift. You are next given jars of capacity 23, 39 and 3 pints, and asked to make 20 pints. If you have stopped thinking, and are now applying your new-found rule mindlessly, you will solve the problem – but you will not spot that there is now a much simpler solution. The problem looks the same, but this particular one admits of two solutions, one of which is more elegant and economical than the other. [insert added by author]

While there is generally agreement on the components of innovation (i.e. creativity and implementation), there is often disagreement on what deserves the title 'innovation'. Today it seems to be fashionable to call everything 'innovation', from the redesign of packaging to the introduction of hydrogen powered cars, basically everything that used to be called 'new product development' in the past. The literature is full of attempts to categorize different levels and types of innovation and we will have a look at several below. Olson *et al.* (1995) for example suggest the following four levels:

- New-to-the-world products (products that are new both to the company developing them and to the marketplace using them)

- Line extensions (products that are new to the marketplace but not to the company)

- Me-too-products (those that are new to the company but not to the marketplace)

- Product modifications (existing products that have been simply modified, i.e. they are new neither to the company nor to the marketplace)

As early as 1942, Schumpeter made some observations regarding different types of innovation, which he referred to as 'discontinuities'. The two types of discontinuity he identified are, first, a competence-destroying discontinuity, which renders obsolete the expertise required to master the technology that it replaces, and second, a competence-enhancing discontinuity, which builds on existing know-how embodied in the technology that it replaces.

While building on Schumpeter, more recent literature, with minor variations, refers to four types of innovation. They are architectural innovation, market niche innovation, regular innovation and revolutionary innovation (Abernathy and Clark 1985; similar, Tidd 1993):

Architectural innovation – Innovation of this sort defines the basic configuration of product and process and establishes the technical and marketing agendas that will guide subsequent development.

Market niche innovation – Innovation of this sort is opening new market opportunities through the use of existing technology, the effect on production and technical systems being to conserve and strengthen established designs.

Regular innovation – Innovation of this sort involves change that builds on established technical and production competence and that is applied to existing markets and customers. The effect of these changes is to entrench existing skills and resources.

Revolutionary innovation – Innovation of this sort disrupts and renders established technical and production competence obsolete, yet is applied to existing markets and customers.

The categories of innovation seem closely related to the categories of design devised by Morley and Pugh (1987) and Slusher and Ebert (1992). Heany's (1983) categories of innovation (style change, product line extension, product improvement, new product, start-up business, major innovation) are also similar to the different product categories introduced earlier. Heany provides a check list for the categorization of innovations, based on six different categories, which is shown in Table 1.1.

Looking at Abernathy and Clark's definitions of innovation, one could equate their first three categories with a competence-enhancing discontinuity and the fourth category, revolutionary innovation, with Schumpeter's a competence-destroying discontinuity. A common categorization of innovation is to differentiate between (a) product innovation, the things an organization offers, and (b) process innovation, the ways in which they are created and delivered (e.g. Tidd *et al.* (1997)). Combining levels of innovation with different categories we arrive at the following matrix (see Box 1.2).

Table 1.1   Degrees of Innovation (reproduced from (Heany 1983))

Is the market for product established?	Is the business already serving the market?	Do customers know functions and features?	What is the design effort?	What is the design effort?	Then innovation is a
			Product	Process	
yes	yes	yes	minor	nil	Style change
yes	yes	yes	minor	minor	Product line extension
yes	yes	yes	significant	minor	Product improvement
yes	yes	yes	major	major	New product
yes	no	yes	major	major	Start-up business
no	no	no	major	major	Major innovation

BOX 1.2   Levels and categories of Innovation (based on Tidd *et al.* 2001)

	Product	Service	Process	Business model
Transformation	Cars instead of horses	Internet banking	Pilkington's floating glass	Internet
Radical	Hydrogen powered cars	A new kind of mortgage	Gas-filled thermo glass panes	Online sales and distribution of computers
Incremental	New car model	Different mortgage feature	Differently coloured glass	Selling in business parks instead of town centres

I have taken the liberty to provide examples, and added 'business model' though it could be argued that some of this would be covered under 'process'.[2]

It is important to understand varying degrees of innovativeness as they flourish within different processes and structures and we will come back to that in Chapter 3.

However, most of these categorizations tend to focus on the outcome (i.e. the product or service), but say little about the process, and the context which is necessary to enable innovation. An approach that focuses too strongly on process is not likely to succeed in creating a continuously innovative organization. To achieve that, existing behaviours, beliefs and mental frameworks need to be understood and shifted. It is often our expertise and experience – the things that we know to be right and that work – that prevent us from coming up with something truly new. Processes can support this shift, but on their own will not achieve it. That is why I define innovation as a frame of mind. Innovation is the art of making new connections, and continuously challenging the status quo – without changing things for change's sake.

CREATIVITY

The uncreative mind can spot wrong answers, but it takes a very creative mind to spot wrong questions.

Anthony Jay

In the previous section, we talked about some characteristics of creativity. In this section we take a brief look at the origins of creativity, what kind of characteristics tend to be associated with creative people, and the creative process.

In her article 'Making sense of creativity', Jane Henry (1991) summarizes different views on the origin of creativity, identifying five sources:

- Grace – this is the view that creativity comes through divine inspiration, it is something that comes to us, or not, something magic which is out of our control; it is this view that believes 'you either have it or you don't', and companies subscribing to this particular view could only enhance their creativity by hiring people who are graced with divine inspiration.

- Accident – under this view creativity arises by serendipitous good fortune and various scientific discoveries have been attributed to this kind of creativity (e.g. Penicillin) – a view that is not particularly helpful to an organization striving to become more creative!

- Association – under this theory creativity occurs through the application of procedures from one area to another. Lateral thinking and brainstorming are methods supporting this approach to creativity. Henry points out that we often miss such opportunities, quoting as an example Sigmund Freud's insight that a side effect of cocaine is numbing of the mouth without realizing the resulting potential as a dental anaesthetic. Following this view, companies would provide training for their staff with the aim to improve levels of creativity.

- Cognitive – here the belief is that creativity is nothing special but that it relies on normal cognitive process such as recognition, reasoning and understanding. Under this view the role of 'application' is crucial, and examples given include the wide range of different filaments Edison used before coming up with a functioning light bulb. The emphasis here is on hard work and productivity, and proponents of this theory such as

Weisburg (1986) point out that ten years of intense preparation tend to be necessary to lead to a creative act. As Henry puts it, 'The logic of the cognitive position is that deep thinking about an area over a long period leaves the discoverer informed enough to notice anomalies that might be significant.' Companies might like this view best – just make people work harder and the result will be creative solutions. However, the research by Amabile suggests that while a challenge is conducive to creativity, demanding too much can be counterproductive. This approach also works only if the problem has been clearly identified and it is about finding the solution. This approach is less likely to result in identifying the right questions, so it could be argued that the cognitive approach is about implementation, not creativity.

- Personality – here creativity is seen as a particular human ability, an intrinsic part of life and growth and Henry points out, 'Viewing creativity as a natural talent directs attention towards removing mental barriers to creativity to allow an innate spontaneity to flourish.' Given this explanation, I would find the title 'skill' much more appropriate for this view than 'personality' as the latter seems to suggest that creativity is something that we are born with.

To a certain degree, the different views as to what lies at the origin of creativity are also time dependent. For example, the view that creativity is based on 'grace' has dominated human thinking until the beginning of the last century. Only since the late 19th and early 20th centuries people have begun to entertain the thought that creativity could be encouraged and trained. It probably started in 1880 when the American psychologist William James declared, 'The only difference between a muddle-head and a genius is that between extracting wrong characters and right ones. In other words, a muddle-headed person is a genius spoiled in the making.'

And most other suggested origins of creativity make some assumption that creativity is not just something that happens to us, but that it is something that can be encouraged and perhaps even trained. But even when accepting that creativity can be learned, there are some people who are just more creative than others, and much research has been undertaken to identify what their characteristics are. The report entitled *The Creative Age*, published in 1999 by the government think-tank Demos, has a rather short list:

- Creative people have the ability to formulate new problems rather than depending on others to define them.
- They have the ability to transfer what they learn across different contexts.

While these characteristics certainly make for a creative person, to be an innovative person it would, as a minimum, be necessary to add persistence and the willingness to take risk. To make things happen you often have to overcome high levels of resistance – often for no other reason than that your path has not been trodden before, as emphasized in John Locke's introductory quote to this chapter.

> **Persistence...**
>
> Charles Goodyear, discover and inventor of vulcanized rubber, as well as Chester Carlson, inventor of electrostatic copying, the Xerox process: xerography, worked for over 30 years trying to find a solution that would work.

The most extensive list of habits of creative people I have found was developed by 1990 Robert Alan Black.[3] While it is titled '32 traits of creative people', I would rather credit innovative people with these characteristics: some of these characteristics are not necessarily important to come up with ideas, however, they are essential for their implementation (see Box 1.3).

The fact that it might be quite difficult to find all these characteristics in one person makes teamwork such an important aspect of innovation.

BOX 1.3   32 Traits of Creative People (Black 1990) (reproduced by Permission of Black, A.)

1. Sensitive

2. Not motivated by money

3. Sense of destiny (believe that you have a special mission or purpose in life you plan or hope to fulfil)

4. Adaptable

5. Tolerant of ambiguity (accept multiple answers or causes to a single problem or challenge)

6. Observant

7. Perceive world differently

8. See possibilities

9. Question asker

10. Can synthesize (see the big picture) correctly, often intuitively

11. Able to fantasize

12. Flexible (willing to try things in many different ways)

13. Fluent (produce lots of ideas or possibilities when working on a challenge or simply choosing a restaurant to go to)

14. Imaginative

15. Intuitive

16. Original

17. Ingenious

18. Energetic

19. Sense of humour

20. Self-actualizing (focus on developing yourself to the best you can be and to discover your specific unique talents)

21. Self-disciplined

22. Self-knowledgeable

23. Specific interests

24. Divergent thinker (looks at things in many different ways at the same time)

25. Curious

26. Open-ended (don't fix on a single idea, keep looking for many different ideas or ways to do things)

27. Independent

28. Severely critical

29. Non-conforming

30. Confident

31. Risk taker

32. Persistent

I would like to conclude the exploration of traits of creative people with a final list, mainly because I like the fact that it highlights one of the underlying reasons for the difficulties that companies have in the realization of innovation: their paradoxical nature. When exploring the questions in their research, what kind of people are creative, and what kind of traits lead to creativity, Csikszentmihalyi came to the following conclusions:[4] 'There may be certain neurological physiologies that predispose you to one or another type of creativity, but it doesn't seem to take a particular talent or genius to be very creative.' He continues, 'However, we do find typically creative individuals have curiosity and interest, and also a certain blend of characteristics often thought of as opposites':

- Divergent and convergent thinking – can think 'outside the box', while also being good at synthesizing a number of ideas into a single concept

- Energy and idleness – high levels of energy, even at a great age (though they may have been sickly as children), but at the same time almost all of them are sometimes seen as being lazy as they don't let themselves be pushed, or keep routines (this is related to incubation, and they feel guilty about it, but they also feel that it's necessary)

- Introversion and extroversion – often being caught up in themselves, but also being interested in a wide range of things, interacting with others and seeking stimulation

- Masculine and feminine – creative people tend to be psychologically androgynous (men who are shy, less aggressive, sensitive; women who are feminine but also dominant)

- Passionate and detached – highly intrinsically motivated, loving what they do but at the same time able to stand back, especially when it comes to evaluation

- Rebellious and traditional – confronting and challenging the existing but at the same time building on the past. As Isaac Newton pointed out: 'If I can see farther than other men, it is because I stand on the shoulders of giants.'

These lists can be used as starting points for designing training and development programmes by managers who want to improve their employees' creativity (and innovativeness).

De Pree (2001) makes suggestions for how to manage creative people. The first point he makes is that leaders should be open towards creative people and acknowledge the contribution they can make. He further suggest that it might be a good idea to protect such people from bureaucracy and legalism and help protect great ideas from being watered down – certainly a problem mentioned in interviews conducted with members of the Innovation Exchange (von Stamm 2001). De Pree quotes Peter Drucker as saying, 'When you have a real innovation, don't compromise.' However, at the same time he emphasizes that this does not mean giving creative people carte blanche. He points out that 'Creative people, like the rest of us, need constraints,' and continues, 'One of the most striking characteristics of the creative person I know is their ability to renew themselves through constraints.'

Once people realized that creativity might not just be a god-given, but that it could be taught, research into the creativity process started. In 1926 Wallas summarized his own and other people's research into the creativity process in *The Art of Thought*, concluding that there were the following four steps:

- Preparation – identification and definition of an issue or problem, based on observation and study

- Incubation – this often involves laying the issue aside for a time, what was seen to be the 'magic' bit at the time and which in Claxton's terms would be associated with the tortoise mind

- Illumination – the moment when a new solution or concept is finally emerging, often associated with 'the flash of inspiration, out of nowhere', but more likely a result of the ability to make a new connection between extensive and varied bodies of knowledge

- Verification – checking out the applicability and appropriateness of the solution for the originally observed problem

Comparing the various models of the creative process that have developed since, Paul E. Plsek (1996) has drawn the following conclusions:

- The creative process involves purposeful analysis, imaginative idea generation, and critical evaluation – the total creative process is a balance of imagination and analysis.

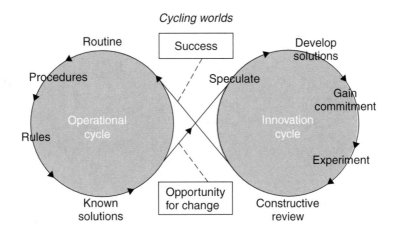

Figure 1.2   Cycling Worlds, Synectics (reproduced by permission of Kogan Page)

- Older models tend to imply that creative ideas result from subconscious processes, largely outside the control of the thinker. Modern models tend to imply purposeful generation of new ideas, under the direct control of the thinker.

- The total creative process requires a drive to action and the implementation of ideas. We must do more than simply imagine new things, we must work to make them concrete realities.

Again, it is obvious that creativity and innovation have been used interchangeably, which I believe contributes to the confusion that exists around creativity and innovation, and the problems that exist in establishing an innovative organization.

To clarify, during the creative process intuition and thought are required — as well as for the implementation, analysis and action. However, each of the two processes requires different skills and is successful under different conditions. This has been expressed in the model of 'cycling worlds' by creativity consultants Synectics, whereby I would read what they call 'innovation cycle' to be the creative process, and what they call 'operational cycle' to be the implementation cycle (see Figure 1.2).[5]

Successful innovative organizations manage to balance the tension between the two cycles without compromising either.

DESIGN

Good design is about looking at everyday things with new eyes and working out how they can be made better. It is about challenging existing technology.

James Dyson, Ford Magazine, *summer 1999*

In the last section of the chapter I take a closer look at what design actually means, explore different approaches companies take towards design, and suggest what why it might be worth considering design and designers in the context of innovation and creativity. A brief overview of the history of design as well as an introduction to different categories of design can be found in Appendix II.

Looking up the work 'design' in any dictionary provides a long list of entries. The *Concise Oxford Dictionary* offers 11 different meanings, and in the *British Encyclopaedia* we even find 33 different entries. In addition to a wide range of options of what 'design' refers to, there is also potential for further confusion due to national differences. Even though 'design' is a word used in many countries, its meaning varies. For example, according to a German dictionary, it only means to 'sketch' or 'pattern'.

In the context of innovation, three relevant interpretations of design can be found:

- Design is the tangible outcome, i.e. the end product of design such as cameras, cars, etc.

- Design is a creative activity.

- Design is the process by which information is transformed into a tangible outcome.

It seems that the last, design as process, is the most commonly used, and it is how I understand the word. For me design is the act of conscious decision making so I would vary the definition slightly and add the word 'conscious'. So my definition reads:

> **Design** is the conscious decision-making process by which information (an idea) is transformed into an outcome, be it tangible (product) or intangible (service).

Design is about doing things consciously, and not because they have always done in a certain way, it is about comparing alternatives to select the best possible solution, it is about exploring and experimenting.

Whereas earlier literature on the subject has looked at design primarily from a designer's perspective, it seems that more recent books on design and design management invariably make a strong link to new product development (e.g. Oakley 1984; Pilditch 1987; Walsh *et al.* 1992; Bruce and Biemans 1995). This seems to be correlated with the growing awareness of the importance of design for a company's success, and a call for a wider use of designers in the new product development process. For example, latest research by the British Design Council (2002) found that 75% of small and medium-sized businesses (50–249 employees) declared that design was

---

Three meanings of design can also be found in the British Standard BS 7000, *A Guide to Managing Product Design*. The Standard refers to design as verb (to generate information from which a required product can become reality), as noun (a set of instructions necessary to construct a product), and as process. Three different types of design process are distinguished:

1. Conceptual design – the process in which concepts are generated with a view to fulfilling the objective.

2. Embodiment design – the process in which a structured development of the preferred concept is carried out.

3. Detail design – in which the precise shape, dimension and tolerances are specified, the material selection is confirmed and the method of manufacture is considered for every individual part of the product.

Evolution of 'Design'

In the traditional understanding, 'design' is often associated with a person who is involved in both the design and production of an object. This concept began to change with the outset of the Industrial Revolution, which initiated the division of work and the need for specialization. Resulting from this, two strands of design evolved, 'design as art' and 'design as engineering', each with a different meaning and different emphasis in education. Part and consequence of the development into specialization was the separation of industrial and engineering design about which Ivor Owen (1990), a former director of the Design Council, says, 'I strongly believe that the schism between engineering design and industrial design has been one of the most damaging issues in manufacturing industry imaginable.' Sir William Barlow (1988), a former chairman of the Design Council, asserts this by pointing out that almost every product requires an appropriate balance of both.

'integral' or 'significant' to them, up from 54% in the previous year. As early as the mid-80s, Kotler and Rath (1984) have heralded the coming of design as necessary organizational competence, declaring in their article 'Design, a powerful but neglected strategic tool' that 'Design is a potent strategic tool that companies can use to gain a sustainable competitive advantage yet most companies neglect design as a strategic tool. What they don't realize is that good design can enhance products, environment, communications, and corporate identity.' However, though other management gurus such as Tom Peters (e.g. 1994) too are great proponents of design, ten years later Davies and Hom (1993) still observed a lack of a strategic use of design.

One of the reasons might be that the close association and overlap of design management, new product development and innovation has caused confusion about the boundaries between the three areas. A further contributor to the confusion around design is that, while it is commonly understood that design is undertaken by designers, research has revealed that a significant part of design or decisions influencing design are not made by designers but by other people in the organization such as engineers, programmers and managers (Hales 1986; Norman 1988). These non-designers who have such a significant impact on the design outcome without being aware of it have been titled 'silent designers' (Gorb and Dumas 1987).

Another reason is the differences between designers and managers on a number of issues, and a widespread belief that designers – or creative people in general – cannot be managed. However, David Walker (1990) quotes from a letter of Geoffrey Constable, Head of Industrial Division, Design Council, of 17th March 1987, in which Constable states, 'It is important to argue that design must be managed and can be managed. There is considerable misunderstanding on both points. Some managers believe that design is something outside normal business practice and does not benefit from being managed but due to creativity and other uncertainties is regrettably unmanageable. In fact design has to be managed just as much as anything else and the uncertainties that are involved are no more serious or disruptive than the uncertainties inherent in any other task within industry that has to be managed, for example, commissioning a new factory or exploiting a new market.'

Walker blames the educational gap for the problem. Whereas managers' education and training tends to focus on analytical studies such as accounting and finance, designers are educated and trained to deal with projects that involve unfamiliar concepts, are predominantly visual rather than verbal, involve fuzzy problems and high levels of ambiguity, and assessments which are 'Variously, subjective, personal, emotional and outside quantification.' He comes to the conclusions that 'The divergence between managers and designers can be detected in personality traits, in habits of thought and work, as well as in educational background.' A comparison between managers and designers is shown in Table 1.2.

Whether or not design actually contributes to the success of a product and a company's performance is critically influenced by management's attitude towards it (Hart and Service 1988; Hart et al. 1989). To provide managers with insights into the implications of different approaches to the management of design, Dumas and Mintzberg (1991) have described five different ways and an evaluation of each option (see Table 1.3). In their view the fifth style, infusion, is the one most likely to lead to the most successful and comprehensive employment of design. However, while the suggested categories give a description of what has been found in companies and are important for understanding different levels of commitment of a company to design, the article does not give any indications as to how or what to do to achieve a particular level of design awareness, nor does it help a company choose the approach to design management most suitable for their situation.

The categories devised by Dumas and Mintzberg are not dissimilar to a differentiation between different levels of understanding of design given by Fairhead (1988) (Figure 1.3).

Table 1.2 Differences between Designers and Managers (reproduced from (Walker 1990))

Characteristics	Managers	Designers
Aims	Long term profits/return	Short term product/service quality
	Survival	Reform
	Growth	Prestige
	Organizational durability	Career building
Focus	People	Things
	Systems	Environment
Education	Accountancy	Crafts
	Engineering	Art
	Verbal	Visual
	Numerical	Geometric
Thinking styles	Serialist	Holist
	Linear	Lateral
	Analysis	Synthesis
	Problem oriented	Solution led
Behaviour	Pessimistic	Optimistic
	Adaptive	Innovative
Culture	Conformity	Diversity
	Cautious	Experimental

Table 1.3 Styles of Design Management (based on Dumas and Mintzberg 1991)

Style	Critique
1. Design champion	Whether patron, crusader, team or consultant, may not be sufficient condition for the full realization of design in an organization, but he/she or it may constitute a necessary first step
2. Design policy	Is fine as long as it clarifies the beliefs that already exist in a company; by itself a design policy is of little consequence
3. Design programme	Sometimes causes a specific change in an organization and even has a lasting effect when that change serves as a model for other initiatives. But these follow-up initiatives must be implemented and that is commonly considered to require the next approach
4. Design as a function	For the vast majority of companies, the influence of design is as likely to be measured by the performance of marketing or production as by its own independent efforts
5. Design as infusion	The permeation of design throughout the organization. Infusion is informal; the ultimate intention is to have everyone concerned with design (silent design)

So we have already heard that design is an important strategic tool, but why think about it in particular in the context of innovation? Look at the 32 traits of creative (innovative) people and consider what we have heard about innovation.

In Table 1.4 I have highlighted the traits that are often associated with designers too and we find that they share many characteristics of creative people (perhaps not surprising as the design profession is considered to be part of

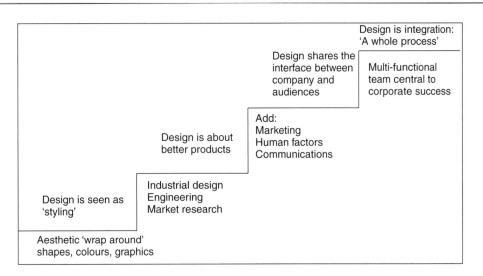

Figure 1.3 Design – The World is Growing (Fairhead 1988) (reproduced by permission of HMSO)

Table 1.4 Creative Traits and Designers

1.	Sensitive	12.	**Flexible**	23.	**Specific interests**
2.	Not motivated by money	13.	**Fluent**	24.	**Divergent thinker**
3.	**Sense of destiny**	14.	**Imaginative**	25.	**Curious**
4.	Adaptable	15.	**Intuitive**	26.	**Open-ended**
5.	**Tolerant of ambiguity**	16.	**Original**	27.	**Independent**
6.	**Observant**	17.	**Ingenious**	28.	**Severely critical**
7.	**Perceive world differently**	18.	**Energetic**	29.	**Non-conforming**
8.	**See possibilities**	19.	Sense of humour	30.	**Confident**
9.	**Question asker**	20.	Self-actualizing	31.	**Risk taker**
10.	**Can synthesize**	21.	Self-disciplined	32.	**Persistent**
11.	**Able to fantasize**	22.	Self-knowledgeable		

the 'creative industry'). This does not mean that innovation should be left to the designers, only that designers might have an important contribution to make to the innovation process, and that they might be valuable members of innovation teams. Even though the link between skills and abilities of members of the creative industries and the skills and abilities required for innovation seems quite obvious, not many organizations seem to employ it to their benefit. As the UK Government White Paper on Competitiveness (1995) states, 'The effective use of design is fundamental to the creation of innovative products, processes and services. Good design can significantly add value to products, lead to growth in sales and enable both the exploitation of new markets and the consolidation of existing ones.' It continues, 'The benefits of good design can be seen as:

● Processes improved by gradual innovation
● Redesign of existing products in response to user needs, new markets and competitor products
● Development of new products by anticipating new market opportunities.'

The case study presented in Chapter 2 gives an illustration of the interplay of innovation, creativity and design in a 'real world' situation.

READING SUGGESTIONS

ON INNOVATION

Tidd, Joe, Bessant, John and Pavitt, Keith (2001) *Managing Innovation; Integrating Technological, Market and Organizational Change.* 2nd edn. Chichester, UK: John Wiley & Sons

Comment: A very comprehensive overview of issues around innovation, slightly biased towards technology

ON CREATIVITY

Henry, Jane (ed.) (2001) *Creative Management.* 2nd edn. London: Sage

Comment: A good collection of articles around creativity, authors include Theresa Amabile, Henry Mintzberg, Daniel Goleman, Michael Kirton, Charles Handy and Rosabeth Moss Kanter

ON DESIGN

Cooper, Rachel and Press, Michael (1995) *The Design Agenda, A Guide to Successful Design Management.* Chichester, UK: John Wiley & Sons

Comment: Nothing earth shattering but a good introduction to design and its place in business

SOME USEFUL WEBSITES

ON INNOVATION

www.innovation.gov.uk

Comment: The UK's government website set up with the aim to help organizations become more innovative, much of it is still under development; it also offers an electronic version of the Design Council's (*www.designcouncil.org*) tool for the assessment of an organization's innovativeness (click on 'managing successful innovation')

www.thinksmart.com

Comment: The website of the US-based Innovation Network, a rich source of articles, book recommendations, a great tool for understanding innovation called *Innovation DNA* and much more

www.fastcompany.com

Comment: The website of the magazine with the same title, loads of interesting articles on and around innovation, well worth a visit

ON CREATIVITY

http://creativeideas.20m.com/articles.htm#General

Comment: Website with lots of links to interesting articles and other information relevant to creativity and also innovation

ON DESIGN

www.designcouncil.org

Comment: The Design Council get increasingly involved in design's role in innovation, and innovation more generally. They have developed a number of tools, and also provide a wide range of case studies and stories on their website

www.dmi.org

Comment: This is the website of the Design Management Institute, some aspects of the website are only available to DMI members

NOTES ON CHAPTER 1

[1] Interview for the Innovation Exchange, 1999 (for a full interview, see http://iexchange.london.edu).

[2] In his book *All the Right Moves* (Harvard Business School Press, 1999), Costas Markides expands on how to pursue innovation at the strategic level (business model innovation).

[3] See http://www.cre8ng.com/newsletter/news2.html or http://creativeideas.org.uk/

[4] Extracted from *Student Colloquium: Problem Finding and the Creative Process*, Dr. Mihaly Csikszentmihalyi, Thursday, 11th November, 1999, notes by Anne K. Gay; see http://www.eng.uwaterloo.ca/~akgay/creative.html

[5] See Jonne Cesevani (2003) *Big Ideas – Putting the Zest into Creativity and Innovation at Work*. London: Kogan Page; or http://www.synecticsworld.com/helpdesk/fill-me-in.htm

2 Innovation = Creativity and Commercialization

CASE STUDY 1: BBC'S *WALKING WITH DINOSAURS*

HOW IT ALL STARTED

I wanted people to think that dinosaurs were real animals – not monsters. The only other place you'd see really good digital images of dinosaurs was in Jurassic Park. Our idea was to create a 'David Attenborough' of the prehistoric world.

Tim Haines, Series Producer

Tim had been fascinated by dinosaurs almost all his life and recalls, 'There was a footprint in the Tunbridge Wells Museum which I saw when I was five and I have been interested in dinosaurs ever since.' Over the years, many films have attempted to depict dinosaurs – often with rather comical results. However, the arrival of computer-aided animation opened up new possibilities, first demonstrated in the highly successful Hollywood movie *Jurassic Park*. Dinosaurs had been a neglected subject for television-makers, and no one had attempted to use the same techniques for the small screen.

Introduction to Dinosaurs

- Dinosaur – from the Greek words *deinos* meaning terrible and *saurus* meaning lizard

- Coined by British scientist Richard Owen who founded the Natural History Museum

- The first dinosaur fossils were actually identified as belonging to an extinct reptile in 1824

- The oldest, or earliest, dinosaurs found so far are prosauropods from the Late Triassic, around 130 million years ago. These were found in 1999 in Madagascar. The animals are thought to be quite closely related to the great sauropods such as *Apatosaurus* which evolved much later.

- Weighing 70 tons the *Brachiosaurus* is the heaviest found, equivalent to 14 elephants

- The longest dinosaur is the *Diplodocus* tons, at 45 m, equivalent to five London double decker buses

- The biggest carnivore is a marine reptile called *Liopleurodon*, it is 25 m long and has a mouth 3 m wide

- The largest flying animal is the *Ornithocheirus* with a wingspan of 12 m (40 feet) and a weight of (only) 100 kg

- The *Torosaurus* (horned dinosaur) has the largest skull: 2.6 m long

- In *Jurassic Park*, a company lawyer is eaten by a *Tyrannosaurus*. Scientists have worked out that it would need 238 average sized lawyers a year to keep it going

- A sauropod's stomach could hold up to half a tonne and had large stones inside it – gastroliths – to help grind down and digest the food

- A single *Diplodocus* produced about one tonne of dung per day

Tim has a degree in zoology, specializing in entomology, but went into medical journalism after graduation. From there he moved on into radio and TV, always specializing in science, medicine and the environment. He was just about to start a new series on Ice Mummies, but before that had a couple of weeks to think of new ideas, and he knew that the BBC was looking to create a landmark series. Having seen *Jurassic Park* he felt that there was a

'Like anyone who sat watching *Jurassic Park*, or who has studied dinosaurs has asked themselves what they were really like, I thought, I'd love to see them alive. They are tremendous evocative creatures, quite unlike anything we have seen before.'

Tim Haines

level of reality to dinosaurs that people expected which was not reflected in past or current television programmes. The technology had so much potential, yet there was a gap in the market for documentary approaches. He wanted to create a programme that could offer the same quality of special effects that had been used in films such as *Jurassic Park*, but with his programme he wanted to recreate, as far as possible, a true representation of the period – environment, flora and fauna, and so forth. His aim was to produce a documentary-like film that would make dinosaurs look like real animals. 'I came up with the idea of doing it as a natural history programme because that's how we are used to seeing real animals, but I wanted to make it with top level graphics.'

Having identified his objective his challenge was twofold: (a) he had to consider what kind of money would be required to realize his idea – and whether it would be realistic; and (b) he had to identify some people who could actually make such a film happen. Further considerations were target audiences, viewing time, film length and, very important for the costing of the film, how much time per show of animated film he would be looking for.

SELLING THE IDEA – PHASE I

The first step for Tim was to raise money for a pilot. With the programme idea being unusual and very innovative, he felt that, to raise the money necessary to make the programme, it was essential to be able to show people what he had in mind.

Securing some finance was one thing but equally, if not more important, was to find a company who could realize the animation. Initially he contacted the people who had been involved in making *Jurassic Park*, but they quoted a production cost of $10,000/sec. With that level of cost for animation they would end up with 3–5 minutes of animation per 30-minute programme. This was not what Tim had in mind, and it clearly indicated that they were not really interested. It seemed that people in the US were generally more interested in film work and not TV, so the work would have to be done in the UK.

After generating a short list of companies that might be able to do the computer animations, he invited proposals from four companies. The responses from the first three were rather disappointing: Company A's suggestion was so extremely poor that it was not worth taking any further; Company B could not be bothered to respond;

> 'I started ringing around and I whittled it down quite quickly; there are only a handful of people who would be comfortable and capable of trying to realize this and I went round and saw several of them.'

and Company C had changed their focus, which meant they were no longer suitable. This left Company D. The company, called FrameStore, founded in 1986, specialized in visual effects and computer animation for commercials, feature films, television dramas, video games, promotional graphics and title sequences.

On 8th August 1996, while still filming for the Ice Mummies documentary, Tim Haines went to meet with Mike Milne, Computer Animation Director of FrameStore, and a few of his colleagues. Mike remembers, 'In a lot of meetings we are asked to do things that are just impossible. Initially the one with Tim seemed to be one of those. It seemed that what Tim was asking for was a Jurassic Park for a TV documentary budget, but he was not

> FrameStore won an unprecedented three consecutive Primetime Emmy awards in the late 90s for the visual effect (Gulliver's Travels, The Odyssey and Merlin), and since then added a further five Emmys including one in 2000 for 'Outstanding Animated Programme' for Walking with Dinosaurs.

presumptuous, as a first step he was asking us whether we had the technical expertise to do it and how much it would actually cost – but even at that point the other people in the meeting still felt it was not quite realistic.'

However, Tim had got his timing right, Mike was fascinated by the idea and had also reached a point in his career where he was interested in moving on from the commercials he had been doing for the past years. He felt that Tim's series was something different, a piece to get his teeth into – and also something that was more meaningful. He liked the idea of a documentary, and, 'Working with researchers and scientists who all had a great aim in life – and were pursuing it for not too much money.' He knew he would desperately try to make it work. It also helped that Tim had a reputation for good documentaries and had worked with Horizon/BBC2. And finally, Tim pointed out that it would not have to be highly detailed shots. They agreed that Mike should create a short piece of animation to illustrate how he would realize the task.

When Tim went back to look at Mike's first pictures a couple of months later he was impressed. Mike, who had spent time in the London Zoo and the London's Natural History Museum thinking about the project, had also looked at some animal documentaries and realized that the level of detail was often not that great, it was often fast moving and even a bit blurred. So Mike took a misty shot of a rhinoceros and put some very simple dinosaur silhouette figures on top and then composited it in, so the actual amount of animation was quite limited. The detail of the animal was almost nonexistent and the compositing with all that mist around was fairly simple – but the picture at the end was utterly convincing. Tim knew they were thinking on the same wavelength when they met again on the 17th October. He recalls, 'The lesson was, don't throw in 500 animators and all the skin designers in the world realizing something on which you can see every scale on its body, if you don't need to. It's just as evocative to see an animal in the mist walking towards you.' That's how the cooperation started.

The very basic and short video Mike had produced was a great help in raising money for the pilot. Tim's boss bought into the idea straight away, and BBC Worldwide was quite interested too. This meant that Tim was able to raise

£100,000, which would be enough to produce a 2–3 minute pilot. Mike did not waste any time, and while Tim was seeking to raise the money he started planning for the pilot.

But not only did Mike start working pro-actively, Tim ensured that the project would move forward in his own time too. While on holiday in Cyprus over Christmas 1996 Tim shot some background footage for the pilot. In January 1997 Mike and his colleague, Andrew Daffy (now head of commercials at FrameStore), started working on the pilot. It took about 12 weeks to complete, and looking back into his diary Mike commented, 'I worked 60 days straight without a day's break during that three-month period.' The results were impressive, better than Tim had anticipated both in terms of animated time produced and visual effectiveness. 'But,' Mike says four and a half years later, 'while it was great at the time now we would hate anyone to see it.'

Once the pilot was done Mike had to sit down and work out the budget. He remembers, 'The costing for the project was based on scaling up the pilot, i.e. cost and timing for the 5-minute pilot times 6 = 30 minute for each programme, and again multiplied by 6 for the series; six times two animators would be needed plus technical staff and admin, etc.' This was quite different from how a project would normally be costed within the industry. Work in the industry would normally be based on a 'rate card,' which is generally available in all meeting rooms. It means a project is costed based on hourly rates for both people and equipment – but this would have pushed the budget far beyond its limits. So Mike went to see the financial director and together they worked out how to do it another way. One decision was to recruit college graduates rather than experienced animators, another was to get second-hand equipment. However, compromising quality of equipment was not an option for compositing. They realized that they did not have the required number of machines for compositing available, but new machines would have cost £800,000 apiece, which was out of the question. So they decided to make do with the machines available but to run them around the clock, manned with junior staff. As Mike recalls, 'We basically treated the project like a start-up.' The original idea had been to hire a warehouse for 18 months to bring the team together, but eventually it proved more workable to use a floor in the building where FrameStore was located.

The proposal they finally came up with was based on cost plus a small profit – and that was exactly how they presented it to the BBC, being entirely open about cost and profit. Tim ended up with a total cost for the series of £6.2 m, including all shooting, location, puppets, sculptures, music, expenses for travel, and so on.

SELLING THE IDEA – PHASE II

The budget the BBC is willing to commit to any programme depends upon the broadcasting slot and the target audience for the programme. It also depends upon the type of programme, for example, a soap opera can be made for much less than £1 m an hour – Tim needed about twice that for his series. A project of this financial scope was new ground for the BBC. However, the BBC was always looking for innovative and new programmes, and Tim was convinced, 'If we could produce the programme how we imagined it, then it would not only be very novel but also likely to attract a wide audience. The programme was not aimed at dinosaur buffs but whole families who could sit down together and watch it. This was something which the BBC was very keen to encourage.'

Armed with the pilot and budget requirements, Tim set about securing funding for the series. As Tim had anticipated, the pilot made all the difference. Alix Tidmarsh, Global Intellectual Property Director, BBC Worldwide, remembers, 'It enabled people to understand what was in Tim's head and what they would get for their money.' Or in Tim's words, 'When we showed the pilot to people they immediately understood what we were planning to do – and bought into it.'

Within the BBC fund raising did not prove too difficult. It was decided to take the idea forward because it seemed simple and achievable, and nothing like that had been done on television before. Between them BBC Broadcasting and BBC Worldwide contributed £3.5 m. In total Tim ended up with six investors: besides the two departments of the BBC, ProSieben of Germany, TV Asahi of Japan, France 3 and the Discovery Channel (US) put up money for the programme. While the level of funding was unusually high for the BBC, it still meant that they would not be able to afford more than £1 million per show – not an overly generous budget for a programme that would rely almost exclusively on computer animation.

THE DEVELOPMENT AND ITS CHALLENGES

While the fact that they had been able to gain support from television companies around the world was a great success, it also had its downside, as it meant that Tim would have to please six masters. The issues were not so much about content, that was clearly the domain of the producer, but different countries had different requirements in other respects, particularly with regards to programme length. This caused big discussions about the format of the series, i.e. how long each programme should be and how many parts the series would have. For example, the BBC would develop 30-minute programmes, commercial stations would be looking for 50 minutes of production plus 10 minutes for advertising. In the end there was no common format, but individual countries would follow what was most appropriate for their environment: in the UK the series was scheduled to run in six 30-minute sessions, the US planned to broadcast a three-hour session with scientists' comments in between, and Japan planned to incorporate its own work too. However, in the end all changes had to be approved by the BBC and individual countries were not allowed to alter the creative content of the product. It was Tim's responsibility to negotiate and give his final approval – though, as Alix pointed out, 'One has to realize that it can be very difficult if not impossible to control, in the end it becomes a matter of trust and relationships, and it is very important that everyone gets on board early and buys into the idea at the outset.'

As the team wanted to make sure that the dinosaur world came alive with as much realism and accuracy as possible, they set about the challenge to making something that was scientifically rigorous as well as being dramatic and entertaining. This meant that important preparatory work had to be done before they could start:

- The right locations had to be found
- Dinosaurs to be featured in the series had to be identified
- The time periods covered in individual programmes had to be agreed

This meant consulting with experts in the field. As Tim recalls, 'We spent a year and a half designing the storyboards. In the process we consulted over 100 palaeontologists, their area of expertise varying from dinosaur footprints to dinosaur movement to dinosaur dung, all to ensure the programmes would be informed by the latest scientific thinking. In addition, we had a dedicated palaeontologist working with us in that time, and a further seven who acted as scientific advisors – each series had its own specialist.' Before Mike and his team could go to work, Tim arranged for several of the world's leading palaeontologists to visit FrameStore to give staff a two-day intensive course.

As well as the palaeontologists, there were the palaeobotanists and palaeoentomologists and palaeoclimatologists, geologists, etc. What the team was not quite prepared for was that the palaeontologists would all disagree with each other; there did not seem to be one single truth. In the end it was about making the best possible judgement given the information available. The discussions and debates throughout the cooperation were not only educational for the BBC team. The scientific community does generally not have the kind of money that is available for television work, so scientists would otherwise not have been able to spend the amount of money and time on investigating a particular aspect of dinosaurs, for example how dinosaurs might have moved. It was in the interest of all parties to work together to generate the best knowledge possible, because in the end it was all about testing theories that could never be proven. In addition to seeking scientists' advice, the team drew on the BBC's natural history library, making cuts of every animal documentary they found to give the animators stimulating ideas about how animals might move.

All the creatures that the team 'created' had to give a realistic impression of scale. Tim comments, 'The scale is a very difficult thing if you don't have a human there, you can't tell specific sizes. Since we couldn't put humans in, we tried very hard to get that moment of "wow, isn't he big!" through the way we designed the shots! Using low camera work and wide angles we tried to achieve a sense of their enormity.'

Walking with Dinosaurs took over three years to produce, with 18 months spent on research and two years on production. Asked how long it took to shoot a typical scene producer, Jasper James, answered, 'In terms of person-hours, the programmes took 75,000 times longer to make than to watch – the animation was the slow bit not the filming – a five-minute scene takes about four days to shoot.'

LOCATIONS AND DINOSAURS

Location was the first big challenge for the desire to make the film as realistic as possible. Finding the right locations for the filming was not as simple as it may seem. Tim explains, 'There was no grass in the dinosaurs' world and no birds (at least, none until the very end of the dinosaurs' reign), so finding places where the pictures looked right and weren't disturbed by today's local wildlife was rather tricky.' Joanna Wright, a colleague of Tim's, travelled the globe twice for about three months to find suitable film locations where prehistoric plants had survived and there was no grass, flowers or deciduous trees. They ended up with locations as diverse as New Zealand, Australia (particularly Tasmania), Bahamas, New Caledonia, Chile and California.

Over a period of 14 months they filmed in these locations for a total of 27 weeks. Jasper James, recalls, 'We were on location about one month at a time, very long hours, hard work, sometimes wonderful, sometimes horrible – nearly

> **How do you know what Vegetation was around at the Time of the Dinosaurs?**
>
> Plants get fossilized just like animals do, although those without hard woody parts tend to get preserved less frequently. Also we have fossilized dung – called coprolite – which tells us not only what plants were around but what the animals were eating! The pollen from plants, too, is often fossilized. This may sound strange, but many millions of pollen grains are produced by plants, and they also have a relatively tough coating, so they do fossilize quite well. It is possible to identify pollen grains from different plants (though not always possible to identify which plants it came from), so they can be very useful in telling what species were around when – and where.

always uncomfortable, but the places were beautiful.' The plan was to shoot between 10 and 12 *set-ups* a day, but the schedule had to be flexible to allow for incidents. For example, on one occasion in Tasmania they had three days of heavy rain mixed with snow, and were unable to film a single frame. However, on one of their best single day's shooting they covered 26 set-ups. The film crew averaged ten people (in comparison, a mini series can have a crew of up to 100 strong).

Choosing the dinosaurs was simpler in comparison. While it was a long process in as much as it required the gathering and sorting of much information, they basically went for the ones that are best researched. They made sure that there was a very large fossil site underlying each programme. As Tim pointed out, 'There is so little to go on from the fossil record that we need as much help as possible!' (See Appendix 1 for a list of the stars of the show.)

ATTENTION TO DETAIL

Whatever was decided on, the team tried to stick to what they could reasonably predict rather than speculating wildly. They wanted to avoid any uncertain aspects. Though, as Tim points out, 'Of course the simple fact that dinosaurs don't exist any more meant that the production team faced a number of challenges! The research was straightforward enough but we encountered a huge range of conflicting scientific opinions. So, a consensus had to be reached based on the theories with the most evidence to support them.' Fortunately, many palaeontologists were happy to help because the programmes would be the first time their research would be brought to life. *Jurassic Park* had certainly been spectacular, but it had not been an accurate portrayal of dinosaur life.

With regards to details on individual dinosaurs, stature and size were probably the easiest to ascertain. Fossilized bones gave a lot of clues as to where muscles would have attached and how big each animal would have been. Other aspects were not as clear-cut, for example speed and motion of dinosaurs, as well as skin colour and behaviours. For all aspects the team sought best advice and then made the best possible decision on the knowledge gathered. For example, as to how they determined at what speed a certain dinosaur would travel, researcher Alex Freeman explained, 'It was difficult, but not impossible, to estimate the speeds of dinosaurs from their trackways. By measuring the spacing between the feet it should be possible to calculate the running or walking speed – if only we knew the length of the legs. It is rare that we can identify footprints as belonging to a particular dinosaur, but it is possible to estimate roughly the length of the legs of the dinosaur from the size of its feet! Therefore we can make a good guess at the speeds of different dinosaurs.'

Detailing the skin was another difficult issue. Initially, they tried to use photographs for the skin – but that did not work. However, in some cases they were lucky and some dinosaur skin imprints had been found which showed exactly what some dinosaurs' skin had been like. But there was no direct evidence of any dinosaur's colour, so they had to make guesses using modern animals' colours as a guide. They were also lucky in finding an expert during their recruitment process. A chap called Daren Horley rang up and asked whether they had someone to do the skin for the dinosaurs. He explained that he was a commercial artist but that he had learned everything one possibly could about dinosaurs and their skin. The BBC had originally employed a graphic designer, but the first dinosaur that had come to FrameStore had not been too realistic, so when Mike showed Tim a dinosaur painted by Daren, Daren got the job. He'd painted highly detailed skin in Photoshop, which was then pasted onto the models.

Just like the colour, sounds were very difficult to speculate about, as Tim explains, 'A little brown bird can make an extraordinary set of sounds. In the end, we created sounds that seemed to fit the size and shape of the body.'

THEORY INTO PRAXIS

In preparation for the project FrameStore decided to hire people rather than put them on time contracts, as was often done in the industry. Mike believed that after the making of *Walking with Dinosaurs* this kind of business would take off. He strongly believed this business had a future – he just knew it would be big. However, one problem was to get the right people. For computer-generated imaging there were not many skilled people in the UK. Unlike in the US, at the time no one in the UK offered proper training in that area. Mike points out, 'Computer animation is an animation job, not a computer job.' Not being able to rely on conventional avenues of recruitment he approached two people from a games company he had come across in an animation software user group. Though the games industry was generally not too well regarded in the industry, these people tend to be quite skilled at animation, work fast and know what they were doing. And, as Mike recalls, 'They were desperate to get out and get into something more meaningful. And,' he adds, 'these two turned out to be our secret weapon.' He ended up with a team of about 30, made up of 15 computer animation staff, including nine animators, three technical support staff, one skin designer, two part-time programmers, a team of six to eight worked on the compositing aspects, putting the images together, with the remaining seven to nine working on production and administration.

The project was set-up in a completely isolated unit – one reason was to get away from 'infection'. People tended to work on a number of projects and there was always one going wrong, Mike did not want the bad tension to affect the team. Instead he wanted everyone to be 100% committed to the project, own it, feel responsible for its success and for solving problems. He wanted people to feel part of a family, of 'being in it together'. He deliberately wanted to create an atmosphere of 'us and them' in the organization – which was very much not what people at FrameStore were used to. He highlighted another reason, 'If people work on more than one project and come up against a problem that is tricky, they move onto another project and solve all easier problems first. People tend to postpone working on the most difficult tasks – at least working on the less difficult tasks gives people the sense that they achieve something. If there is only one project to work on, you cannot avoid working on the tricky problems.' Mike also decided to emulate American working conditions and divide tasks up among his team according to individual skills. Normal practice in computer graphics across Europe was for staff to become generalists. FrameStore decided that, to meet the BBC's deadline and produce the highest quality work, the team should make the maximum use of individual skill, and over the course of the project each team member became a specialist in their own area.

Walking with Dinosaurs was produced using a combination of CGI (Computer-Generated Images) and 'animatronics'. CGI means that the images come out of the computer rather than being externally generated and then manipulated by the computer. 'Animatronics' – animated models – were used for many of the close-up shots. Whilst computer graphics were good, they were better for long-distance shots. Animatronics were more realistic in close-up work, such as a dinosaur eating or drinking. Mike estimated that about 80% of the series had been done in CGI, the remaining 20% using animatronics (made by a UK-based company called Crawley Creatures). An animatronic model could take between two weeks to two months to make. The result was 20 minutes of animation per 30 minutes session; in *Jurassic Park* in comparison there were about 7–8 minutes for the entire film.

Tim drew up storyboards thinking he might have to accept that his ideas could not be realized. 'I had an ideal that I wanted to aim for, but I was always prepared to forget things and try to find another way round things. But Mike Milne and FrameStore have this foolish "can do" policy, so they threw themselves at everything we asked them to do and, as time passed, in fact the reverse happened. They would say, "You know how the script says that this

> 'Whilst *Jurassic Park* is hugely regarded by the industry and is considered to be a benchmark in this kind of animation, we established very early on that *Walking with Dinosaurs* would be made in the style of a wildlife documentary, with the viewer watching the dinosaurs going about their normal activities in their natural habitat.'

dinosaur does this? Well, why don't we have him walk right into the camera?" so the whole thing fed off itself and as you are riding the crest of the wave, things just get better and better. None of us was complacent, we were all perfectionists saying, "no, we can do better" and "no, let's try that again" and that's fundamental.' Mike's praise was just as fulsome, 'Tim proved to be very flexible, he was willing to change the brief/the story if the way he initially proposed was too difficult or too expensive to do.'

But the biggest challenge remained how to make something unreal look real. To get an idea about dinosaur movement and behaviour, much time was spent studying existing natural history documentaries. FrameStore realized that a range of techniques would be needed to make the film look as realistic as possible. Tim explained, 'The majority of shots in a documentary have a moving camera, either hand-held, panning or tilting. These we had to create without the assistance of motion control or repeatable memory heads, this was especially difficult for several interaction plates that needed to match seamlessly. We also gathered technical information for every shot which would be used later for creating lighting.'

THE MAKING OF DINOSAURS

The BBC commissioned three sculptors to produce highly detailed scale models of each of the dinosaurs, based on their skeletons and the most up-to-date research. These were then scanned using Soho Cyberscan, FrameStore's state-of-the-art scanning system, specially developed for the project, and which, by using a laser scanner on a robot arm, could build up an incredibly detailed and accurate image. A major challenge was preserving the skin detail of the dinosaur models without overloading the database – a challenge met by a breakthrough in programming made by team member Andy Lomas. A crude version of each character was generated to allow animators to track movements and check positions without overloading the system with too much data. Only towards the end of the process was minute detail, such as skin colour and texture, put back into the image. 'One of the fundamental needs for animators are systems that operate with enough speed to enable them to animate intuitively,' explains Mike Milne, 'SoftImage does not allow animators to switch between simple and complex images swiftly, so another of our team members, Alex Parkinson, built a system that could.'

Daren Horley, responsible for designing the dinosaurs' skin, looked at different species in detail, and found himself facing a dilemma. 'Ken Carpenter, a palaeontologist from the University of Colorado, was kind enough to leave me some casts of skin impressions from a Stegosaurus. The thing that struck me was the small size of the scales, on a large animal they would be all but invisible at a distance. I discovered that to make the scale texture show up at TV resolution I had to make them reasonably large; it became an informed compromise between what was scientifically accurate and what looked right. The BBC suggested a look that utilized a lot of colour, but I felt that we might risk a toy-like appearance and favoured a muted colour palette.'

BRINGING THE DINOSAURS TO LIFE

Putting dinosaurs into a background was not an issue, that was something FrameStore did all the time, but the question was, how to get life-like creatures with life-like movements? A first idea was to use real animals and transfer their movements to the dinosaurs, that was what Mike had done for the pilot (rhinos, elephants), but Mike felt that if only they could get the movements right they would not have to worry too much about the rest. The problem was that there were not many animals around they could use. The right people at the right time helped overcome this issue, Mike remembers, 'We were very lucky. The two people I recruited from the games industry were absolutely brilliant, they could not only make

> **How long on average did it take to make a fully rendered Computer-Generated (CG) Dinosaur?**
>
> On average: two weeks to build the CG model from the scanned maquette, two weeks to paint the textures, three to four weeks to animate the basic walks, runs, etc., another four to six weeks to animate all the shots, about three weeks for the computer to render all the frames, and then a couple of weeks to combine the images with the live-action backgrounds.

movement look just right, they were also very fast doing so. Had we not found them it could have been a big problem.'

But even the animation of the animals was only part of the equation. The computer-generated dinosaurs needed to be placed onto live action backgrounds – and they needed to interact with the environment. So it was decided to film various bushes, trees, plants, driftwood and rocks against a portable bluescreen. Using a bluescreen would allow the placing of individual elements together or adding aspects into a scene without encountering problems with the background. The BBC crew also scaled trees and tweaked branches with string to simulate a dinosaur's shoulder brushing against it, and threw stones into streams to create splashes where the dinosaur's feet would tread. In the studio dust clouds, splashes, water sprays, drips, etc., were also filmed against a bluescreen backdrop. All camera angles and lenses had to be measured meticulously to make sure that the dinosaur animation matched the movement in the background plates. Lighting references had to be taken (using high-tech equipment such as footballs) to ensure a perfect match for compositing.

Footage was loosely cut together, crude block animations were then placed onto the background plates to give a sense of timing, followed by the modelling and animation. Subtle effects such as reflections in water and shadows were then added and the grading matched between each shot. Once this had been completed the most detailed images of the dinosaurs were composited onto the background plates, using Inferno and Henry, and bluescreen layers were added. Simulations of hand-held camera effects such as pans and tilts were added towards the end of the process, along with other effects such as motion blur to lend realism to the shots. (For more details on the stages of the animation process, please refer to Appendix II.)

> **Computers and Software behind the Dinosaurs**
>
> FrameStore used SoftImage, a specialized animation software, costing about £10,000, for all modelling, animation and rendering. The combining of images with live-action was done on special machines called 'Henry' and 'Inferno' which cost nearly half a million pounds. In terms of hardware they used Silicon Graphics Octanes for the animation, dual Pentium II's for the rendering. The Octanes were not all that powerful – about 200 MHz with 256 Mb RAM – but they had special graphics boards for really fast previewing. The rendering machines had twin 700 MHz processors with 1 Gb RAM.

IF I ONLY HAD TIME . . .

They created a word 'blockmatic' – block out animation. Mike explains, 'It meant you had to decide two things. First, how many creatures are in the picture and second, how fast they are going to move, no more. Setting up the entire episode like that helps the producer to get a feel for the whole flow and it does not require a great creative genius to achieve that. That completed Tim would then decide what actions he would want the dinosaurs to do in each scene. The advantage of breaking it down into such steps is that they are non-threatening and achievable.' 'And,' adds Mike, 'at any time you have got something you can deliver.'

'When working in the creative industry,' Mike comments, 'it is essential to know when to stop.' Creative people tend to want to refine and refine and refine. During the making of *Walking with Dinosaurs*, Mike took the shots out from the previous day first thing the next morning and put them onto the computer. That way he knew exactly what/how much had been done. He would make the decision when something was finished, which members of the team might have argued with, saying that they would want to spend more time on a particular scene, but he had the final say. In his view it was preferable to be able to deliver than refine the product endlessly. He explains, 'One has to set limits in one's own mind as to what it is people get out of the documentary rather than getting it 100% right.' Another way to manage a huge task was to break down the creative tasks into manageable chunks. 'But,' he emphasizes, 'you need to do it all in parallel, so at any time there is a finished product and you can see it all at the same level [of quality], then elevate it to the next level, etc.'

However, seven months into the project they had still not a single episode completed. FrameStore's MD was getting really worried. Mike, on the other hand, felt that the learning from the first episode would enable them to do the rest much faster later on. They were also developing a set of behaviours that could be used in all scenes. About 1/6 to 1/10 of the scenes would be special and more detailed, but going over the same ground again and again was kept to a minimum.

When they were just about one year into the project, Mike decided to call a crisis meeting, he felt they had a serious decision to make. They had lost too much time in the beginning and were now running out of time. Mike went to the team and suggested they hire more people to get the work done. This would mean that the profit would get blown out of the window, but at least they would be able to deliver on time. The team, though, did not agree with this. Mike remembers, 'They just said, "no way, not a good idea". But the good thing was that a few days later they came back with a counter-suggestion: the existing team should split in two and just get on with it. Their argument was that they would have to spend so much time training the newcomers they might as well do it themselves. Splitting the existing team in two meant that they could work on the two most straightforward episodes simultaneously.' Though the arithmetic seemed a bit strange, it worked, though Mike admits that the quality for one of the two suffered a bit. However, on the upside, the episode for which quality was slightly compromised was set under water where the scenery was so beautiful that it did not need such high quality to have a positive impact on the viewer.

WORKING WITH BBC GLOBAL BRAND MANAGEMENT

In the late 1990s the BBC decided to respond to an increasingly globalized marketplace of television and entertainment. In 1998, about half way through the development of *Walking with Dinosaurs*, the BBC set up the Global Marketing and Brand Development Department (GMBD) to coordinate and manage products that would sell across media and globally. Part of the responsibility of the new department was to create and ensure brand consistency across the range of products developed in association with a programme.

The new department was part of BBC Worldwide, the commercial arm of the BBC whose responsibility it was to maximize revenues from BBC properties (programmes, brands) so as to generate cash to be re-invested into quality BBC programming. As part of BBC Worldwide, GMBD's remit was to coordinate and raise investment for new projects, liaise with production to develop ancillary products appropriate to the brand, and position those products effectively in market, thereby generating revenues for BBC Worldwide and the BBC.

GMBD played an essential part in realizing new productions. First and foremost, BBC Worldwide would acquire the rights from the BBC in return for its investment. Secondly, they would cooperate with production to develop a brand proposition in keeping with television and translate this into brand and style guides (see Appendix III) – this process aided the crystallization of a unique selling proposition of a production. Prior to the setting up of GMBD, such decisions would have been left to the discretion of the producer. Thirdly, GMBD tended to take a strategic perspective on the development of BBC properties. It would look to identify opportunities across new media, new channels and routes to market.

Throughout programme development the team in BBC Worldwide would also make sure that producers were aware of the commercial necessities. For example, in countries such as Japan, the use of a presenter can cause problems. The Japanese audience would not have responded positively to a British presenter and would require their own. A similar reaction could be expected in France, where the issue has more to do with the French perception that the presenter format 'talks down' to the audience. While many producers are aware of commercial necessities when developing programme content and structure, there can be a conflict between commercial and creative interests. And while this may not be explicitly expressed Tim comments, 'BBC Worldwide would rarely directly object to any project by a producer, but whether they thought it was worth it or not would be reflected in the money they are willing to put up. In the end getting a film off the ground means ensuring that everyone's needs are met.' Paul Clarke, Head of Factual Global Marketing, BBC Worldwide, adds, 'Collaboration at all levels is the only way to ensure successful acquisition of funds for new programming and ensuring that the brand is marketed effectively.'

In the process of programme development there are two main points of contact between commercial and production: tagging meetings and the development of the concept for a production.

If and when required, commercial would call tagging meetings. During these meetings, producers present treatments (synopses of what the programme or series is about plus initial budgeting) and GMBD assess them as to their commercial value and tags those it is interested in. Evaluation criteria would include whether the programme would be likely to be transferable into more than four countries, whether it would have potential to be exploited through a range of media, i.e. video, book, merchandise, etc. and whether it would have some permanence in the marketplace, i.e. promises to be a series rather than a one-off. As Paul explains, 'To effectively market a title such as *Walking with Dinosaurs* requires significant marketing investment, and therefore you need to sustain brands for the long term rather than launch new titles every quarter.'

Before the setting up of the GMBD department, much of the interaction between commercial and production tended to rely on personal contacts and initiative. Now there were four main kinds of meetings between GMBD and production:

1. *Commercial hours meetings*: ensuring an understanding between production, GMBD and BBC public service of the demand and supply of science, natural history and history, arts and documentaries programming. Insights from the meeting would direct the allocation of investment.

2. *Editorial meetings*: between production and GMBD: allowing GMBD to preview up and coming titles and share ideas with production.

3. *Title launch meetings*: GMBD would align production with stills/specific requirements to facilitate cross-media exploitation; it would also allow production to update GMBD on latest changes to programme treatment.

4. *Title review meetings*: ongoing and *ad hoc* as necessary.

Once a treatment had been selected and budgets have been signed-off, an initial development meeting would be held between commercial and production to discuss the latest treatment, as this could change during the first phase, as well as identify stills requirements. It was important to do this early on as production used to work on these aspects towards the end, but as the production of books could have lead-times of 18 months or more, programme and related products would not be available at the same time. Early agreement on ancillary products was important for another reason: different media have different demands on the quality of images. For example, pictures for the book need a higher resolution than those for the film, which meant that additional money would be needed. It was further important to agree to time-lines, particularly as people in production would not always be aware of ancillary product time-lines, which often varied widely from those for television production.

Finally, BBC Global Brand Management would engage in the brand development and positioning. Generally this would involve the following:

*   An outline on how to position the programme
*   Developing a brand guide
*   Developing marketing plans

Effective positioning development would rely on close cooperation between production and GMBD. By necessity this had to be an iterative process given that the ideas would initially be primarily in the producer's head and could change, especially in the early stages. The visual identity would be developed out of the brand positioning and marketing plans would be developed in collaboration with BBC public service marketing media format teams (publishing, video and DVD, etc.) and applied to international markets.

For *Walking with Dinosaurs* the process was slightly different, as GMBD did not exist when the series went into production. Alix remembers, 'The *Walking with Dinosaurs* series was started before we came into being. Half the auxiliary products had already been initiated and we were not too happy with the consistency – or lack of it – across the products.' However, in many ways the series was seen as a test case for the new approach, signifying a shift from programmes primarily driven by production to programmes developed in close cooperation with GMBD. It was a first not only in its scope of international outlook, but also in terms of developing merchandise for a factual – rather than fictional – programme.

THE RESULTS

Initially it was quite difficult to get licensees to understand the difference between *Jurassic Park* and *Walking with Dinosaurs*. The difference was not in the animation, but in the fact that *Walking with Dinosaurs* was aiming to be a documentary, whereas *Jurassic Park* was made up, beginning to end. In addition, *Walking with Dinosaurs* would not have used human beings in their film or anything else that would not have been consistent with the world in those days.

Still, there was some criticism from some palaeontologists. Though Tim Haines pointed out, '90% of the palaeontologists I talked to are delighted, and anyone who is involved in museums or institutions that thrive on public interest are also delighted. It is interesting to look at some of the criticisms from the Natural History Museum, which has used *Walking with Dinosaurs* in its advertising campaign to get people to attend. Dismissing the series as invalid, because it's based on speculation, betrays a deep-seated elitism.'

It was felt that there would have been room for improvement. Transmission in the UK was October 1999, a lot of the products only came out about 12–18 months later. Another issue with the product was that one cannot trademark the 'truth'. Had production been aware of this they could have 'personalized' the dinosaurs, e.g. a broken tooth, a scar, etc., which would have helped to brand merchandise. Had they been able to liaise with Tim earlier, they could have alerted him to that fact and individual dinosaurs would have been more trademarkable. As a consequence, BBC Worldwide has now developed a philosophy guide that clarifies unique selling points. In addition, there is a brand guide as well as a style guide that outlines how to use the logo.

Despite these issues, the series has gone from strength to strength and the results are impressive:

- In September 99, even before the first broadcast the series had generated more than £1.30m in television pre-sales.

- The series has been the 19th most popular programme ever at the BBC, and it has done incredibly well because it is not linked to any particular culture and can be translated into any language.

- In the US it broke all records; it was the highest non-sports cable programme; in spring 2000 over 40m people in the US watched all or some of the programme on the Discovery Channel.

- By December 2000 the series has had a total retail marketing value approaching £35 million and has generated more than £1.7 million in programme sales with TV deals in 22 countries; BBC Worldwide hold all publishing rights to the series, advance orders and sales of the video and books alone have already been made to the value of £1.25 million.

- By mid-2001 the series had been licensed to over 50 countries.

- By mid-2001 Tim's book had sales in the UK in excess of 700,000 and about the same number of the children's book were sold; the book had also been Number 1 in the *Sunday Times* Hardback 'General' category for two weeks.

All in all, the programme has made a turnover of more than £25 m and won several awards (see Appendix IV). Tim explains the success as follows, 'TV is there to entertain. Also to educate but that is not the primary objective. On TV you want to give people relaxation and *Walking with Dinosaurs* is both highly entertaining and highly educational.' He also points out that, 'The first programme was even better than the pilot in that is was even more realistic. This was just as well as expectations had been raised through the excellent pilot. As a producer you have a problem, you want people to be excited about a programme but the more fuss people make about a programme the more the pressure is on for the producer to meet or exceed expectations.'

> '*Walking with Dinosaurs* is the first major example of global brand marketing in the factual area and is, with all ancillary marketing products, pointed to become one of BBC Worldwide's top earners. It has already broken audience records for ABC in Australia and has been a massive hit in Germany for Pro7 – it is a worldwide phenomenon.'
>
> *BBC Worldwide Chief Executive Rupert Gavin*

QUESTIONS

1.   What are possible mechanisms for ensuring both creativity and commercial realism?

2.   Drawing on both your own experience and the case study, what does it take to make an innovative project happen? [What are aspects of innovative projects (a) generally (b) in this case? How were they addressed?]

3.   What are the considerations in innovating for a global market?

4.   What are considerations for developing a global brand?

APPENDIX I: MEET THE DINOSAURS

Starring in each of the series:

1.   New blood – 220 million years ago

   —   *Coelophysis* – meaning hollow form (because of his thin bones) dinosaur; carnivore, meat and fish eating, cannibalistic scavenger

   —   *Placerias* – mammal-like reptile; herbivore

   —   *Cynodont* – meaning dog-toothed; half mammal, half reptile; omnivore

— *Postosuchus* – archosaur; carnivore

— *Peteinosaurus* – early pterosaur; insectivore

2. A time of titans – 152 million years ago

— *Diplodocus* – meaning double beamed lizard; dinosaur, herbivore

— *Allosaurus* – meaning different lizard; dinosaur, carnivore

— *Stegosaurus* – meaning covered lizard; dinosaur, herbivore

— *Anurognathus* – meaning without tail and jaw; pterosaur; insectivore

— *Orchitholestes* – meaning bird robber; dinosaur, carnivore

3. Cruel sea – 149 million years ago

— *Ophthalmosaurus* – meaning eye lizard; ichthyosaur, carnivore

— *Liopleurodon* – plesiosaur; carnivore

— *Rhamphorhynchus* – meaning beak snout; pterosaur; carnivore

— *Eustreptospondylus* – meaning well-reversed vertebrae; carnivore

— *Cryptoclidus* – meaning hidden collar bone; plesiosaur; carnivore

— Hybodus shark – cartilaginous fish, carnivore

4. Giant of the skies – 127 million years ago

— *Polacanthus* – meaning many spined; dinosaur; herbivore

— *Ornithocheirus* – meaning bird hand; pterosaur

— *Tapejara* – meaning old being; pterosaur; carnivore

— *Iguanodon* – meaning iguana tooth; herbivore

— *Utahraptor* – meaning robber from Utah; dinosaur; carnivore

5. Spirits of the ice forest – 106 million years ago

— *Leaellynasaura* – named after daughter of palaeontologist Tom; dinosaur; herbivore

— Dwarf allosaur – meaning strange lizard; dinosaur; carnivore

— *Muttaburrasaurus* – named after a township in Australia; dinosaur; herbivore

— *Koolasuchus*; named after a palaeontologist; amphibian, carnivore

6. Death of a dynasty

— *Anatotitan* – meaning giant duck; dinosaur; herbivore

— *Torosaurus* – meaning bull lizard; dinosaur; herbivore

— *Ankylosaurus* – meaning fused or stiff lizard; dinosaur; herbivore

— *Tyrannosaurus* – meaning tyrant lizard; dinosaur; carnivore

APPENDIX II: STAGES OF THE ANIMATION PROCESS

Adapted from FrameStore's website (http://www.framestore.co.uk)

1. DIGITIZING/SCANNING

All dinosaur models in this series began life as a physical maquette. These are high detail scale models sculpted in clay, from which a resin cast is made, which are used directly for scanning and building the computer graphic models. Upon receipt of the finished maquettes, the digitizing process begins. This is represented by three key stages:

1. Preparing the maquette for scanning; which entails cleaning and then covering the model with a diffuse and optically opaque white paint.

2. Scanning, with an in-house high resolution laser scanner.

3. Data cleanup, and creating a range of digital models at different resolutions for animation and rendering.

In cooperation with Soho Cyberscan, FrameStore developed a suite of software tools, to faithfully capture the three-dimensional form and texture detail represented in the original physical maquettes. Once scanned, the model data is initially just a very large cloud of over six million three-dimensional points. At this stage the data is too dense, it has to be reduced to about one million points and linked into a polygonal lattice. A refined form is created using even fewer polygonal facets, however still maintaining the level of detail seen in the original model. Finally, a low resolution version is made for animation purposes, this enables us to see creature movement playback in real time.

2. MODELLING

When the project started there were originally 24 dinosaurs to be modelled. By the time the last episode was complete, this number had grown to 40. New creatures were introduced as the series evolved, and extra model detail was called for in some sequences.

Animation model

Upon receiving the high and low resolution polygonal models from the laser scanner, they were adjusted to the correct scale and orientation, so as to match the camera and scene data for each shot. A simple animation model is built from the low resolution scanned data. This is generally made from a series of cylindrical components.

Patch model

By carefully observing the form 'flow lines' running over the high resolution scanned data, an efficient implicit surface model is built using up to 88 patches.

Fully textured model in neutral position

Finally, capturing the fine surface detail seen in the original maquettes involved combining advanced proprietary computer modelling techniques, with the more traditional skills of an illustrator.

3. SKIN DESIGN

The process of painting the dinosaur skins began with the creation of colour designs which were sent to the BBC directors for approval. In designing dinosaur skin, various factors had to be taken into account – habitat, possible lifestyle, whether the dinosaur was a carnivore or a herbivore, and body size. The size of an animal has a bearing on its colouration; large animals tend to have dull skin colours (like elephants or rhinos), with bright colours and patterns reserved for smaller, tropical animals such as parrots or lizards. As colour pigment does not fossilize, there is no historical evidence of dinosaur skin colour; however, there is evidence that dinosaurs had scaly reptilian skin. Once the designs were approved, the skins were ready to be painted. The first step was to paint a black and white (or greyscale) image, called a 'bump map,' that the computer interprets as bumps in the surface. This creates shadows and highlights, giving the illusion of a rough textured skin.

Next a 'colour map' was painted containing all the skin colour and pattern information. These were then applied to the model. As the maps were two-dimensional images projected onto a three-dimensional model, it was necessary to paint multiple maps to cover the entire surface of the dinosaur. These were combined into one seamless map.

4. ANIMATION

Computer animation is a technique for creating the illusion of movement and life, using computer-generated characters, or in this case photo-realistic dinosaurs. The process is divided into two main parts, primary and secondary animation. Primary animation involves the main articulation and motion of a creature. Secondary animation is all the other movement, such as flesh and muscle movement.

1. After the model has been built, a 'skeleton' is constructed, which will be used for animating all the movements of the dinosaur.

2. Onto this skeleton an interactive model is built, a low detail representation of the very complicated complete model. This is done so the animator can quickly and easily manipulate the dinosaur. The creature can then be animated by moving and rotating different 'bones' or joints. Now that the skeleton and interactive model are created animation can begin.

3. With the help of the BBC a library of live action wildlife reference material was built up, which was used to help form ideas about the kind of movements and behavioural characteristics the dinosaurs would have. The first stage is to get the dinosaur walking. This initial animation helps visualize the animal's weight, size, posture and character. Each 'bone' is then individually animated to create realistic, fluid movement.

4. In a process called 'enveloping,' the final model is attached to the animation skeleton. A walk cycle for the complete dinosaur is then rendered on a 'turntable' so that the skin and movement can be fully tested.

5. Extra 'bones' are added (ribs, for example). These make sure that skin, muscles and wobbling fat behave correctly. Finally, eye blinks and breathing are added, these small details really help bring the creatures to life.

5. LIGHTING AND RENDERING

Once the animation is completed for a shot it is ready to light. Lighting involves illuminating the computer-generated scene with virtual lights, to match the direct and ambient light in the live-action backplate(s). This is first accomplished by using survey data and reference information collected on location at the time of filming. Range data enables the setting up of a virtual camera and set its position. Reference frames of a 'lighting-ball' are filmed at the same time. Using a 'lighting-ball' it is possible to understand the proper direction and intensity of the dominant light sources in the scene. After carefully balancing the virtual lights to match the graded live action scene, the shot is ready for rendering. As part of this project proprietary methods were devised to maximize render throughout, but to also offer complete flexibility over lighting balance and shadow density, right through to the final composite. This enabled the generation of over 28,000 frame elements in one 12-hour period.

6. COMPOSITING

Computer-generated 3D elements are rendered to tape, with up to five layers for each creature. These consist of a colour, form, shadow, highlight and secondary shadow passes (as shown below). Each layer is added one on top of the other, and at each stage careful adjustments are made to ensure that the dinosaurs' shading and shadow density match those of the live action background plate. At this stage bluescreen elements such as extra tree ferns, rocks and other foreground items are added.

When colour grading underwater creatures, the colour saturation decreases with depth. By using a 3D depth matte, a creature can be made to appear and disappear from the blue depths. For the larger land-based dinosaurs we were also able to control the depth of field along the length of their bodies. The team of five Henry and five Inferno compositing artists produced over 1000 shots.

7. MASTERGRADE

When all the compositing is finished the final shots are dropped into the edit. In telecine any final 'look' or matching of colour balance is carried out. It was decided to make *Walking With Dinosaurs* 'future protected'. This means safe for 4:3 and 16:9 widescreen viewing. The plates or backgrounds were shot on 35 mm film 'open gate'. This gave us excellent steadiness and detail. Prior to *Walking with Dinosaurs*, almost all documentaries were shot 16 or S16 mm, which was felt not to be high enough quality for this project. The film master was finally transferred to digital tape as '16:9 anamorphic'; this is then unsqueezed at the point of broadcast.

APPENDIX III: EXCERPT FROM BRAND GUIDE

Brand positioning

—   the real-life experience with the most extraordinary creatures that ever lived

Brand substantiators

—   travel back in time and watch living, breathing dinosaurs in their natural habitat

—   it feels completely real; a primeval environment is created by leading-edge computer technology, animatronics and footage from locations around the globe where ancient plants still survive

—   story-led programmes which show us the anatomy, life-cycle and behaviour of dinosaurs — familiar favourites like *Tyrannosaurus Rex*, as well as less familiar creatures like *Liopleurodon*, the world's largest carnivore at 25 meters long

— the latest palaeontological theories on the magnificent prehistoric animals which roamed the earth for 160 million years

Target audience

— broad family appeal – adults and children alike

— everybody who loved *Jurassic Park*

— everybody with an interest in natural history or palaeontology

How does it make me feel?

— Wow, that was amazing

— I feel I could reach out and touch them… the detail is fantastic

— When you see the dinosaurs in the forest crashing through the trees, splashing in the water, chasing insects – it's like being on a dinosaur safari

Brand values

— real, captivating, cutting edge

Associated products

— home videos

— adult trade books

— children's books (photo book, sticker book, Q&A book, 3D poster book)

— DVD

— Music CD

— Merchandise

— Online site

APPENDIX IV: AWARDS AS OF 30th OCTOBER 2001

WALKING WITH DINOSAURS – THE PILOT

- Prix Pixel-INA Monte Carlo 1998 'Content Graphics'

- London Effects and Animation Festival (LEAF) 1997 'Education and Training Award'

- Australian Effects and Animation Festival 1998 'Education and Training Award'

- CGIX Amsterdam 1998 (category not recorded on the award, and I can't remember!)

WALKING WITH DINOSAURS – THE SERIES

- 3 Emmys (US)

  — Outstanding animated programme

  — Outstanding music composition for a mini series, movie or special

  — Outstanding achievement for non-fiction programming – sound editing

- Royal Television Society – team award for *Walking with Dinosaurs*

- BAFTA – innovation award; also nominated for the Lew Grade Award (voted by readers of *Radio Times*)

- Voice of the Listener and Viewer Awards – best new television programme

- London Effects and Animation Festival (LEAF) Gold Award 1999

- Royal Television Society Craft and Design Awards 1999/2000 'Design and Craft Innovation Award'

- Royal Television Society Programme Awards 1999 'Team Award'

- Creative Freedom Awards 2000 'Factual Television Programme Award'

FRAMESTORE

- 2001 Outstanding Animated Programme: *The Ballad of Big Al*

- 2000 Outstanding Visual FX: *Walking With Dinosaurs*

- 2000 Outstanding Animated Programme: *Walking With Dinosaurs*

- 2000 Outstanding Main Title Design: *The 10th Kingdom*

- 1999 Outstanding Special FX: *Alice in Wonderland*

- 1998 Outstanding Special Visual FX: *Merlin*

- 1997 Outstanding Special Visual FX: *The Odyssey*

- 1996 Outstanding Special Visual FX: *Gulliver's Travels*

3 Structured Processes for Developing New Products

For most companies wanting to become more innovative, which they will almost certainly associate with the development of new products, the starting point is the introduction – or revision – of a new product development process. While structured processes for the development and management of new products are no guarantee for improving innovativeness, they are nevertheless an important part in an organization's armoury to improve new product introduction rate and maximize the benefits from a company's product portfolio.

This chapter briefly reviews the evolution of the new product development process, expands on the stage-gate process and product portfolio management, as well as the role of the project leader, concluding with some insights into best and worst practice.

> In a survey conducted in 2000 with members of the Innovation Exchange, a networking initiative based at the London Business School, only about half of the participants declared to have a systematic new product development process, with another 24% saying they were starting to work on it.

THE EVOLUTION OF THE NEW PRODUCT DEVELOPMENT PROCESS

One of the biggest influences on how companies approach product development in the West has been a concept developed by NASA in the 1960s, introduced to make the management of large scale, complex defence projects easier. The first version, 'Phased Project Planning', as it was called, described a basically sequential approach consisting of four phases:

- Preliminary analysis (phase A)
- Definition (phase B)
- Design (phase C)
- Operation (phase D)

In addition, checkpoint reviews were introduced to ensure that mistakes would not be carried forward into the next phase. Whilst this approach was originally applied to complex, large scale projects only, its principles were soon scaled down and translated for new product development in a more general way. The fundamental principle – phases and checks between them – are still valid today, and reflected in the now most commonly used kind of process, the stage-gate process, to which we will come back in the following section. Figure 3.1 shows the NASA process as seen in Peter W. Morris' book *The Management of Projects*.

A further influential study, with regards not only to the development process but to new product in general, was undertaken by Booz Allen Hamilton (1982). When they researched how companies define product development stages, they found the following steps:

Figure 3.1   The NASA Management Process (Morris 1994) (reproduced by permission of NASA)

1.   Development of new product development strategy[1]
2.   Idea generation[2]
3.   Screening and evaluation[3]
4.   Business analysis
5.   Development
6.   Testing
7.   Commercialization

These categories are used with variations throughout the literature, and there is a body of literature discussing each of the steps individually. If more steps are proposed, they are generally a breakdown of one of the steps above. Cooper (1986), for example, describes 13 steps whereby the additional steps result from separating activities such as market research and business analysis. Another, broader way of segmenting the development process, identifying three main stages, is provided again by Cooper (1988):

1.   Pre-development activities
2.   Product development and testing
3.   Commercialization

In his 1992 article, Rothwell provide a useful summary of how the new product development process has evolved over time (shown in Table 3.1).

In the shift from a linear, sequential development process towards a more integrated and dynamic one, the need for increased speed has been one of the main drivers. Takeuchi and Nonaka (1986) have written one of the most influential articles on this subject, alerting companies to the need to move away from the linear approach. The sequential approach is described as 'relay race' where the baton is passed from one department to the next, often requiring changes to accommodate requirements of a downstream department. This approach could probably also

Table 3.1 Five Generations of NPD Models (based on Rothwell 1992)

Generation	Type of model	Characteristics of model
First	Technology push model	Simple linear sequential process; emphasis on R&D, the market is a receptacle for the fruits of R&D
Second	Need pull model	Simple linear sequential process; emphasis on marketing; the market is the source of ideas for directing R&D; R&D has a reactive role
Third	Coupling model	Sequential but with feedback loops; push or pull or push/pull combinations; R&D and marketing more in balance; emphasis on integration at the R&D/marketing interface
Fourth	Integrated model	Parallel development with integrated development teams; strong upstream supplier linkages; close coupling with leading-edge customers; emphasis on integration between R&D and manufacturing/design for makeability; horizontal collaboration (joint ventures)
Fifth	Systems integrating and networking model	Fully integrated parallel development; use of expert systems and simulation modelling in R&D; strong linkages with leading customers (customer focus at the forefront of strategy); strategic integration with primary suppliers including co-development of new products and linked CAD systems; horizontal linkages; joint ventures; collaborative research groupings; collaborative marketing arrangements etc.; emphasis on corporate flexibility and speed of development (time-based strategy); increased focus on quality and other non-price factors

have been called 'Chinese Whispers', as information passed on is often incomplete or insufficiently explained, leading to misunderstandings and confusion. One of my favourite sketches on this subject stems from Michael Smith (see Figure 3.2, reproduced as seen in Lorenz 1990).

Takeuchi and Nonaka contrast the relay race with a, then, new approach they compare to a 'rugby game', in which the product is passed back and forth between the different departments, like the ball in rugby. They explain that advantages of the new approach include not only increased speed, but also greater consistency and integrity of the product, because of the early consideration of concerns and requirements from all departments involved in a product's development process.

Building on the insights and positive results companies experienced through the early and continuous interaction between all departments, a large number of articles in the early 90s has heralded the use of cross-functional teams as the solution to many a development problem (e.g. Ancona and Caldwell 1990; Oakley 1990a; Belbin 1991; Nadler 1991; Faust 1993). However, companies implementing teams as a consequence were often disappointed. This may have been attributable to a considerable extent to the fact that people were told to work in teams – without being given any training or other kinds of support that would aid the shift in working practices. We shall come back to the subject of teams in Chapter 10.

A final aspect that has received a great deal of attention in the literature is what is often described as the 'fuzzy front end' of the development process. There are two aspects to the fuzziness: the first refers to the uncertainty, and the other to the lack of structure often associated with the early stages of product development. However, early stages of product development are critical as over 80% of a product's production costs are locked in during these early stages (e.g. Dixon and Duffey 1990; Smith and Reinertsen 1995). A lack of attention here can lead to costly

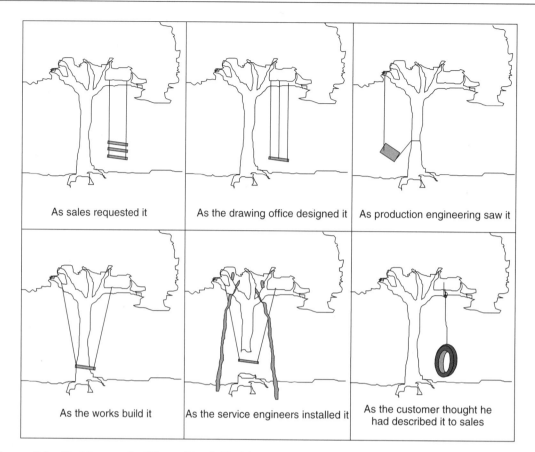

As sales requested it

As the drawing office designed it

As production engineering saw it

As the works build it

As the service engineers installed it

As the customer thought he had described it to sales

Figure 3.2   Barking up the Wrong Tree? (Smith, in Lorenz 1990) (reproduced by permission of Basil Blackwell)

and time-consuming changes later in the development process. Smith and Reinertsen point out, 'The calculated cost of delay is often 500–5000 times higher than the visible cost of assigned personnel. Managers unaware of these costs will tend to ignore the fuzzy front end. Those who understand these costs will instead focus a great deal of attention on this phase.' Khurana and Rosenthal (1997) who have undertaken research into the fuzzy front end of new product development found that success factors related to this stage can be grouped under two headings:

1.   *Foundation* – including aspects such as the existence of a product strategy, the management of the product portfolio (rather than individual projects), the existence of a specific product development organization structure including a project leader, a core team, an executive review group, a good communication structure.

2.   *Project-specific* – referring to the existence of the following: a concept statement, thorough evaluation, a product definition, value chain considerations, front-end project planning and definitions, and recognizing interrelationships.

However, there are also those who emphasize that different stages of the development process require different cultures, particularly if innovation rather than incremental improvements are concerned. Zien and Buckler (1997) describe what they call three micro cultures of innovation:

1.   *The Fuzzy Front End (FFE)* which is experimental and chaotic; requires high tolerance for ambiguity and uncertainty; for people with high structure needs it often seems 'unreasonable'; but people who like it enjoy it for the quest itself; it *is* unpredictable, and it depends on much individual activity.[4]

2.   *The Product Development Process (PDP)* which needs to be disciplined and focused on numerous quantitative goals and measurements; it requires commitment to the goal; is schedule-oriented and urgent; can be trained, and is generally not receptive to new ideas; teamwork is of paramount importance.

3.   *Market Operations (MO)* where we seek predictability and order; it has a strong financial orientation; it relies on commitment to established values and businesses; is oriented to rules and routine and slow to change; has to be highly organized and does not welcome revolutionary ideas; tends to be of large size compared to FFE or PDP.

THE STAGE-GATE PROCESS

I have mentioned earlier that the principle of the stage-gate process go back to the work undertaken by NASA on project management. As the original NASA process, the stage-gate process suggests that a project has to be reviewed at certain points in its development, and a go/no-go decision should be made. This way an organization can avoid throwing good money after bad – it is never

Sunk Cost

Past expenditure, which is often thought to be irrelevant to future decisions as the best decisions tend to maximize future cash flow

The Oxford Concise Dictionary of Business (1990)

advisable to keep spending money on a project just because quite a lot has been spent on it already (sunk cost).

The stage-gate process as now known and used in product development has been devised by Robert G. Cooper and his colleagues. Both Figure 3.3 and the overview in Box 3.1 are based on Cooper and Kleinschmidt's (2001) article 'Stage-gate process for new product success'.

In their article, Cooper and Kleinschmidt also share some insights into how to maximize chances for new product success. This includes the already mentioned necessity to pay careful attention to the early stages, which includes doing background research as well as a 'sharp and early' definition of the product. Other points include the need for market orientation, teams and strong cross-functional cooperation and, most importantly, the need

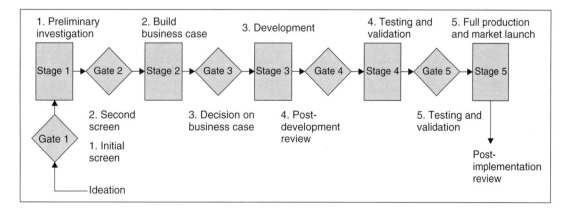

Figure 3.3   Stage-Gate Process (reproduced from (Cooper and Kleinschmidt 2001))

BOX 3.1   Process Overview (Cooper and Kleinschmidt 2001) (reproduced by permission of Cooper & Kleinschmidt)

Gate 1	Gate 2	Gate 3	Gate 4	Gate 5
First decision to commit resources, signalling tentative commitment; criteria tend to be qualitative and few in number: strategic alignment, technical feasibility, competitive advantage, opportunity attractiveness; looking at 'musts'	More rigorous screen; commitment of resources more substantial; often a scoring model is used to measure synergies, market attractiveness, competitive situation, product advantage, profit potential; looking at 'musts' and 'shoulds'	Last point to kill project before heavy spending; sign off product specification; pass criteria should be tough and rigorous; looking at 'musts' and 'shoulds' again as well as financial and risk review	Recheck continued attractiveness of project; check against product specification and performance expectations	Criteria here are largely on quality of efforts to date, appropriateness of the production and launch plans, financial viability

Stage 1	Stage 2	Stage 3	Stage 4	Stage 5
Quick review of project, looking at technical and marketplace merits	Development of business case to verify attractiveness; 'critical homework stage' that is often neglected; studies may include: user needs/wants; competitive analysis; concept testing; technical and manufacturing appraisal; legal, patent and regulatory assessment; detailed financial analysis	Deliverable at end of this stage is a lab-tested prototype; emphasis is on technical work, marketing and manufacturing activities run parallel	Testing and validating: the product itself, production process, customer acceptance, economies; activities may include: in-house product test checks (quality and performance); user field trials; pilot production; pre-test market; revised financial analysis	Putting marketing launch plan and production or operations plan in motion

Post-implementation review

Often companies review the project and the products performance about 6–18 months after launch to draw out lessons learnt for a superior product. This last point is still the major differentiator between a successful and a less successful or even completely unsuccessful product. And finally, as we mentioned speed earlier, it is interesting that the authors warn to be careful about speed. Or rather, agreeing with the idiom 'more haste, less speed', they say that companies should be careful not to let speed become a goal in itself. The goal should always remain the introduction of a successful new product. Cutting corners, particularly in the early stages, generally has to be paid for, manifold, later.[5]

A further note of caution: in applying a stage-gate process companies should be careful not to let the process become an end in itself. If applied too strictly and rigidly it can hinder rather than help the development of new products, as an Innovation Exchange member pointed out, 'There can be a tyranny of the process!' Leading-edge companies have come to realize this and now talk about using the process as guideline, rather than 'bible' or 'rule book'. Gates become more fluid and more than one stage can be worked on simultaneously. This prevents individual gates from becoming bottlenecks that delay progress of a project unnecessarily. In fact, Robert Cooper himself pointed this out as early as 1994, announcing it to be time for the third generation new product development process, one that is characterized by four 'Fs':

- *Fluid*: it is fluid and adaptable, with overlapping and fluid stages for greater speed

- *Fuzzy gates*: it features conditional go decisions (rather than absolute ones) which are dependent on the situation

- *Focused*: it builds in prioritization methods that look at the entire portfolio of projects (rather than one project at the time) and focuses resources on the 'best bets'

- *Flexible*: it is not a rigid stage-and-gate system; each project is unique and has its own routing through the process

The four 'Fs' are not only important for the application of the process, they also apply to the treatment of the process itself. It is important to continuously assess and adjust a company's new product development process to make sure it reflects latest insights, the context of the organization, and particularly its ambition. What I mean by the last term is that a process for the development of incremental improvements or routine projects should be different from one that aims to produce radical ones – as alluded to earlier.[6] Changes in a company's structure can also have implications for the new product development process, for example, product development in a functionally oriented organization is likely to be executed differently from an organization with a project or matrix structure (for characteristics of functional, project and matrix-based organizations, see Table 3.2). Whichever process is chosen, it is essential that reward systems support the behaviours required to fill the process with life – in fact, all systems and aspects of an organization need to enhance and support each other, a theme which we will come back to again and again throughout the book.

DEVELOPMENT FUNNEL AND PRODUCT PORTFOLIO MANAGEMENT

Next to the stage-gate process the most known and popular tool in the armoury to improve new product development is the 'Development Funnel', a tool developed by Harvard Business School professors Kim Clark and Stephen Wheelwright in the early 1990s (see Figure 3.4). It encourages managers to take an integrated approach to new product development. Rather than making decisions on individual projects, their approach suggests the management and coordination of product development activities from a company-wide perspective, starting with a link to company strategy. It is interesting to note though that much of the literature seems to treat the development

Table 3.2   Types of Organizational Structure[1]

Type	How it works	Appropriate for	Problems
Functional structure (basic structure)	The project is planned and executed within a functional structure with moves from department to department in a pre-arranged sequence (relay race) Responsibilities must be clearly defined Need for integration of sequential activities	Improvements of existing products. New products of low innovation Sequential processing possible Fosters deep specialization and expertise	Often strong pressure on the departments to give top priority to the short term Conflicting demands on staff (prioritization of projects) Balance between short-term projects (order and discipline) and innovative projects (freedom and flexibility) Integration of functions
Independent project organization	Self-contained group, full-time members from various different functions The project manager has full responsibility for the project and is given the necessary resources for planning and implementation Team should be co-located	Large projects which justify employing experts from different functions on a full-time basis For new solutions or new products Firms in dynamic markets	Issue of re-integration of staff Isolation from the rest of the organization Dispensing people to the project full time might cause problems in the basic organization How to maintain specialization and carry forward learn from previous projects
Matrix organization	Decision-making responsibility rests with the project team Project manager negotiates with heads of functional departments on necessary resources (manpower and equipment) Staff is assigned on part-time or full-time bases Task often broken down into independent activities, allowing simultaneous processing High demands on social and political skills of project manager Clear goals and well-understood technology will result in an effective balance of power	Complex projects which require simultaneous efforts of experts from several disciplines Large projects: here the project manager is often supported by team leaders within the individual functions	Authority can be split between the project manager and the functional manager Projects are cutting across the authority lines of the functional departments (leading to authority ambiguity) Conflict of loyalty of part-time staff who work on more than one project simultaneously Problems of re-integration into functional structure If project is broken down into sub-tasks the need for coordination goes up Competition for resources also leads to an increased need for coordination Time-consuming decision-making process

[1]Based on Earle (1973), Kingdon (1973), Sayles (1976), Baker and Wilemon (1977), Davis and Lawrence (1977), Kolodny (1979), (1980), Vasconcellos (1979), Rowen *et al.* (1980), Greiner and Schein (1981), Brown and Agnew (1982), Holt (1987) and Ulrich and Fluri (1988).

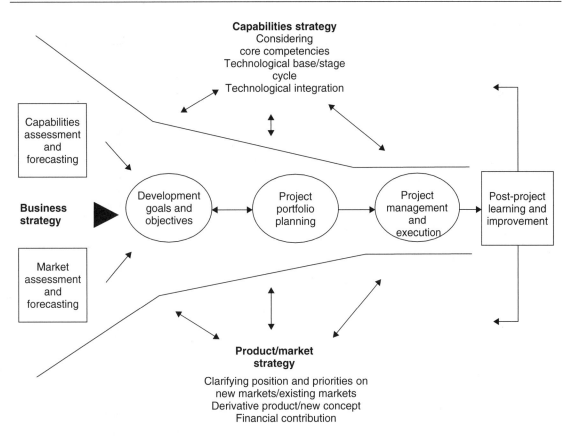

Figure 3.4 The Development Funnel (reproduced from (Clark and Wheelwright 1993))

funnel as a variation on the theme of stage-gate processes albeit with a strong emphasis on the need to generate many ideas, and to narrow them down quickly as the project is progressing through the process. I believe that the main advantage of the development funnel is the requirement to take a company-wide perspective.

In the following we will look at the factors behind each of the individual components of the development funnel.

For *Capabilities Assessment and Forecasting* a company would undertake an analysis of the current and future product/service capacity, look at current and planned new product/service developments, investigate the efficiency of current processes and review technologies to determine the company's current position.

Market Assessment and Forecasting would involve an analysis of existing clients to identify current needs and areas of improvements, as well as an analysis of competitors to identify new areas of expansion and, finally, a trends analysis to capture the direction of the industry.

Development Goals and Objectives comprises the development of a set of specific measures and targets for key portfolio criteria, including:

- strategic fit
- revenues and profits
- client fit

- dates of new product/service introductions and technology achievements
- new product/service performance objectives and criteria

This component also involves the establishment of targets for entering new segments, developing new technology and technical skills, or creating new markets, as well as acting as a guideline for investment decisions.

Project Portfolio Planning involves the definition of a set of current and future projects and the allocation of resources to them. Careful resource planning and management are critical, as successful product development is prevented in many organizations due to 'project constipation', too many projects with too little resource. Clark and Wheelwright found that a person should work on no more than two projects if he or she is to provide a maximum of value added activities (Figure 3.5).

When developing a portfolio, companies should consider

- specifying the types and mix of projects along with the key portfolio criteria
- explicitly linking projects to firm and service line strategies
- identifying existing capacity for development
- identifying capability requirements for development of current and future generation products/services
- providing a resource capacity plan for development efforts
- acting as the framework for communicating the portfolio

In the context of innovation it is particularly important to review the product portfolio in terms of the mix between radical and incremental innovation. Most organizations are focusing on incremental innovation, thereby putting the future of their organization into jeopardy. Many organizations that have started out with a major innovation or with being very innovative become stale and complacent over time, neglecting three out of the four quadrants that a company's product portfolio should address (see Figure 3.6). Unless an organization keeps putting new products into the far three quadrants, over time all its products or services will end up in the bottom left corner. What

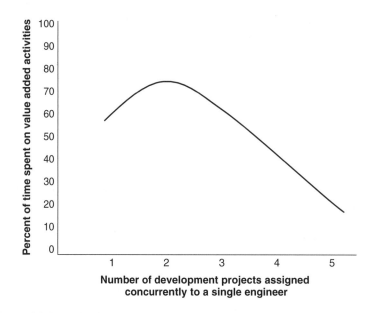

Figure 3.5   Value Added Per Project (reproduced from (Clark and Wheelwright 1993))

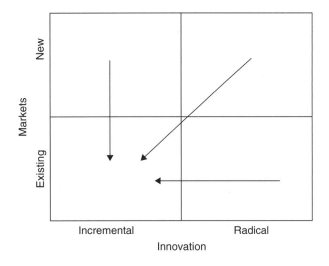

Figure 3.6 Innovation Categories

the appropriate split between the four different quadrants is will depend on each company's specific context and innovation ambition – but without some activity in each, decline is certainly pre-programmed. And by the way, most organizations concentrate about 80% of their efforts on incremental innovation, and 10% on incremental innovations for new markets and radical innovation for existing markets – and none in radical innovation for new markets.

Project Management and Execution implies the definition of appropriate stages and gates a project must pass through. This process has to facilitate ideation, guide projects efficiently from idea to launch, ensure untenable product/service projects are terminated, identify tasks for each stage, specify clearly identified decision points, and provide information on required documentation and decision criteria. While some seem to view the development funnel as a substitute for a stage-gate process, I rather see the stage-gate process as a tool during the *Project Management and Execution* stage. And what Cooper calls 'post-implementation review', though not officially part of the stage-gate process as such, covers Clark and Wheelwright's last box, 'post-project learning and improvement'.

However, the execution of a development funnel as described above seems to be an ideal scenario, not matched by what Clark and Wheelwright (1993) found (see Figure 3.7). While their three scenarios certainly do not give the impression of a happy ending, companies should also be wary not to 'overdo things', particularly when it comes to perfecting a product before launch. Members from Innovation Exchange member companies explained that working on the '100% right theory' can delay product introduction indefinitely!

One of the reasons for a lack of successful introduction of stage-gate processes and development funnels might be that managers often seem to forget that new processes require support from and adjustments in other areas of the organization, e.g. training, alignment of reward structures and communication systems and role definitions.

Another is that top management's attention to any one particular project seems to come at the most inconvenient time: towards the end, when most parameters have been fixed and changes are costly and time consuming – as shown in another graph from the 1993 book by Wheelwright and Clark (Figure 3.8).

This means that a particularly critical, and fairly new role, is that of a project leader who sits at the centre of the hourglass of management and project team.

Figure 3.7   Development Funnel Realities (reproduced from (Clark and Wheelwright 1993))

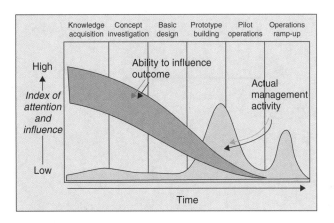

Figure 3.8 Senior Management Attention (reproduced from (Wheelwright and Clark 1993))

THE ROLE OF THE PROJECT LEADER

The issue of 'the project manager' was first brought onto management's radar through a 1959 *Harvard Business Review* article by Paul Gaddis. He was the first to alert management to the fact that a new bread of corporate animal was required, the project manager.

In his book on project management, Harvey Maylor (1996) suggests that project managers should receive the following from their organization/management:

- Responsibility
- Authority
- Accountability
- Credibility

He goes on to explain that the exact role a project manager takes on will depend upon aspects such as the nature of the project (complexity, scale, position in hierarchy of projects), the nature of the organization that it is being carried out in (sector, activities, organizational structure), the personality of the project manager, and the specific constraints under which the project team is working. He also provides a list of characteristics desirable in a project manager (see Box 3.2).

BOX 3.2   Characteristics of Successful Project Leaders (reproduced from (Maylor 1996))

- A desire not just to satisfy but to delight customers and stakeholders alike

- Accepting of both challenges and responsibility

- Being focused on action, rather than procrastination – getting the job done rather than avoiding critical or difficult decisions

- A desire to make the best use of all resources – minimize waste in all activities

- Does not lose sight of the light at the end of the tunnel – is goal focused

▶

- Has personal integrity – people find it very difficult to respect and take the authority of a person who has low integrity

- Is flexible about the route that must be taken to achieve the stated end goals

- Has personal goals that are consistent with those of the project organization – the project team perceives that the project manager and the organization are going the same way

- Ability to determine the real needs/desires of the customer; this is done through 'getting close' to the customer via visits and both formal and informal discussions, and asking the relevant questions

- Analytical skills to turn data into information and break down the project in comprehensible component parts

- Technical skills – the project manager need not be a technical specialist, but must at least be capable of comprehending the work that is being carried out and 'speaking the language' of the people involved

- Team skills – many battles have been won against poor odds by the ability of individual to motivate and enthuse a team

- Ability to delegate effectively – not try to do everything personally

- Ability to manage your own time – you cannot expect to manage other people unless you can show that you can manage yourself

- The balancing of stakeholders' perceptions of project progress (otherwise known as being able to 'sell ideas')

- Negotiation skills – resolve potential conflict to create a win–win situations

- Problem solving/facilitating problem solving

- Question all assumptions made by stakeholders at all stages of activity

That the project-specific context not only influences the role of the project leader but also that the project leader needs different characteristics depending on the context has been pointed out by a colleague of Clark and Wheelwright, Takahiro Fujimoto. In his 1991 article, Fujimoto categorizes products by looking at two aspects: the difficulty (a) of achieving internal product integrity, and (b) of achieving external product integrity. He suggests that each of the four possible project types requires a different type of project manager, or 'integrator', as he calls them.[7] The four product categories he defines are 'Component-driven Products', 'Complex Products', 'Simple Products' and 'Interface-driven Products' (see Figure 3.9). He suggests that to manage each product type a different set of skills is required, for example, for highly complex projects a manager might be the best integrator, whereby he sees the manager as someone with general, political and negotiation skills – rather than someone with, for example, a particular specialist technical expertise. The more complex a project – or the more innovative – the greater also the need for effective communication and internal selling.

But the skill set required of a project leader may not only vary from project to project, they may also change during the course of the project, particularly for large and complex projects. The following example from the Eurostar, the high-speed train that connects the capitals of Belgium, France and the UK, illustrates this (von Stamm 1999).

While the members of the central project team and most other key people remained unchanged throughout the project, the person for the manufacturing consortium changed twice during the development process. The first

Figure 3.9 Types of Products and Project Integrators (Fujimoto 1991) (reproduced by permission of Design Management Journal)

change took place in 1991 after time and cost overruns had come out in the open, the second in 1993 when the project went from the development stage into production. Each of the three project managers had a different skill set which was seen to be most appropriate at the time.

The first project manager had been responsible for the development of the TGV Atlantique, the latest version of the French high-speed train which has been regarded as the blueprint for the Eurostar. However, he had not managed international projects before, and failed to acknowledge the issues and complications arising from this. He also seems to have underestimated the technical complexity arising from the need to operate the train on four different railway systems (Belgium, France, UK and the Eurotunnel). His withdrawal from the project was a signal to the customers, the three national railways, that the imminent problems regarding time and cost overruns had been acknowledged, and that action for change and improvement had been taken.

His successor was chosen for his technical competence – he had high credibility with the engineers working on the project – and his extensive experience in managing international projects. His main aim was to bring the technical problems under control and the project back on track.

When the third project manager took over, the major technical problems had been solved and someone was needed who could make sure that production would progress at satisfactory speed. In fact, someone was needed who had sufficient authority with the French factories to ensure manufacturing would actually happen because here the Eurostar had to compete for capacity with the various TGV models.

So whether it is the structure and design of the new product development process, or the choice of project leader, the company- or project-specific context and requirements need to be taken into account. Off the shelf solutions can only be a starting point, not the final solution.

Perhaps one final comment on project leaders. The choice of the 'right' project leader is important for another reason: one of the key differentiators between projects that are successfully introduced to market and those that fail, or disappear into the black holes of an organization is often quite simply the enthusiasm and passion of the project leader. This is particularly important for innovative projects where there is inherently a lot of uncertainty as well as potentially also a lack of understanding of the concept, and therefore a greater need for selling and communication. And who is most likely to feel passionate about any particular project, extremely keen to tell anyone who may or may not want to hear about it? Who else but the originator of the idea. This has led some organizations that have previously given innovative ideas to professional project managers for development to reconsider their approach. They now provide the idea originators with the training necessary to bring them up to speed with project management best practice, or have a professional project manager work alongside them to complement their skills.

READING SUGGESTIONS

ON NEW PRODUCT DEVELOPMENT

Clark, Kim and Wheelwright, Steven (1992) *Revolutionizing Product Development: Quantum Leaps in Speed, Efficiency, and Quality*. New York: Free Press

Comment: A classic on tools and frameworks for new product development, introducing the development funnel, amongst other things

Baxter, Mike (1995) *Product Design, Practical Methods for the Systematic Development of New Products*. London: Chapman & Hall

Comment: While it is written primarily with designers in mind, it provides useful insights into aspects on and around product development, including creativity and innovation. At the end of each chapter Baxter provides a useful summary of key concepts, as well as lists of 'Design Toolkits' for various aspects of the development process

Smith, P.G. and Reinertsen, D.G. (1997) *Developing Products in Half the Time*. 2nd edn. New York: Van Nostrand Reinhold

Comment: While focusing on the acceleration of new product development, what problems are and how they can be overcome, this book has lots of useful insights for new product development in general

Bobrow Bobrow, E.E. (1997) *The Complete Idiot's Guide to New Product Development*. New York: alpha books

Comment: A bit basic but a good introduction to lots of subjects relevant to new product development

ON PROJECT MANAGEMENT

Maylor, Harvey (1996) *Project Management*. London: Pitman

Comment: I found this a very useful introduction to project management with all sorts of evaluation and assessment techniques

SOME USEFUL WEBSITES

www.pdma.org

Comment: The website by the Product Development and Management Association provides a useful glossary on NPD terms, as well as book recommendations on and around the subject

www.stage-gate.com

Comment: This is the website of the consultancy founded by Robert G. Cooper and Scott G. Edgett who are seen to be the originators of the stage-gate process; it provides useful articles, book references and latest insights on and around the stage-gate process

NOTES ON CHAPTER 3

[1] Aspects related to strategy are covered in Chapter 6.

[2] Aspects related to idea generation are covered in Chapter 22.

[3] More on evaluation and measurement in Chapters 22 and 25, respectively.

[4] This is very much the point made in the introduction about the difference between creativity, which relies on individuals, and implementation, which depends on teams.

[5] Further articles on the stage-gate process are available on http://www.stage-gate.dk/articles.

[6] By the way, this may be one of the factors that contribute to companies' difficulties in dealing with radical innovations. I am not sure that there are many organizations that devise different processes for different types of innovation.

[7] With 'internal product integrity' he refers to problems in achieving consistency among the functions and structures of the product itself, and with 'external product integrity' he refers to the difficulty in coordinating the interface (functions and features) between product and user.

4 A Note on Globalization

While global aspects play only a secondary role in the BBC case study, I would nevertheless like to take the opportunity to expand on that subject as many organizations are grappling with the issue. There are some words that need explaining before one can start a discussion on it, like 'innovation' and 'globalization' is one of them. People have different expectations and concepts in their mind when talking about it. The varying perceptions cause confusion and misunderstandings about scope and implications of globalization. And as academic Wood (2000) points out, 'Globalization is fiercely controversial and triggers strong emotions.'

Is globalization a myth or reality? What does globalization actually mean? What drives and hinders globalization, what are the advantages and downsides? What does globalization mean in the context of new product development – does a global product exist? Is globalization for everyone and what are structures that might facilitate global innovation? This chapter explores these questions and attempts some answers.

MYTH OR REALITY?

Within 5 years there will be two kinds of managers – those who think in terms of a world economy and those who are unemployed.

Peter Drucker

Recent research suggests that globalization is a myth.

Rugman and Hodgetts

Williamson stated in 1994 that, 'Thinking and acting globally has become the order of the day in many corporations, both in the US and overseas. The proliferation of telephone service, fax, and electronic mail make it possible for even small companies to have a global reach.' A more recent literature review by Ulijn *et al.* (2000) noted that, 'Commentaries on organisational vision, effectiveness, direction, and mission usually noted the necessity to innovate and expand beyond normal limits and borders.'

Rugman and Hodgetts (2001), on the other hand, who define globalization as 'the activities of multinational enterprises engaged in foreign direct investment and the development of business networks to create value across national borders,' declare that, 'recent research suggests that globalisation is a myth. Only in a few sectors, such as consumer electronics, is a global strategy of economic integration viable. For most other manufacturing, such as automobiles, and for all services, strategies of national responsiveness are required, often coupled with integration strategies. Successful multinationals now design strategies on a regional basis; unsuccessful ones pursue global strategies.'

In his book *The End of Globalization*, Rugman (2000) argues that the bulk of world trading activity is regionally rather than globally based and that multinationals must improve their ability to analyze what drives success on a regional, rather than global basis. In fact, he states that trade is taking place primarily what he calls 'triad-based', meaning trade between the United States, the countries of the European Union and Japan – rather than globally. As a consequence, so Rugman suggests, companies need to develop a distinctive competence or sustainable competitive advantage within their home region.

During an Innovation Exchange workshop held in spring 1999, this was certainly the view of a member of a FMCG company too, who declared, 'Global innovation does not work. We have experienced repeated problems in developing a global brand and found it much more useful to develop a product aimed at – and fulfilling the needs of – one particular market.' This seems to be supported by a survey of six multinational consumer product firms (Colgate-Palmolive, Kraft GF, Nestlé, Procter & Gamble, Quaker Oats and Unilever) in 67 countries on five continents undertaken by Boze and Patton (1995). Their findings indicate that less than 1% of brands were global brands, whereby global was defined as being found in 90% or more of the countries surveyed.[1] On the other hand, Nestlé does only 2% of its business in its home country, Switzerland, and the remaining 98% abroad (Espey 1991).

There is evidence for and against the scope, or even existence, of globalization. Two comments that might put this into perspective. First, what all these statements have in common is that they are backward looking, which limits their predictive power for the future. While Rugman might be right that trade currently takes place primarily between three marketplaces, the European Union, the United States and Japan, it does not imply that it will be the same in the future. Could it not rather be argued that globalization is happening, but that it takes time, just as all change? No one can expect immediate and complete globalization just because academics have become aware of a trend. Change takes time. As Paul Judge wrote in *Management Today* in August 2001, 'Most talk about globalisation is primarily economic. Human beings are even more complex than economies, and are much slower in going global.'

Consider cross-functional cooperation and teamwork: these concepts were first promoted about 30 years ago, and as has been pointed out in the previous chapter, they are key to successful product development. But does this mean that today all organizations operate with cross-functional teams? Or rather, does the fact that not all organizations are operating this way mean a trend does not exist? One simple answer as to why not all organizations are following the trend may be that it is just not appropriate for all types of organizations or industries. It is certainly a fact that it has never been easier for a company to enter a marketplace beyond its national boundaries and promote its services or products abroad than today. There is little doubt that the interconnectedness between different parts of the world has increased. To quote Wood (2000) again, 'The marriage of telecommunications and computers greatly accelerates the process of global economic integration.' The degree to which cross-border activities involve one or many countries will depend on product, industry and size of the company in question. And actually, I am not alone in my view. Lowell Bryan *et al.* state in their book *Race for the World*, 'The process of economic integration is not new. It has been under way, at a slow pace, for thousand of years. What is new is the pace and the scale.'

Secondly, some say globalization exists, some that it has never happened. Maybe by looking at globalization at different levels a high degree of agreement can be reached. What are people meaning when they talk about globalization, and what are implications for understanding global innovation?

DEFINITIONS

The term 'globalization' entered our language in the 1980s, and the magazine *The Economist* defines globalization, short and sweet as 'international economic integration'. In his book *The Lexus and the Olive Tree*, the journalist

Tom Friedman goes beyond the purely economic context stating that, 'It is the inexorable integration of markets, nation states, and technologies to a degree never witnessed before in a way that is enabling individuals, corporations and nation states to reach around the world farther, faster, deeper, and cheaper than ever before.'

GLOBAL OR INTERNATIONAL?

But is this global integration reality for companies today? And are we talking truly global or rather international? Where is the borderline? Williamson (1994) defines the difference as follows: 'International organizations house only portions of functions at foreign sites or operate independent business units. In contrast, the global company locates functions based on economic advantage or regulatory considerations.'

The discussion might become less confused when trying to understand globalization on three different levels:

- economic
- organizational
- product

It is the economic level Tom Friedman, author of *The Lexus and the Olive Tree*, is referring to when he defines globalization as 'The inexorable integration of markets, nation states, and technologies to a degree never witnessed before in a way that is enabling individuals, corporations and nation states to reach around the world farther, faster, deeper, and cheaper than ever before.' Between the developed world and emerging markets the dollar trade volume has gone up from $802 billion in 1986 to $2 trillion in 1996.

Talking about globalization at the organizational level, we have to consider which industry we are talking about. According to a McKinsey report (quoted in Bryan *et al.* 1999), the degree of globalization in petroleum, timber, aluminium or chemicals is somehow higher than in shoes, luxury goods or legal services, and definitely higher than in funeral homes or large scale production materials. The question here is, in how many countries is an organization operating and trading?

Finally, at the product level the discussion is about whether or not it is feasible to (a) develop products in a global team and (b) sell it to a global customer, and we will come back to that later.

Assuming that a trend towards globalization exists in at least the first two of the three levels introduced above, we now turn to what enables globalization, what drives organizations to become (more) global and what the advantages are. This will be followed by an investigation of the obstacles to globalization, as well as some potential downsides.

ENABLERS AND DRIVERS OF GLOBALIZATION

There are three main enablers of globalization:

- Deregulation
- New communications
- Increasing mobility of capital

Governments are reacting to market pressure to deregulate and open markets to foreign trade. Trade alliances (EU, NAFTA, ASEAN (Southeast Asia), MERCOSUR (South America)) and a changed political climate (Cold War, China) help to open up new geographical markets. Digital technology enables cheaper and faster communication than ever before also helping to overcome problems of geographical dispersion. And finally, more and more money crosses borders – the foreign exchange transactions amount to $1.5 trillion per day.

If deregulation, technology and mobility of capital are enablers at the economic/national level, what are the drivers at the organizational level to pursue globalization? Beside the usual drive to cut cost, there are several other reasons underlying the quest for globalization:

- *Competitive pressures* and a concern for remaining at the forefront of business development are one reason organizations are induced to start thinking globally.

- Access to new markets is not only used to increase trade. More and more companies locate departments based on the best/*most effective conditions* not only for manufacturing. For example, Branscomb *et al.* (1999) found that the United States rely increasingly on foreign resources for their innovation efforts.

- Another driver is the need to respond to increased *consumer awareness*. Through travel consumers encounter new products or find out about product offerings from other countries through the media, this latter trend has been accelerated by the internet revolution (Gray 2001). But there is also a dichotomy: people want variety and experience 'exoticness' when abroad but at the same time they want things they are familiar with and of which they know exactly what to expect. This is particularly applicable to food.

ADVANTAGES OF GLOBAL INNOVATION

While cutting cost is often one of the reasons companies pursue globalization strategies, increased efficiencies, reduced complexity and duplication in a company's product portfolio are some of the other benefits gained by the same token.

Along with globalization strategies, companies often increase centralization, as this is seen to be necessary to coordinate brand consolidation and reduction of product variety. Pooling of resources, better integrated portfolio management as well as closer alignment to the company's overall strategy can be further positive side effects of global product management. Operational benefits are seen to be the need for fewer manufacturing plants, longer production runs, reduced changeover time, and fewer products to stock.

THE FLIPSIDE OF THE COIN

As with everything, global innovation too has some disadvantages and problems. One of the most important questions is, does a truly global customer really exist? Judge (2001) points out that human beings are slow to change, and that it will therefore take some time for them to become 'global'. The question then is, is it really possible to develop a product that satisfies the needs of a Danish consumer as well as those of a consumer in Nigeria, Chile and Korea? And even if we manage to develop such a global product, a product that must be blander if it wants to satisfy different tastes and needs, do we not leave too much room for a perhaps smaller competitor who focuses on the needs of one country only and can therefore match requirements much better? How many tastes can we satisfyingly integrate before the end result becomes something unexciting and meaningless?

On the other hand, an increase in the travelling population can cause a conflict if a company's strategy is to consolidate brands while maintaining a degree of local adaptation. A consumer used to a certain consistency of a cosmetic product or taste of a particular drink or food encountering variations when consuming the seemingly same product in a different country will be confused and upset by the inconsistency. The variations between countries in the degree of sweetness in toothpaste is one example, the degree of spiciness in a McDonald's is another.

And while the consolidation of brands has great advantages, companies aiming to reduce their product portfolio by 300% create high pressure for those remaining to perform. It also brings up the question as to what criteria should be used for the development of future brand. Is it possible to identify brands with global potential early enough to ensure they are not weeded out by accident? The introduction of a new brand on a global basis is highly risky and costly. Will this result in boring products that are perceived to be safe? What will happen to the innovation aspect of global innovation? And again, will the global company leave its doors wide open for competition from the small and nimble?

Another of the advantages, the pooling of resources, has its disadvantages too. The coordination of development efforts on a global basis leads to increased complexities, where errors of judgement will have far reaching and costly consequences. Under regional control local managers will have made decisions based on their local insights and their experience. Will this expertise be called upon, or will decisions be made by people at the centre who just assume that they know what is best for the regional markets?

OBSTACLES TO GLOBAL INNOVATION

And beyond the potential downsides of global innovation there are also cultural issues within organizations that need to be addressed. Many of the organizations following the goal of globalization have previously had strongly regionally oriented structures, with considerable power and autonomy given to the local managers. What actions are taken to ensure that 'we' within an organization is perceived to encompass the entire organization? Because when headquarters makes decisions on what projects to take forward it will do what is best for the entire organization – which may not be what would have been best for any particular region. Will people be able to associate with the distant headquarters, rather than be upset that another department's project has been chosen over their own?

How much will the feeling of 'us and them' hinder successful development – and more importantly, implementation? Gray (2001) highlights the need to 'Remove local subjective prejudices – often founded on old research data and myth – and focus on objective issues'. In the Innovation Exchange workshop on global innovation, the problems arising from local protectionism were emphasized too. Members of participating companies had experienced that local managers had become protective of their organization and previous power, using perceived regional differences in taste as a pretext to boycott the introduction of new products that had been developed without their involvement, as well as to justify local product development. In such a situation, are centres able to establish *true* rather than *perceived* or assumed consumer preferences? And more importantly, are these organizations capable of building a culture that overcomes such protectionism?

To achieve global innovation existing structures will have to change. As Monge and Fulk (1999) point out, 'A hierarchical, bureaucratic structure is less responsive in such an environment, and a flatter, more responsive organizational pattern is required.' Have those companies seeking to become global innovators flattened their hierarchies and implemented faster and easier ways of communicating?

Consistency of raw materials and quality of production are further aspects that can hamper globalization. For example, 3M pointed out that minor variations in raw material for its sand paper production lead to significant inconsistencies in the product's performance, requiring continuity of suppliers and in product formulation, making transfer of production and formula between locations difficult, if not impossible (von Stamm 1999).

Finally, perhaps the greatest obstacle to global product development is the differences that exist between nations in a variety of aspects. Areas where nations differ include

- *Differences in consumer preference and habits.* Take, for example, washing machines. Whereas front-loading machines seem to be the preferred option in most European countries this is not so in France. Here top-loading ones are the norm. Take food, where there are also considerable differences in habits. Gray observes that clues to divergent responses can be found by looking at national attitudes to the environment. For example, Germans tend to be ecologically vigilant, while the French believe food and wine are more important than environmental campaigning. He also reports that when Unilever was developing a new chicken dish, it had to bear in mind that in the US chicken is traditionally cooked in the oven, rather than on top of the stove, which had implications for the consistency and ingredients of the sauce itself, as well as for the instructions on the packaging.

- *Differences in environmental requirements* such as environmental regulations or attitude, e.g. emission levels in the States are different from those in Europe.

- *Differences in general legislation and company law.* For example, in Germany one cannot just decide to produce and sell leather belts, an accreditation by the responsible crafts guild is required, otherwise the person will be liable to fines.

- *Differences in health and safety regulations* can mean that materials acceptable in one country cannot be used in another, or that medication freely available in one country is a prescription drug in another.

- *Differences in patenting laws* also exist, for example, if an employee in the UK develops a product for which a patent can be registered within his normal remit of work, the patent will be held by the company, which will also receive the royalty payments. In Germany, on the other hand, the patent will be in the name of the inventor who will also be the beneficiary of royalty payments.

- Finally, even *differences in the physical environment* such as climate variations and variations in distribution patterns can have an effect.

Fundamental differences between countries remain which, when ignored, cause significant problem at best, complete failure at worst. Barkema *et al.* (1996) point out 'Unexpected culture differences might lead to serious failures as demonstrated by a statistical study of foreign entry.' Zuckerman (2001) emphasizes the need to consider cultural issues when promoting change, 'Nothing can sink a global logistics operation faster than ignoring the cultures and mores of any given region.' Cultural differences are quite fundamental and will be explored in more depth in Chapter 15.

WHAT DOES GLOBAL MEAN IN THE CONTEXT OF NEW PRODUCT DEVELOPMENT?

Focusing on the product level, globalization can take two meanings: (a) it can refer to a product that is developed for a global consumer – either by a central or by a global team – or (b) it can mean that a product is sold on a worldwide basis – be it exactly the same product worldwide or variations of a product under the same name (see Figure 4.1). The difference is important as it has implications for the development of new products.

While the 'development team' aspect will have implications primarily during the design and development process, the number of nationalities that make up a product's 'market' is likely to have implications for the outcome itself. It is important to understand differences in two situations:

Figure 4.1 Degrees of Globalization

(a)   When developing products for a specific country (1 nationality), and

(b)   When developing products across countries (many nationalities).

The first is necessary to understand what the 'order winner' in that particular country is. The second is necessary to understand whether one and the same product can be a success in a number of countries, or whether adjustment would improve the odds for success – or may even be necessary. This does not mean that one can expect people of a certain national background to behave exactly as predicted by the stereotypes! For example, I am German but I cannot stand beer. I believe I have some sense of humour (but I know what people mean when they refer to the Germans as not having one...). I am a freak for punctuality – but then I know Germans who aren't. What I tend to say is, if you meet a German, you will more likely or more frequently be able to observe certain behaviours and characteristics. Or put differently, when you have a group of 1000 French people and 1000 Danish people, you will find certain behaviours and values more frequently in one group than the other.

Assuming that there is a global consumer means that marketers will aim to develop a product that is appealing to people around the world. Such a product must therefore consider and address a great variety of preferences.

The most difficult scenario is probably the development of a product for a 'global' market developed by a global team. In such a scenario, the result is very likely the result of a series of consensus decision, which most likely reflect the lowest common denominator. Such a watering down of concepts in the attempt to satisfy a global audience has been observed by Martin Smith, former Chief Executive of the advertising agency Grey Worldwide London, in an *FT* article (Smith 2001). 'Sorry, that's too interesting for us,' he laments. 'A loss of subtlety and nuance in ads caused by risk averse marketers dulling them down to accommodate a global audience.'

Another consequence of aiming to find a consensus between varying design tastes can be a lack of ownership. Each party assumes that the result reflects the other parties' preference – while in actual fact it does not please anyone. A story from the development of the high-speed train connecting the capitals of Belgium, France and the UK, the Eurostar, in which all three countries were involved, may serve to illustrate the point. Those who have travelled on the Eurostar may recall the pink-frosted lampshades in the first-class carriages. The French press referred to them as 'typical English pink', whereas the UK press associated them with 'typical bohemian French'. Each side thought it was the other country's taste that had influenced the decision, while no one seemed to be happy with it. If that happens when coordinating tastes between three countries, and all of them European, what would happen to a global product?

There are products that might not necessarily have been developed with the 'global' consumer in mind, but have ended up being sold globally – Coca-Cola or McDonald's are examples. Such products often have a strong national association – which is part of their attraction. Coca-Cola, widely cited as a 'truly global product', started off as a product that was developed in response to a specific local need in a specific local market. Marketing and the drink's taste that appealed to a wide audience mean it is today one of the most widely available products around the globe. Coca-Cola has become global, but it was not developed with that intention in mind. And, as Rugman (2000, p170) points out, even the Coca-Cola formula is not quite the same everywhere, the amount of syrup used is varied to cater for regionally preferences in the degree of sweetness.

Another product often assumed to be global is the car. An example of a successful 'global product' is Chrysler's PT Cruiser. As Tom Lockwood (Global Brand and Design Strategy Manager, StorageTek) writes, 'A decade ago, the differences between cultural design preferences and the communication inefficiencies caused by geographical distance could have made this kind of international appeal difficult, if not unthinkable. But the internet now allows designers, engineers, and marketers to disseminate ideas globally in a matter of seconds and keep close track of cultural preferences, trends and design processes.' The car is selling 175,000 a year instead of the expected 70,000 both sides of the Atlantic. However, even here it may only hold true for the base model. Having been involved in an international exhibition by the motor company Ford, I realized that different aspects of the car were highlighted as standards, depending on the nationality of the audience. Each country addresses national preferences by varying fittings, colours and standards. Such adjustments can put a question mark over concepts of global production and distribution.

While emphasizing the need to understand the differences, I would by no means like to suggest that the attempt to develop global products is always futile. In fact, Kleinschmidt and Cooper (1988) reported that 'industrial products that are developed for world applications and are targeted at export markets will have more success.' It will depend on the industry and product in question, and to what degree consumer taste are truly compatible. And again the issue might be one of definition. Does global mean *exactly* the same – or 'variations on a theme'? Products that vary at the following levels may still be considered 'global':

- Different product formulations (e.g. for cream, toothpaste, scents, etc.)

- Product features (e.g. for cars, washing machines, mobile phones)

- Packaging varying to address different design preferences (e.g. for toys, pharmaceuticals)

- Different distribution channels, depending on the host country's existing infrastructure

- Different approaches to marketing depending on consumer preference (e.g. different types of sales promotion, 2 for 1, vouchers, bundling, etc.)

- Different approaches to advertising (different types of humour, play on words, etc.)

None of the above is detrimental to the concept of a global product, the questions should be, how easily – effort (possibility) and cost – could we adapt an existing product? When faced with a decision of whether or not a product has global potential an organization might want to consider the following aspects of new product development:

- *Product ideas* – is there a consumer group to which the product is relevant that exists in more than one country? Are there differences at the systems level, e.g. regulation, power supply?

- *Manufacture* – is manufacture possible in more than one country? If not, is transportation easy and cost efficient; are raw materials sufficiently consistent across markets?

- *Marketing/advertising* – what are consumers' preferences in approaches to marketing; are tastes, preferences for advertising compatible?

- *Approach towards sales and distribution* – to what kind of sales promotions do consumers react favourably? What distribution channels do they use?

- *After sales service* – what are expectations towards after sales services? What services are to be included in the purchase of the product, what is an 'extra'?

Depending on the degree of overlap, product managers might want to decide to launch a 'global' product or to develop a local brand.

WHAT TO CONSIDER WHEN GOING GLOBAL

Larry Roelling (Executive Vice President at Enterprise IG consultants in San Francisco) has the following recommendation for developing a global brand:

- Create a captivating name, wordmark or symbol that is understood and has positive connotations around the world/in all applicable markets

- Determine whether it is best to accentuate or play down country associations

- Be willing to modify strategy to accommodate cultural diversity

- Devise packaging that strengthens brand impression

- In the development and execution of product or service, be sensitive to environmental, social and ethical considerations

- Research the laws of each country as they affect sales and marketing

- Balance economies of scale with a local presence

Gray has some similar advice, 'What most global brands have in common is a powerful identity. Successful global brands often feature abstract brand names, as well as identities that are single-minded and memorable, but not literal.' He continues to give the following recommendations:

- *Develop a holistic brand brief* that encompasses all communication of the brand at every consumer interface. This brief should be the bible against which everything is objectively measured – all research must be designed and implemented tightly against the objectives set out in the brief. Ensure that the bible is bought into at all relevant levels through all markets – failure to do this will invariably result in confrontation down the line.

- *Create a strong, simple visual brand icon* capable of instantly identifying the brand through all communication and flexible enough to incorporate local detail.

- *Communicate the brand consistently, cohesively and repeatedly* and do not allow creativity to get in the way of simple communication.

In addition, much of the best practice identified for new product development and innovation is equally applicable to global innovation. As for all initiatives that are to be taken seriously, it is important for *the top to lead the way*.

Research by Heiss and Fraser (2000) found that top corporate executives who consider their companies very successful globally spend 40% of their time on global issues, compared with 25% of executives overall. A way to give weight to the importance and seriousness of global would be, for example, to give profit relief to global innovation projects as they may take longer to become profitable – and to develop alternative metrics for innovation, e.g. the number of intellectual property rights gained.

If a *clear and focused strategy* is important in any scenario, it becomes paramount for the successful implementation of a globalization strategy – more on the role of strategy and vision in Chapter 6. Communication plays a critical role, as emphasized by Heiss and Fraser in the following statement: 'Best-practices companies are balancing the global-local challenge of overall communication – advertising, branding and media relations. These companies are synchronizing international operations and coordinating these activities in communicating information from local subsidiaries to headquarters. Globalization has increased the need for clear, consistent and central corporate messages with adaptation at the local level.'

The desire to maximize benefits from globalization companies tend to lean towards a *centralization of new product development* activities. This was considered necessary to avoid duplication and allow maximization of existing resources. A further advantage of a centralized approach was seen to be the opportunity for cross-funding over a longer time horizon. Project that might otherwise have fallen prey to the consequences of quarterly or bi-annual reporting could be pursued for the long-term benefit of the organization – and taking a global perspective on new product development might also help to smooth the waves of economic turbulences across countries.

The *sharing of knowledge* should be supported by establishing global networks and the facilitation of effortless communication between different parts of the organization. As Heiss and Fraser found, 'Best-practices companies are using research to develop a better understanding of their global constituencies-and communicators must immerse themselves in the research process.'

Global innovation is built on *collaboration and relationships*. Without people working together, sharing insights and information global innovation cannot happen. Selectron's Vice President of Global Logistics, Jim Molzon, states that he can't get 'buy-in' to company goals in overseas operations unless it's a collaborative process (in Zuckerman 2001).[2]

Dedicated resources are needed. An Innovation Exchange member commented as follows (von Stamm 2001): 'We have a very limited number of global projects – or rather projects with global potential. At no time is the project managed from the centre, the leadership is always with one of our innovation centres. But as the local centre does not always have the right skills and resources to execute the project, we will second people or give part of the project to the central research facility, establishing virtual teams – but the leadership always stays local.'

While it makes sense to centralize some activities, others should remain with the regions. Examples are accounting and payroll systems. In addition, to accommodate local differences in custom and law, some companies are sorting their portfolios of activities according to their applicability on a local, regional, or global basis and obtaining economies of scale by rewriting those that can be used globally (Williamson 1994). Best-practices companies are balancing the global–local challenge even though seeing the benefits of such an approach may take some time, as one Innovation Exchange company reports, 'The matrix we are using to *balance global and local requirements* was time consuming to start with. And it was frustrating to get consensus and to get consistency across the process but we have managed it now. How have we overcome the initial problems? Because of the commitment of the people and the clarity everyone shares about business direction.'

However, sometimes the findings will indicate that differences are so fundamental that the development of a product appropriate for a variety of markets will be impossible. For an organization it is important to remain open and accepting of such situation – particularly if the product is widely believed to have global potential. Gray provides the example of research undertaken by a design consultancy that, when charged with the development of a new stationery range for a global office products company, came across significant differences in expectations of children's pencil cases: in the US, pencil cases had to be bigger to be best, while in Germany it needed lots of compartments and in France there was a more haphazard approach. As the designer commented, 'It became apparent there was no way we could design a global pencil case.'

SUMMARY

This chapter has addressed the following questions:

- What does globalization actually mean?
- What are the drivers and obstacles to globalization?
- What does this mean for global new product development?
- What to consider when developing global products?

Globalization means different things to different people but for the purpose of this volume is it refers to the fact that companies are increasingly broadening their geographical reach and that they adjust their structures and processes, new product development in particular, accordingly. Planning and coordination takes place at a global/international level rather than the national/regional one – which does not preclude new product development at the regional level, it only means that decisions about which projects are taken forward are being made at the centre.

While globalization may not have reached its full potential, strategic planning in companies considers actions and planning for the global (or at least international) level rather than the national/regional one. Truly global products, in the sense that exactly the same product satisfies consumer needs in countries around the globe, hardly exist. But sometimes quite simple and small variations will address varying consumer needs and in such a situation the planning and developing of 'global' product may make sense.

READING SUGGESTIONS

ON GLOBALIZATION IN GENERAL

Rugman, Alan (2000) *The End of Globalization*. London: Random House

Comment: In his book Rugman pursues the line that there is no globalization and never has been, as the connectivity and exchange is primarily happening between three regions, North America, the European Union and Japan; the author discusses the implication of this different view of globalization for managers and strategy planning

Lowell, Bryan, Frazer, Jane, Oppenheim, Jeremy and Rall, William (1999) *Race for the World*. Boston, MA: Harvard Business School Press

Comment: Written by four McKinsey consultants, the book paints the picture of a world that is increasingly connected with any one company operating in more and more markets. The authors suggest how managers can prepare their organization to be in the pack that 'leads the race for the world'

SOME USEFUL WEBSITES

http://www.globalisationguide.org/

Comment: Starting more from an economic perspective, this site provides some insights on questions such
                as, 'What is globalization and where did it start?', 'Who are the players?', and 'What are the costs
                and benefits of free trade?'

NOTES ON CHAPTER 4

[1] Procter & Gamble has the most global brands, with 8% of the brands studied distributed in 50% or more of the
countries. The majority of brands (50% to 72%) are available in three or fewer countries.

[2] Selectron is a contract manufacturer of computer boards and equipment for companies such as Dell Computer
and Compaq and has 60 manufacturing operations in 28 countries and five continents.

5 Innovation and Branding for the Web

CASE STUDY 2: ihavemoved.com – PART A

WHAT NEXT?

In July 2000 the four founders of ihavemoved.com sat at their boardroom table in the grip of a mild panic. Having launched their website in November 1999 and secured £2.5 m finance in March 2000 – signed just before the NASDAQ crash – they were faced with significantly dropping registration rates. The advertising campaign they had run in May and June 2000 to raise awareness had a positive impact on overall brand awareness, and had attracted lots of visitors to their website, but actual sign-ups to their services were dropping significantly. What

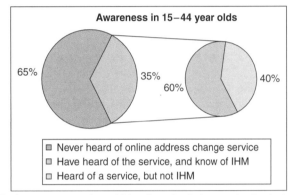

Awareness in 15–44 year olds

65%   35%   60%   40%

☐ Never heard of online address change service
☐ Have heard of the service, and know of IHM
☐ Heard of a service, but not IHM

were they to do next to secure the future of the company in which they had invested all their personal wealth?

THE STARTING POINT

The ignition point for ihavemoved.com (IHM) occurred during the MBA at London Business School in 1997. For their second year project, David Anstee and Niko Komninos teamed up to develop a business plan. Internet ideas were still hip and cool back then, so the original idea was devise a website on which people could view properties for free and the company would make money from selling mortgages. Their idea got nominated to represent LBS at the European Business Plan competition at INSEAD, France, in June 99. As soon as they arrived they found out that people from Imperial College had a very similar idea which led, not surprisingly, to a lot of frantic activity on both sides to fine-tune presentations and impress the jury. Custom-made folders were produced for each judge and glasses of vodka with mango juice were handed out – a potent subliminal reminder of the company's name: 'MangoHomes'. But not only that, as David remembers, 'We also did a fake *Business Week* cover with "MangoHomes wins" which was put under the judges' hotel room doors overnight.' But to no avail, whereas Imperial achieved 3rd, they did not even get placed.

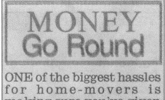

Also realizing that the time lapse between identifying a property and dealing with the mortgage might cause problems, they started a major rethink of the original idea, deciding that they should find a value proposition that would integrate better into the service.

The revised idea was sparked by a conversation over the breakfast table between two of the later company directors, Francesco Benincasa and David, who rented an apartment together. Occasionally at weekends they used to sit down and go through all the mail that would pile up during the week. They used to get stacks of mail, addressed to other people, obviously previous tenants who for one reason or another hadn't bothered to tell their friends, debt collection agencies and utility suppliers that they had moved. Francesco and David wondered where the people had moved to and what they were missing out on by not receiving their post. They also thought about how much money companies were wasting by posting out information to people who would never receive it. They expressed their vision as: 'ihavemoved.com will enable individuals and companies to change address for every piece of mail that crosses their threshold; quickly, easily and conveniently.' The idea for a change of address service was born in summer 1999.

They presented their revised business idea at London Business School in Kathy Hammond's class 'New Media Markets', but the feedback they got from students, who were quite concerned about privacy issues, was quite negative! However, this time they were not dissuaded by the negative feedback and decided to push on.

By this time, the team had grown to four, Onic Palandjian, a childhood friend of Niko's had joined, bringing his sales experience to the party, an ideal complement to David's background in finance, Niko's marketing expertise and Francesco's knowledge of internet business gleaned from running an internet consultancy (more details of their professional background can be found in Appendix I). Not only were the professional skills complementary, they also got on well at a personal level, which was considered very important as Francesco emphasized, 'I'd lived alongside David for a year before we worked together and Niko and Onic grew up together, so we all knew how each other would react in a fast-growing business.'

To avoid complications and disappointment, the autumn was spent not only refining the idea, seeking lawyers' advice and developing a website, but also for lots of meetings to talk about where people felt they should be in five years' time and what they wanted out of life.

MARKET OPPORTUNITY AND COMPETITION

The population of the UK is just under 60 million, of which around 10% move each year. Nearly 80% of all movers are aged between 15 and 44. This corresponds closely to the demographics associated with internet usage, with 78% of users falling into the same age group. From this information, they deducted that there are at least 2.3 million online movers each year in the UK.

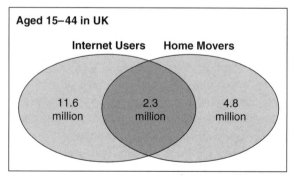

When ihavemoved.com launched their website there were about 100 property sites around, but they were the only company offering an online change of address service in the UK. In contrast to mail forwarding with the Post Office, their service was free to movers. It was not until July 2000 that a competitor emerged, being a close copy of how IHM's site looked at the time. 'Company X'

had started as an offline service but launched an online version just after ihavemoved.com's advertising campaign. As David remembers, 'We responded to their threat by also offering an offline form, figuring that if they were entering "our" market, we would enter theirs and increase the pressure.' In autumn 2000 Company X, employing six staff (of whom five were directors drawing no salary) and averaging about three address changes a day, was seeking £750k in funding. With the very tough market, raising money was almost impossible, especially with a clear market leader in IHM distancing itself from them apace.

Jun 99	Leave LBS
Jul 99	Set up company
Aug 99	Demo site
	— put up companies
	— process first CoA
Sep 99	HSBC loan
Nov 99	Bluewave site launch
Dec 99	British Gas
Dec 99	PowerGen
Mar 00	Rothschild funding

FROM IDEA TO REALITY

ihavemoved.com ltd was registered in July 1999. Then, to prove the concept and have a prototype to show potential partners and investors, Francesco built a functioning demo site. The founders skimmed the fax or email addresses for customer service departments off bills and websites of key companies, and used this to pass on the trickle of change requests that came through the site. Whilst a bit cheeky and only marginally legal, this 'rapid prototyping' approach proved the concept, boosted the learning cycle and gave the impression of progress and credibility.

Through the UK Government Guarantee Scheme, the company was able to raise £30k in an unsecured loan from HSBC, due to a relationship Francesco had from his previous company. This enabled IHM to retain Bluewave, a web design agency selected from a shortlist of three firms for their understanding of the opportunity and their enthusiasm for the project.

Equipped with initial screen shots from Bluewave and a healthy dose of enthusiasm, it was time to start selling. Two factors made the utility sector the most amenable to IHM's offering. Deregulation in the electricity and gas markets had resulted in intense competition for customers. Secondly, moving home requires disconnection and reconnection, and this is the perfect point to capture a new customer... or lose an existing one. Utilities were the companies to hit, and Centrica (British Gas) was the biggest game in town.

VALUE PROPOSITION

Basically, companies would pay for clean information delivered at the time of moving, in a format easily incorporated into their customer database. This would save costs and make it easier to stay in touch with customers. For movers, this free service would save time and hassle, as well as acting as an effective reminder for all the tasks easily forgotten during the stressful moving process. ihavemoved.com made a high gross margin

Using the website
- Log on
- Enter old and new address
- Select the companies which need to be informed
- Enter specific data where required
- That's it

revenue stream from notifications and commissions. They also collected rich and timely information about its users. This was seen as the likely real long-term value of the company.

THE REVENUE MODEL

The team came up with a number of revenue avenues, including charging users of the site, however, after investigating the options, it seemed the following were the best options:

- *New customer commission*: the service provider partners offer significant commissions on new customers, cross-sales and up-sales. In the case of a Telco, this ranges from £5–£90, depending on the product sold. From one energy company, a new dual fuel customer can generate up to £40.

- *Digital update service*: ihavemoved.com partners pay £1.00 per notification of a customer address change in a digital format compatible with their existing database. This pales in comparison to the expenses associated with call centres, data entry and administration.

- *Banner advertisements*: the type of traffic ihavemoved.com attracts, and the ability to target specific ads at very narrowly defined demographics, has enabled the company to sell banner and sponsorship space at above average rates.

LOOKING FOR FUNDING

Having the idea seemed easy, but how and where to get the money for the investments necessary to get the business going? The four partners had used their own money – around £100,000 in total – to get the business off the ground, but they now needed serious money to put the company on a proper footing: offices and more staff were needed to enable growth. In addition, they realized that they would have to upgrade the website, which did not work quite as they wanted to. The usability both from the user as well as their perspective was not satisfactory, it was inflexible and unintuitive.

With the website up and running, first customers and companies signed up and with first revenues coming in they had not anticipated how difficult it would be to find investors, especially as money seemed to be handed out to almost any business ideas during this time, the dotcom boom. Initially they were quite protective about their idea – but got more relaxed as time went on. Without introductions it was literally impossible to get through doors – and even with an introduction it was hard work to get even the chance to present the idea. David remembers, 'Rising above the noise was difficult. Venture capitalists were seeing so many business proposals and dotcom ideas that they were difficult to contact, were frequently rude and usually devoted very little time to each new idea. It did not help that many operate on a black-ball system where one vote against it is sufficient to reject the proposal. While we could usually convince the people we met of the merit of the idea, it was very difficult to get in front of people in the first place. In a way venture capitalists are quite risk averse, they want proof that something has worked before – but what if what you do is so new it does not have a point of referral?' It was an interesting experience to find that venture capitalists should prefer to invest in 'me toos'.

After contacting over 40 VCs, and presenting at dozens of meetings, the breakthrough finally came on the 18th January. The following Tuesday saw them holding their regular networking evening at the Mermaid Theatre in London. CNN were filming the funding frenzy, and they followed the ihavemoved team as they worked the room. At the dinner that followed, Francesco sat next to Zoe Appleyard of Continuation Investments N.V. ('CINV' – the principal private equity vehicle for the Rothschild investment banking group.) Zoe was the executive responsible for bringing in new business at the firm. Not only did she like the business concept immediately, it also fitted very well with CINV's investment strategy, which focused on investing in TMIT businesses (telecom, media, internet, technology). While most investors had been sceptical about the business idea, CINV immediately saw some unique selling points such as a first-mover advantage, a good concept that was simple and obvious, and further possibilities once the data had been collected. In addition, there were synergies with another CINV investment, upmystreet.com (incidentally ihavemoved.com and upmystreet.com entered a business relationship in July 2001). The investment proposal went to committee mid-February and the contract was signed on the 8th March 2000.

After a first investor was secured, others followed suit: Hyundai, who saw them on the 19th of January CNN broadcast, Nicholas Negroponte whom they met through a Greek connection of Onic's, and Internet Indirect (later acquired by New Media Spark). By the time they signed the investment agreement for £2.5 million in March 2000, things were desperate: they had sold houses and stretched out their credit cards to the limits, BT had already cut off the phone, and they were seriously short of cash. The timing was tight from another perspective too: just two days after they signed the agreement the dotcom crash happened and the NASDAQ index went into free fall.

PUTTING THE MONEY TO WORK

With fresh money available, the founding team was now able to put structures and systems into place that would set the company up for future growth. Immediate steps were to get offices and hire five more people (an operations manager, an operations assistant, a sales manager, a marketing assistant and a website manager). The total number of staff grew from seven in March 2000 to 12 in May and 17 in July.

Next on the agenda was an upgrade of the website by Bluewave to sort out problems with the functionality of the site and to improve the user experience. Then they commissioned Conquest to design an advertising campaign to boost awareness and position themselves as a first-mover. This ran in June 2000, to coincide with the re-launch. Costing £600,000, this was quite a moderate amount for an internet start-up. So far they had only deployed one successful PR campaign with most major national newspapers covering the story.

To mark the re-launch of their website they decided to celebrate with a high-profile event at the Royal Opera House. Their breakfast seminar on the 2nd of June 2000, for which they had secured high-calibre speakers such as Nicholas Negroponte, founder of the MIT Media Lab and *WIRED Magazine* and Alex Allen, the UK e-Envoy, the event was attended by their other investors, 200 delegates from the UK's largest companies as well as CNN.

The results of the medium-sized launch produced good results, about a third of the target population of 18–44 year olds knew that they could change their address online, 60% of whom also knew that the place to do it was ihavemoved.com. The team were also pleased to find that all service providers they contacted seemed to have heard of ihavemoved.com. While the campaign had been great in promoting awareness of ihavemoved.com's services, it had also alerted competition to a great opportunity: in July 2000 a competitive site went online. Company X had previously offered their service offline and now decided to offer their services online too.

While the re-launch had been a great success, they had struggled greatly to get Bluewave to complete the redesign of the website for the re-launch, despite quite close operation and making extra funds available to boost resource

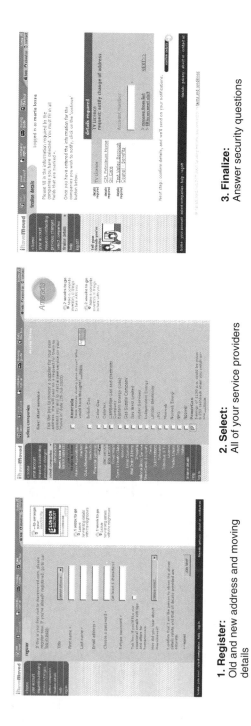

1. Register:
Old and new address and moving details

2. Select:
All of your service providers

3. Finalize:
Answer security questions

input at Bluewave. Even with only two weeks to go to the start of the advertising campaign and the re-launch party, the website had been far from ready. Frustrated at the progress, they decided to get technical and design expertise in-house and hire a Chief Technical Officer. However, this was quite a risky move as none of the directors had the knowledge necessary to assess the technical capabilities of the new recruit. Using their network they found Andrew Day who turned out to be just what they needed. Not only was he able to immediately identify major flaws with the newly redesigned website, he was also able to fix them. Having the design resource in-house not only gave them more control, it was also much cheaper.

Andrew Day

Information technology has been a part of Andrew's life since he was 13 years old, when he wrote the first published machine code version of the game *Space Invaders* in 1977. After four years in the banking sector, in 1995 he founded a company to offer online information services – he could be viewed as one of the original dotcommers. Before joining ihavemoved.com in June, Andrew provided consultancy services to Virgin Mobile Phones.

THE NEED TO ACCELERATE GROWTH

So far so good. The company had successfully secured funding, re-launched its website, and the advertising campaign had given the company a profile in the crowded dotcom scene. High levels of interest from the media had helped too: between 1st November 1999 and 31st August 2000, the company achieved 161 mentions in the press, averaging four a week. This reached a cumulative 46.7 million people in the UK. In addition, the company and website had won several awards. However, the high levels of awareness did not seem to be translating into actual customers, sign-ups to the services were lower than expected and they needed to grow faster to meet revenue projections and financial commitments.

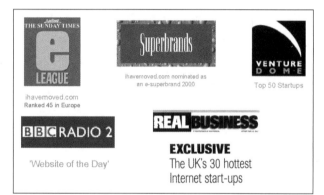

When the directors were pondering what steps to take to accelerate growth, they revisited the arrangements they had with one company, PowerGen. In December 1999 PowerGen and ihavemoved.com had come to an arrangement under which PowerGen had incorporated ihavemoved.com's service into their own website. PowerGen had understood immediately the benefits that 'clean' and formatted data would provide, and had wanted to ensure that more of its customers would be using the system. It also meant that they would be able to offer a better service to their customers who, when visiting PowerGen's website, would find an address changing service as part of the site's offerings. The website would of course be branded with PowerGen's look and feel. ihavemoved.com would lose its branding and the only reference to IHM would be 'powered by ihavemoved.com'. The question was, whether it would be feasible and sensible to offer such a structure to other customers. Many organizations had to re-acquire their customers when they move, and these organizations are very keen to find newer, more efficient ways of doing this.

This was an interesting proposal but quite threatening too. If a strong brand was considered increasingly important for a 'bricks and mortar' company, it was said to be essential for a web-based one. Over the months they had managed to build up very good awareness for their brand, would they lose all that by having their concept integrated into another organization's website?

And how would PowerGen's competitors react if ihavemoved.com put their services on PowerGen's site? Would they stay with ihavemoved.com or would they withdraw?

Finally, the production of custom-made pages for different providers took development time and resource, which cost money. Could ihavemoved.com get companies like PowerGen to pay for this production when essentially this initiative helped promote the ihavemoved.com service and create revenue for the company from the backend notifications? Would the partners instead seek to charge ihavemoved.com or request revenue share for promoting them on their websites and should ihavemoved.com pay?

QUESTIONS

- Why was it important to position ihavemoved.com as a first-mover?
- What would you do to take the company forwards?

APPENDIX I: BACKGROUND TO THE FOUR FOUNDERS

E. David Anstee

BCom (Melbourne), MBA (London Business School)

David has four years of experience in equity raising and corporate finance with Merrill Lynch Australia. He spent his summer break working with Arts Alliance, a London-based venture capitalist, vetting business plans, meeting portfolio companies and working on a business plan under a scholarship scheme. With a focus on

1997–99	London Business School
1995–97	*Travel, National Geographic*
1991–95	Merrill Lynch Australia
1994–99	*3D World* newspaper, Sydney

entrepreneurial studies both at London Business School and while on exchange to the Haas School of Business at UC Berkely, David is responsible for the financial performance of the company, German operations and investor relations.

Francesco Benincasa

BSc (Cardiff), IOD

As managing director and founder of the Chameleon Group, Francesco has worked in web communications and strategic planning since 1995. He has delivered pioneering web strategies to McKinsey Consulting, the BBC, NCR, Evolution Consulting, McGregor Boyall and TrustWorks. Francesco's responsibilities include online marketing, relationships with key partners, and white label integration.

1995–99	Managing Director of Chameleon Strategic reviews for BBC, BT, Dixons. Online branding for Freeserve
1992	RAF Officer Cadet Pilot
1989–92	BSc Hons University of Wales

Nicholas Komninos

BA, BAS (Penn), MBA (London Business School)

Prior to his MBA, Nicholas was a Flight Sergeant for the Hellenic Air Force, dealing extensively with HR-related issues, and Account Executive for OgilvyOne advertising where he planned, conducted and evaluated international marketing campaigns. He has an academic background in psychology and practical experience in designing HRM systems during his summer internship at Qualco Management Consultants. Nicholas was one of the co-founders of a private tutoring service for the students of the American College of Greece. He is responsible for maintaining the fast growth of ihavemoved.com as marketing director and human resources manager.

1997–99	London Business School
1999	Qualco Consultants
1995–97	OgilvyOne Worldwide, Athens
1989–93	University of Pennsylvania USA BA in computer science and psychology

Onic Palandjian

BSc (Bentley), Bus. Admin. (Harvard)

With experience as a venture capital executive in the US, Onic has evaluated and refined the business models of a variety of internet and e-commerce enterprises. He has conducted business in the former Soviet Union under uncertain and difficult circumstances, and worked on the financial and operational areas of a global shipping company. Onic works on securing partners and alliances for ihavemoved.com, as well as the commercial offering.

1998–99	Eagle Venture Capital USA
1996–98	Dorian Ships, Piraeus and USA
1992–95	John Hancock Financial USA
1994–95	Harvard Extension School
1989–92	BSc, Bentley College USA

6 Strategy – Emergent or Planned, and Other Issues

In the ihavemoved.com case study the attitude of the four founders towards the development of their company's strategy, and the flexibility they have shown in responding to emerging opportunities were quite important to the success of the company. The decision to allow other companies to brand the website, acknowledging ihavemoved.com only through a reference to 'powered by', was not an easy one, but essential for the company's financial well-being and growth. Flexibility and open-mindedness were required, though; in fact, the new offering did not distract from the founders' vision but rounded it. In the first chapter of his book *Contemporary Strategy Analysis*, Robert M. Grant introduces three stories of outstanding corporate success, proposing that in each case success was due neither to access to superior resources nor to sheer luck. Though he continues, 'In all three stories lucky breaks provided opportunities at critical junctures. But none of the three organizations was subject to a consistent run of good fortune. More important was the ability of all three [organizations] to recognize the opportunities when they presented themselves and to have the clarity of direction and the flexibility necessary to exploit these opportunities.' (1991, p3). The openness towards opportunities and the mental and organizational flexibility that allows taking advantage of them are part of what differentiates innovative organizations from their less innovative counterparts.

In this chapter, we first expand on the differences between emergent and planned approaches to strategy, and what this means for innovation. We then take a closer look at what innovation best practice in the context of strategy looks like, and follow up by discussing a few strategy frameworks that

1. Help companies to define their starting point and context (Porter's five forces).

2. Provide insights for how companies can align their organization to an innovation ambition (Higgins' application of Peters and Waterman's 7S framework to innovation).

3. Suggest an approach that helps strategy implementation (Hays and Williamson).

The chapter concludes by taking a closer look at design from a strategic perspective.

STRATEGY – PLANNED OR EMERGENT?

The strategic aim of a business is to earn a return on capital, and if in any particular case the return in the long run is not satisfactory, then the deficiency should be corrected or the activity abandoned for a more favourable one.

Alfred P. Sloan Jr

There are probably two distinctive approaches to strategy development. The first is planned – top management devises the strategy, middle management translates it, and supervisors and employees implement it. This approach

Table 6.1 Planned versus Emergent Strategy (based on Hatch 1997 and Mintzberg 1990)

	Planned strategy	Emergent strategy
Starting point	External and internal context of the organization (traditional SWOT[1] analysis)	Action within the organization, trial and error learning though still aimed at implementing an overriding strategy
Leading to	Identification of key success factors (external) and distinctive competencies (internal)	Insights from experiments that in turn influence future action
Resulting in	The creation, evaluation and implementation of a strategy	Review and revision of the overriding strategy
Flow	Top down	Bottom up as well as top down
Level of uncertainty (driven by complexity and rate of change)	Low	High

[1]SWOT stands for strength, weaknesses, opportunities and threats; the first two are internally focused, the last two externally.

it also referred to as 'rational model' of the strategy process. The problem with this approach is that it represents a linear process, not allowing for feedback to be integrated in a flexible and timely fashion. The second approach, on the other hand, combines top down planning with structures that allow for reactions to insights and activities from all levels of the organization. This approach is also referred to as 'emergent strategy'. Table 6.1 summarizes the description of the sections on 'Strategy as rational decision making' (planned strategy) and 'Emergent strategy' in Mary Jo Hatch's book *Organization Theory* (1997).

One could argue that in today's fast moving environment there is little choice but to follow an emergent strategy development process. It is important to point out that emergent strategy should not be confused with not having a direction or strategy at all. When embracing the white label strategy, ihavemoved.com did not change what their company was all about. They knew what they wanted to provide: a web-based offering that would provide a one-stop-shop address changing service to home movers. Had they insisted on providing the website itself that was offering the services they would not have entered into collaborative agreements with other companies. So it is not only the ability and willingness to respond to unforeseen opportunities that lie at the core of innovative organizations, but also a strategy that is formulated broadly enough to prove flexible when necessary. It is probably the lack of a broad enough vision that prevented Xerox from exploiting the inventions coming out of its research lab in Palo Alto (see Chapter 1). By the way, it is often the shift from a product- to a service-based strategy that makes the difference. Think about train operators in the US. Had they thought of themselves as being in the business of transporting people from one place to another rather than being in the train business, their chances of survival would have been much higher.

However, being flexible and responsive can also be quite threatening. What if the new opportunity threatens the core of the existing business? In an interview by the magazine *Quisic*, Peter Skarzynski, co-founder and CEO of the strategic consultancy Strategos, was asked, 'You've been quoted as saying that for companies to innovate, they may have to stop doing some things that made them successful in the first place.' His response was, 'They have to critically look at the things that have made them successful and understand which of those keep them from radical growth, keep them from transforming the industry. So yes, sometimes it means stopping or changing the very thing that drove the success.'[1] The larger the organization, the larger the part of the organization that is under threat, the less likely it is that the opportunity will be taken up.

It seems to me that the description of characteristics of a success-generating new product development process given by Robert G. Cooper (1994) is equally appropriate for a company's strategy. The four characteristics identified by Cooper are:

- *Fluid*: it is fluid and adaptable, constantly reviewing the company's environment to enable early identification and fast response to changes or opportunities

- *Fuzzy gates*: it features conditional go decisions (rather than absolute ones) which are dependent on the situation

- *Focused*: it builds on the company's skills and capabilities (rather than on existing products and markets) and focuses resources on the 'best bets'

- *Flexible*: it does not stick religiously to its formulated strategy if changes in the wider environment render it obsolete

I would also like to emphasize that one approach does not exclude the other, and argue that both are needed. A company needs to have its overriding goal or ambition, but needs to be flexible in how it achieves it. No good insisting on the production of typewriters when the world has moved on to personal computers – unless one wants to become a specialist and niche player. As has been pointed out, sometimes organizations need to give up what has made them successful in the past to be able to succeed in the future.

Companies aiming to become more innovative have to embrace the thought of allowing their strategy to emerge. To be innovative is to pursue opportunities that were neither known nor available before, and which cannot possibly be planned or scheduled. As research by Slevin and Covin (1997) found, 'Planned strategies are positively related to sales growth among firms with mechanistic structures and operating in hostile environments. Emergent strategies, on the other hand, are more positively related to sales growth among forms with organic structure and operating in benign environments.'[2]

STRATEGY AND INNOVATION

Before looking at strategy best practice in the context of innovation in particular, some more general insights into strategy best practice follow. In his aforementioned book on strategy analysis, Grant identifies the following four characteristics of successful strategies:

- They are directed towards unambiguous long-term goals.

- They are based on insightful understanding of the external environment.

- They are based on intimate self-knowledge of the organization's capabilities.

- They are implemented with resolution, coordination, and effective harnessing of the capabilities and commitment of all members of the organization.

To become a successful innovator, the first and last point are most important. We have just discussed the importance of flexibility while maintaining an overall strategic direction. The first point also implies clarity and sharedness, and we will come back to that in a moment. The last requires determination and commitment – something that research by Repenning (2002) has found to be fundamental to innovation success. His research into understanding the dynamics of innovation implementation led him to the following conclusion: 'Managers should not adopt an innovation unless they are prepared to be both fully committed to the effort and patient in the month between adopting the innovation and crossing the motivation threshold. A half-hearted approach or early termination can severely limit the value of an otherwise useful innovation.' (See Box 6.1.) What is true at the project level is equally true for the company level. Managers should not embark on the journey of creating a more innovative organization unless they are prepared to continue on the path and commit the necessary resources.

BOX 6.1   Repenning's Experiment

He conducted two experiments concerning the implementation of an innovation that were identical up to a certain point in time, and the only aspect varying after that was the level of senior management commitment. In one scenario visible senior management commitment was discontinued after 24 months, under the other scenario it was continued. Perhaps not surprisingly, in the first scenario the commitment amongst employees dropped down to zero in a short period of time, leading to failure, whereas in the second scenario employees remained committed, leading to successful implementation of the innovation.

And to clarify, in a vision a company states its goal. Its strategy is, as defined by James Brian Quinn in *Strategies for Change: Local Incrementalism*: 'The pattern that integrates an organization's major goals, policies, and action sequences into a cohesive whole. A well-formulated strategy helps to marshal and allocate an organization's resources into a unique and viable posture based upon its relative internal competencies and shortcomings, anticipated changes in the environment, and continent moves by intelligent opponents.' Or in much simpler terms, a strategy is a plan for action. So if to become more innovative is part of an organization's goal, managers will have to develop a plan of action to achieve this. Putting it into the annual report and adding it to the company's values is not sufficient. Most importantly, it ignores that becoming (more) innovative is about changing behaviour, and an innovation strategy provides 'a plan for action' on how to achieve this.

Research into innovation best practice with Innovation Exchange member companies emphasized the need for a strong link between a company's vision and its innovation strategy, i.e. both vision and strategy should be used when setting the agenda for innovation and new product development activities. And while this book focuses on innovation, I do not want to ignore the fact that there are other positioning strategies companies can pursue. Jones (1997) identifies four different types of new product strategies (see Table 6.2), each of which will require a different approach, structures and strategies to realize its respective ambition.

Looking back at the characteristics of planned and emergent strategy (Table 6.1) and comparing them to the characteristics of the four different new product strategies above, we find that an emergent strategy is much better suited for achieving innovation.

However, something even the most innovative organizations need to balance are the diverging need of innovation on the one hand and operations on the other. It is the conflict between creativity and implementation introduced in the first chapter. Table 6.3 compares aspects of an operating organization with those of an innovating organization. However, how many organizations that claim to be innovative truly have all the characteristics of the innovating organization? And another questions is, is there an innovative organization that could survive long term without also providing the conditions of an operating organization?

Table 6.2 Product Strategies (Jones 1997) (reproduced by permission of Butterworths Heinemann; Jones, T.)

Type	Characteristic	Examples
Offensive	• Innovators	Pilkington – float glass
	• Research-intensive	Du Pont – Teflon
	• High risk/uncertainty	Polaroid – instant film
	• Current information	Hoover – vacuum cleaner
Defensive	• Followers	Matsushita – VHS video
	• Incremental innovation	IBM – personal computers
	• Production quality	WordPerfect – computer software
	• Market focus	Nissan – cars
Imitative	• Low cost manufacture	Compaq – computers
	• Licensed technology	Molson – dry beer
	• No R&D	Daewoo – cars
	• Localized markets	Samsung – microwave ovens
Traditional	• Established markets	Barbour – clothing
	• Constant demand	Aga – cookers
	• Niche market	Zippo – cigarette lighters
	• Low technology	Mont Blanc – pens

Table 6.3 Comparing Operating and Innovation Organizations (based on Jay R. Galbraith and Robert K. Kazanjian 1986, as adapted by Grant, p240) (reproduced by permission of Professor R. Grant)

	Operating organization	Innovating organization
Structure	Bureaucratic, specialization and division of labour; hierarchical control	Flat organization without hierarchical control; task-oriented project teams
Processes	Operating units controlled and coordinated by top management which undertakes strategic planning, capital allocation and operational planning	Processes directed towards generation, selection, funding and development of ideas; strategic planning flexible, financial and operating controls loose
Reward systems	Financial compensation, promotion up the hierarchy, power and status symbols	Autonomy, recognition, equity participation in new ventures
People	Recruitment and selection based upon the needs of the organization structure for specific skills functional and staff specialists, general managers and operators	Key need is for idea generators who combine required technical knowledge with creative personality traits; managers must act as sponsors and orchestrators

What does this mean for managers? For one it means that large, operating-oriented organizations that also want to be innovative have to find a way to balance the demands of both the operation and the innovating company. It might also mean that large operating organizations are just incapable of dealing with radical innovation in the existing structures, and that to allow truly radical innovation to flourish, they have to create alternative structures that meet the requirements of an innovating organization.

Finally, some insights into strategy best practice for innovation. Research into innovative organization tends to highlight three aspects about strategy and vision that differentiate the innovative from the less innovative organization:

- Clarity
- Sharedness
- Attainability

If having a clear and shared vision and strategy is important for any organization that wants to achieve an ambition, it is essential for an organization aspiring to change – and what does the ambition to become more innovative imply but the need for change? While the implications of 'clarity' and 'sharedness' are quite straightforward – everyone in the organization needs to know and understand, and share the same interpretation of the strategy – attainability is a bit more ambivalent and without explanation might be interpreted wrongly.

One could understand this third aspect either to read: it has to be easily achievable or it has to be just about achievable. Theresa Amabile, whose framework was introduced in Chapter 1, refers to this with 'pressure' (represented by workload pressure and challenging work). The goal set needs to be attainable, but at the same time it needs to provide a stretch, a challenge. Something too easily attained does often not seem worth pursuing, whereas something too unrealistic puts people off. Having said this, if the external pressure is sufficient it is surprising what people can achieve. Think about the public pressure to perform created by Kennedy's public announcement that he wanted to put a man on the moon, or the challenge to engineers at the NASA during the Apollo 13 flight, when the lives of their colleagues and the entire mission depended on their ability to create a pump that could convert carbon dioxide into oxygen out of the most bizarre array of objects imaginable. It is often that need, the urge, the crisis, however you like to call it, that is missing in organizations wanting to become more innovative, companies where people tend to think, 'everything is going just fine, thank you, why change?'.

People need a reason to change – and not just one that appeals to their minds. John Kotter (2002) emphasizes, 'People change what they do less because they are given analysis that shifts their thinking than because they are shown a truth that influences their feelings.' It is 'getting people's hearts as well as their minds' that matters and management writer Charles Prather has translated this into a formula for change:[3]

$$\text{Change} = \text{Vision} \times \mathbf{X} \times \text{Felt need to change}$$

Change only happens when there is a vision of where to go, when there is a *felt* need for change, and when there are some specific steps to be taken ('$\mathbf{X}$'). If any part of the equation is zero, there is no change. This also enforces the point made earlier, that a clear strategy and vision are so important in realizing an innovative organization.

By the way, Rosabeth Moss Kanter's book *The Change Masters* explores the dilemma of change, and provides a host of useful insights as to why change may not be happening, and how to overcome the hurdles. Though the list of 'rules for stifling innovation' she provides in her book (see Box 6.2) might make you smile, I am sure there are some – if not many – that can be observed in organizations that you know.

BOX 6.2   Rosabeth Moss Kanter's 'Rules for Stifling Innovation'

1. Regard any new idea from below with suspicion because it's new, and because it's come from below

2. Insist that people who need your approval to act first go through several other levels of management to get their signatures

▶

3. Ask departments or individuals to challenge and criticize each other's proposals (that saves you the job of deciding; you just pick the survivor)

4. Express your criticism freely, and withhold your praise (that keeps people on their toes). Let them know they can be fired at any time

5. Treat identification of problems as signs of failure, to discourage people from letting you know when something in their area isn't working

6. Control everything carefully, make sure people count anything that can be counted, frequently

7. Make decisions to reorganize or change policies in secret, and spring them on people unexpectedly (that also keeps people on their toes)

8. Make sure that requests for information are fully justified and make sure that it is not given out to managers freely (you don't want data to fall into the wrong hands)

9. Assign to lower level managers, in the name of delegation and participation, responsibility for figuring out how to cut back, lay off, move people around, or otherwise implement threatening decisions you have made. And get them to do it quickly

10. And above all, never forget that you, the higher-ups, already know everything important about this business

So attainability means finding a balance between realistic but boring and unrealistic but exciting, and providing people with a motivation and ambition to achieve it.

USEFUL CONCEPTS AND FRAMEWORKS FOR STRATEGY DEVELOPMENT

With all the above managers are still facing three important questions:

1. *Outward looking* – no organization operates in a vacuum. How to understand our context and define our starting point?

2. *Inward looking* – what aspects should our innovation strategy address?

3. Once we have established our innovation strategy, how to ensure implementation?

The three frameworks I am suggesting are:

1. Porter's five forces to help companies define their starting point and understand their industry context.

2. Higgins' application of Peters and Waterman's 7S framework to innovation to provide some insights for how companies can align their organization to an innovation ambition.

3. Hay and Williamson's strategic staircase to provide valuable insights into strategy development and implementation.

Before developing an innovation strategy for their organization, managers should make sure that they understand the context in which they operate and what their position in the playing field is relative to other players. Porter's (1980) five forces framework allows organization to do just that by requiring managers to take a closer look at customers, suppliers, possible new entrants, possible substitutes for its existing products and its industry's overall competitive position. Figure 6.1 summarizes the aspects to be considered for each of the five forces. The insights gained from the analysis can inform both the company's overall as well as its specific innovation strategy.

Once context and positioning have been established, the company's overall strategy can be developed. Closely linked to the overall strategy should be the company's innovation strategy. The 7S framework developed by McKinsey consultants Peters and Waterman (1982) provides a useful reference point to make sure that all aspects of the organization are aligned to the innovation ambition. Higgins (1996) has used the 7S framework to suggest how to implement an innovation strategy. He states that 'Everything in business must start with strategy. Your organization's innovation strategy reflects the demands of its future environment, and how the organization plans on reacting to or changing that environment to meet its needs. Strategy leads to everything else. The other Ss must be pointed in the same direction as strategy.' He too suggests that the strategy determines, and must be supported by, values which need to be set by top management and shared throughout the organization. Based on the strategy and values,

Figure 6.1 Porter's Five Forces (Porter 1980) (reproduced by permission of The Free Press)

Table 6.4 The 7S Framework (based on Higgins 1996) (reproduced by permission of Innovative Leader)

7S	To consider
Strategy	Should reflect the demands of future environment, and how the organization plans to react to or change that environment to meet its needs; everything else must follow
Structure	Teams, innovation centres, lines of communication, alliances, idea evaluation
Systems	Align rewards and remuneration, management information systems, celebration of innovation and creativity, idea assessment beyond financial evaluation, systems for implementing process, marketing, and management innovations
Style	Accepting of failure, suspending judgement, transformational leaders
Staff	Recruit creative people, develop innovation champions, train people, provide time for reflection, provide physical facilities
Shared values	Strategy determines shared values; changing existing values will take time
Skills	Create opportunities, improve and innovate continuously, start knowledge management and organizational learning initiatives, invest in R&D

managers then need to set to work to develop and select the right structure, the right systems, the right style, and the right staff with the right skills. Table 6.4 lists what managers need to consider for each of the seven Ss.

Once the context is understood, and plans have been made for how to change the organization's 7Ss to reflect the innovation ambition, there is still the most difficult step, and two problems. First, how to develop the strategy from which the other six Ss follow; and secondly, how to implement it and fill the strategy with life.

I would like to refer to two articles written by Michael Hay and Peter Williamson in 1991 and 1997, respectively. Both articles investigate why strategy often fails at the implementation stage, and suggest an approach that might help to overcome the problems.

In their first article the authors identified lack of clarity, a preference to continue in accustomed ways, and the fact that most organizations seem to use the past as a predictor for the future as the main reasons underlying implementation failure. They found that many organizations describe a large number of priorities, each with several key performance measures, which means that it is difficult for managers to prioritize their efforts. If everything is first priority, where to focus resources? If innovation is not top priority, innovative projects tend to get axed at the first sign of difficulties, partly because they are seen to be high risk, partly because benefits cannot be reaped in the short term.

In addition, Hay and Williamson found that the different priorities can be in direct conflict with each other, which they felt made implementation efforts even more difficult. In her book *When Giants Learn to Dance*, Rosabeth Moss Kanter (1989) pick up on some of the contradictions managers face:

- Think strategically and invest in the future – but keep the numbers up today.

- Be entrepreneurial and take risks – but do not cost the business anything by failing.

- Know every detail of your business – but delegate more responsibility to others.

- Speak up, be a leader, set the direction – but be participative, listen well, cooperate.

- Continue to do everything you are currently doing even better – and spend more time communicating with employees, serving on teams, and launching new products.

While I agree that the contradictions are difficult to manage, I also believe that increasingly innovative companies and individuals have learned to do just that. Innovative organizations manage their existing business through structured and efficient processes, while at the same time providing some flexibility and slack for creativity and innovation to flourish.

But back to strategy development. In their second article, Hay and Williamson probe deeper into possible causes of implementation failure. Interviewing managers about strategy and probing deeper into statements made about strategy, they found that managers' perception of what strategy means and involves is the true show-stopper to implementation (see Table 6.5).

Realizing that what seems to get distilled from the strategy are targets and forecasts, they comment: 'But what often gets lost in this distillation process is the broader strategic perspective.' And it is just this broader perspective that is essential to innovation. From the above, they distil three reasons for implementation failure:

1.   Confusion about what exactly a 'strategy' is and, specifically, the difference between the various levels at which it operates. How, for example, should a mission, individual objectives and the budget be linked?

2.   An abiding sense that episodic bouts of strategy and the reality of managerial life rarely connect. How, therefore, is one to link strategy to action?

3.   Frustration that the constituent parts of the organization more often pull apart than together with department X thwarting the best efforts of department Y, and vice versa. In other words, can strategy be coordinated and made consistent across the organization?

The approach they suggest involves the following sequential approach:

Step 1:   Provide clear definition of goals, explain what they actually mean for day-to-day management, be specific about actions and targets.

Step 2:   Establish what the specific goals mean in terms of requirements on the firm's resources.

Step 3:   Think about what your company would look like when the strategy has been achieved. Then identify what specific actions you need to take to achieve your goal, working back from the future and considering all resources, skills, capacity, structure, etc. required (now also known as 'backcasting')

Table 6.5   A Deep-Seated Scepticism Characterizes the View from Below

On the surface	Revealed below
Strategy is about the long term	Far enough in the future so that you don't need to do anything about it now
Strategy depends on forecasts	Strategy is about crystal ball gazing
Strategy influences profitability	Budgets are about profitability, strategy is about mountains of paper and thick folders
Strategy is about a common mission, pulling together	Everyone agrees we should have a strategy as long as it doesn't constrain any of our individual departments
Strategy needs periodic review	Strategic planning is a comfortable part of the corporate ritual; a once-a-year 'binge' and it's back to the in-tray

With that process in mind, they then suggest that companies develop the following in a strictly methodical fashion:

A vision	that has two dimensions: external and internal; defining a vision provides the firm with an essential set of bearings: a map of the changing terrain on which it is competing; underpinning the vision there has to be a set of guiding beliefs and values
A mission	that should encapsulate an organization's *raison d'être* or guiding purpose; the destination to which that purpose leads; and the rationale behind the purpose
A plan	that focuses on how it is to be done, identifying specific steps
Key initiatives	each step of the plan it to be broken down into specific initiatives
Individual objectives	employees' objectives need to be derived from the set of initiatives being pursued; where individual objectives and strategic requirements are at odds with each other, then strategy will surely fail
Budgets	the revenues and costs identified in a budget have to be linked to individual initiatives

To qualify what Hay and Williamson call a 'first class strategy', it should provide the following:

- *Inspiration* in the form of a worthwhile, relevant goal.

- A *linkage* that helps individuals to connect their own task with the initiatives being undertaken elsewhere in the company.

- *Guidance* to individuals about the trade-offs and prioritization decisions they have to make on a daily basis.

- *Discretion* for the individual to manoeuvre by loosening some existing constraints and generating some new options.

- The facilitation of *communication* by establishing a common language which everyone in the company can use.

If a strategy fulfils the criteria above, it should provide a sound foundation from which managers can build an innovative organization.

DESIGN AND STRATEGY

A design strategy is the effective allocation and coordination of design resources and activities to accomplish a firm's objectives of creating its appropriate public and internal identities, its product offerings, and its environments.

Olsen et al. (1998)

In the final section of this chapter, I would like to talk about design's role in and connection with business strategy. For the last 20 years, management gurus have promoted the strategic value of design, starting with Kotler and Rath declaring in 1984 that design is 'a powerful but neglected tool', quoting companies such as IBM or furniture maker Herman Miller as examples of companies that have used design to achieve a superior market position. Tom Peters soon joined the ranks of the illustrious promoters of design – but so far, it seems, without too much success! There still remains much confusion about what design means, what its use involves, and how it can actually contribute to a company's competitiveness. People continue to confuse design with styling – the latter being something that is applied to an existing product towards the end of its development process, whereas the former is an integral part of a product's development process right from the outset.

Differences in education, resulting in different approaches to problem solving, can partly be blamed for managers' lack of understanding of the contribution design can make to business success. Managers are taught to think rationally, to analyze and measure. They are taught to avoid risk and focus on answering questions. Designers, on the other hand, are taught to express themselves (be emotional), to explore and experiment. They have a great tolerance for ambiguity and focus on understanding the question. Managers are concerned with facts and figures, whereas designers are driven by intuition and inspiration. The lack of acknowledgement and understanding of the differences leads many managers to view design and creativity as something close to a black art, something that cannot be managed and is therefore better left alone. Creating an awareness for the differences and bringing designers on board as early as possible can help to maximize the benefits that can be gained by harnessing the differences.

It also helps to communicate clearly the benefits that design and designers can bring to a business. Kotler and Rath explain that design and the conscious management of design can add value by:

- Creating corporate distinctiveness in an otherwise product- and image-surfeited marketplace
- Creating a personality for a newly launched product so that it stands out from its more prosaic competitors
- Reinvigorating product interest for products in the mature stage of its life-cycle
- Communicating value to the consumer
- Making selection easier (standing out) and increase consumer satisfaction
- Helping to inform consumers in a more efficient way

Kotler and Rath continue to identify what constitutes effective design, namely performance, quality, durability, appearance and cost benefits, but state that to achieve this it is necessary that senior management recognizes and understands the contribution design can make, and that designers are an integral part of the new product development team, right from the outset.

Considering the above, and referring back to the Porter framework, design can thus help

- To create barriers to entry by providing product differentiation and creating emotional switching costs

- To reduce suppliers' bargaining power by high levels of differentiation, enhancing product quality, and increasing hurdles for possible substitutes

- To reduce buyers' bargaining power again by higher levels of differentiation, increased desirability and product quality, and decreasing price sensitivity by preventing direct comparability (due to differentiation and quality)

- To reduce customers' receptivity to substitutes and decrease price sensitivity

- To reduce the impact of the number of players and excess capacity, e.g. Apple computers are less likely to be affected by excess capacity than bog standard computers

But even if management realizes the value of design, the next question then is, how it can be harnessed, where it applies, and what part design can play in realizing a company's strategy. Cooper and Press (1995) have identified three distinct areas of design activity in an organization, and associate specific design strategy issues with each:

- The development of corporate identity – this is about communications and, of course, identity; it requires the understanding of the corporate values, the relationship between corporate image and corporate goals, whether the focus lies on the corporation, the division or the product line, what the necessary design competencies are, and what the intangible messages of the corporation are. To implement these strategic issues, designers need to work with members of the PR, advertising, HR, finance, R&D, marketing and IS departments.

- The design of saleable products and services – this is about the relationship between the factors involved in product or service design (price, quality, standardization) and corporate goals, and requires the understanding of price point constraints and production costs and capacities, about having insights into the features that are valued by customers, about having the competencies necessary to design and deliver the planned products, and understanding the intangible messages that designed products and services carry. To implement these strategic issues, designers need to work with members of the marketing, R&D, operations, and, to a lesser extent, finance and accounting departments.

- The design of operating environments – this is about the relationship between corporate values, image, environment and goals. It requires the understanding of the competitive strategy adopted by the firm or division, knowing how work is conducted within the firm and the critical interrelationships between functions, understanding consumer shopping preferences, having the competencies necessary to design corporate environments, and understanding the intangible messages that corporate environments carry. To implement these strategic issues, designers need to work with members of the marketing, operations and HRM departments, as well as architectural firms and public zoning agents.

> **Summary of Design Management Process**
> (based on Olsen *et al.* 2000)
>
> 1. Clearly articulate the firm's competitive strategy to designers and design managers.
>
> 2. Develop a detailed understanding of the design requirements inherent in the adopted competitive strategy.
>
> 3. Ensure open lines of communication among the design group and other functional units.
>
> 4. Create, review and approve design briefs.
>
> 5. Compare performance outcomes against the objectives established in design briefs.

However, having said all that, and emphasized the contributions design can make, I would like to give voice to a designer (!) who, while many seem to suggest that design should take over the world, suggests that, 'In a successful relationship, you will often find a dominant partner and a quiet one – a leader and a supportive follower. In the business-design relationship, business must be the leader, and design must be the supportive follower.' For that to happen, Turner (2000) realizes, design has to redefine 'its relationship with business – not in terms of design strategy versus business strategy, but at a much more fundamental level'. He suggests that design take the role of coordinator, facilitator and interpreter, rather than that of the leader it often aspires to. He also suggests that, as design touches so many parts of a business, 'It can bridge the gap between a company's ambitions and the things that go on every day in the factory, the showroom, or the office in a way a mission statement never can.' This certainly is a strong argument for design, and for the potential to become reality, companies need to integrate design into their DNA – or treat design as, what Gorb and Dumas call 'design as infusion' (see Chapter 1), which means everyone in the organization understands and values the contribution design can make.

I would like to conclude this chapter with some questions senior management might want to ask about design that I have extracted and adapted from the British Standard 7000, *Guide to Managing Product Design*:

- Have the corporate objectives for design and new product development been properly defined and, thereafter, periodically reviewed?

- Are these corporate objectives understood by all involved, and have they inspired enthusiasm?

- Is the company's product strategy compatible with its corporate objectives?

- Have significant resources been provided to match the product strategy?

- Are procedures in place to ensure that up-to-date information about market requirements are available to the design and development team?

- Are the collaborative, information and evaluation links between the design and development team and other parts of the organization operating properly?

- Are the organizational policies and procedures for managing the design and development process adequate?

- Is there a sincere and visible commitment to high standards of product design?

- Are achievements and expenditure being monitored against time?

- Are results being properly evaluated, and is this evaluation being communicated to all concerned?

READING SUGGESTIONS

ON STRATEGY

Grant, Robert M. (1991) *Contemporary Strategy Analysis: Concepts, Techniques, Applications.* London: Basil Blackwell

Comment: Introduction to strategy analysis and development, makes several references to innovation and the innovating organization

ON CHANGE

Moss Kanter, Rosabeth (1985) *The Change Masters*

Comment: One of the classics on change, with particular insights for and emphasis on innovation

Moss Kanter, Rosabeth (1989) *When Giants Learn to Dance*

Comment: On how large organizations manage to become innovative, and thrive on change

SOME USEFUL WEBSITES

www.strategos.com

Comment: Website of Strategos, the consultancy set up by management guru Gary Hamel which provides a listing of their publications as well as insights into their research findings
www.smsweb.org

Comment: This is the website of the Strategic Management Society, which provides a list of useful links (www.smsweb.org/reference/web_sites.html), as well as influential books on strategy

(www.smsweb.org/reference/inf_books.html)

NOTES ON CHAPTER 6

[1] For full interview see http://www.quisic.com/cgi-bin/ic/ic_article_display.pl?nav=2&channel_id=1&content_id=104.

[2] See also Table 3.2 in Chapter 3 for a comparison between different types of organizational structure whereby 'mechanistic structure' corresponds with 'functional structure' and 'organic structure' with 'matrix structure'.

[3] 'Leading innovation: enabling your organization', presentation given at the 2002 Innovation Network conference in Minneapolis, 22nd–25th September 2002.

7 Branding and Innovation

'Our brand is our most important asset,' explains Joe Middleton, European President of Levi Strauss. 'It's more valuable than all the other assets on our balance sheet. It is more valuable than our factories, our buildings, our warehouses and our inventory'.[1]

Strategy and branding issues were closely related in the ihavemoved.com case study, and brands can provide a shared framework within which innovation can take place. This chapter looks at what 'brands' and 'brand equity' actually mean, what their role in innovation can be, and what role brands play for web-based companies.

WHAT IS A BRAND?

Some may ask, why actually talk about brands in the context of innovation? On its website the British Brands Group (www.britishbrandsgroup.com) declares: 'In a world that is ever more complex and sophisticated, brands stand out as beacons of familiarity and reliability. As reference points with known characteristics with which consumers can identify and trust. As symbols of hope and new prosperity in the fast emerging markets of the world. As vehicles for delivering continuously improving value.' People might want to argue that if familiarity is a major characteristic of a brand, then surely brands must be a rather unsuitable subject to discuss for innovation? Well, I think that is just why it is important to discuss brands. There are two reasons. First, as Haigh (1996) points out, 'It [the brand] must be separable from the underlying product or service, permitting transfer of loyalty between products and categories over time', which means that a brand can be used as a platform from which to launch innovation. The advantage of using an existing brand as a springboard for innovation is that consumers, customarily slow to embrace something entirely new, might transfer the trust and liking they have for the existing products or services associated with the brand to new ones, hence accelerating its acceptance.

The second reason is, in understanding the power of a brand, managers launching an innovative product or service should focus on building a strong brand quickly, thus accelerating the development of trust and acceptance rates amongst its potential customers. The Orange campaign comes to mind. By the time the services were launched, consumers already seemed to have a good familiarity with the brand, leading to a faster take-up of the product than might otherwise have been the case. Don't forget, what influences people's decision making is,

> A brand starts its life as a statement or guarantee about a single product. As the reputation of that product grows, the brand may be used as a promise of assurance in relation to be products launched under the same umbrella. The brand has also developed a third and more subtle role, in which it says something both about the product and about its users and their lifestyles.
>
> *The British Brands Group*

first and foremost, experience, then feelings, and rationality only comes in when absolutely necessary (often as post-purchase rationalization). Focusing on developing a strong brand can help acceptance and market penetration.

What else do brands do for consumers and companies? As the British Brands Group's booklet *A Guide to Brands X* points out, when brands were 'invented' around the middle of the 19th century, their main purpose was 'to differentiate a product from its competitors by stressing particular features such as quality, consistency and reliability'. They also declare that, 'Brands help us to decide what to wear, eat and use, how we shop, travel and manage our money.'

Now that we have established why we should talk about brands, what does 'brand' actually mean? Allen (2000) suggests a rather short and straightforward definition of a brand: reputation = brand = behaviour, which I understand to mean that a brand rises and falls with its reputation, which in turn depends on the behaviour people associate with it. However, his definition seems to confuse 'brand' and 'brand equity' which need to be differentiated. *A Marketing Glossary for UK Public Companies' Annual Reports*[2] offers the following definition for 'brand':

A brand is a name, term, symbol or design (or a combination of them) which identifies one or more products (mostly used in the US)

Or

> A brand is a specifically defensible piece of legal, intellectual property manifested in logos, identities and advertising to which an incremental stream of revenue is attached. It therefore represents a secure flow of future earnings.
>
> *Haigh (1996)*

The identification plus the product itself and its packaging, i.e. the gestalt (mostly used in the UK), e.g. 'A product is something that is made, in a factory; a brand is something that is bought, by a customer. A product can be copied by a competitor; a brand is unique. A product can be quickly outdated; a successful brand is timeless.' Stephen King

To put a bit more flesh on this definition, it might help to take a look at the characteristics of brands as identified by the non-executive of one of the world's largest advertising companies, WPP, Jeremy Bullmore:

- Products are made and owned by companies – brands [images], on the other hand, are made and owned by people... by the public... by consumers.

- A brand image belongs not to a brand, but to those who have knowledge of that brand.

- The image of a brand is a subjective thing – no two people, however similar, hold precisely the same view of the same brand.

- People come to conclusions about the brand as a result of an uncountable number of different stimuli – many of which are way outside the control of or even the influence of the product's owner.

- Much of what influences the value of a brand lies in the hands of its competitors.

- It is universally accepted that brands [brand equity] are a company's most valuable asset, yet there is no universally accepted method of measuring that value.

> **Brand Image**
>
> Perceived impression of a brand by its audience. A multidimensional concept that is hard to measure precisely but can be defined by its associations, e.g. Martell cognac is associated with expensive sporting activities.

With his list, Bullmore makes also clear the difference between a product and a brand, but even though most of the above seems to imply that the management of a brand and its reputation are beyond a company's control, this is certainly not the case. This rather means that companies have to consciously manage their brand (whether this refers to the product or the company level) and take actions to reinforce the desired image of the brand, counteracting any negative reflection competitors' action might cause if necessary.[3]

In his last point, he refers to brand equity which the *Marketing Glossary* defines as:

An important tangible asset for the company, it can be seen as the reservoir of results gained by good marketing but not yet delivered to the profit and loss account.

Awareness, attitudes, associations, memories and habits, which cause people to choose/recommend the brand more often and/or in larger quantities and/or at higher prices than would otherwise be the case.

'Customer brand equity' is part of the total brand equity in the minds of customers as distinct from other stakeholders, e.g. employee brand equity which is the reputation of their employer in the minds of employees.

Similar to reputation which is often used for corporate brand equity but excludes product availability. Can also be described as 'goodwill'. The financial value of brand equity cannot (in the UK) be included on a balance sheet although the cost of acquired brands may be so long as the cost is not more than their financial value.

What, then, are characteristics of brands, particularly successful ones? The following traits have been combined from Ambler (1997) and the website of the British Brands Group (BBG):

- They provide a strong bond of trust between the brand owner and the consumer – successful brands meet or even exceed consumer expectations and aspirations.

- They come with an implicit guarantee of quality.

- They are consistent – the assurance is not only about quality, but also about consistency, wherever and whenever the product or service is bought the experience is the same.

> The four dimensions of 'brand manners' as identified by Pringle and Thompson (1999) are:
>
> - *Spiritual*: the brand must make the consumer feel a better person
>
> - *Political*: consumers must feel comfortable with how the brand was made, etc. (was it right for me)
>
> - *Emotional*: the brand must give us the feeling 'I would like to do that again'
>
> - *Rational*: the brand must function, perform and over-deliver

- Leading on from the previous point, successful brands are also widely available.

- They have a distinctive difference – successful brands stand out from the crowd. As the BBG points out, 'Consumers will not purchase a product that is simply a mild variation on a theme, a brand should provide a distinctive difference.'

- And finally, they have a clear personality – consumers are clear what the brand stands for and what its rational and emotional values are.

You will find out about the true strength of a brand really when disaster strikes. Think about the Elk-test disaster of the Mercedes A-Class. Though there was a lot of negative press, the Mercedes brand, and of course how the crisis was managed by the company's management, meant that the success of the product was merely delayed, not prevented. I believe that the saving grace was not the brand in itself, but the consistency of the management's behaviour with the brand values: admitting the problem and acceptance of responsibility, open communication, and rectification of the problem in the shortest possible time.

Given that consumers seem to be obsessed with labels – spending £20 bn on branded fashion goods in the UK alone – and that brands are increasingly seen to be a company's most valuable asset, there are increasing attempts to put a value on brands and to measure the brand equity.

So what, then, is brand equity, and where does it come from? In his aforementioned presentation on innovation and brands, Ambler says, 'Brand equity is a marketing asset, it is the consequence of good marketing. It is primarily formed by the brand experience, but also by advertising and marketing, and can be described as "What everyone has between the ears about the brand".' Or as David Aaker (1991) defines it, brand equity 'is a set of assets (and liabilities) linked to a brand's name and symbol that adds to (or subtracts from) the value provided by a product or service'. He identifies aspects that feed into brand equity: brand loyalty, brand awareness, perceived quality, brand associations, other proprietary brand assets.

But how to put a value on a brand? David Haigh, author of the report *A Review of Current Practice – Brand Valuation* (commissioned by the Institute of Practitioners in Advertising (IPA) in 1996) has observed four different financial valuation methods:

- *Cost based* – based on what it would actually or theoretically cost to create the brand; Haigh suggests that this approach is backward looking and no guide for current value.

- *Market based* – this approach assumes the existence of comparable transactions of brands or companies against which a brand can be valued; however, he identified two problems with this approach, the difficulty of making direct comparisons between brands, and the availability of sufficiently detailed data to make a judgement.

- *Income based (royalty relief)* – assumes that brands are licensed to operating companies, which in turn pay royalties, which in turn could be used to determine the value, using Net Present Value (NPV) or Discounted Cash-Flow (DCF) calculations; problems with this approach are that (a) brands are more often than not 'used' by the companies that own them, and (b) if brands are licensed it is often difficult to get the data necessary to make a judgement.

- *Income based (economic use)* – based on estimating the difference in gross profit from selling a branded as opposed to an unbranded product; an approach pioneered generally using the discounted cash-flow approach (a method pioneered by the brand consultancy Interbrand); this approach evaluates the brand against a number of different aspects, such as geographic spread and protection, using the identified 'brand risk' to discount future cash flow.

BRANDS AND INNOVATION – A CLOSER LOOK

For owners of brands. . . , the successful management of brands depends on a never ending quest to bring the brand closer to the consumer's ideal. In a dynamic economy, brands are not only a guarantee of quality and replicability, they are also the means for delivering innovation. Innovation which depends on the long term commitment of brand owners to make substantial investment in the future of their brands.

http://www.britishbrandsgroup.com

Earlier in this chapter we established why it is worth taking a closer look at brands and branding in the context of innovation, i.e. the provision of focus for innovation around an existing brand, and the need to establish a strong and consistent presence quickly if a new brand is concerned. In this section, we take a closer look at what this actually means.

In the chapter about strategy and vision, the need to provide some focus for innovation was emphasized. A strong brand is one way of providing such focus. As SGS, a company specializing in the verification, testing and certification of new product declares, 'Innovation and brands are interdependent. A brand can focus innovation on the requirements and aspirations of the consumer which can help build brand equity.'[4] If everyone is familiar with the brand and what it often referred to as the brand's DNA (the core values reflected by the brand), this will make it easier for them to come up with new ideas that strengthen the brand and move it forward, though companies must ensure that the new product and services are aligned with the brand promise – unless the innovations are to be used to help reposition the brand. Allen (2000) describes the brand promise as the intersection of three aspects: corporate communication, corporate behaviour, and corporate strategy (see Figure 7.1).

But the question is not only 'What can the brand do for innovation?', it is also 'What can innovation do for the brand?'. To quote from the British Brands Group's website again, 'In order to meet the changing needs of consumers and to stay ahead of the competition, the manufactured brand must strive for continuous innovation and improvement.' Ergo, innovation and brands are interdependent. Innovation is not only a means for staying ahead, it also helps to achieve another criterion for brand success: differentiation.

However, the association of brands and innovation is not all positive. A strong and clearly defined existing brand can be limiting innovation, restricting the avenues that can be explored. It becomes a question of how far a brand can be stretched – the issue of 'brand extension'. Recent research into this topic by Hem *et al.* (2001) led to the following insights:

- Perceived similarity of brand extension and parent brand is crucial for the acceptance of brand extension of services.

- The reputation of the parent brand is a crucial factor: a favourable reputation of the parent's brand has a positive impact of the success of the brand extension (this is true for FMCG, durable goods and services alike).

- The perceived risk[5] associated with the brand extension is an important influence for brand extensions of durable goods and services.

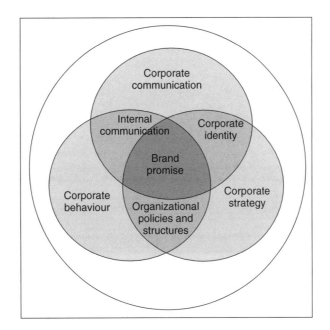

Figure 7.1   Brand Promise (Allen 2000) (reproduced by permission of Design Management Journal)

- Consumers who have generally a positive attitude towards innovation tend also be more open towards brand extensions.

So it is important to decide what kind of strategy a company wants to pursue, innovation within or outside existing brands, and, in deciding a company's strategy towards branding, a categorization by Vishwanath and Mark (1997) might be useful, particularly as they comment on each quadrant's position on innovation (see Figure 7.2). They suggest that a company can have one of four approaches towards brand positioning:

- *Hitchhikers*: gain share by lowering prices dangerously, it is usually in their best interest to follow the leader's pricing moves. Innovation might help.

- The *High-Road Brands*: key to success here is innovation, consumers tend to be loyal and willing to pay a premium.

- The *Low-Road Brands*: feature-inflated cost structures and lack of differentiation, to improve situation review cost structure.

- The *Dead-End Brands*: According to the authors, you don't want to be here and should try anything to get into a different quadrant!

Each of the four types of brand is associated with a different level of innovation, and in the end the success of a company will depend on the level of alignment that is achieved across all aspects of the organization.

Finally, not all brands live up to expectations, and Keller *et al.* (2002) have identified five possible reasons as to why that might be:

- Walk before you can run – companies sometimes attempt to build brand awareness before defining a clear brand position. The authors suggest that many dotcoms have succumbed to this kind of pitfall.

- Identify what matters – sometimes companies focus on promoting something consumers don't care about. The authors give the example of analgesics where companies focused on the length of the relief – rather than what mattered really to the customer: the speed with which it took effect.

- Focus on differentiators – a brand will get into trouble when the main selling point can easily be copied, e.g. price advantage.

Figure 7.2   Branding Categories (based on Vishwanath and Mark 1997)

- Watch what you are copying – copying a product feature because a competitor has been successful with it does not mean that you will benefit too. The authors quote the example of General Mills introducing Honey Nut Cheerios, based on the perception that honey is healthier. When Post decided to re-brand its Sugar Crisp into Golden Crisp, it actually lost market share.

- Think carefully before re-branding – trying to reposition an existing brand can be very difficult if not impossible. The authors give the example of Pepsi-Cola's attempt to move the brand away from its youthful image, only to revert back to it when it became clear that the repositioning only led to a loss in market share.

BRANDS AND THE WEB

This final section briefly looks at brands in the specific context of the web, finishing with some considerations about website development in general.

What do companies planning to set-up a website need to consider? In their article 'Branding: leadership strategies',[6] Plant and Willcocks (2000) have identified four components:

- *Technology* – how are we attempting to leverage the technology, and with what consequences for our brand?

- *Service* – what level of service at what cost will we deliver through this channel, and how will this affect the brand?

- *Market* – what is our segmentation strategy, and how can we define brands across our segments?

- *Brand* – what is the website going to do for our brand, create a new one, reinforce or change an existing one, or are we just following what everyone else does?

The authors found that market leaders will not focus on one or a few of these aspects, but address all of them. While branding cannot compensate for shortcomings in the competitive positioning, the pricing strategy or levels of service provided, it can play a powerful role in creating a successful web presence.

As indicated above, the authors have identified a number of different strategies a company can pursue in setting up its website:

- *The creation of a new brand* – e.g. the setting up of a new company such as amazon.com or eBay.com. The strength here comes from being the first-mover, and developing a high visibility fast, and most importantly, adding value for the consumer

- *The reinforcement of an existing brand* – giving the BMW website as an example (www.bmw.com), the authors describe this as an 'intermediate strategy for organizations that have established distribution channels and cannot risk alienating existing customers and distributors (e.g. philips.com), or that can inform but not sell to certain segments such as drug manufacturers (genentech.com).'

- *To support the repositioning of a brand* – for example, United Parcel Services (www.ups.com) moved from being a parcel delivery company with a rather static site in 1996 to being a logistics solutions company whose website reflected the 'information delivery component' of the brand.

- *To be a brand follower* – the 'me-too' approach, driven by the fact that everyone else in the market has done it, often mimicking the first-mover without adding any particular value that would be specific to their site.

Needless to say, the authors believe that the last option is the one least likely to create value for the company.

But apart from which strategy a company pursues, what should managers consider when setting up an internet site? Upshaw (2001) points out that managers of dotcoms seem to fail to realize that 'in a selling environment in which the product is not touchable and services are promised by companies that came into being only months before, businesses must entice prospects into active involvement with their brands, not just their sites.' His advice for companies seeking to introduce a web-based brand includes:

- Adopt a name that will provide maximum flexibility for the brand.com business model, e.g. if the 'click' business is to move into 'mortar' too.

- Establishing marketing strategies that are self-sustaining, e.g. make sure that all marketing and advertising activities reinforce each other.

- Construct a masterbrand that creates superiority online, not just differentiation, e.g. not only the choice but also the legendary service of amazon.com.

- Design a user interface that is specifically suited to create maximum brand involvement, not just simple interaction, e.g. personalized pages when the site is revisited.

- Forge a proactive customer service operation that is an integral part of a greater relationship-building engine, e.g. life online support.

And whether the company is entirely web-based or whether it is a 'mortar' company that decides to set-up a website, what are the aspects to consider maximizing chances of a success? Lorraine Justice (2001) has some suggestions. First she recommends reviewing who should be involved during the web development. Quite obviously, the website development team should include representatives from a number of different disciplines such as design, computer programming, marketing, social science, information architecture and those related to production. The second group are the visitors (one-off) and users (repeat) of the site; ideally the website should be designed in a way that people who have visited once would come back. The third group, and not to be underestimated, are the decision makers, who may or may not be the client. She further suggests that it might sometimes be advisable to bring in an independent expert team that has the expertise to comment on technology and usability, and who is not prone to 'Betriebsblindheit', a nice German word for describing the problems that arise from being too close to a situation to be able to see its problems and limitations. Even though this might incur some extra costs, getting the site wrong would be much more expensive.

Justice has also identified a number of issues that often go

> **Web development process (Justice 2001)**
>
> Define the site purpose
>
> - Corporate communication tool?
> - Provide which content to which audience for what experience?
>
> Research/information gathering
>
> - Set the information hierarchy, navigation system, and ideas for visual/emotional appeal to use for the prototype
>
> Ideation/problem solution
>
> - Informal prototype and site solutions generated
>
> Production of the site
>
> - Pulling components together, visualizing the site
>
> Final evaluation
>
> - Successful, not successful, partly successful
> - Plans for future updates and redesigns

wrong in website development – though looking at the list it seems to me that it is not only website development that suffers from these ailments, but these are characteristics of projects that are not planned properly, and that do not have a high profile within the organization:

- Poor team development caused by personal conflict, control issues, politics and power struggles.

- Poor definition of the website's purpose, varying views on what it is to achieve, a lack of hierarchy/importance to guide the structure, and poor research methods.

- Poor development process, namely being overly descriptive, or too unstructured, e.g. missing clear stages and sign-off points (see also Chapter 3).

- Lack of technical or artistic support, which are both essential for the successful development of a website.

- Unrealistic time or cost constraints.

Beyond the more procedural contributors to website success, Robin Cleland (2000) has identified the following ten elements of web branding success:

- A compelling value proposition.

- A high-quality online experience (convenience, content, customization, community, connectivity, customer care and communication).

- A reputation for excellence (delivering their e-promise).

- Strong communications programme and efficient customer acquisition strategy.

- Unique positioning concept and distinct brand image.

- Strong partnership and strategic alliances.

- Intense customer focus.

- First-mover and early-mover advantage.

- Relentless innovation.

- Ability to leverage offline brands and assets.

READING SUGGESTIONS

ON BRANDING

Upshaw, Lynn B. and Taylor, Earl (2000) *The Masterbrand Mandate*. Chichester, UK: John Wiley & Sons

Comment: The book identifies what differentiates successful from less successful branding strategies. Emphasizing the need to foster a sense of community both within and outside the organization the authors analyze successful megabrands, such as Sun Microsystems, Charles Schwab & Co and America Online

Kapferer, Jean-Noel (2001) *Reinventing the Brand: Can Top Brands survive the New Market Realities?* London: Kogan Page

Comment: A review in the Market Research Society's publications described the book as, 'Useful insights into brand strategy and management. Kapferer provides a holistic overview of the marketing industry and market research's place within it'

Klein, Naomi (2001) *No Logo*. London: Flamingo

Comment: High-profile and controversial book suggesting that 'ever powerful brands' reflect a potential danger;
                provides a historic account of the development of brands

                Plant, Robert T. (2000) *e-Commerce: Formulation of Strategy*, London: Financial Times/Prentice Hall

Comment: Drawing on his interviews and research with leading e-commerce organizations, Plant explores four
                key drivers of e-commerce success: brand, technology, service and market. The book is aimed at
                board level to develop an understanding of all aspects associated with internet strategy
                development and execution

                Bedbury, Scott (2002) *A New Brand World: Eight Principles for Achieving Brand Leadership in the 21st
                Century*. New York: Viking Books

Comment: Written by the former Head of Advertising at Nike and, more recently, Senior Vice President of
                Marketing at Starbucks. Provides a counterpoint to Naomi Klein's book. It tells the story behind the
                success of Nike and Starbucks, and how it can be applied to any growth business

                Dowling, Grahame (2000) *Creating Corporate Reputations: Brands, Identity, and Performance*. Oxford,
                Oxford University Press

Comment: Corporate reputations are a valuable strategic asset for every company. Good reputations have
                been shown to help firms attain and sustain superior financial performance in their industry. This
                book outlines how high-status companies become corporate superbrands, and it presents managers
                with a framework to enhance their corporation's desired reputation

SOME USEFUL WEBSITES

                www.interbrand.com

Comment: The Interbrand website has lots of useful and interesting articles on the subject of brands, most of
                which you can either view or download. Interbrand are the pioneers in brand valuation

                www.britishbrandsgroup.com

Comment: The British Brands Group website has a host of useful information on and around brands

NOTES ON CHAPTER 7

[1] Quoted in the article 'Consumer products – branding', which can be found on http://www.sgs.co.uk/consulting/
industries/consumer/branding.htm.

[2] The glossary has been edited by Tim Ambler, London Business School, and can be downloaded from
www.london.edu/marketing/glossary.

[3] In his book *Company Image and Reality*, David Bernstein makes a persuasive argument as to why companies
should communicate: people will talk anyway so you might as well influence what they have to say.

[4] See http://www.sgs.co.uk/consulting/industries/consumer/branding.htm.

[5] The authors identify two components of perceived risk: (a) uncertainty about the consequences of making a mistake, and (b) uncertainty about the outcome. Consumers rely on brands to minimize perceived risk.

[6] The full article can be found on http://www.brandchannel.com/papers_review.asp?sp_id =58; the website also makes reference to Plant's book *E-commerce: Formulation of Strategy*, Financial Times/Prentice Hall, 2000.

8 The Value of Market Research

CASE STUDY 3: BLACK & DECKER'S QUATTRO

IF I ONLY HAD TIME...

'We need a decision soon, the trade fair in Cologne is in March next year and we need to commission tooling if we want to be ready on time. We do not have time to market test the new design. The original design had great results so we know people would like it. I know this new design is a bit different, but...'

Nigel Robson, industrial designer at Black & Decker's design centre in Spennymoor, UK, had been working furiously to produce an alternative design for a new cordless multifunctional tool that was to be introduced to the world at the trade fair in Cologne in March 1998. It was already April 1997 and a decision on the design needed to be made soon.

Due to internal resource constraints, the initial design had been developed by an external consultancy with which Black & Decker had worked successfully before. The result was alright, but Lawrie Cunningham, Director of Innovation and Industrial Design, thought it quite traditional and felt that this new product category could be made more exciting. Even though marketing were very happy with the original design – which had researched very well – he decided to ask Nigel Robson from his industrial design team to refine it. Nigel, who was relatively new to the company, felt very strongly about not just 'rounding the corners', as he put it.

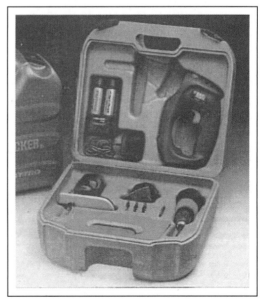

In his view, this new multi-purpose tool ought to look different from what existed already, and it was certainly not to look like a drill. He pointed out, 'The question for the designer is always how to differentiate your product on the shelf.' The main reason the existing design looked like all other cordless drills was the location of the batteries. Nigel started looking for alternative locations. At the same time he reviewed the ergonomics of the product. It was not very well balanced, making it uncomfortable to use. By reconsidering ergonomics and battery location, he not only achieved better handling of the product but also increased functionality.

However, there were not only upsides. The new design was more expensive, it needed some extra parts, being less able to rely less on existing – hence proved and tested – parts. On top of that there would not be time to market test the new design. At least with the first design they knew that customers would like it.

A NEW CONSUMER TREND

Lawrie Cunningham explains, 'Black & Decker are always keen to stay in touch with changes in customer preferences, to react to or even anticipate consumer trends.' He continues, 'We are continuously trying to get a portrait of our buyers and take time to look carefully at what exactly it is the consumer wants.' As a consequence, most new product ideas are researched intensively by marketing who define what is needed, but generally leave it to the designer how to execute it. Concepts are developed around user profiles that are defined by motivation, knowledge and ability.

In addition to the desire to respond to market demands, there were also other reasons for Black & Decker to pursue the concept. They were operating in a market with a lot of competition, where prices had dropped considerably. A significant manufacturing base had grown in China and, for example, in 1996 one could get a sander for £19.95, a product that had previously been two to three times that price. So the opportunity to introduce a product that was different and would offer new benefits to consumers was very welcome.

Marketing had become aware that in the DIY tools market, the emphasis was increasingly on multifunctionality. Earlier in 1996 Black & Decker had already introduced a multifunctional sander, which had been very successful. Their aim was now to develop another even more successful tool around the concept of multifunctionality. The multi-purpose tool was a response to an ever increasing need for simple tools that users of limited experience could feel confident working with. The challenge was to create a product that would be truly innovative and exciting in a highly competitive market – particularly as in the past add-ons had been perceived to be inferior. This meant that they would have to ensure that performance for all functions was equally high – which would be a challenge, given that the battery available would only have 7.2 volts.

> Millions of people rely on powered hand tools to make their lives easier. All of these people have different needs. Tool manufacturers have responded with a seemingly bottomless toolbox of powered drills, grinders, sanders, saws and so on. To keep their customers satisfied, and attract new ones, manufacturers have been offering lower cost tools with improved ergonomics and a wider range of features. One of the most popular feature is battery power. Battery-powered or cordless tools are one of the fastest growing categories in power tools, with advances in rechargeable batteries spurring development.
>
> Machine Design, *17th April 1997*

BLACK & DECKER – THE COMPANY

Black & Decker had been founded in 1910 by Duncan Black and Alonzo G. Decker in Baltimore, Maryland. In the 1920s the company started its global expansion by setting up wholly owned subsidiaries in Canada (1922), the UK (1925) and Australasia (1929). Interrupted by the war, expansion continued so that today Black & Decker sells its products in 130 countries around the world (see also Appendix 1). In 1996 the consumer products division of

Black & Decker was operating in three distinct areas, CPT (Consumer Power Tools), Outdoor and Household, of which CPT was the largest.

In 1965 the British subsidiary purchased a 100,000 sq ft plant at Spennymoor near Durham, which is recognized as one of B&D's flagship sites. One of the company's three design centres is located here. Of the other two design centres, one is in Black & Decker's homeland, Maryland, the other in Hong Kong. Each centre designs products not only for its region but for the global market. One hundred people work in the European Design Centre, as Spennymoor's design department is known. However, only about 40 out of these are designers/industrial designers; the rest are technicians, 3D specialists, and so on. But, as Danny Bone, Innovation Manager, emphasizes, 'We all share a passion for power tools.'

> Power tool maker Black & Decker has been drilling away at plant optimization using kaizen. The continuous improvement program at the Spennymoor plant under the guidance of U.S. consultant TBM has proved so successful that last month the company hosted a week-long event to demonstrate the kaizen approach to 43 senior managers from Rolls-Royce, TRW, Alstom, JCB, Polaroid and others.
>
> *Professional Engineering, 10th May 2000*

At Spennymoor about 14 million tools are produced every year – equivalent of 360,000 tools per week – 79% of which are exported. The throughput as well as the number of different products – about 2000 product variations leave Spennymoor every month – creates much opportunity for process improvement. This is why Black & Decker embraced first kaizen and then 6 Sigma.

Besides quality, branding is very important to Black & Decker. To allow a clearer brand proposition Black & Decker had separated its consumer and professional lines in 1994, re-launching its professional products under the brand name 'DeWalt'. In the States this move pushed them from being number three to being number one in professional power tools.

From its inception, Black & Decker was an innovative, market-led organization with focus on new product development. Today about 65% of its products are less than three years old, and as Danny points out, 'We often have products that are ahead of the market.' To facilitate innovation they have established flat structures and work through peer-led groups, use product and process-based teams, and have mechanisms to maintain close contact with their customers.

To facilitate sharing of knowledge and the dissemination of ideas, Black & Decker have established a database to which every engineer has access. Into the database, which has been upgraded recently, all test data is entered. When asked about how people would find out about projects or find people with a particular expertise, Shaun Loveless, a Senior Electrical Engineer, answered, 'You find out about existing projects by contacting other people, by emailing around. How to find some special expertise? Project files are created at the end of each project. The files used to be microfilmed, but today it is all put onto CDRom. If you look there you can find out who was on the project.' 'And,' he adds, 'Everyone here at B&D is happy to go and ask for help and advice.'

To help minimize common conflicts between marketing and engineering and ensure that the two functions would work together, both functions, as well as the Director of Industrial Design Europe, report into the same person, the European Marketing Director. Though Stephen Bird, European Marketing Director and Vice President of Consumer Power Tools at the time, remembers, 'There used to be a lack of cooperation between marketing and engineering as well as between the UK and the rest of Europe. Particularly the latter has improved since we have started bringing people from all over Europe to work with us at Spennymoor.'

DEVELOPING CONCEPT AND PROTOTYPE

The idea for the new product was conceived on the 1st of November 1996 during a video conference involving Stephen Bird, Marketing Director Europe, Lawrie Cunningham, Director of Innovation and Industrial Design, and Danny Bone, Innovation Manager. They were discussing the success of the recently introduced multi-sander, and felt that there should be further scope in developing multifunctional or perhaps even multi-purpose tools, though in the past the argument had been that having different function heads would technically not be feasible.

Still, intrigued by the idea, Stephen asked Lawrie and Danny to think about it – and, as Stephen remembers, 'Danny had this gleam in his eye and I knew he already had something in mind. Danny came back a fortnight later with this rough but fully working prototype. The idea was great and he could prove that interchangeable heads were technically not a problem. Danny's trick was to develop a separate gearbox in front for each of the tools. Although each feature already existed in many guises from a number of manufacturers, we wanted to combine forward thinking views of changing marketplace requirements with highly innovative patent pending design solutions.'

> The idea for a multi-purpose tool was based on:
>
> - A strong DIY market in Europe with an increasing number of men and women doing DIY
>
> - Main trend: less experienced female on the increase; more people living on their own – growing number looking for small products (space constraints)
>
> - People do a small number of small DIY tasks; in contrast, many existing B&D products had the tendency to be over-engineered
>
> - Market for drills is mature – need to do something different
>
> - Recent success with the multi-sander (combining three functions), sold at a premium price

Danny, who had been working in the area of new product development since 1989, had been promoted to Product Innovation Manager in 1995. While nominating an individual to be the 'Innovation Champion' can cause problems, not least because of the NIH (not-invented-here) syndrome, this did not seem to be the case in Black & Decker. Danny attributes this to a culture where design and innovation are valued and appreciated. It also helps that Danny has a track record in successful new product development, which give him credibility with colleagues across all functions. He describes his role, 'One aspect is that I act as catalyst between engineering and marketing.' He also points out that he has many colleagues with whom he can discuss ideas, and who are able to ask each other the right questions.

He strongly believes that in new product development it is important to move to prototypes and models quite quickly as it helps marketing and other departments to understand how an idea could work. He says, 'I see being a translator as another important part of my job. If you have a model to show people they are much more likely to buy into the idea and get a feel for the benefits we are trying to achieve through the new product. The great benefit of my position is that I am given time to explore and experiment. My scope goes across all product groups within the consumer business.' Though there can also be a problem with prototypes, as Danny points out, 'Sometimes there is a necessity to translate between the different functions, for example, marketing don't always understand the difference between a prototype and a product; if they see a working prototype they think it can be in the shops the next day which of course is not true.'

Once the concept had been developed, the next step was to present it at one of the worldwide product meetings. When Stephen went to present it at the global new product development meeting in the US later in November 1996, it was clear that he was very excited about the idea. However, the meeting did not go well. In fact, they did not like the idea of it at all, and not only that, he was told to stop working on it. Thinking about it afterwards,

Stephen reflected, 'The market in the US is very different from the market in Europe, much more macho, powerful, and about tools for a specific use – rather than easy to use and multifunctional.' But he said, 'It is a rare occasion for me to call something "my baby" – but if ever there was one, this was it. I really wanted to do this.' So he disobeyed the ruling and decided to develop the tool one step further.

He commissioned an external industrial design consultancy to develop the concept into a model and did some preliminary market testing. When he re-presented his idea at the next meeting six months later in March 1997 with some positive market response to back him up the response was, 'We thought we had told you not to do it!' But he dug his heels in and focused on communicating the importance and potential of the new idea. In the end he got the go-ahead for at least some further development. Looking back he comments, 'The good thing about Black & Decker is that people are not afraid to throw up ideas and fight for them, that's nothing unusual. I even had a few disasters, but this was OK. As long as it does not become a habit, B&D accepts a bit of failure.'

> We wanted our industrial design execution to make the tool desirable to own and use by both male and female consumers. For example, comprehensive flexibility and neat storage was seen as a clear user benefit.

The plan was to introduce the new product complete with a kitbox at the big trade fair in Cologne in spring 1998. Meeting that deadline was important if they wanted to make it into the shops for Christmas 1998. This meant that they had to work towards a tight time schedule, having less than a year for development and tooling. It could take about 16 weeks alone just for the tools to be made, and as this had to be outsourced, it was out of the hands of the Black & Decker team. Taking it to a trade fair would also mean that it had to be very robust, as visitors at a trade fair – particularly from competing organizations – would test the product thoroughly.

However, when Lawrie saw the prototype based on the design consultancy's design he was not quite happy. He felt that they should be able to do better with the design. Given the time frame, Stephen was not too pleased with going for a second design, in fact as he recalls, he was quite negative about it – but he was also open-minded and in the end Lawrie persuaded Stephen that there would be some value in giving it another go.

So when industrial designer Nigel Robson came back from a two-week holiday, Lawrie asked him 'to come and see me once you have sorted yourself out'. Nigel knew something was up and went to see him straightaway. Lawrie explained the project to Nigel and outlined his thoughts on the need for a rethink of the industrial design. A project of such scale was a first for both Nigel and Senior Design Engineer Brian Wadge; both were very excited by the idea. Nigel recalls, 'The first thing I did was to familiarize myself with competitor products. Power tools as a category tended to be quite traditional – but consumers were not. I felt that we could do with being more innovative and daring.' However, he also pointed out that, 'If it had been just a sander we would have had a lot of time to develop the product – but the product would have three different heads which all needed careful design and engineering input.'

Chris Burke from purchasing commented on the time schedule as follows, 'Was time pressure a good thing? In a way, yes. There was no room for things to go wrong and we knew we had one shot at things, true. But then, if you have 6 months you fill the 6 months, if you have 6 years you fill them too. It really focused our minds.'

A first team meeting was held early in April 1997 with representatives from engineering, purchasing, manufacturing, finance, marketing, industrial design and quality, other people would join the group if and when needed. While Brian was dedicated full time to the project, for other people it was one project amongst others. However, it was soon made clear that this project should get first priority. Brian went to great lengths to ensure that everything was documented and made available for future access.

For many people on the team such as Andrew, Brian and Nigel it was their first big assignment and Davie Skaife remembers, 'The key players were all keen and ambitious – and being relatively new to the game they did not have any pre-conceived ideas.' The group was quite closely knit and many people knew each other from previous projects.

The Project Team	
Representative	Department/function
Andrew Eyre	Programme Manager
Danny Bone	Innovation Manager
Brian Wadge	Senior Design Engineer
Richard Jones	Senior Design Engineering
Nigel Robson	Industrial Designer
Shaun Loveless	Senior Electrical Engineer
Alan Baldwin	Finance
Davie Skaife	Quality Engineer
Chris Burke	Purchasing
Norman Spence	Manufacturing Engineer
Etienne Bourgeois	Marketing Europe
Kirsten Smith	Marketing North America

After the initial meeting the group would meet on a weekly basis, chaired by the programme manager, Andrew Eyre. Outside contractors would be brought in for tasks such as model making – they used a lot of 3D, as opposed to 2D, as there was seen to be much less margin for (wrong) interpretation. Using SLS, which stands for selective laser sintering, they were able to get a prototype within three days – rather than the 16 weeks it used to take in old days. The models were not only for demonstration purposes but also for communicating with other departments. Brian comments, 'As the models are made straight from the drawings you can see mistakes straightaway.'

While Nigel was working on the design the rest of the team were putting the information together for the CAR – the Capital Appropriation Request. The document combines information from all disciplines, outlining resource requirements for the development and manufacture of a new product, which can be quite time

> Up to $400,000 a project can be signed off in Slough, generally within a couple of weeks; above that it has to go to the States where sign-off can take up to a couple of months – if no changes are required.

consuming. Alan Baldwin from finance comments, 'Marketing being based in Slough can be a bit of an issue. They can take an awful lot of time at the outset and we here do not get into the project soon enough, they don't always involve us early enough. At times we also have to wait for artwork and packaging which are marketing's responsibility. However, we are trying to remedy this by bringing some marketers here to Spennymoor.'

Getting costing right for new products has a high priority at Black & Decker, which means that purchasing gets involved very early on. Once a design is available Chris Burke from purchasing starts working back from the launch date to determine what needs to be available when. For the Quattro he worked closely with Brian to ensure everything would be available as and when needed.

A lot of the costs are driven by the purchasing agreements Black & Decker has with its preferred suppliers. But project teams tend to cooperate closely with the suppliers to ensure best possible solutions, both in terms of functionality and cost effectiveness. Davie Skaife explains, 'We visited the suppliers and involved them early on. We went as a group, design engineering and quality engineering, which meant that there was always a good level of knowledge around the table. We went through all functions of new parts before doing anything else.'

With the new design Nigel had clearly moved away from the traditional pistol handle generally found for drills. The new handle also added extra functionality, Nigel had put quite some effort into making it stand up, which was particularly tricky for the top-heavy jigsaw module. While the two designs were not too different in terms of the mechanics, the second required some new tooling – which had cost and time implications. The newness also implied that it was more difficult to get accurate cost estimates, they could not use previous projects as a benchmark. First estimates ended up well above the original target cost – whereas the original design, with a greater number of existing parts and no additional costs for tooling, came out much cheaper.

When Nigel first showed the 2D drawings of his new design to marketers they did not like it – but his reaction was, stuff it! He was convinced that his design had benefits to offer and continued to refine it. Once he had modelled both designs the development team went back to present it to marketing and management. Many people had a vested interest in sticking with the traditional design, not least because it seemed less hassle, would be cheaper, quicker to develop, and based on tried and tested components. But Nigel kept arguing vehemently for the radical and at every opportunity.

Management was faced with a difficult decision, the traditional design had researched very well – and no one outside the company had seen the new one, and there was no time to conduct lengthy market research. Then there were also the additional new parts that would require tooling and extensive testing (all components need to be tested for consistency (gauge reliability and reproducibility), whereby the variation between two measurements has to be less than 9%) and marketing had already started 'selling' the initial design and was reluctant to go back on it. On the other hand, as Brian pointed out, 'In order to get innovative products you have to take risks. You have to move away from what you have always done.' But then again, individuals were rewarded on successful market introduction and were answerable to any costs occurring from repairing damaged products, so there was not much incentive to take too much of a risk. Nigel sums it up saying, 'There was no confidence to make a clear decision.'

QUESTIONS

1. Given the situation, what would you do; which design would you take forward and why?
2. What is your definition of market research and what is/should be the role of market research in new product development?

APPENDIX I: COMPANY HISTORY

FROM COMPANY HISTORY

1910	B&D founded by Duncan Black & Alonzo G. Decker in Baltimore, Maryland
1911	First advertisement placed in *Manufacturers Record and Horseless Age*
1912	Adopted B&D hex as company trademark
1913	First cash dividend paid
1914	Filed application with US Patent Office for pistol grip and trigger switch drill (patent awarded in 1917)
1917	Build new plant at outskirts of Towson, Maryland
1918	Opened first company-owned product service centres in Boston and New York
1919	Passed the $1 m sales level
1922	Incorporated B&D Mfg. Co in Canada
	Expansion of factory
1924	Erected two-story admin building in Towson, still B&D International HQ
1925	B&D as wholly owned subsidiary in London, UK
1927	Listed B&D on the Baltimore Exchange, production starts in 1928 in leased plant in Slough
1929	Established B&D Australasia
1933	Reorganized sales operations to promote regional management control

1939   Build a 65,000 sq ft plant in Harmondsworth, UK

1942   Formed B&D post-war planning committee; decision to develop the do-it-yourself market for power tools

        First use of plastic by company (replacing metal drill housing)

1946   Introduced world's first line of popularly priced drills and accessories

        Opened sales, service and warehousing facilities in São Paulo, Brazil

1948   Subsidiary in Mexico

1951   S. Duncan Black dies

1955   Subsidiary in South Africa

1956   Alonzo G. Decker dies

1957   Subsidiary in Belgium

1958   Subsidiary in New Zealand

        Subsidiary in Germany

        Subsidiary in the Netherlands

1960   Acquired DeWalt

1961   French subsidiary (bought out company)

        British company opens sales and service branches in Denmark and Sweden

        Acquired Italian company

1962   Subsidiary in Norway

1964   Passed $100 m sales level

        Began multi-programme schedule of US network television to advertise the broad range of B&D products

1965   British company purchased 100,000 sq ft plant on 53.7 ha at Spennymoor, Durham, UK

        Subsidiary in Venezuela

1966   Subsidiary in Austria

1967   Subsidiary in Spain

1968   Introduced new management concept which established geographical areas of operations, each under a
        vice president who serves as general manager with responsibilities for all markets in the group

        Subsidiary in Finland

1969   Passed $200 m sales level

        Subsidiary in Japan

        British company opens sales and service branch in Israel

1970   British company opens sales and service branches in Portugal, Cyprus, Greece, Iran

        180,000 sq ft added to Spennymoor

1971   Subsidiaries in Nigeria, Argentina, Singapore

1974   Introduced management concept which establishes four operating focus, US Power Tool, European
        International, Pacific International and McCulloch Corporation (acquired in October 73), each under a
        corporate officer

        Joint venture in Yugoslavia

        Subsidiary in Zambia, Panama, the Philippines

PRODUCTS

1916   The world's first portable 1/2" electric drill with pistol grip and trigger switch utilizing a universal motor
        marketed

1922   First electrical screw driver

1936   First electric hammer developed with a special B&D patented design proved more effective and easier
        to handle

1940	First electric Quick-Saw with table and radial arm attachments
1946	First portable electric 1/4" drill for consumers
1953	First finishing sanders and jigsaws for consumers were marketed, thus expanding the consumers' ability to do-it-yourself
1957	Move towards outdoors with first lawn edgers and hedge trimmers for consumers
1961	First cordless electric drill powered by nickel-cadmium cells
1962	First cordless outdoor product (hedge trimmer)
1963	First all-insulated drills and sander grinders
1968	First power head for the Apollo Lunar Surface Drill used to remove core samples from the moon
1973	Workmate (combination of workbench, vice, and sawhorse)
1979	Introduction of the Dustbuster, a hand-held cordless vacuum cleaner for household markets
1981	Heatgun – introduced into consumer markets
1984	Powerfile
1992	Snakelight
1996	Multi-sander
1998	Quattro
1999	Mouse
2000	Quattro selected as Millennium Product by Design Council

APPENDIX II: CAPITAL APPROPRIATION REQUEST SUMMARY EXTRACTS

Marketing overview

- Driven by the desire to dramatically improve the penetration of the VersaPak business by providing a hero product for 1998 and beyond

- Multifunctionality has been extremely successful in the sanding category (575 k sold in Europe in 1996 at 179.00 DM)

- The concept has been extensively researched, with outstanding results, being 'better than multi-sander' and in the top 5% of projects researched by the research company

- The multi-sander was received as new, interesting and highly giftable

- Price point of 249.00 DM with gross margins of 45% within Europe

- High promotion spend (15.3% NSV year 1) will support the launch and volumes of 1290 k are anticipated over three years

- TV media spend will commence in November 1998 for European launch countries

- Cannibalization of volumes has been shown within the CAR as the Quattro will replace the majority of multi-tool kitboxes sold

Competitive position

- No competition at point in time
- Designs will be heavily patented for future protection

Global requirements

- Major market is seen to be Europe (up to 400 k/annum) with a level of interest in the US and eastern hemisphere (up to 80 k/annum)
- Spennymoor will provide the global requirements

Engineering plan

- Project is fast track, therefore the intention is to use as many existing components as possible
- Use of modern draughting and rapid prototyping techniques

Manufacturing plan

- Incubated in Spennymoor for approximately 12 months and then relocated to an attack plant
- A new production line will be laid down, using low levels of assembly automation to facilitate transfer

Purchasing plan

- Complete analysis of capacities of current components has been undertaken and there will be no requirement to extend these as part of this project
- For new components, tools will be laid down with minimum capacities of 864 k/year vs. 475 k/year anticipated annual sales volumes

Quality plan

- Aligned to Milestone process
- All of the 'critical to quality' performance dimensions are detailed in the plan
- Test programmes will be discussed and utilized to simulate high levels of customer abuse modes of operation, so that failure potential is minimized
- Ongoing quality post-bulk will be controlled through clearly defined standards, test bench data and market feedback through the early warning system

Financial summary includes

- Exchange rates
- Capital investment
- Sales potential
- Product cost/profitability
- Return measures
- Sensitivity analysis
- Alternative production plant

Signed-off in June 1997

9 Approaches to Market Research

Market research tends to be an important part in a company's armoury to develop and verify new products and services. Not least because best practice literature has shouted for years about how important it is to meet consumer needs for a product to be successful. Most companies translated this into the need to conduct market research and involve consumers throughout the development process. However, what managers need to be careful about is what kind of approach to market research they take, and how much they let results influence their decisions. In the case of Black & Decker, should the market research data available dictate which design to take forward? Rather the devil you know?

Particularly in the context of innovation, there is a considerable problem with market research: if you ask people what they want, they will refer to something they are familiar with. Kaplan comments, 'Customers seldom articulate needs they don't know they have. Ten years ago, how many people would have asked for a subscription to anything like America Online? Thirty years ago, how many people would have asked for a calculator that fits into a shirt pocket-or a microwave, or a VCR, or a Walkman?' So it is important to understand the limitations of market research, and more importantly, to understand the need to match the approach taken to market research with the development aim in mind.

There are two main different approaches, quantitative and qualitative. The former involves surveys and questionnaires, the latter interviews, focus groups and observations. After some general insights on market research, this chapter looks at traditional market research methods and the most recent developments.

WHAT IS IT ABOUT MARKET RESEARCH?

Research with members of the Innovation Exchange revealed that most companies are dissatisfied with the results of current market research practices. Taking a closer look at how many companies conduct their research gives an indication why; more often than not, the activity is outsourced to an external agency. This means that the information the company gets back has been filtered through the market research agency's lenses, or as a member of the innovation exchange put it, 'You generally only get a summary of the research but researchers do not necessarily have the knowledge and understanding of the market to interpret the results "correctly".' As Bobrow recommends in his book *Complete Idiot's Guide to New Product Development* (1997), 'Use it [market research]. Don't believe it.' You may have already heard the following story that illustrates this point:

A car manufacturer, just having finished a prototype of its new small car, commissioned a market research agency to find out what consumers would think about it. When the research report came back the engineers were surprised to read that consumers were not quite happy with the engine performance. It was only a small car and the engine was already quite powerful. But still, give the consumer what the consumer wants. So the engineers reworked the engine, and the revised model was market tested again. But still, the results said that consumers wanted more power. This circle was repeated a few times until the engineers threw their hands up and said, 'This cannot be true! Let us speak to the researchers or even better, be present when they conduct their research.' And indeed, a good idea it was. When the engineers were present and could actually observe the consumer and talk to them directly they realized that not the *real* power of the engine but the *perceived* power was the issue. What consumers were missing was the feeling of gently being pushed back into the seat when accelerating – something that could be fixed easily – and quickly as well as cheaply – by changing the upholstery.

This story illustrates very clearly that it is not about getting data, but interpreting the feedback correctly, and applying insights and expertise to come to the right conclusions, extracting meaning from the data, converting it into information. When selecting a particular method for a piece of market research, the two critical questions are, will this type of research be able to collect the data we need, and secondly, will the way the data is treated maximize its value?

Another issue with market research is that it is often undertaken to confirm results or beliefs, rather than to gain new insights. Market research is sometimes commissioned with the aim of generating some 'ammunition' to help sell a particular concept – and when the answers are not as desired, they often get ignored.

But even if market research is taken seriously and conducted appropriately, the results are not necessarily a good indicator for what is going to happen upon the introduction of the product. Let me just give you a couple of examples:

- 190,000 consumers testing the *New Coke* against the existing formula overwhelmingly declared that they preferred the new taste, but its launch was a failure (Martin 1995).

- In consumer research, McDonald's found that consumers wanted healthier burgers – but when they launched their diet burger, McLean, it was a flop. People continued to buy the nice fatty, greasy burgers (Martin 1995).

If market research does not seem to be a good predictor for market success, its predictive power of market failure is similarly (un)impressive: Kaplan (1999) reports, 'When tested through market research, the HP35 calculator, the first videocassette recorder, the fax machine and Federal Express all received negative ratings!' or as another story from Martin's article shows:

> When Compaq first thought about introducing Systempro, PC-based servers, everyone in the industry declared that this, surely, was beyond personal computers and had to be done on a mainframe. Gary Stimac, then Compaq's senior vice president who led the team recalls, 'By the end of 1990, Systempro's first year in the market, it generated only $200 m in revenue. But we did not give up and continued to educate the market. It typically takes 12–18 months to get good read on whether what you are hearing is surmountable scepticism or a downright lack of market acceptance.' In 1994 Compaq sold $1.8 bn worth of Systempro, equalling 17% of the company's revenue.

These insights – failure of current market research practices to deliver accurate results and the problems of misinterpretation through external research agencies – lead companies to reconsider their approach. Involving people from within the organization in market research exercises is a possible solution, as a quote from a government website on best practice in service acquisition illustrates,[1] 'In the past, it was not unusual for technical staff to conduct market research about marketplace offerings, while contracting staff conducted market research more focused on industry practices and pricing. A better approach is for the entire integrated solutions team to be a part of the market research effort. This enables the members of the team to share an understanding and knowledge of the marketplace – an important factor in the development of the acquisition strategy – and a common understanding of what features, schedules, terms and conditions are key.' Another is to send out your staff to observe your product or service in action.

Another good source for customer insights many organizations ignore are the front-line sales people. They have direct contact and can often observe the customer using the product. However, mechanisms need to be put in place to ensure that the feedback that comes from the front line is honest and straight. Most sales people are not motivated to feed back if there are any 'problems', nor are they rewarded for ideas, they are rewarded for sales. This may also influence their listening ability: they listen to sell, not to learn. Companies can improve the process by putting systems in place that encourage sales staff to feed back any useful information, e.g. introduce customer visit feedback forms and ensure that rewards are not counterproductive – but don't forget to train the sales people so they know what they are expected to do and look out for.

> 'The starting point for innovation is to connect with the consumer. This has been a weakness over past 4–5 years, we were too removed from the consumers. We are now asking our people to go and talk to consumers where they spend their lives – in bars, sports fields, shopping centres – to find out how they actually live. We can already see that where we understand the consumer more we have great success.'
>
> From an interview with a manager from an Innovation Exchange member company

TRADITIONAL APPROACHES TO MARKET RESEARCH

Keeping the above in mind, what are approaches to market research? Traditional approaches to market research all have one thing in common, they are based on asking the consumer what he or she wants, through the collection of either quantitative or qualitative data. Under the category of quantitative research we find different distribution methods of surveys and questionnaire: per mail, over the telephone, in person, either in home or office, or 'on the street' and more recently, via email or on the internet.

The three main qualitative market research methods are interviews, focus groups and observation – or in fact, a combination. Qualitative approaches have the advantage that they generate a deeper level of understanding of consumer needs and viewpoints. However, artefacts such as drawings, prototypes, or the finished product can be used for either. As mentioned before, it is horses for courses. Table 9.1 by Steven Cohen (1996) compares methods of quantitative market research, whereby the last two columns also shed some light on the benefits of qualitative interviewing.

But there are not only different approaches to consider; managers should also think during which stages of the development process they seek to involve consumers. Bruce and Cooper (1997, p86) suggest that market research has a part to play in all stages of product development. Conveniently, Mahajan and Wind (1992) provide a matrix with different approaches to market research on one axis and different new product development stages on the other, suggesting which approach is appropriate for what stage (see Table 9.2).

Another questions is, how many people to ask to get some meaningful insights? Cohen (1996) has collected data that provides some guidelines on typical sample sizes for different types of quantitative marketing research studies (Table 9.3).

Table 9.1 Comparing Approaches to Market Research (Cohen 1996) (reproduced by Permission of John Wiley & Sons Ltd)

	Survey method			
	Mail	Telephone	In person (home or office)	In person (intercept)
Use of incentives	Recommended	Not necessary except on rare cases	Recommended	Recommended
Cost per interview	Low	Depends on population to be reached	High	Moderate
Ability to use visuals and physical prototypes or do taste tests	Visuals only	Not possible	Yes	Yes
Possible interview complexity	Few skip patterns, many complex question types possible	Complex skip patterns, many question types not possible	Both complex skip patterns and question types are possible	Both complex skip patterns and question types are possible
Awareness, open-ended questions, and probes	Not possible	Possible	Possible	Possible
Speed of response	Slow	Fast	Moderate	Moderate
Security	Low	High	Moderate	High
Survey length	Long surveys possible	Moderate length	Long surveys possible	Long surveys possible
Control over who responds	Low	High	High	High
Control over conduct of interviews	Low	High	Moderate	High

The reliability of the data will vary from industry to industry, and with varying user groups. For example, research that involves professional users and buyers tends to be much more reliable than research undertaken with consumers stopped in the street, and insights from research for Fast Moving Consumer Goods (FMCDs) tends to be more reliable than those from research regarding capital expenditures goods.

THE FUTURE

Given that traditional approaches to market research do not seem to work too well, particularly in the context of innovation, what then are approaches that might help? Sanchez and Sudharshan (1993) recommend what they call 'real-time market research'. In their words, real-time market research involves 'To offer batches of actual new product models to consumers to learn their exact and varied preferences as to alternative product configurations, features

Table 9.2 Use of Models and Methods of Market Research Across New Product Development Activities (Mahajan and Wind 1992) (reproduced by permission of Blackwell Publishing)

	Focus group	Limited rollout	Concept tests	Show test/clinic	Attitude, usage studies	Conjoint analysis	Delphi panel	QFD	Home usage test	Product life-cycle models	Synectics
New product idea generation	x	x	x				x	x		x	x
New product screening	x	x	x	x	x	x	x				
Market study for concept development	x	x	x	x	x						x
Market identification positioning, marketing strategy specification	x	x	x		x	x			x	x	
Business/finance analysis		x			x	x				x	
Product development		x	x	x		x		x	x		
Consumer test of products	x	x	x	x		x			x		
Pre-market volume forecasting				x		x					
Market test/trial sell		x		x							
Market launch planning	x	x	x	x	x					x	

Table 9.3 Sample Size for Market Research Studies (Cohen 1996) (reproduced by permission of Blackwell Publishing)

Study	Minimum size	Typical size (range)
Market studies	500	1000–1500
Strategic studies	200	400–500
Test market penetration studies	200	300–500
Concept/product tests	200	200–300/cell
Name tests	100/name variant	200–300/cell
Package tests	100/package variant	200–300/cell
TV, radio commercial tests	150/commercial	200–300/commercial
Print add tests	150/advertisement	200–300/commercial

Table 9.4 Traditional Models of Market Research and their Shortcomings (Mahajan and Wind 1992) (reproduced by permission of Blackwell Publishing)

Models	Major shortcomings
Focus group	Market complexity not captured
Limited rollout	Too much time to implement
Concept tests	Forecast inaccuracy
Show test/clinic	Too much time to implement
Attitude, usage studies	Forecast inaccuracy
Conjoint analysis[1]	Expensive, complexity not captured
Delphi panel[2]	Market complexity not captured
Quality Function Deployment[3]	Forecast inaccuracy, too much time
Home usage test	Expensive, too much time
Product life-cycle models	Forecast inaccuracy
Synectics[4]	Expensive, forecast inaccuracy

[1]Bobrow (1997) describes conjoint analysis as 'a technique for separating and measuring respondents' judgements about complex alternatives, usually product characteristics or attributes, into distinct components'.

[2]Delphi technique – elicits ideas from participants by means of a series of highly structured and progressively more focused questionnaires; initial questionnaire is sent out, questions are summarized and rephrased into a new set of questions which is re-sent to initial participants; process is repeated.

[3]Quality Function Deployment (QFD) – a matrix with product characteristics and attributes on the one axis and customer needs on the other is used to determine where to focus development efforts.

[4]I would not necessarily classify Synectics as a tool for market research. I would rather describe it as a structured team approach to problem solving and idea generation, promoted originally by a company of the same name.

and performance levels. This approach, so they claim, overcomes some of the limitations and time requirements of traditional market research methods – for a list of what Mahajan and Wind (1992) consider to be the major shortcomings please see Table 9.4.

However, real-time market research does not really overcome the problem of people knowing what they like and liking what they know. There are two possible ways of addressing this issue. The first is, if innovative products or ideas are concerned, work with a group of people who are known to like change and new things, don't work with traditionalists who always prefer the 'good old days'. Find the 'Vorreiter', the pioneers of new products and technologies who like nothing better than a new toy. They are more likely to be open and positive towards new things. The most leading-edge market research and launch strategists go even further; rather than launching a product or service and leave it to advertising and other sales-enhancing techniques to establish the product in the marketplace, they aim to identify trend leaders and let them promote the product instead. If the right people can be identified, marketers can achieve a market pull – instead of the company push – for their innovation, an approach called 'viral marketing'. The art lies in identifying who the right people to create a market are. However, it is also very expensive.

The second way is not to ask people what they want, but observe what they actually do. This approach is particularly useful at the idea generation stage, as it helps to identify latent consumer needs – those needs of which the consumers might not even be aware – but if you are able to identify such a need, and develop a solution for it, you are on to a winner. One company well known for this approach is IDEO (www.ideo.com).

Harvard academics Leonard and Rayport (1997) called this approach 'emphatic design'. They explain, 'Emphatic design calls for company representatives to watch customers using products and services in the context of their own environments. By doing so, managers can often identify unexpected uses for their products. They can also uncover problems that customers do not mention in surveys. Companies can engage in emphatic design, or similar techniques such as contextual inquiry, in a variety of ways. However, most employ the following 5-step process:

1. Observation,
2. Capturing data,
3. Reflection and analysis,
4. Brainstorming for solutions,
5. Developing prototype of possible solutions.'

In Table 9.5, Leonard and Rayport contrast the traditional approach of asking people what they want with the observation approach.

It is approaches such as 'emphatic design' and 'infectious marketing' that are more likely to identify seed for innovations than market research methods that count 'ticks in a box' and rely on statistical analysis.

Table 9.5 Comparing the Traditional Approach with Emphatic Design (Leonard and Rayport 1997) (Reprinted by permission of Harvard Business Review. From 'Spark innovation through emphatic design' by Leonard, D. and Rayport, J.F. November–December, 1997. Copyright @ 1997 by the Harvard Business School Publishing Corporation; all rights reserved)

Inquiry	Observation
People can't ask for what they don't know is technically possible	Well-chosen observers have deep knowledge of corporate capabilities, including the extent of the company's technical expertise
People are generally highly unreliable reporters of their own behaviour	Observers rely on real actions rather than reported behaviour
People tend to give answers they think are expected or desired	People are not asked to respond to verbal stimuli, they give nonverbal cues of their feelings and responses through body language, in addition to spontaneous, unsolicited comments
People are less likely to recall their feelings about intangible characteristics of products and services when they aren't in the process of using them	Using the actual products or a prototype, or engaging in the actual activity for which an innovation is being designed, stimulates comments about such intangibles as smells or emotions associated with the product's use
People's imagination – and hence their desires – are bounded by their experience, they accept inadequacies and deficiencies in their environment as normal	Trained, technically sophisticated observers can see solutions to unarticulated needs
Questions are often biased and reflect inquirers' unrecognized assumptions	Observation is open-ended and varied; trained observers tend to cancel out one another's observational biases
Questioning interrupts the usual flow of people's natural activity	Observation, while almost never totally unobtrusive, interrupts normal activities less than questioning does
Questioning stifles opportunities for users to suggest innovations	Observers in the field often identify user innovations that can be duplicated and improved for the rest of the market

READING SUGGESTIONS

Kelly, Thomas (2001) *The Art of Innovation*. New York: HarperCollins Business

Comment: Written by one of the founders of one of the leading innovation consultancies, IDEO, this book provides some great insights into the company's practices and processes. An anonymous reviewer on amazon.com wrote, 'The key strength of this book is Kelly's hands-on experience that crackles through every page. This book is not permeated by academic detachment but a bubbling and infectious enthusiasm.'

Hague, Paul (2002) *Market Research*. London: Kogan Page

Comment: Aimed at practitioners and students alike, this book does not require previous knowledge of the subject. It provides advice as well as real-life case studies that provide insights about how to set up market research. It covers all steps from planning, desk research, qualitative and quantitative research, over sampling and questionnaire design to data collection and analysis. Also useful is the listing of research agencies, codes of practice, quality schemes and a contact list

SOME USEFUL WEBSITES

www.rbg.org.uk

Comment: The *Research Buyer's Guide* is a directory of organizations offering market research and related services

http://www.marketresearch.org.uk

Comment: With over 8000 members in more than 50 countries, the Market Research Society is the world's largest international membership organization for professional researchers and others engaged or interested in market, social and opinion research

NOTES ON CHAPTER 9

[1] From http://oamweb.osec.doc.gov/pbsc/step3_take.html, a government website on a project on developing best practice for service acquisition.

10 A Note on Teams

Since the early 1990s, teamwork, which played an important role in the Black & Decker case study, has found widespread attention in the management literature in general, and the innovation and new product development literature in particular. Teams are often described as the backbone of innovation. For example, Tidd *et al.* (1997) certainly agree, stating that, 'Innovation is primarily about combining different perspectives in solving problems, and there is thus much potential value in team working.' But what actually is a team?

We believe that organizations only truly innovate and grow when three fundamental elements are all firmly in place (http://www.innovaro.com):

- The ability to conceive and exploit new ideas
- A clear strategic vision focused on value generation
- Aligned and empowered teams to drive progress

In their work, Katzenbach and Smith (1993) define a team as 'a small number of people with complementary skills who are committed to a common purpose, performance goals and approach for which they hold themselves mutually accountable'. They differentiate between five different types of teams whereby the distinguishing factor is the degree to which performance can be delivered (see Box 10.1).

BOX 10.1   Different Types of Teams (based on Katzenbach and Schmidt 1993)

Working group	'There is *no significant, incremental performance need* or opportunity that would require it to become a team.' The purpose is exchange of information, best practice, perspectives, etc.
Pseudo team	'There could be to significant, incremental performance need or opportunity, but *it has not focused on collective performance and is not trying to achieve it.*' There is no real interest in shaping a common purpose, and the sum of the whole tends to be less than the parts. Of all types of teams this performs worst.
Potential team	'There is a significant, incremental performance need, and *that really is trying to improve its performance impact.*' Often lacks clarity of purpose and collective accountability.
Real team	'A small number of people with complementary skills who *are equally committed to a common purpose, goals, and working approach for which they hold themselves mutually accountable.*'
High-performance team	'All conditions of the real team, and has *members who are also deeply committed to one another's personal growth and success.*' This type of team outperforms all others.

For teams to succeed in innovation they have to be at least real teams. But while there is general agreement that teams are essential for innovation, companies often complain that they do not seem to work. Responding to the discontent, Denison et al. (1996) point out that teams have been implemented before there was any empirical evidence about their effectiveness. Research undertaken by Henke et al. (1993) confirms this. Their findings, based on interviews in dozens of US firms, suggest that most firms are not using teams as effectively and efficiently as they could and should. Majchrzak and Wang (1996) provide one explanation, 'Managers often underestimate the difficulty of breaking the functional mindset. Many managers do away with functions but fail to change their own positions. Our research indicates that if companies are not ready to take the steps required to change their culture they may be better off leaving their functional departments intact.'

However, Henke et al. also found that organizations interviewed experienced the following benefits when using teams:

- The shortcomings of hierarchical structures are overcome by the team's ability to cut across traditional vertical lines of authority.

- Decision making is decentralized and therefore faster.

- Hierarchical information overload is reduced at higher levels.

- Higher quality decisions can have a significantly greater potential of occurring than with individual decisions.

To what extent benefits can be reaped depends, to a large degree, on team composition, structure and level of responsibility, and that all of the aforementioned is appropriate for the task at hand.

When Wheelwright and Clark (1995) took a closer look at teams in the context of product development, they found four different types of teams:

- functional
- lightweight
- heavyweight
- autonomous

Each team has its advantages and disadvantages, and each is better suited to some kinds of problems than others. Table 10.1 summarizes their characteristics, strengths and weaknesses and Figure 10.1 provides a visual representation of the different team structures.

Wheelwright and Clark have also identified four different levels of innovation – breakthrough, platform, derivative and enhancement – and combining the two sets of insights, they provide a matrix that suggests which type of project team is particularly relevant and appropriate for which type of innovation (see Figure 10.2).

These categories relate to the portfolio categories introduced in Chapter 3 on new product development, and Figure 10.3 shows how both categorizations integrate.

Beyond structuring and composing a team that is appropriate for the development challenge, there are some more general rules for team success. Tidd et al. (1997) found that successful teamwork tends to depend on the following:

- Clearly defined tasks and objectives
- Effective team leadership
- Good balance of team roles and match to individual behavioural style

Table 10.1 Types of New Product Development Teams (based on Wheelwright and Clark 1995)

Team structure and associated characteristics	Strengths	Weaknesses
Functional Members are answerable to their respective functional heads; team is abandoned upon completion; projects evolve in a serial fashion as tasks pass from one function to the next; assessment not as team but by functional managers	Brings functional expertise to problem solving Function managers control resources for the tasks they own Clear career path Clear control, functional accountability	Judged based on adherence to functional processes rather than overall project results Cookie cutter approach to solving varied problems Team does not own business results Narrow levels of expertise Disjointed development Turf battles possible
Lightweight Most common; heightened degree of coordination due to 'administrative' oversight; individuals continue to be focused primarily on their function, not on overall project results; improved communications	Same as functional Oversight of collective functional responsibilities helps to ensure timely project completion	Same as functional The lightweight manager has little organizational clout and little power to affect critical decisions
Heavyweight Core team members are representatives of their functions on an integrated development team; heavyweight manager is the heavyweight in the organization	Heavyweight manager has broad control over the decision-making processes, resources used and targets established	Team members still report to functional head; rewards and responsibilities are disconnected from project deliverables Political tightrope – project manager has about the same stature as functional heads
Autonomous Team members are co-located and answer only to the heavyweight project manager; the team has extreme latitude to devise solutions to the problems it has responsibility for; sets own objectives; truly integrated cross-functional structure	Focus on results No conflicting forces pulling at team members Speed and ability in solving challenging, novel problems Complete functional integration, the broadly skilled team is independent	Less control; team tends to expand on original project description Little use of existing process solutions Independent/lack of integration with others Unique product and process solutions may be difficult to integrate into existing business

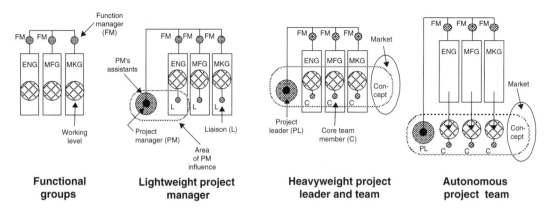

Figure 10.1   Types of Development Teams (reproduced from (Wheelwright and Clark 1995))

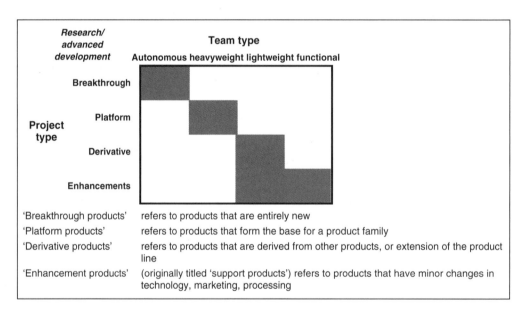

Figure 10.2   Levels of Innovation (reproduced from (Wheelwright and Clark 1995))

Figure 10.3   Levels of Innovation and Product Portfolios

- Effective conflict resolution mechanisms within the group
- Continuing liaison with external organization

And while Smith and Reinersten (1995) look at how to accelerate the execution of new product development products in particular, their insights are valid for successful teamwork in general. In their experience the more of the following criteria the team satisfies, the faster it will develop products:

- A team should have fewer than ten members.
- Members should volunteer to serve on the team.
- Members should serve on the team for the time of product concept until the product is in production.
- Members should be assigned to the team full time.
- Members should report solely to the team leader.
- The key functions, including at least marketing, engineering and manufacturing, should be on the team.
- Members should be located within conversational distance of each other.

However, I would like to point out that it is generally the case that the more innovative a project, the more difficult it is to give accurate time predictions. It is in the nature of innovation to carry a degree of uncertainty and unpredictability – if everything was known and predictable it would hardly be innovative!

There is one characteristic that is particular to innovation teams which did not show up on either of the above lists: diversity. During a speech at the 2002 Innovation Network (www.thinksmart.com) conference held in Minneapolis, Dough Hall, author of *Jump Start your Business Brain* provocatively – but quite to the point – said, 'If you have complete consensus within a innovation team of ten, nine of these people are a cost savings opportunity!' Innovation happens when you connect different bodies of knowledge. If there is no intellectual tension and questioning of each other's assumptions, there will be no innovation. Hence, team composition is very important, and it pays to consider carefully whom to second to the team. And that is why in the last section of this chapter we take a closer look at different personality and preference tests that might help you to compose a diverse team.

TEAM COMPOSITION

In this last section, we investigate tools for determining and understanding team diversity. By the way, one point that is also essential when putting together a team is to select its members based on their merit, i.e. on the skills they have to offer, rather than just choosing someone who happens to be available at the time (which seems to happen rather a lot. . .). This is something the innovation consultancy IDEO sees as a cornerstone of their continued innovation success, even if it requires bringing together people from their eight offices around the world for the duration of a project.

The six instruments introduced here are:

- *Belbin* suggests eight different roles that should be represented in a team to make sure all necessary skills are available

- *Myers Briggs* investigates four opposing pairs of behaviour and attitudes

- *C.A.R.E.*, developed by Allen Fahden and Srinivasan Namakkal, identifies individual behavioural and thinking approaches

- *Kirton's KAI Inventory* looks at people's preferred problem-solving style

- *Innovation Potential Indicator* (IPI), a tool for the assessment of individuals' potential to innovate, developed by Dr Fiona Patterson

- *The Adversity Index* (AQ), developed by Paul G. Stoltz, PhD, is based on the theory that how a person responds to adversity is a valid and broad predictor of, amongst other things, individual and team performance and capability for change.

(1) Belbin's Team Roles

Dr Meredith Belbin and his colleagues developed this tool specifically to help organizations to compose better teams. They found that in a 'perfect team' eight different roles are represented, whereby one person can hold more than one role, i.e. a team does not necessarily have to have eight members. The test they have developed is based on four principal factors:

1.   Intelligence
2.   Dominance
3.   Extroversion/introversion
4.   Stability/anxiety

Table 10.2 lists the eight roles, their specific traits, as well as their benefits and downsides.

(2) Myers Briggs Type Indicator (MBTI)

The second instrument is the MBTI, developed by Isabel Myers and Katharine Briggs in the 1950s. It has been designed to facilitate the understanding of psychological types as described by psychologist Carl Jung. The MBTI identifies four individual preferences:

- Extroverts versus introverts (E vs I)
- Sensers versus intuitives (S vs N)
- Thinkers versus feelers (T vs F)
- Judgers versus perceivers (J vs P)

The first three choices describe a person's orientation toward life, the last one a person's orientation to the outer world, resulting in 16 possible types. The MBTI is considered one of the oldest, most reliable and valid of the personality instruments. It has been given to millions of people, and has proven to be a useful tool in understanding human dynamics both at work and on a social level. The authors suggest that it is an effective tool in team building, communication and career exploration. Table 10.3 provides a summary of each of the eight preferences.

In Kenneth Allinson's book *The Wild Card of Design*, I found the reproduction of some typical professional profiles for some of the 16 MBTI types interesting in the context of this book (see Box 10.2).[1]

BOX 10.2   How Professions Score on the MBTI (based on Allinson 1995)

•	Architects	INTJ	• Computing professionals	INTJ
•	Designers	ENFJ	• Managers, administrators	ESTJ
•	Fine artists	INFJ	• Engineers	ISTJ
•	Craft workers	ISTJ	• Accountants	ISTJ

Table 10.2 Summary of Belbin's Team Roles

Title	Characteristics	Upsides	Downsides
Chairman	Calm, self-confident, controlled, tolerant, warm, enthusiastic	Capacity for welcoming all contributions and treating them on their merits without prejudice. Strong sense of objectives	No more than ordinary in terms of intellect or creative ability
Company Worker	Conservative, dutiful, predictable	Organizing ability, practical common sense, hard working, self-disciplined	Lack of flexibility, unresponsiveness to unproven ideas
Shaper	Full of nervous energy, highly strung, very high achievement motivation, wants to win, aggressive, extrovert	Drive and a readiness to challenge inertia, ineffectiveness, complacency or self-deception	Prone to provocation, irritation and impatience
Plant	Innovative, introverted, independent, individualistic, serious-minded, unorthodox	Genius, imagination, intellect, knowledge	Up in the clouds, inclined to disregard practical details or protocol
Resource Investigator	Extroverted, warm, enthusiastic, curious, communicative	Capacity for contacting people and exploring anything new. An ability to respond to challenge	Liable to lose interest once the initial fascination has passed
Monitor Evaluator	Sober, unemotional, prudent, detached, intelligent	Judgement, discretion, hard-headedness	Lacks inspiration and the ability to motivate others
Team Worker	Socially oriented, rather mild, sensitive, trusting, perceptive, diplomatic	An ability to respond to people and situations. Promotes team spirit	Indecisive at moments of conflict
Completer Finisher	Painstaking, orderly, conscientious, anxious, consistent	Capacity for follow-through, perfectionism	Tendency to worry about small details. A reluctance to 'let go'

(3) C.A.R.E. Profile (CARE)

The third instrument, the CARE, was developed by Allen Fahden and Srinivasan Namakkal. It identifies individual behavioural and thinking approaches using four categories:

- *Creator* – likes to come up with new ideas, reframe problems and explore alternatives; good at visualizing the bigger picture, prefers to focus on the future.

- *Advancer* – recognizes ideas and new directions early on and advances them; when thinking about implementation prefers to rely on past experience; works within existing norms and expectations.

- *Refiner* – likes to challenge concepts and wants to understand consequences before acting; prefers order and being methodical.

Table 10.3   Characteristics of the Eight MBTI Types (adapted from Hipple *et al*. 2001)

Extroverts (E)	**Introverts (I)**
Are action-oriented and impulsive	Enjoy privacy and quite time
Like to think out loud and tend to present rough drafts	Tend to prefer fully developed ideas
Outgoing and social	
Sensers (S)	**Intuitives (N)**
Look at what is known and real	Perceive abstract things meanings, relationships and possibilities through insight
Rely on actual experience and proven results	Like complexity, theoretical relationships and connections between things
Approach change slowly, carefully, incrementally, and critically	Able to see future possibilities, often unusual and abstract ones, using imagination and theory
Thinkers (T)	**Feelers (F)**
Use the process of logical and impersonal decision making	Arrive at conclusions through process of appreciation with a system of subjective personal values and standards
Apply logical analysis to weigh facts and examine consequences objectively	Typically exhibit a warm understanding of people, compassion, empathy and the need for harmony
Judgers (J)	**Perceivers (P)**
Convergent, driving towards closure and results	Divergent, open, flexible and unconstrained
Organization, schedules, plans, and priorities are important	Try to keep things open for new possibilities as long as possible and donot want to miss anything

- *Executor* – focuses on high quality and ensuring the implementation process runs smoothly; prefers proven to the new and pays attention to detail.

The instrument is based on the theory that those working together toward a common goal combine their behavioural preferences and thinking into a specific approach. Identifying individual approaches to teamwork, clarifying roles, understanding and encouraging innovation and problem solving are all components of CARE. The authors suggest that over the course of a project the idea is passed back and forth between the four different roles, each bringing a particular skill to the party.

(4) Kirton Adaption-Innovation Inventory (KAI)

Developed by Dr Michael Kirton, the fourth assessment tool is primarily focused on thinking styles with particular interest in how people show their creativity, solve problems and make decisions. It measures style, not level or ability. Scoring takes place on a continuum that includes *Highly Adaptive* (low score) and *Highly Innovative* (high score) at opposite ends of the scale. The three components measured are: originality, attention to detail, and conformity to rules with each receiving a numeric designation placed on the continuum. Each of the components is added to arrive at the total KAI score. The KAI takes an in-depth look at problem-solving styles, and is useful in teamwork when coping behaviour is needed between team members with diverse styles. It also provides knowledge and awareness of both individual style and team style, and can thus be a useful tool in providing the right balance of adaptors and innovators in a group. Table 10.4 shows their characteristics, and what they think of each other.

Looking at their propensity to embrace change – and what is innovation but change – each type is very different, as Figure 10.4 shows.[2] This difference can lead to quite some conflict, depending on the level of respect between individuals involved, as Prather indicates in Figure10.5.

Table 10.4 Summary of Kirton's Adaptor and Innovator (based on Hipple *et al.* 2001) (reproduced by permission of American Chemical Society)

Adaptor (Conserver)	Innovator (Originator)
Efficient, thorough, adaptable, methodical, organized, precise, reliable, dependable	Ingenious, original, independent, unconventional
Accepts problem definition	Challenges problem definition
Does things better	Does things differently
Concerned with resolving problems rather than finding them	Discovers problems and avenues for their solutions
Seeks solutions to problems in tried and tested ways	Manipulates problems by questioning existing assumptions
Reduces problems by improvement and greater efficiency; aiming at continuity and stability	Is catalyst to unsettled groups, irreverent of their consensual views
Seems impervious to boredom, able to maintain accuracy in long-term spells of detailed work	Capable of routine work (system maintenance) for only short bursts; quick to delegate routine tasks
Is an authority within established structures	Tends to take control in unstructured situations
Tends to view innovators as:	*Tends to view adaptors as:*
Unsound, impractical, abrasive, undisciplined, insensitive, one who loves to create confusion	Dogmatic, compliant, stuck in a rut, timid, conforming, inflexible

Figure 10.4 Adaptor versus Innovator (based on Kirton 1980)

Figure 10.5 Acceptance of Person (reproduced from (Prather 2002))

(5) Innovation Potential Indicator (IPI)

This test for identifying the innovation potential in existing and potential employees was developed by Dr Fiona Patterson. It looks at four main areas of behaviour which can be used to establish whether a person is an innovative thinker:

Motivation to Change (MTC)	Describes whether an individual is open to frequent change and new ways of tackling issues at work
Challenging Behaviour (CB)	Describes an individual's degree of active engagement in championing change or maintaining the status quo
Consistency of Work Styles (CWS)	Describes an individual's preferred approach to work
Adaptation (AD)	Describes an individual's preference to adopt tried and tested work methods as opposed to doing things differently

The behaviours identified by the scale are shown in Table 10.5.

(6) The Adversity Index (AQ)

Finally, the Adversity Response Profile, developed by Paul G. Stoltz, PhD, is based on the theory that how a person responds to adversity is a valid and broad predictor of individual and team performance, capability for change, ability to learn, persistence, motivation, productivity, and mental and physical health. The profile looks at four factors:

- *Control Dominance* – How much control a person believes he has over a given event or outcome.

- *Origin and Ownership Dominance* – How much a person feels ownership for the outcome even when the origin of the event was someone or something else.

- *Reach Dominance* – To what extent a person lets bad events impact on other areas of his or her life.

- *Endurance* – How long a person allows adversity to last.

The tool provides a measure of a person's adversity capacity, called AQ™ (Adversity Quotient). A person's AQ also measures their subconscious patterns of response to adversity. It is plotted on a scale of low to high, the higher the AQ, the greater the tendency to outperform others, learn from mistakes, take risks, and stay emotionally healthy. The lower the AQ, the tendency is to repeat mistakes, feel helpless, avoid risk, become depressed, and be debilitated by stress.

Table 10.5 Innovation Potential Indicator (based on Patterson 2000)

Individuals with high MTC	• Are tolerant of ambiguity and issues that are less 'clear-cut' • Are likely to be interested in new ways of thinking and to strive for achievement • Show intellectual curiosity and enjoy solving problems for the challenges they may offer • Actively seek change and are open to new experiences
Individuals with low MTC	• Do not welcome shifting work goals and too frequent change • Prefer stable environments and are keen to resolve ambiguity • Approach new ideas and ways of working with caution and prefer the familiar
Individuals with high CB	• Believe it better to seek forgiveness than to ask for permission • Are unlikely to bow to authority if they hold strong beliefs about a particular issue • Will challenge others' points of view
Individuals with low CB	• Strive for group consensus • Are less likely to take risks • Will accept the group consensus and harmony even if they hold strong beliefs about a particular issue
Individuals with high CWS	• Prefer to engage in a disciplined and structured work style • Are highly conscientious • Actively seek organization and a structured environment
Individuals with low CWS	• Prefer an unstructured environment and variety • Prefer to juggle lots of conflicting demands • Do not enjoy situations that require a methodical and planned approach
Individuals with high AD	• Do not believe they need to be radical to achieve significant progress • Prefer analytical step-by-step approaches and 'precision'
Individuals with low AD	• Are more likely to work outside current systems and parameters to find new ways of tackling problems • Look for novel ways to achieve solutions and aim for originality

Except for the last one, which seems to imply a 'right versus wrong' attitude, all tools are just describing different approaches and preferences. When reading through the description you will find that some roles and preferences provide a better fit with the requirements of radical innovation, step changes, challenging, etc., while others are ideal for situations where incremental innovation, continuous improvement and increased efficiency are required. In the end, for bringing a project to a successful conclusion, all skills are needed at some point or other. The question each manager needs to ask him or herself is, where is our emphasis and what are the characteristics of the project for which we are assembling a team? To ask someone with a ESTJ Myers Briggs profile to come up with a radical innovation is as inappropriate as it would be to as a INFP type to bring a project to a successful conclusion! What all these tools do is provide some help in (a) putting the right person on the right job or project, and (b) giving people a means through which they can explain and understand their differences. Difference in preferences and language, if not understood and acknowledged, can cause major misunderstanding between individuals, as well as disruptions in the execution of projects.

One last observation on this subject: Prather and Grundy (1995) comment on the tension that can exist within commonly used job classifications. We often put accounting and finance or sales and marketing under one person's

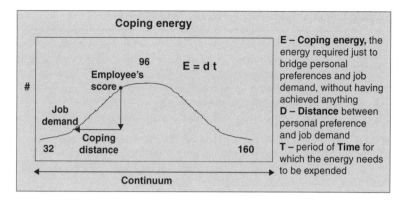

Figure 10.6   Coping Energy (Prather, 2002, based on Kirton)

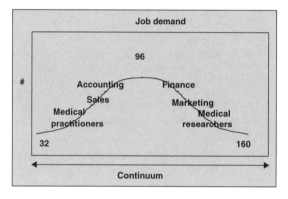

Figure 10.7   Coping Energy (Prather, 2002, based on Kirton)

responsibility. If we look at how they actually score on the KAI, we find that individuals focusing on one of these positions actually score quite differently. So people in positions that combine responsibility for both spend a lot of energy doing work they'd rather not be doing. Prather and Grundy call energy expended on such tasks 'coping energy' (see Figures 10.6 and 10.7). They explain, 'Essentially, coping energy is zero-return energy – that is, it brings you up to zero so you can begin doing the work.' I really liked this concept as it helps to explain why it takes one person forever to complete a task while another can do it in the shortest period of time – it is about liking what you do, doing what you like, and therefore being good at it.

For characteristics of team leaders you may want to refer back to the Team Leader section in Chapter 3.

READING SUGGESTIONS

Skopec, Eric and Smith, Dayle M. (1998) *How to Use Team Building to Foster Innovation Throughout Your Organization.* New York: McGraw-Hill

Comment: In their book the authors discuss how to develop and organize a well-balanced, productive team, how to lead, motivate and reward teams, deal constructively with mistakes and obstacles to successful team building

Katzenbach, Jon R. and Smith, Douglas K. (1993) *The Wisdom of Teams*. Cambridge, MA: Harvard Business School Press

Comment: With their book, Jon Katzenbach and Douglas Smith provide a very valuable insight into a great variety of aspects surrounding teams. In Part One of the book they address questions such as why teams are useful, why they might be resisted, how to define a team and what its characteristics are. Part Two is concerned with different types of teams, how teams work, what kind of leader do they need, what might prevent them from performing and how to address this. The third part looks at the role of teams in major change, the role of teams at the top and why they are different, and, last but not least, the role of management.

SOME USEFUL WEBSITES

http://www.ccmd-ccg.gc.ca/research/publications/html/innovation/focus-e.html.

Comment: On this page the Canadian Centre for Management Development argue for and explain the use of teams in innovation
http://www.american-book.com/Articles/arwilsonp3.htm

Comment: On this page Phil Wilson introduces his book, *Inspired Innovations: A Guidebook to Highly Efficient New Product Development*, in which he discusses how development teams can be used to routinely produce award-winning, commercially successful innovations. The book is available from http://www.pdbookstore.com

http://www.kdla.net/statelib/SLS-GSCResources-DHPT.htm

Comment: On this page of the Kentucky State Library you find an extensive list of books relevant to creating high-performance teams

NOTES ON CHAPTER 10

[1] Originally from G. Macdaid, M. McCaulley and R. Kainz, *Atlas of Table Types*, Centre for Application of Psychological Type Inc., Gainesville, Florida 1986.

[2] Adapted from a presentation by Charles Prather at the 2002 Innovation Network conference in Minneapolis, 21–25 September.

11 Collaboration – Innovation in Manufacturing

CASE STUDY 4: THE LOTUS ELISE

THE PHILOSOPHY BEHIND LOTUS AND THE ELISE

A proper sports car should weigh little, handle and ride superbly, and deliver high levels of driver satisfaction.

Colin Chapman, Lotus founder

The Lotus Seven, launched in 1957, had been Chapman's first car to be built on a commercial scale – previous models had been built exclusively for racing purposes. By taking his cars to market he wanted to transfer some of the excitement of racing cars to the road.[1] The Lotus Seven offered racing car qualities at kit-car prices, with performance achieved through lightweight construction rather than a powerful engine. Chapman was quoted to have said, 'It is a bit like a four-wheeled motorbike.'

In 1966 Lotus, which had started off on a site in Tottenham, London, moved to its current site in Hethel, Norwich. The site, which had been the home of a USAAF Liberator squadron in the Second World War, was chosen not only because it would offer ample room for expansion, but also because it would allow the building of a great test track on what was the former runway and the airfield perimeter road. While keeping the driving fun, Lotus moved decidedly upmarket with the development of the £60 k Esprit in the 1970s, a direction that was substantiated through the introduction of the Elan, a two-seater sports car, in the 1980s. Neither of the cars has ever been built in large quantities.

Group Lotus plc consists of two parts: Lotus Cars Ltd building the Lotus vehicles, which at time of Elise development had about 500 staff, and Lotus Engineering, acting as a consultancy to the automotive industry, which had about 800 employees. Both parts of the business, each generating about half of the company's revenue, are located on the same site. While they normally operate quite independently, they operated closely on the development of the Lotus Elise.

While the company had taken on engineering work for outside companies on a consultancy basis before, a separate Design and Engineering side of Lotus was set-up in

> The only other car manufacturer that entertains an automotive engineering consultancy is Porsche.

1986. In 1998 35 designers and modelers were employed by Lotus. Russel Carr, Chief of Design, explains, '50% of all the work that Lotus Design does is for third parties. The volume of work has increased several-fold over the last five years.' At Lotus' new design centre in Hethel with its two independent units, officially opened by the prime minister of Malaysia in October 2000, they can now run two vehicle programmes independently of each other.

In its drive to deliver lightweight, fast cars innovation has always played an important part. Says Kenneth Sears, Head of Vehicle Engineering, Lotus Engineering, 'One of the things that people identify with the company is gaining some performance advantage through the development of new technology.' Explaining what Lotus means by innovation a company representative explained, 'Innovation must combine elements of knowledge, information and creativity. This means that engineers now and in the future need to combine individual and team working skills.' It also means that the company is strongly committed to research and development, and the development of new products.

Previously owned by the Italian company Bugatti International, which had bought Lotus Group in 1994, the Malaysian car manufacturer Proton took a 64% stake in the company for £51 m in October 1996 with its chairman, Tan Sri Yahaya, buying an additional 16%. When Yahaya died in a helicopter crash, his share was bought by Proton in June 1997, bringing the company's share in Lotus to a total of 80%. The remaining 20% are still held by Romano Artioli.[2]

CONCEPTION AND CONCEPT

Don't follow the crowd and copy what they are doing.

Alastair Florance, Lotus Cars

There were several threads that together led to the conception of the idea for the Lotus Elise, or project M1-11 as it was originally called. The company was looking for a follow-up product to the Lotus Elan, which had proved far too expensive to produce and was rather complex to manufacture. The last straw had been that the Japanese company that had supplied the engines for the Elan had closed down. With the discontinuation of the Elan in June 1992, 200 jobs were lost.

The Elise started with a clean sheet, the only guideline was that it had to be true to the spirit of the founder. To fund the experimentation and development necessary for an entirely new car it was agreed that money would be diverted from the research budget of Lotus Engineering under the condition that the new car should be a demonstration of Lotus' engineering and technology skills. In fact, it was the research budget of two years that was 'liberated' for the development of the Lotus Elise.

It was agreed that the money available should be invested in the development of those parts that would really make a difference, parts that would contribute to the car's character and advancements in technology. In addition, a member of the development team was tasked with maximizing the number of components that were readily available and would not compromise the car's design and character. For example, the cost involved in developing a door mirror in-house would have been in no proportion to the value created through its uniqueness, so a readily available model, from the Rover Metro, was used instead.

The design brief started from a corridor conversation of a few people – including Kenneth Sears, then Head of Technology Strategy, and Roger Becker, Head of Vehicle Engineering – about what a new Lotus car should look and feel like in November 1993. Soon after the design team began its discussion about the philosophy for the new car concept. Unusually, rather than starting with an engineering specification, this project started in the design centre. A few parameters were clear from the beginning: it had to be an open two-seater sports car that would be fun to drive, and it should not cost the world. Three

years were anticipated from conception to production, as was a production run of a couple of thousand cars.

The designers started by putting together theme boards through which they explored customer characteristics and defined the mood and feeling that the car should have. Such boards would be covered with pictures of cars, aircraft, fashion items, celebrities, advertisements and motorcycles such as Ducatis, a passion for which was shared by Richard Rackham, Head of Engineering, and Head of Lotus Design, Julian Thomson. Richard went into raptures about it, 'The bike has some awesome performance. You will never use all of it, but you know it is there. It is a bit of a toy that you just love owning. And if you take the clothes off a Ducati you see lots of nice things, that's what we wanted to achieve with the Elise.' Richard and Julian kept discussing the concept in all its aspects during work as well as when they met socially.

Once a philosophy had been agreed the designers would spend about six weeks developing sketches. Through the sketches key aspects were discussed and agreed: it was to be a step-in two-seater with the engine located at the back, set quite low. The question always asked was, is this in the spirit of Lotus, would driving such a car be fun? The team also used a buck made out of fibreboard, mounted on a wooden frame called the 'seating buck', through which the relationship of driver to driving controls, such as the steering wheel, pedals and gearstick, could be explored. In addition to mood boards,

sketches and the cardboard model the team brought in a whole host of previous Lotus models.

With some key aspects and overall lines agreed, a first scale model was developed. This initial 1:3 scale clay model would demonstrate how the car was anticipated to look

A very clever aspect of the models is that only half a car is built – and then set against a mirror.

and what the basic elements would be. Rather than using the clay model for presentations, a plaster case would be taken from it from which fibreglass models would be made. This had the advantage that the original clay model could be used for further development, while the presentation model would be much more attractive and representative of a real car than a clay model could be. Once completed, the fibreglass model showed some flaws. For example, the proportions of the car did not seem right, it was too short and the overall height had to be reviewed.

Even though the Lotus Board had approved the development of a new car in-house in January 1994, the team faced its first big challenge only a month later. Unbeknown to the Lotus team, Artioli had invited other design consultancies to come forward with designs for a new Lotus car. Julian recalls, 'Mr Benedini, Bugatti's representative, got the Lotus Board down to decide which design they liked best.' It was fortunate for the in-house team that their idea was considered to be the most progressive,

innovative and different – and more aligned with the key brand values of the company than the other designs. While following a similar philosophy to the Lotus Seven, the design team had made a conscious effort to differentiate the new product from the existing ones.

During a body review meeting held in spring 1994, for which a refined second 1:3 scale model was used, questions were posed as to the feasibility of a step-in design. Finding a satisfying engineering solution, mainly to achieve the necessary stiffness, would require time and was likely to add weight to the car. On the other hand, developing doors and windows would be quite costly too, and particularly the designers were very keen to stick to their original idea. As a compromise it was decided to give the team four weeks to come up with a solution. But before the four weeks were up vehicle legislation

engineer Ken Evans dropped a bombshell: legislation decreed a maximum step-in height of 750 mm off the ground, a running board, i.e. a step, would be required. Ken pointed out that the line would only have to come down by 30 mm but the designers felt it would compromise the lines of their design. A major rethink was required, resulting in additional costs of about £1/2 million.

While the second-generation design changed several times, it showed many aspects found in the final car such as the side air scoops, the top-exit radiator duct, the character of the headlights and the round indicators.

The surface of the 1:3 scale model was scanned to develop a set of drawings from which a full-scale model would be developed. Developing a full-size model is quite an involved process, and often scaling problems mean that proportions have to be revisited. Richard compared this to scale toy models where certain aspects of the car look right only because they have been overemphasized. In developing the first full-size model, wood and foam would be applied to a steel frame which would then be sent away to a specialist. At the specialist the foam would be milled to 40 mm below

the surface and spiked with pegs sticking out 60 mm, making the model look like a giant hedgehog. Upon return to Lotus, the model makers there would apply clay to the height of the pegs before sending it once again to the specialist who would then copy-mill it into the final, but still only initial, clay buck. At the time Lotus employed ten model makers, bringing in additional modellers on a contract basis if and when required. A team of four to six would work on a full-size clay model at any point in time, each on a specified area. The role of the model makers was to help designers and engineers to refine the design. Based on the clay model that returned to the factory in May 1994, the design was signed off and both Romano Artioli and Gianpaulo Benedini of Bugatti were part of the decision making-body.

A lot of the actual design was done 'on the object', for example height and positioning of the headlights. Clay had the great advantage of being easy to manipulate and change, bits could be taken away and added back on. By doing so any curve or shape could be achieved. Refinement can take quite some time and might leave some people wondering whether anything has actually changed, but spending time and effort here could make the difference between the end result being 'great' or 'exceptional'.

While the full-size clay model was developed, the latest 1:3 scale model was tested in the wind tunnel by aerodynamicist Richard Hill. For lightweight cars to achieve high speeds efficient aerodynamics are particularly important. Hill found what he had anticipated when first seeing the low, stubby design: the car had quite a high drag factor. Another aspect contributing to the high drag factor was the radiator duct. By reducing the lift at the front, the radiator duct caused an imbalance at the back, meaning that the car would lift under aerodynamic load. Not something one would want to experience in a rear-drive car. To address the problem Richard Hill used clay, Styrofoam and tape to build up the surfaces until the optimum aerodynamic performance was achieved.

When presented with the result Julian was quite taken aback. Not only did he feel that the design had been spoilt, there was also the question of whether this meant that the design had to go back to the Board for renewed approval. Richard Hill explained that he had taken the changes to the ultimate limit and that a compromise would have to be found. Project Manager Tony Shute commented, 'The car was as aerodynamic as a brick! However, the car had style and whatever happened, we did not want to lose that.' Richard Rackham too was a strong supporter of Julian's design and keen to help find solutions that would maintain the visual identity. Under the mediation of other team members a compromise was finally reached, and a spoiler added.

Julian commented on the design process, 'The important thing is to remember that all those decisions governing the size and layout of the package that are given by the body engineering department are relevant to us. We talk about the styling but my group is very much involved with the

> Occasionally they would come up against what founder Colin Chapman had described as, 'the old school engineers' of whom he had said, 'The trouble with experts is they know what can't be done.'

concept of the car; you find that all companies offering truly innovative products have to have a level of understanding between both groups. You can't just have engineers produce something and then decorate it with different styles, they have to complement each other.' Richard agreed saying, 'Chassis design is more than just a structure, it's part of the style of the car as well, because it's so visible in the design.' The team worked to progress engineering and design issues in parallel, as well as considering interior and exterior as each would impact on the other. The efforts were supported by the geographical closeness between the design and the engineering department, and a presence of key concept engineering personnel in the design studio.

A lot of attention was paid to detail. Having a single windscreen wiper was part of the desired look. But not only would it look racy, it was also cheap, and most efficient aerodynamically. The choice of a single wiper had

> Later in 1997 the French company approached Lotus, being interested in buying the wiper mechanisms Lotus had developed.

implications for the size of the windscreen and with it the proportion of the whole vehicle. There were many legal requirements and from the outset there had been some doubts internally as to whether a single wiper would work. Julian remembers, 'Our engineers were more interested in developing wiper systems that would fit any car.' Lotus had also approached a French company specializing in complex wiper systems. But the tight schedule for the project meant that Lotus was looking for a solution within four months – rather than the 12 the French company declared necessary – which meant that they decided not to get involved. Determined not to give up, Richard Rackham experimented until he found a solution that worked. He commented, 'The fact that I was familiar with the Citroen AX system probably helped to see what would be possible. I just tilted the wiper motor spindle and it worked.' For the manufacture they eventually found a UK-based company but the design was, in the end done, entirely in-house by Richard.

Probably the tallest challenge for the team was to achieve all other ambitions within a limited budget – if you have lots of money you can achieve almost anything! To make the car widely affordable the price tag had been set at the

> We wanted to make the frame out of as small a number of components as possible. We wanted to join each piece.

£20,000 mark. To meet all challenges the team decided to strip out anything that was not absolutely essential, and have as many parts as possible with more than one function, so for example the front structure of the car, which was crash structure, also provided support for the radiator, aerodynamic wing and attachment for a tow hook.

CHASSIS DEVELOPMENT

While Julian and his team were working on the overall design, Richard Rackham, who had been involved in the development of the M1-11 even at seating buck stage, started to think about the chassis design. The target weight for the new car had been set at 650 kg – to put this into perspective, a Renault Spider Sport weighs about 930 kg and the MGF brings about 1.1 tons to the scale.

Some Key Players in the Development Team set up in January 1994 and their Roles

- Tony Shute – Project Manager, product engineering background, philosophy behind the car, its gestation period, has done a lot of the development driving

- Julian Thomson – Head of Lotus Design, designing the shape, styling process

- Richard Rackham – Head of Engineering Design, responsible for the design of the chassis and suspension, engineering issues, issues during productionizing process

- Luke Bennett – Manufacturing Engineering Manager

- Morris Dowton – Manufacturing Manager, Lotus Production

- Ben Wright – Purchasing and Procurement Manager

- Dave Minter – Executive Engineer, responsible for honing the ride and handling

- John Miles – details of damping set-up

- Alastair McQueen – Chief Test Driver

To determine the dimensions of the chassis, Richard and his team, together with Julian, started with a full-size plastic sheet onto which the outline of the car was pasted. The tapes that were used for the lines could be moved and reapplied whereby different colours were used for different parts, i.e. chassis, engine, and passenger. 'Using this,' said Richard, 'helps us understand the interaction between car and "agent orange", so called because for the occupant we use orange lines.' From the full-size drawing computer drawings are produced which then allow working with the chassis and the positioning of individual components.

Before the start on the M1-11 project Lotus had been working with a British car manufacturer on exploring the use of lightweight extrusions for car structures, a liaison that had been set-up by Hugh Kemp, Technical Director at Lotus at the time. When Lotus' collaboration partner was taken over by a German manufacturer the relationship ended rather prematurely. However, Richard had got hooked on the idea and decided to explore possibilities for the M1-11, and Tony commented, 'It is nice to have a big brother when exploring new territory but we are quite used to doing such things on our own. Our Board saw the visionary product and felt that our people had not only the necessary expertise and knowledge but also a good dose of enthusiasm to see the project through.' Richard contacted a company they had worked with previously, the Danish company Hydro Aluminium, whose core expertise was in the building industry, but which had recently set-up a new division, Hydro Automotive Components.

> The aluminium is shipped to England for bending, then goes back to Denmark for heat treatment, machining and the assembly of the chassis before being shipped to Lotus.

Welded aluminium had been used for car structures before, but not to the extent Richard planned to use it. Using extruded aluminium would mean that the frame would be not only lightweight but also durable and corrosion resistant. A constraint inherent in the choice was that extrusions tend to be straight. Any bend would not only cost time and money, it would also create a weak point in case of a collision. Finding a solution that would use only straight parts and be aesthetically pleasing turned out to be impossible, and in the end two bends had to be integrated into the back part of the chassis. Hydro's experience and expertise came into its own and a special and complex piece of equipment was developed for the bending. However, the bending had to take place in a part of Hydro located in England; this meant that the chassis parts had to be shipped back and forth a few times. It was agreed that once Hydro's new plant in Worcester would be completed, production would be moved to the UK.

Aluminium versus Steel

The most critical aspect of strength in automotive structures is for safety. Modern vehicle structures must retain the integrity of the occupant cell without significant distortion in crash conditions and provide controlled energy absorption. Aluminium alloys have a range of strength to weight ratios which is broadly similar to typical automotive steels whereas the dynamic behaviour may be different. Aluminium, for example, tends to exhibit no effect or a softening. Aluminium generally cannot support such high values of elongation before failure.

Tooling for a particular aluminium extrusion can cost as little as £2000 whereas tools for a pressed steel part can require as much as fractions of millions.

While open cars are often compromised structurally, requiring extensive stiffening to make them sufficiently rigid, the Lotus Elise with its aluminium chassis needed no additional measures. Despite its structure weighing as little as 154lb, it met all safety standards and proved to have great torsional rigidity.

However, welding aluminium tended to reduce its strength, which would have to be counterbalanced by thickening the material. And there were more downsides, (a) welding would only hold the parts together at the seam, (b) as welding changed the properties of the material there was also the concern that corrosion might occur here and (c) heat-induced distortions could occur. The team did a lot of investigating and much research took place into possible solutions. In the end, to avoid an increase in material, and inspired by the use of glue in the aircraft industry, Richard decided to explore bonding. He

found a partner in crime in Peter Bullivant-Clark at Hydro Aluminium Automotive Tønder, Denmark, who had been involved in Hydro's previous explorations of the use of aluminium extrusions for vehicle spaceframes. He spent two years with the Lotus engineers encouraging them to 'think extrusion' and 'think bonding'.

Hydro had used chemicals for bonding aluminium before, but there were no industry standards which meant that there would be no ready made solutions. Several companies were visited and interviewed before they signed up

Ciba, based near Cambridge, UK, to help address the problem. Bonding had several advantages: rather than just holding different parts together at the seam, it would bind them together through a patch. Bonding would also not be given to distortion. However, a downside was that

> The material used for the bonding does not cure entirely until the chassis has been into an oven for 4–5 hours. This means that parts could be adjusted and even dissembled during experimentation stage.

once a bonded joint started to peel it would have the tendency to separate suddenly – and the idea of the Lotus Elise disintegrating suddenly in the case of an accident was not particularly appealing. To overcome the problem, special aluminium screws were used right at the edge of the joints. In fact, the screws, which were made of soft aluminium, when driven into the parts were actually slightly melting so they acted more like rivets and were hence called 'screw rivets'. These screw rivets did not have to be very strong as their main function was to prevent the onset of peeling. Testing took place to ensure that corrosion would not be likely to happen.

But not only was the chassis made of aluminium. Richard recalls, 'Once I got hooked I started looking at every part thinking, could this be an extrusion? For example, I looked at the ugly Metro pedal box we had initially intended to use. Next to it I had sketched an idea pedal – and suddenly thought "extrusion"! The resulting pedal did not only look elegant, simple and functional, but also turned out to cost a fraction of their steel equivalents.' Other parts that were made of extruded aluminium included the door hinges, suspension uprights and the steering column mounting bracket.

The Elise derived part of its structural stability from two high-sided members on either side of the car, which were connected in front and rear by torsion boxes. Attached to the chassis were front and rear clamshell body sections made from lightweight composite materials.

> The pedals and brake disks are aluminium, the aero-dynamic body is made from lightweight composite material and the oil dips are made of plastic. And, because of its weight, the car does not need power brakes or power-assisted steering.

The body panels were made of very light composite materials. Lotus had been involved in glass-enforced composites since the 1950s. About 20 different types of matting were used in the production of the panels. There are two different ways of producing panels. One

> The switch-over point where the high investment in machinery for steel panels becomes preferential to the high labour cost for glass fibre panels is around 20–30k units per year.

was to use a closed mould, the other to use a number of moulds that are joined together. The latter required layering of the glass fibre by hand which was time consuming but had the advantage that several sections could be joined together and would come out as one piece. For example, for the front panel eight sections are joined together, 11 for the back. Matting would be laid up in a mould that had been prepared with a gel that would form a smooth, paintable surface. Sufficient curing times for the panels were important, the panels had to remain in the oven for 5–6 hours at 60°C, then stand for 24 hours before being put into the oven for another hour at 80°C. If cured too fast the panels would develop a tendency to buckle and distort.

Once the body parts had cured they would be prepared for painting. The first step was cleaning up and smoothing the edges, which was done with a water jet cutter. Next the panels would get two coats of primer, after which imperfections would be sanded off and another coat of primer would be put on. After that panels would be checked once more for flaws before a colour and clear coat are applied. That done the panels would be placed into an oven to dry for 80 minutes at 80°C. Another quality check would take place before panels would be moved on for assembly. In total there were 16 build stages for the Lotus Elise, each lasting between seven and 36 minutes.

Another type of composite material was used for the brakes, aluminium and silicon. It was much lighter than the conventionally used cast iron, and, given that it conducts rather than absorbs heat, it had the additional benefit that such brakes would not overheat.

> The brakes were produced by Lanxide. When the company went under in mid-1998 Lotus quickly changed to race car specification cast iron discs.

GETTING APPROVAL

Getting approval for a new model could be a lengthy and frustrating process. There were about 25 major tests a car had to pass for obtaining European-type approval. More often than not a new type would fail in several of them, which would mean that the programme could be put back by as much as six months. The Elise team had worked hard and systematically to anticipate and avoid any major reasons for a reject. They tested everything they possibly could under a range of circumstances and conditions. The testing facilities at Hethel, such as the track and rigs, were used extensively to ensure any problems would be detected before the car went for approval. One example was noise emission. Instead of measuring noise emission on the finished product, a silencer was incorporated right from the outset, meaning that it was an integral part of the product as well as the production process – rather than having to be put in as an afterthought.

Several internal measures supported quality control efforts. People from engineering and process control met at the end of every day to discuss any issues that had come up during the day. Everyone could find out performance criteria such as production cost, delivery against targets, materials issue and so on from noticeboards that had been distributed around the shop floor. To ensure everyone could see how their work fitted into the whole, an instruction booklet was available, providing information on the parts used, sequence of assembly, move-up times, duration of each build stage, and so on.

Some of the initiatives had been prompted by the preparations for QS 9000 certification which Lotus obtained in 1997. QS 9000, the car industry's equivalent of ISO 9000, had been a requirement from some of their major clients such as Ford and General Motors.

The team decided to go for approval in the Netherlands – not that the tests there were much different from those in the UK, but the team there had been particularly cooperative and helpful. There was only one aspect that had to be redressed for the Elise, the angle of the front windscreen which was considered to be too shallow. This had escaped the attention of the team as it became only obvious in the prototype – today, where everything would have been done on CAD, it could have been identified earlier.

But even that did not prevent the Elise from becoming the first car in the world to obtain the full European vehicle-type approval the first time around.

> Lotus have copyright, design registration, trade mark and patents for the Elise, and several items on the car are the subject of new patents.

THE MARKET AND RESULTS

Strong design requires strong leadership.

Richard Rackham

When the car was first shown at the international motor show in Frankfurt in 1995 it caused a bit of a stir. Not only because of its exciting design but also because of the extensive use of aluminium in a way thought impossible before. Richard recalls standing next to the car and being approached by someone who turned out to be the project manager for the Renault Spider. The French project manager was completely taken aback by the fact that Lotus had managed to come up with a bonded aluminium chassis – just as he had aimed to do, but he had

> 1997: *Car* magazine named the Lotus Elise as the most innovative new car in production in its 2nd annual Design and Technology Awards. The chassis and brakes on the Elise also picked up the Best Innovation in Production Award.

been told by his engineers that it was entirely impossible. Upon which Richard commented, 'The car would probably not have been as daring both in terms of its design and components had decisions been made by consensus.'

While it had originally been planned to produce around 700 cars per year, since start of production in August 1996 it had become obvious that demand would by far exceed this mark. In May 1997, with a daily production of eight cars expected to go up to 12 by the end of that year, Lotus had an order book of 2000, which translated into a waiting list of 18 months. In handling that kind of demand Lotus' dedicated, well-trained dealership was seen to be essential. Increased demand also meant that Lotus had to invest significantly in increasing production capacity, but even in January 2002 they had waiting

times of approximately three months. And all that despite, as Tipler writes, 'While other cars seem to have a clearer customer profile, it is not quite clear what attracts someone to Elise ownership.' But Lotus were not too worried about customer profiles at that point in time, to quote Julian, 'We don't want to get overly involved in marketing, market research and clinics, that sort of stuff; that's a lot of hassle. But I think what is important is how you pitch our car in terms of its image, how you separate it, how you use a brand. The luxury for us is that we don't have to find hundreds of thousands of customers, we only need to find a few thousand. And the product we do can be even stronger for those people. That's what we've done with the Elise: we've found a product that isn't for everyone but definitely is for some people. And those people would never be seen dead in an average sports car. That's our luxury. We've got a fantastic name. We've only got to find a maximum of 5000 customers a year, and we know there are nuts who'll put up with all sorts of things. And we can build our brand and make it stronger. We can do a total enthusiasts' car, we don't need to do electric windows or NHV, or worry about a walnut facia. We can get away with blue murder compared with the others, and we can make a fantastic car that enthusiasts are going to love.'

THE FUTURE

In the *Autocar* magazine of 12th February 1997 Proton, the company's Malaysian owner, outlined the following agenda for the company:

- Treble Elise production at Hethel.
- Establish Elise assembly in Malaysia.
- Launch third model, possibly slightly larger Elise-based V6 coupe, by 2000.
- Replace Esprit with V8 supercar by 2000.
- Establish post-grad college for automotive engineers at Hethel by autumn 1997.
- Consider Lotus re-entry to F1 for Malaysian GP of 1999.
- Double earnings from engineering.

QUESTIONS

1. What can be learned from the use of prototypes at Lotus?
2. Discuss the role of collaboration with external companies.
3. Given the demand for the new product, what steps should the company consider?

NOTES ON CHAPTER 11

[1] Interesting to note that 25% of all Lotus Seven built have, at some point or other, been driven in races.

[2] In the late 1990s Artioli sold Bugatti to the German car manufacturer BMW.

12 The Role of Prototypes

On a list of, say, five things would-be-innovation starts should be, working at creating a full-blown culture of rapid prototyping surely merits inclusion.

Tom Peters (in Machlis 1996)

During the development of the Lotus Elise, the team made extensive use of different types of prototypes, from very simple ones made of cardboard, to highly sophisticated computer-generated ones. Extensive experimentation and the use of prototypes are firmly at the heart of innovative organizations, and it is not only restricted to tangible products. While it can be a bit more difficult to apply the concepts of experimentation and prototypes to processes and services, once understood and internalized, they can prove invaluable in keeping an organization agile.

In this chapter I investigate what makes experimentation and prototypes so invaluable to innovation, provide a brief overview of different categories of prototypes, and conclude with Michael Schrage's (2000) insight that innovative teams do not create innovative prototypes, but in fact, innovative prototypes create innovative teams.

WHY USE PROTOTYPES?

In recent times, more and more companies have cottoned on to the benefits of using prototypes. And Michael Schrage (1993), research associate at the MIT Media Lab and a Merrill Lynch Forum Innovation Fellow, strongly believes, 'Companies that want to build better products must learn how to build better prototypes.' Companies renowned for their innovativeness, such as

> Almost immediately after thinking of a promising concept, a development team at a place like IDEO or Design Continuum builds a prototype, shows it to users, tests it, and improves it. The team then repeats the sequence over and over.
>
> *Hargadon and Sutton (2000)*

IDEO (www.ideo.com) and Hewlett Packard (www.hp.com) and Sony (www.sony.com), to name but a few, are firm subscribers.

So what are reasons that more and more companies subscribe to prototyping, particularly innovative ones? In the following, we look at each of the arguments listed below in turn:

- It helps to bridge language barriers between departments and create a shared vision
- It provides focus
- It facilitates involvement
- It allows failure at the early stages
- It contributes to the learning process
- It saves time

- It helps to communicate the unknown
- It works for services too

IT HELPS TO BRIDGE LANGUAGE BARRIERS BETWEEN DEPARTMENTS AND CREATE A SHARED VISION

Leonard Barton (1991) likens today's development teams to the seven blind men of the fable describing their encounter with an elephant. As each of them has touched the animal they all believe to have shared a common experience and to talk about the same thing. However, as they have each touched a different part of the elephant – having had a different starting point – each has come to a different conclusion as to what the object in question is. The one who has touched the trunk thinks he felt a snake, the one who has touched its flank asserts he has touched a wall, and the one who has touched a leg believes to have encountered a tree trunk.

The diverse people involved in new product development today are like a group of blind men touching an elephant, each assuming they discuss the same thing while each perceives a different aspect of the whole. Working with prototypes makes sure that all members of a project team share the same vision of the outcome when discussing and

> Language barriers between disciplines can inhibit a team's productivity in the early stages of a development process, when that productivity is important.
>
> *Sisodia (1992)*

developing a new product. This can be particularly important in the early stages, when there is a need to develop an understanding of what the project is all about and what its aims are.

Prototyping specialists IDEO go a step further. Whereas most organizations would start with a specification as the foundation for product development, founder Kelley comments (in Perry 1995), 'We believe in a prototype-driven culture, not a specification-driven culture.'

IT PROVIDES FOCUS

But beyond establishing a shared vision, there is another benefit to using prototypes as early as possible. Sisodia (1992) points out, 'In addition, the involvement of engineering and production people in the team at early stages can lead to emphasis on product capability instead of usability and can build unnecessary manufacturing costs into the final version of the product. Some of these difficulties can be mitigated by using early-stage models and prototypes (getting physical fast) as a way of spanning language barriers and increasing the likelihood of developing consensus among team members.' Prototypes are tangible and easy to understand, which means that they are also useful for resolving crucial questions quickly and unambiguously.

IT FACILITATES INVOLVEMENT

It is not only within the development team that prototypes prove useful; they also help communicate with other constituencies within and outside the organization. Many people have difficulties visualizing what is described to them and, as the saying goes, a picture says more than a thousand words. True, but if you can offer something three-dimensional, even better. How many times has someone described something to you and in the end said, let me draw it for you? And if you can touch the object, it becomes even more convincing and real. So being able to show a prototype can help in the explanation and selling process, and to get buy-in.

Prototypes also allow a constituency larger than the project team to contribute to the development. Leonard and Rayport (1999) comment that prototypes 'enable the team to place its concept in front of other individuals who work in functions not formally represented on the team'. This means that prototypes make it easy for 'outsiders' to contribute and provide feedback to a project under development. Of course, this applies not only to 'outsiders' within the organization, but also those outside, i.e. potential customers.

IT ALLOWS FAILURE AT THE EARLY STAGES

The possibility to get early feedback from a wide range of audiences (internal and external) has a further benefit: it allows to weed out mistakes early. Mistakes or even failure as a result of feedback in the early stages can play an important role in putting the team on the right track. Steve Deak of Hasbro says (in Perry 1995), '[By using prototypes] we do design iterations a heck of a lot quicker. We can weed out wrong ideas much earlier. Once you get a prototype, a lot of things become obvious, because you can hold it and feel it.'

Avoiding 'barking up the wrong tree' and early elimination of mistakes are quite important, as about 80% of manufacturing costs are decided during the early design stages of a product (e.g. Sisodia 1992).

IT CONTRIBUTES TO THE LEARNING PROCESS

Insights into mistakes and wrong approaches early on also feed into an organization's learning process. However, this requires that the process is carefully recorded and iterations, reasons for rejection or improvement are noted and stored in a form that is easily accessible to later project teams. This is also pointed out by Barkan and Iansiti (1993), who say, 'When effectively exploited, prototypes are an essential part of the learning process – providing benefits in speed, quality, and productivity.'

IT SAVES TIME

Being able to put product ideas to internal and external audiences early also means that time can be saved. According to Perry (1995), organizations that used rapid prototyping – generating prototypes directly from 3D CAD data – cut between 10–15% of development time. A great benefit in many industries times where time-to-market is a significant contributor to the successful introduction of new products.

IT HELPS TO COMMUNICATE THE UNKNOWN

What I find particularly important in the context of innovation is that it helps to sell the unknown. Let me tell you a story to illustrate what I mean. Imagine you, a person of the 21st century, are meeting a person from the

> 'What use could the company make of an electric toy?' Western Union upon turning down rights to the telephone in 1878

middle ages, and have to explain to them the benefits of products such as a car or a microwave without being able to demonstrate it. You may want to role play this and experience first hand how difficult this can be! This is how people with an innovative idea feel like, like someone from the future trying to sell people the benefits of a product they just cannot imagine or understand. Personal computers, telephones and small photocopiers are famous examples where people just could not see the value – and hence the potential – the product had. So the more radical an innovation, the harder it is to understand, the more important and valuable prototypes become.

IT WORKS FOR SERVICES TOO

And though it is not obvious immediately, prototypes not only work for tangible products, but they can be a great help for intangible products too.[1] Rettig (1994), for example, suggests the use of paper-based prototypes for the development of software and websites. Pointing out that the development of 'real' (i.e. computer-based) versions is expensive and time consuming, he suggests the use of paper-based versions which allow potential users to play with possible elements (see Box 12.1).

> **BOX 12.1 Problems with Hi-fidelity Prototyping in Software Development (based on Rettig 1994)**
>
> - Take too long to build and change
> - Reviewers and testers tent to comment on 'fit and finish' issues (wrong focus, they should focus on usability, etc.)
> - Developers resist change – once they got so far they are probably not willing to change anymore
> - A prototype in software can set expectations that are hard to change
> - A single bug in the hi-fi can bring a test to a complete halt

Hargadon and Sutton (2000) illustrate the benefits of using prototyping for website development through the following story. Inspired by Dell Computers, Bill Gross of Idealab! thought of selling cars online, using the internet not only to send customers to a dealer but sell cars directly. While other companies often spend as much as $10,000–$250,000 on temporary websites to find out how many people might be attracted to the website and its offerings, Gross quickly assembled a group to try out the idea. Rather than building a complex website that would be able to link dealers or handle large numbers of visitors, the team built something simple just to test the idea. Gross hired a CEO for three months and explained that his only job was to sell one car. The idea was that in case of an order Idealab! would buy the required car from a dealer and resell it to the customer, accepting that this might incur a loss of about $5000. To his surprise Gross found that over 1000 people visited the website on its first day, resulting in the sales of four cars.[2] So there are different ways of using prototypes in the service environment.

PROBLEMS WITH PROTOTYPES

However, as ever it is not all roses – or rather, no roses without thorns. Two problems associated with the use of prototypes are (1) the need to manage expectations, and (2) the need to manage intellectual property rights.

If you are showing a prototype to external audiences – external to the project team – you have to manage expectations quite carefully. Think about the prototype of the Elise Lotus exhibited at the motor show. Many people would probably think that having a working prototype means that the car will go into production shortly. Far from it. It took another 12–18 months before the first customer received the finished product. The same is true for the use of prototypes internally, if a company is not familiar with the use of prototypes, and the different types of prototypes. In the Black & Decker case study, it was mentioned that sales assumed the product was ready to go into the shops, whereas it was only a working prototype, which meant that all tooling, resourcing and manufacturing had still to happen. So in showing prototypes it needs to be made quite clear what the purpose and scope of it is. Another consequence of a mismanagement of expectations is that people might comment on functionality – 'But this button does not work. . .' – where the prototype is about form and usability, or vice versa.

> **Machlis (1996) on the introducing of rapid prototyping**
>
> *Benefits*
>
> – weeding out wrong ideas much earlier
> – being able to see, touch, feel it helps evaluate concepts better and with more confidence

How to implement rapid prototyping

- move to 3D CAD
- determine if you are interested in concept models, functional prototypes and/or a process for speedy toolmaking
- test various processes by prototyping at one or more service bureaus
- don't underestimate the resources needed to run an in-house RP system, including infrastructure and technicians

How to begin using solid modelling

- investigate benchmarks and ease-of-use claims made by software vendors
- invite vendors to demonstrate their software's ability to solve one of your common design problems
- analyze packages for ease of model creation, editing, assembly modelling, and available complementary software packages

The second issue is around the protection of intellectual property. In his article 'Is your prototype yours?', Berner (1997) points out potential problems that can arise when a prototype is shown at trade shows before all important patents are registered. There is not much then to prevent competitors from picking up unique aspects and using them in their products. The timing of patent application and registration generally stirs some debate, and will be explored in more detail in Chapter 19.

WHAT PROTOTYPE?

Prototypes can be anything from crude gadgets to elaborate mock-ups.

Hargadon and Sutton (2000)

From the previous section, it has already become clear that there are many different kinds of prototypes, and which one is most appropriate will depend upon the aim and the stage of the project's development process at which it is to be used. In the development of the Lotus Elise, a number of different kinds of prototypes were used for the development of the body shell, as well as the development of the chassis. Box 12.2 lists the different kinds of prototypes used during the development of the body shell.

BOX 12.2   Prototypes used during the Lotus Body Shell Development

- The team started with mood boards to capture the essence of what the new car was to be about

- This was translated into a 'cardboard buck', which gave a first impression of the overall lines of the car

- Once this was refined, a 1:3 scale clay model was built – but for presentation purposes a plaster case was made, which in turn was used to build a fibreglass model that would be much more realistic than the duffer clay model

- There were several iterations of the 1:3 model, which was also used for testing in the wind tunnel

- The development of a full-size clay model using digital technology (the model is cut directly from the digitized drawings), which was then refined by hand

Today, computers and computer-driven machinery tend to play an important role in facilitating fast and cost-effective prototyping. Machlis (1996) comments that 'A decade ago "rapid prototyping" was little more than a laboratory curiosity.'[3] Today, leading companies make extensive use of the possibilities opened up by computer-aided prototyping. For example, IDEO has computerized milling machines that allow the use of rough sketches as well as detailed drawings to be turned into either rough first concept models, or sophisticated and refined prototypes. They are also known to have built a full-size foam model of an Amtrak train to play with seating arrangements, layout and signage.

In his 1991 article 'Inanimate integrators: a block of wood speaks', Leonard Barton lists the basic categories of prototypes, suggesting that the further down the list, the more senses are addressed. Table 12.1 summarizes the different categories, their manifestations and what their main purpose is.

It has already been emphasized that the use of prototypes can be particularly useful at the outset of a product's development process. An approach which I find particularly powerful is 'Totem Building', a process developed by Dr Angela Dumas that combines words and visual images to create a 'totem' which summarizes and illustrates the vision for a product, or product group. Dumas described totems as 'Object-based metaphors for product development, using words and pictures; helping to build up a vocabulary which strengthens the sense of belonging to the family to which the product belongs.' Box 12.3 summarizes the totem-building process as described in her 1994 article 'Building totems: metaphor-making in product development'.[4]

BOX 12.3   Angela Dumas' Totem-Building Process

The situation   A shoe maker who wants to be innovative/fashionable, but despite trying seems to come up with the same kind of shoe again and again

   Phase 1

Step 1: Building the context

   Company teams were teamed up with fashion design students to go around a circuit of selected shoe shops whereby students were asked to talk about their likes and dislikes while going along, resulting in the purchase of the pair of shoes the student liked most (regardless of price). To enable the company people to get to know the students a little bit better, this was followed by lunch.

   The idea was not to copy the desirable shoes but to understand what made them attractive, and translate that into a shoe that would fit into the same product category; the results would be appraised by the fashion students.

Step 2: Defining the context

   Each company team discussed the shoes chosen by the students, agreeing on subset and ten words associated with the shoes; each person then drew the shoes and put underneath his or her own selection of associated words; the drawings reflected the personal preferences, e.g. some drew the entire shoe, others just a detail – a balance between individual and teamwork is seen to be critical.

▶

Step 3: Building a vocabulary

Each team receives five sets of slides each with different objects (furniture, interiors, textiles, consumer products, and industrial products) with the task to select one slide from each set that matches the set of ten words established in Step 2.

Once the slides are chosen, each team member drew separate pictures to represent the objects shown on the slides, again each individual choose a selection of words from the original ten to apply to each picture.

Participants then drew a picture of what a shoe would look like if the object on the slide became a shoe.

Again the balance between team and individual input is important: the choice of slide was a team decision, the drawing of the shoe based on the slides and the selection of words is an individual act.

Step 4: Refining perceptions

Each team reviewed the ten words originally agreed upon; any words added by individuals were also discussed until a revised list of 6–8 words was agreed.

This is followed by a discussion on the physical qualities of the slides to establish which qualities are shared by five slides; this leads to a description of the 'family' to which the object (shoe) belongs.

Step 5: Distilling the totem

Each team reviews caricatures drawn in step 3 (what if this object became a shoe) comparing them to the five slides to decide which 5–6 caricatures best fit into the 'family'.

Finally, slides, words and caricatures are reviewed, and those items that are least relevant, powerful or helpful are taken out; the remaining words, slides, caricatures and shoes become the totem.

Phase II

Design and prototyping of new products developed from the totem

The results   A range of new shoes very different from the company's traditional range eliciting a very positive (surprised) response from fashion design students.

It has mentioned earlier that the kind of prototype will vary from stage to stage, and audience to audience. In a way, Michael Schrage (1993) turns the process on its head

> 'Prototypes are a way of life.' IDEO founder David Kelley in Schrage (1993)

when he suggests that, by looking at a company's use of prototypes, one can tell much about the company's culture, and whether or not it is innovative. The questions he asks are, how and where are prototypes used: internally or externally, to identify opportunities or manage risk, and are they formal or informal. In his experience 'Within some innovation cultures, prototypes effectively become the *media franca* of the organization – *the* essential medium for information, interaction, integration, and collaboration. In other cultural contexts, prototypes are little more than sales tools and technical stalking horses for the politically adept.' His framework, shown in Figure 12.1, illustrates this.

Table 12.1 Categorization of Prototypes (Leonard and Barton 1991) (reproduced by permission of Design Management Journal)

2D (flat) models	Non-functional 3D models	Functional prototypes	User test models	Organization/system models
• Concept sketches • Drawings • Blueprints	• Mock-ups • White models • Simulations	• Engineering prototypes • Feasibility models • Simulations	• Working prototypes	• First production units • Pilots • Production models
• Specifications • Engineering layout	• Site models • 'Soft' models	• CAD models • Finite element analysis – graphical representations		• 'First article'
Generally require some understanding of 'expert speak'	Emphasis on form and aesthetics, how it feels and looks	Emphasis on functionality/how it operates	Combining form and function; foretelling interaction between user and product	Primarily focusing on the interaction between product and company (e.g. manufacturing)

Within Non-functional 3D models also: Simulations • CAD models • Finite element analysis – graphical representation

— Address an increasing number of senses →

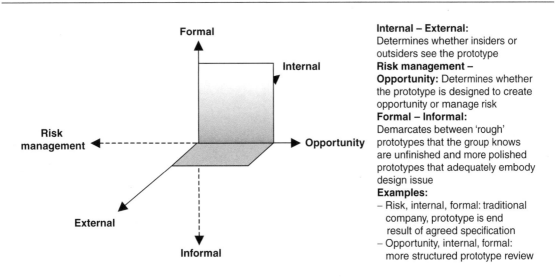

Internal – External:
Determines whether insiders or outsiders see the prototype
Risk management – Opportunity: Determines whether the prototype is designed to create opportunity or manage risk
Formal – Informal:
Demarcates between 'rough' prototypes that the group knows are unfinished and more polished prototypes that adequately embody design issue
Examples:
– Risk, internal, formal: traditional company, prototype is end result of agreed specification
– Opportunity, internal, formal: more structured prototype review

Figure 12.1   A Framework for Understanding Prototypes (Schrage 1993) (reproduced by permission of Design Management Journal)

In his recently published book, Schrage (2000) goes even further, commenting that 'Several companies discovered that, instead of innovative teams creating innovative prototypes, innovative prototypes create innovative teams.' This implies that appropriate and extensive use of prototypes can help an organization to improve its innovativeness. Schrage continues, 'It means that innovation requires improvisation. It means innovation is not about rigorous following "the rules of the game", but about rigorously challenging and revising them. It means innovation is less the product of how innovators think than a by-product of how they behave.' He concludes that the value of prototypes lies not so much in the models themselves as in the interactions they encourage and provoke. So perhaps the choice of prototype should be influenced by the kind of interaction and collaboration that it should facilitate.

And on the comment on collaboration, this is another differentiating factor for innovative organizations; they engage extensively in collaboration, internally as well as externally, which we shall explore in more detail in the following chapter.

READING SUGGESTIONS

Kelly, Thomas (2001) *The Art of Innovation.* New York: HarperCollins Business

Comment: Also listed under the reading suggestions in the market research chapter, this book is also helpful when wanting to find out more about how an innovative organization uses prototypes

Schrage, Michael (2000) *Serious Play – How the World's Best Companies Simulate to Innovate.* Boston, MA: Harvard Business School Press

Comment: The entire book is dedicated to the promotion and explanation of the value of prototypes, and their role in the innovation process

SOME USEFUL WEBSITES

	http://www.radical-departures.net/serious_play_full.asp
Comment:	Here you can find a good summary of Schrage's book *Serious Play*

http://pages.cpsc.ucalgary.ca/~saul/681/topic-prototyping-wong2002/prototyping-wong2002.html
http://www.hotwireindustries.com/hotwire/r_prototype.html

Comment: Under this link you find some information about low-fidelity prototyping
                in particular and prototypes more generally

NOTES ON CHAPTER 12

[1] More insights on insights specific to innovation in the service industry can be found in Chapter 24.

[2] The experiment led to the founding of CarsDirect.com.

[3] 'Rapid prototyping' generally refers to prototypes generated straight from digitized drawings, whereby the models is cut out of blocks of foam or other material that is cut by laser or shaving drill, eliminating the need for hand-crafted mockups or expensive tooling.

[4] For a reprint of her article, contact the Design Management Institute (www.dmi.org) in Boston.

13 Collaborating for Innovation

1 + 1 + 1 = 5
This is how a company participating in the 2001 survey of the Confederation of British Industry (CBI) summed up the benefits of collaboration.

The second aspect that made the development of the Lotus Elise such an innovation success was the company's willingness to collaborate, internally as well as externally. Collaboration is yet another arrow in the quiver of innovation. When considering that innovation happens through the connection of previously unconnected bodies of knowledge, and when assumptions are challenged, it is

> The best innovators aren't lone geniuses. They are people who can take an idea that's obvious in one context and apply it in not-so-obvious ways to a different context. The best companies have learned to systematize that process.
> *Hargadon and Sutton (2000)*

easy to understand why innovative companies are keen collaborators. It is often the assumptions we carry about what we can and cannot do that prevent us from innovation – and if someone comes along and questions us as to why we do things the way we do, it can help us to realize the mental models we have, and hence enable us to change them.

This chapter will shed some light on issues around collaboration, looking at reasons as to why companies collaborate, what benefits they gain, what can be in the way of collaboration, how collaboration can be encouraged, and what different forms of collaboration there are.

SOME BACKGROUND

For decades companies used to pursue development activities – be they a new product or a new strategic direction – within their own boundaries. Collaboration seemed too risky, and if a company decided to collaborate, this would generally be manifested in the form or a merger or acquisition, on a permanent basis – though the reason underlying most of the M&A activities was the desire to grow rather than to collaborate. In the more recent past, collaboration has gained increasing attention in the management literature. Managers have come to realize the benefits of teaming up with other companies for selected projects or developments rather than 'for life'.

One of the reasons that collaboration has become so much more popular is that many organizations feel that they have come to the end of the path of growth through mergers and acquisitions, and that future growth will have to come from new avenues, including innovation and collaboration. France, Kohen and Mahieddine (2001) quote a Booz Allen & Hamilton survey, which reports that four out of five executives said they saw alliances as one important strategy for future growth, and refer to another study that states that by 2002 participating companies expected 35% of their revenues to stem from alliances.

That collaboration is not only a plan for the future, but actually happening show the figures of the 2001 annual survey of the Confederation of British Industry, which found that about 75% of companies surveyed had been involved in external cooperation, with 44% describing themselves as regular collaborators (five or more collaborative ventures per year). Most collaboration lasted between 2–5 years, whereby larger organizations tended to have longer cooperation periods than small organizations. Most likely collaboration partners were other companies (see Box 13.1), though I thought it quite interesting that while partnerships with consultants were almost always described as problematic, fewer problems were reported in business–academia relationships – despite the commonly held view that academia may be too slow and not too reliable in meeting deadlines.

BOX 13.1   Collaboration Partners (CBI Survey 2001)

Who to collaborate with?

Other companies	73%
Academia	48%
Consultants	35%
Government or private research institutes	25%

An interesting trend is that towards collaboration with competitors, as a survey undertaken by the Innovation Exchange in spring 2002 found out (von Stamm, 2002). Of all participating firms, 37% indicated that they were currently collaborating on a small percentage of their projects with direct competitors, and in future as much as 49% envisage this form of collaboration (see Box 13.2).[1]

BOX 13.2   Collaboration Today and in Future (von Stamm 2002)

Within the supply chain

- With distributors and retailers: past → future
  - A small percentage   53% → 60%
  - Majority   11% → 18%
  - Not at all   31% → 20%

- With suppliers: past → future
  - A small percentage   64% → 60%
  - Majority   11% → 22%
  - Not at all   18% → 13%

With customers

- Lead users: past → future
  - A small percentage   44% → 33%
  - Majority   23% → 47%
  - Not at all   24% → 13%

With the competition

- Non-direct: past → future
  - A small percentage   47% → 53%
  - Majority   4% → 9%
  - Not at all   49% → 36%

- Direct: past → future
  - A small percentage   38% → 49%
  - Majority   9% → 9%
  - Not at all   56% → 42%

Other

- Universities: past → future
  - A small percentage   51% → 53%
  - Majority   7% → 11%
  - Not at all   42% → 29%

▶

•	Customers generally:	past → future	•	Consultancies:	past → future
	— A small percentage	51% → 33%		— A small percentage	58% → 62%
	— Majority	33% → 44%		— Majority	16% → 20%
	— Not at all	13% → 13%		— Not at all	22% → 13%

But of course, for innovation not only is external innovation important; even more critical is internal collaboration. The use of a cross-functional team has long been heralded as a cure for many ailments of new product development, and the issue of teams and their role in innovation has been discussed in Chapter 10. While most of this chapter focuses on issues relevant to external collaboration, the discussions of obstacles to collaboration, and some of the insights into how to make collaboration work, are as relevant for internal collaboration as they are for external collaboration.

REASONS FOR, AND BENEFITS OF, COLLABORATION

There are many reasons why companies collaborate externally, and the following will be discussed below:

- To share risk and cost
- To access new or different markets
- To obtain additional resources
- To gain access to knowledge and expertise
- To reduce development time

THE DESIRE TO SHARE RISK AND COST

When asked, 'what motivates companies to collaborate', the most frequent answer is that it allows the sharing of costs and risks involved in new ventures – and more often than not, risk and cost are invariably linked. It seems the higher the risk, the greater the openness towards collaboration. This is supported by recent research findings, which indicate that those companies that engage in R&D activities which aim to introduce innovations new to the market (rather than new to the firm) are more likely to engage in cooperative arrangements than those that engage in more incremental innovation (Tether 2002). But costs can also be an important factor, particularly in industries such as pharmaceuticals, where development costs are prohibitively high.

However, talking of risk, there is always a brand risk attached to collaboration. If the collaboration fails, or the results are too far removed from the image and positioning of the parent companies, it might cause some confusion amongst customers, or even worse, damage the parent brand.

ACCESSING NEW OR DIFFERENT MARKETS

There are also many organizations that seek collaboration to expand into new and different markets. As we read in Chapter 4, globalization is an issue many managers have to contend with. Not many companies have the resources available to expand into new countries at the rate they would like. Collaboration with companies in the target market, or companies that operate in the target markets, can help to accelerate the process of expansion, as well as provide valuable local insights and expertise.

But some organizations are much more ambitious in their collaboration, they collaborate to create new markets. One example is the collaboration between consumer electronic giant Philips and athletics-ware manufacturer Nike, announced in March 2002.[2] In the announcement it reads, 'Royal Philips Electronics and Nike, Inc. today announced an alliance to merge their athletic and digital technology expertise to develop innovative technology product solutions which create a richer, more motivating environment for physical activity.' The article continues, 'Nike and Philips bring unique strengths to the venture. Nike has exceptional expertise in sports and material technology, marketing and innovation. The company transformed athletic footwear with the invention of air technology. Philips is a leading innovator of "wearable electronics" technologies and has a long heritage of technology innovation, especially in the digital arena, as well as intimate knowledge of consumers. Philips originated the idea of wearable electronics in 1995 and has a reputation for introducing high quality, cutting edge electronic products.' Again, innovation happens by bringing together disparate bodies of knowledge to create something that has not existed before.

TO OBTAIN ADDITIONAL RESOURCES

Most organizations will have been through one – or even several – rounds of downsizing, generally with the preamble to have to refocus.[3] This has often led to the contracting out of activities previously undertaken in-house. Whereas there are some activities that almost any organization would have sought collaboration for anyway, such as advertising, some companies have extended this to R&D and product development activities. Even if the functions may have not been disbanded entirely, these departments have often been reduced to a size that makes effective in-house development difficult. During interviews conducted by the author (von Stamm 2001), one participant commented on his company's staffing staff policy: 'It seems to be a good idea to get a company "lean and mean" but I think we might have gone too far and have become anorexic.' If such organizations want to engage in the development activities, collaboration often becomes a necessity.[4]

ACCESS TO AND TRANSFER OF KNOWLEDGE

Closely related to the previous point is the lack of the skills or technologies necessary to execute a particular project. In the case of the Lotus Elise, the company did not have the skills necessary to manufacture the aluminium frames, or to glue the aluminium parts together. Instead of trying to develop the skills in-house, they looked for other companies which they could partner with.

While collaboration can be used to access additional resources – manpower or expertise – it also provides the opportunity to transfer skills between organizations. For example, new product development agencies often use collaboration on particular aspects to gain insights into, and better understanding of, aspects relevant to a particular project, as the following story illustrates (Hargadon and Sutton 2000). New product development agency Design Continuum was commissioned to improve the tools and techniques used in knee surgery. Rather than reading up on or being told about how it works, the engineers decided that observation would provide the most relevant insights. Joining surgeons at a convention, they asked doctors to simulate the surgical procedure so they could observe and ask questions during the process. Hargadon and Sutton report how one of the engineers described the scene: 'We wanted to observe the procedures, so we had a cadaver lab, which was actually in a swanky hotel. One room was the lecture room and the other held 12 cadavers. They had the room chilled down to 50 degrees, with the cadavers in there and a guard 24 hours a day making sure nobody accidentally walked in. We just wanted to see how doctors used the tools, the little blocks and stuff they use for doing the procedures.' From their observation the designers concluded that surgeons often needed a 'third arm' which inspired them to develop a new surgical tool that would function like one. So collaboration can provide some learning by doing – or, in the case above, observing.

TO REDUCE DEVELOPMENT TIME

When Lotus decided to experiment with aluminium frames they had one of two choices: first, develop the necessary skills in-house – after all, they were also a manufacturing company. Secondly, they could seek out a company that had an expertise in this area and engage in collaboration. Following the first route, Lotus would have had to spend significant resources, time and money, to develop the skill to a standard necessary to apply it to their new car. By taking the latter approach, Lotus avoided wasting valuable time and energy on the development of a skill that, while useful, would not be core to their activities. So collaboration is a quick way of gaining access to skills that would take a long time – or at least too long a time – to develop in-house.

And finally, an interesting reason to increase collaboration internally was brought forward in an Innovation Exchange interview (von Stamm 2001), 'The company is split into separate business units and the (cultural) glue is beginning to unravel. To prevent this from happening we are trying to become more interactive and collaborative.' So internal collaboration can help create a shared culture, and help bind different parts of the organization together.

If you would like to find out how supportive your organization is towards collaboration, you may want to take a look at a set of questions published in Snead and Wycoff (1996) (see Box 13.3).

BOX 13.3   What's Your Organization's Collaborative Quotient?
(from Snead and Wycoff 1996) (reproduced by permission of Snead, L. & Wycoff, J.)

The following evaluation will help you determine how well your organization supports collaboration. Rate your organization from 1 to 5 on the following questions.

1 = terrible/never   2 = poor/seldom   3 = average/generally   4 = good/often   5 = excellent/always

1. We stimulate communication by providing conference rooms, whiteboards, bulletin boards, open work areas.

2. We share information widely through group meetings, newsletters, email, closed circuit TV, financial and performance reports.

3. We have a high level of trust and respect for each other.

4. We encourage people to collaborate on projects and allow them to identify potential projects even when it takes time away from 'normal' duties.

5. We have a compensation policy that rewards collaborative efforts as well as individual efforts.

6. Our organization's values, vision and objectives are clearly understood by all and we encourage groups and individuals to clarify their own values and vision.

7. Rewards and risks are shared equitably by everyone in the organization.

▶

8. We have computer-enhanced collaboration tools and groupware in place and everyone in the organization has access to these tools.

9. We encourage informal interaction across departments and functions and have an 'open access' policy for everyone in the organization.

10. Most of the time, most of our people feel pride in their work and frequently talk about work being 'fun'.
    Total

Scores

50 Congratulations! Check your perceptions with the first five people you meet. If they rate these questions the same way you do, call us . . . we would like to hear your story!

45–49 Yours is a rare organization. Somehow you've managed to do what everyone else is talking about doing. Keep up the good work!

40–44 You're on the right track but you need to open your lines of communications. Ask people (all people) what would make their work life better. What tools do they need? What information do they need? Do they understand the work processes and how they fit into the whole?

39 or less Organize a collaboration group to discuss ways to stimulate collaboration . . . before it's too late.

G. Lynne Snead, Vice President with FranklinCovey can be reached at lynne.snead@franklincovey.com

WHAT GETS IN THE WAY OF COLLABORATION?

While there are compelling reasons to collaborate, not everyone is into collaboration, not least because there are often great obstacles to be overcome – a study conducted by Kalmbach and Roussel (1999), Acenture, found that about half of all alliances fail. But not only is external collaboration prone to failure; while often less obvious, internal collaboration has its problems too, ranging from project delays due to a lack of timely responses or lack of provision of information, to suboptimal results, to things just not happening. In the following, we look at some obstacles to collaboration:

- Lack of trust and respect
- Restrictions to knowledge sharing
- Non-supportive reward systems
- One-sided benefits

> The CBI survey found that reasons for not collaborating were:
>
> - Had not really thought about it (48%)
> - Do not want to share ideas (36%)
> - No need, have all resources in-house (32%)

LACK OF TRUST AND RESPECT

If there is one key ingredient for successful collaboration that cannot be overemphasized it is trust. Without trust between the collaborating parties – be they within one organization or across company boundaries – there will be no way that the collaboration will yield the best possible results, and that other benefits of collaboration can be reaped.

In some organizations where collaboration is second nature, you might find that trusting one's colleagues is second nature, and that this may even be extended to external collaboration partners. But for people in a great many organizations, trust is not something that exists naturally – particularly if these organizations have gone through periods of change induced by mergers or acquisitions, or restructuring. Climate surveys undertaken after such a period of change will almost invariably show a reduction in levels of trust – trust between colleagues, as well as trust between management and staff. This means trust is something that needs to be built and nurtured carefully.

I would like to elaborate a bit more on the negative impact of downsizing – or 'rightsizing' as it was subsequently called when the inevitable redundancies had caused too negative an association with downsizing. Consider the atmosphere in a company that goes through 'a round of downsizing'. First people are insecure about their jobs; then they get upset by close colleagues leaving; in the end they are left with an increased workload because the reason for downsizing tends to be the need to cut cost, rather than underutilized resources. So what are the consequences?

- The destruction of trust
- The destruction of internal networks
- The elimination of slack

In times where everyone fears losing their job, they are not likely to be at their most trusting. Sharing ideas and knowledge might lead a colleague to look better or more useful, so people tend to withhold their insights and ideas – not exactly conducive to good collaboration.

Losing people through downsizing is detrimental to innovation and collaboration for two reasons. First, innovation often relies on the ability to locate people with the right skills within the organization if and when they are needed – more often than not, this relies on internal and informal networks. Such networks develop over long periods of time, and when people from the network are removed, particularly if they have been key players or holders of specialist expertise, it will take a long time to close the gaps. The second reason is that those who leave are often the more experienced and knowledgeable people, either because they are close to retirement and are encouraged to take up financially incentivized offers for early retirement, or are happily taking up redundancy packages because they know that they can easily find another job somewhere else. In their research, Dougherty and Bowman (1995) identified the destruction of informal networks, impacting on a company's capacity to successfully develop new products, as a major negative effect of downsizing.

Finally, while it is generally argued that downsizing decreases slack and duplication, more often than not the people left in the organization will feel stretched and overburdened with work. I believe that many organizations that downsize take it too far, cutting out what I call the 'creative fat'. As a consequence, people tend to be so busy that they do not have the time to contemplate, to have a chat in the corridor, to network outside their own organization, be it to attend external events, see customers or meet up with colleagues from inside or out the organization. They have to 'do' all the time. Why do I think that is a problem? Because to come up with new ideas, to make new connections and to be innovative, people need time to doodle and think. But not only that, under time pressure people tend to focus on the most urgent things at hand – this quarter's budget, this month's sales figures – and not things that are long term – as innovation initiatives tend to be.

The issue of respect is critical as this determines to which degree participants believe that their colleagues' actions and words are their best efforts. If I tell you that something can or cannot be done, and you do not respect my professional qualifications and capabilities, you may believe either that I am entirely unrealistic or that I am just too lazy or ignorant to carry out the task. More likely than not, you will try to find a way of making it happen, finding someone else to do it, get a second opinion, and so on. If, on the other hand, you trust my professional judgement, you will either trust me to get on with it, or there will be no time (and money) wasted in exploring the possibility further.[5]

RESTRICTIONS TO KNOWLEDGE SHARING

If people are asked to collaborate but at the same time are told, 'but don't give away any of our company's (department's, team's) secrets' this can create problems – not least as it undermines the development of trust which, as has just been emphasized, is essential in making collaboration work. In collaboration the willingness to share and contribute – on both or all sides – is important. If one party holds back, the other(s) are likely to do the same.

NON-SUPPORTIVE REWARD SYSTEMS

How to incentivize and reward for collaboration is another important issue. If the contribution to a successful collaboration is not part of the assessed performance, chances are slim that people will give themselves entirely to the collaboration. In the end, people deliver and focus on what they are assessed. Reward and assessment systems have to be set-up to encourage and support collaborative behaviour.

There is also an interesting discussion as to the percentage split between collaborators. Some say that it is important for someone to have a majority. Others, such as The Technology Partnership, which is our case company in Chapter 24, swear on 50/50 joint ventures. Their argument is that only equal shareholdings will result in equal interest to make the venture work. They also have the policy of joint ownership of intellectual capital – and in their extensive collaboration experience have achieved great results by following these principles.

ONE-SIDED BENEFITS

Following on from the previous point, collaboration will not work when the benefits are one-sided. The attitude 'the winner takes it all' is not one that is appropriate for collaboration. Unless both parties gain from working together, the collaboration will not be sustainable. Some companies wanting to engage more in collaboration experience that their past is coming back to haunt them. An Innovation Exchange company interviewed about their attitude towards collaboration answered: 'Our cooperation with customers is limited, and with suppliers it is quite difficult as we have generally screwed them for cost in the past.' Similarly difficult is the situation of another company interviewed, which admitted, 'Our company negotiates too hard with its suppliers, which often causes them problems during the contract period, it sometimes even means that they so bust. This means in the end we have to pay more than we would have had we been less aggressive in the first place' (von Stamm 2001).

HOW TO MAKE COLLABORATION WORK

There are a number of things managers can do to help overcome the obstacles discussed in the section above:

- Rationale for collaboration
- Open and frequent communication

- Facilitation of face-to-face meetings
- Dedicated collaboration space

RATIONALE FOR COLLABORATION

Any collaboration should be undertaken for the right reason – just because everyone else is engaging in collaboration is not the right reason – and the type of collaboration should be matched to the objective in mind. France *et al.* (2001), from Ernst & Young, recommend asking the following questions:

- Does each of our alliances align strongly with our corporate culture and business goals?

- How well is our portfolio performing, in the aggregate? Are we leveraging our alliances to capture maximum value?

- Do we need additional alliances? Are we missing key areas of opportunity? Should some be eliminated?

- Are we reaching the best universe of prospective partners?

- Does our alliance portfolio create any new risks?

If it is an external collaboration addressing a strategic need, a joint venture might be the most appropriate form. Tidd *et al.* (2001) have assembled a table that provides an overview of different types of collaboration and their advantages and disadvantages (see Table 13.1).

As everything within an organization that is to be taken seriously, collaboration requires if not the active involvement, at least the support of top management.

Everyone needs to be clear that the reason for engaging in collaborative efforts is its relevance and importance to the company's future – and not because it is the latest management fad that everyone else seems to be doing at the time. Objectives need to be stated clearly, and measures need to be put in place to monitor progress against them. The reward and assessment structure should also be designed to recognize and encourage collaborative behaviours.

Table 13.1 Types of Collaboration (Tidd *et al.* 2001) (reproduced by permission of Tidd, J.)

Type of collaboration	Typical duration	Advantages (rationale)	Disadvantages (transaction costs)
Subcontract	Short term	Cost and risk reduction, reduced lead-time	Search costs, product performance and quality
Cross-licensing	Fixed term	Technology acquisition	Contract cost and constraints
Consortia	Medium term	Expertise, standards, share funding	Knowledge leakage Subsequent differentiation
Strategic alliance	Flexible	Low commitment Market access	Potential lock-in Knowledge leakage
Joint venture	Long term	Complementary know-how Dedicated management	Strategic drift Cultural mismatch
Network	Long term	Dynamic learning	Static inefficiencies

As important as a good and thought-through rationale for entering a collaborative agreement is to think about time frames and possible exit scenarios. Is the collaboration for the duration of a project, for a certain period of time? What happens to equipment and machinery at the end of the collaboration? How are people integrated back into the parent organization? There are many important questions to be considered, not least to reassure people who are delegated to the collaborative venture.

OPEN AND FREQUENT COMMUNICATION

Open and frequent communication between the collaborating team and the parent organization is very important. The parent organization needs to be assured that progress is made against set objectives, and team members need to be reassured that they are still part of the main organization.

For the collaborating team to be flexible and able to respond quickly to changing requirements, it is beneficial to limit the number of people who have to be involved in the decision-making process.

Working in a collaborative venture also means that you bring together different cultures, which is bound to lead to some conflict. It is therefore important that structures are in place which allow for these conflicts to be resolved, including mechanisms for constructive feedback.

FACILITATION OF FACE-TO-FACE MEETINGS

Trust requires a degree of familiarity, and familiarity cannot be built via email or through video conferencing. So to build trust and allow mutual respect to grow, there is only one way: facilitate face-to-face meetings so that those who are expected to work together have the chance to get to know each other.

If you cannot allocate people to the collaboration whose reputation precedes them, you might want to try to find ways that allows collaborations to respect each others' expertise. One way might be to organize exhibitions or presentations of their work, another to develop a game or simulation that allows participants to display their expertise (without 'showing off').

You may also want to consider the use of facilitators to start the collaboration off. One Innovation Exchange member commented on their use of teams, 'We have a strong commitment to teams and this year we are using extra facilitators to help our teams work together – teams don't just happen.'

DEDICATED COLLABORATION SPACE

In addition to supporting the process of collaboration through facilitators, organizations should provide some space where collaboration partners can meet and work together. If such space cannot be allocated to the team for the entire course of the collaboration, it should at least be made available at frequent intervals. IDEO places great value on its project spaces. All project teams have a space dedicated to their exclusive use. One of the benefits of dedicated space is that everything to do with the project can be left on display. IDEO find that it helps people to start where they have left off, and it also has the added benefit of allowing others to come in and contribute their ideas – particularly as there are always some prototypes around (see also the previous chapter).

It is also important to understand that collaboration spaces are different from other office space such as meeting rooms or workstations. The layout of the room should facilitate and encourage collaboration, offering whiteboards, easel pads, pens and sticky notes, and a selection of tables and chairs chosen for comfort rather than adherence to office furniture norms (see Box 13.4).

BOX 13.4   What Collaboration Rooms should Convey (Snead and Wycoff 1996) (reproduced by permission of Snead, L. & Wycoff, J.)

Beauty – Goethe recommended that every day you should read some poetry, see a beautiful picture, get into nature so that we don't lose the sense of the beautiful that's in all of us.

Fun – Play is an important part of creativity and collaboration. Fun breaks down barriers and frees us from the inhibitions that keep us 'in the box'. Bean bag chairs, toys, bright graphics, crayons and silly hats all help create an atmosphere of fun.

Abundance – Of snacks and drinks as well as all kinds of stationery.

Tools – For example, internet connection, a computer with mindmapping and project management software, a printer, an overhead projector and VCR.

In his book *Orbiting the Giant Hairball*, Hallmark's jester and 'creative paradox',[6] Gordon MacKenzie describes how he created the space of the creative design group he led. Instead of selecting from the company's office furniture catalogue, he went to antique shops collecting rolltop desks, using stained glass windows and doors as space dividers and milk cans as wastebaskets – even if getting the milk cans, which were not on the list of approved furniture, past the accountants required declaring them as part of the company's art collection! The environment was not only much more imaginative than any standard office environment, it also cost 20% less.

Exactly how much structure needs to be provided will vary from company to company, and according to the individuals involved. Companies who are used to collaboration and people with tolerance for high levels of ambiguity will need less instruction and structure than those who do it the first time (see Box 13.5). However, too much structure and bureaucracy can prevent people from focusing on the task at hand, being too busy managing the bureaucracy and reporting requirements.

BOX 13.5   Collaboration between TTPcom and Hitachi SIC

The set-up

- Mutual compatibility: one had what the other needed

- Royalty based building on a common objective

- Joint intellectual ownership to ensure each party would be equally interested and protectionism in engineering teams would be dispelled

- Broad areas of responsibility (not bogged down in detailed definitions as to who does what)

▶

Getting started

- Teams were established with complementary as well as overlapping skill sets and direct links from engineer to engineer

- Started by bringing the two teams together for four weeks

- Six face-to-face meetings per year

- Audio and video conference calls

- Both parties being aware of other culture's specifics

- Use of simple English

- Ask face-saving questions etc.

- Working with secondment to transfer skills

READING SUGGESTIONS

A Question of Culture? Collaborative Innovation in UK Business, CBI in cooperation with 3M and the Design Council, February 2001

Comment: This report provides insights into what differentiates innovative from less innovative organizations, focusing on culture and collaboration in particular. To obtain a copy please contact the Confederation of British Industry, Centre Point, 103 New Oxford Street, London WC1A 1DU

Doz, Yves and Hamel, Gary (1998) *Alliance Advantage: The Art of Creating Value Through Partnering*. Boston, MA: Harvard Business School Press

Comment: The book introduces three possible approaches to creating value through alliances, and shows how they evolve over time. Illustrated through case studies on companies such as Xerox, JVC, Corning, Siemens, Airbus, GE, Thomson, Boeing and many others

NOTES ON CHAPTER 13

[1] However, there are also 4% of firms which had undertaken a small percentage of their development work with direct competitors in the past, but indicate that they would not do so in the future.

[2] Press Information 25 March 2002, from Philip's website http://www.philips.com.

[3] A consequence of downsizing with negative implications for a company's ability to innovation, the destruction of trust, is addressed in the section on what gets in the way of collaboration.

[4] Much of the discussion on the collaboration with external designers in Chapter 28 is relevant to collaboration with external partners more generally.

[5] I would also like to emphasize that highly innovative teams will make possible what others have believed impossible before. Accepting and respecting someone's expert opinion should not be confused with giving up at the first hurdle.

[6] This was a title Gordon created for his job at Hallmark's headquarters – read the book to find out what it entailed!

14 Innovation and Industry Context

CASE STUDY 5: ROCHE–SAQUINAVIR

1995 – A NEW CLASS OF HIV ANTIVIRAL

On 6th December 1995 the US Food and Drug Administration (FDA) cleared Roche's new HIV drug, Invirase ® (saquinavir), for use in combination with approved nucleoside analogues for selected individuals with advanced HIV. This decision to approve Invirase as quickly as possible was addressed in the US media as, 'Some of the most hopeful news in years for people living with AIDS. This approval introduces a new class of drugs for treating AIDS.' Until 1995, HIV therapy had been limited to the use of combination regimens comprising two drugs that were designed to prevent the virus from infecting the cell. The introduction of Invirase enabled the use of new combination regimens that would target the virus at two steps in the replication cycle – providing a 'one-two punch' approach. Like many other infectious agents, immunodeficiency viruses have an unfortunate tendency to mutate in such a way that they become resistant to individual substances used to attack them. As many as 40% of HIV/AIDS patients had failed multiple treatment regimens or had developed resistance to existing options.

While AIDS-related deaths had declined since the introduction of Invirase and subsequent HIV protease inhibitors, the number of people living with HIV continued to grow. The use of triple combination therapy, pioneered in Roche's Phase III clinical trials, became known as HAART (Highly Active Antiretroviral Therapy). The use of HAART therapy has been shown to significantly prolong the survival of people living with HIV, and reduce the incidence of opportunistic infections.

While Invirase provided significant clinical benefits, full potential (antiviral effect) could not be realized due to limited bioavailability of this formulation. When Merck launched Crixivan in late spring 1996, a third protease inhibitor, they focused their marketing activities against Invirase upon the greater viral load reductions achieved with their drug.

In addition, a company called Agouron had picked up Roche's patent and had managed to develop a similar compound in just five years with the advantage of achieving higher drug concentrations, and showing a unique drug

> **Criteria for selecting an ideal antiretroviral combination**
>
> - Synergistic or additive anti-HIV activity
> - No cross-resistance between drugs
> - No overlapping toxicities
> - Antiviral activity in multiple cellular and tissue reservoirs of HIV
> - Lack of adverse interaction between component drugs and other commonly used agents
> - Ease of administration

resistance profile that allowed other protease inhibitors to be used following failure of a Viracept-containing treatment regimen.

MOVING INTO HIV DRUG RESEARCH – THE SITUATION IN 1986

In 1982 an unusual collection of clinical symptoms observed in a small number of homosexual men in urban areas of San Francisco was recognized and classified as Acquired ImmunoDeficiency Syndrome (AIDS). Thereafter, the number of individuals diagnosed with AIDS increased rapidly, and it became apparent that AIDS was widespread in many Western countries and sub-Saharan Africa, and had evolved into a worldwide epidemic. AIDS manifests itself as a severe impairment of the human immune system, leaving those affected vulnerable to a wide range of opportunistic infections, resulting in a dramatic loss of weight and ultimately death. At this early stage in the history of AIDS, the life expectancy of an infected individual was around two years.

The search for the infectious agent responsible for AIDS attracted the attention of scientists around the world. In 1983 two research groups, one in the USA the other in France, independently isolated the same retrovirus, which later became known as Human Immunodeficiency Virus (HIV), the causative agent of AIDS.

Molecular cloning and gene sequencing elucidated the composition of the HIV genome. From this data, it was proposed that much of the genetic information required for replication of the virus was contained in just three distinct genes: *gag*, *pol* and *env*. From the nucleotide sequence of these three genes, a number of enzymes were proposed to be encoded by the HIV, giving scientists the first indication that it may be possible to design specific chemotherapeutic agents capable of inhibiting the replication of this deadly virus.

The sheer scale of the problem and the potentially devastating threat to world health mobilized worldwide cooperation. In 1986, six United Nations' organizations took the unprecedented step of joining forces to form the 'Joint United Nations Programme on HIV and AIDS' (UNIAIDS). Its role is to monitor, facilitate exchange and spread knowledge related to HIV and AIDS. The organization also publishes annual estimates on the spread and scope of HIV infection, as well as mortality rates, with the objective to help direct efforts to control the spread of the virus and those infected by it. From a

Scientific background

HIV is a retrovirus. Like all retroviruses, the genetic material of HIV is RNA rather than DNA. When HIV infects a cell, the viral RNA is transcribed by a specific enzyme, called reverse transcriptase (RT) into DNA which is then integrated into the host cell genome. After that viral DNA is copied to produce components of new viral particles, which are assembled at the cell membrane where budding and maturation result in the formation of a new HIV particle.

Scientists continued to isolate and study HIV from infected individuals in those areas where the disease was of epidemic proportions. It became apparent that two significantly different strains of the virus existed, which were classified as HIV-1 and HIV-2. The latter, most predominant in Africa, is less virulent.

Scientists were comparing the genetic composition of HIV with other closely related viruses in an attempt not only to trace its origin but to better understand its replication and also to identify possible model systems to facilitate the evaluation of potential inhibitory agents. The transmission of viruses from animals to humans is known but is not common and is an inefficient process. Most notable is the transmission of influenza from avian species to man, which until the 1997–8 Hong Kong outbreak was thought to require the intermediacy of hogs. Since HIV infects the chimpanzee attention turned to other primates and viruses that infected primates. There is a high degree of homology between HIV and Simian Immunodeficiency Virus (SIV) which infects the African green monkey. This led to the suggestion that HIV may be derived from SIV that may have crossed the species barrier as early as the 17th century and emerged as HIV in the 1930s.

few known cases in the early 1980s, the number of people living with HIV and AIDS was estimated by UNIAIDS and the World Health Organization (WHO) to have grown to 36.1 million worldwide by the end of 2000, with 1.4 million of them being children. This equates to approximately 15,000 new infections every day. The geographic region most affected by HIV is sub-Saharan Africa, with about 70% of all known cases. A further 16%, or 5.8 million, live in South and South-east Asia.

The first two drugs on the market, Retrovir® (or ATZ) introduced in 1987 by Burroughs Wellcome and Hivid® introduced in 1992 by Roche, were both designed to hinder the viral RNA from being transcribed and integrated into the cell. However, they could not prevent the virus from reproducing once the cell had been infected. Other concerns were that these drugs could only be taken in relatively small quantities, as they tended to interfere with the metabolism of human cells, causing side effects such as diarrhoea, vomiting, nausea, fatigue and headaches. In addition, problems started to occur with strains of the HIV that had mutated in such a way that they had become resistant to the drug.

ROCHE TAKES UP THE GAUNTLET

Even in the mid-1980s the speed with which the virus was spreading focused pharmaceutical companies' attention on the problem. All major pharmaceutical companies seemed to be racing against time and each other to find an angle that would allow them to be first in bringing an HIV drug to market. In late 1985, around the same time Glaxo and SmithKline started to engage in research into HIV, Roche's antiviral chemotherapy group in Welwyn, UK, initiated a programme to develop a drug that would prevent the virus from entering the cell. There were also rumours that Burroughs Wellcome was about to introduce an HIV drug.

In May 1986 the current status of the AIDS pandemic was discussed in Roche Nutley with a call for a corporate commitment to AIDS research and the formation of an AIDS task force. Various aspects of research into AIDS therapy and diagnosis were assigned to different Roche research centres. It was decided that Roche Discovery in Welwyn would take on the HIV protease and reverse transcriptase as therapeutic targets. The prior

Rick Kramer, a Roche scientist working in collaboration with the American health authorities performed experiments into which parts of HIV could be produced in yeast cells. In these experiments he deleted parts of the virus to see what effect that had on the other components. He showed that deletions in one gene, suspected of being a protease by analogy with the SIV gene, prevented proteolytic processing of the *gag* and *pol* gene products. This confirmed that the virus encoded a protease which had an essential function in virus maturation and he proposed that this protease could therefore represent a target for an anti-HIV drug.

Protease acts like a pair of scissors cutting into pieces the long protein chains produced by the cell under the influence of the virus. These pieces are needed for the production of a new virus that bursts out of the host cell and then infests new cells. If the protease fails to do its job the resulting immature virus particles are non-infectious.

experience of many Welwyn chemists and biologists in the inhibition of proteases from sources other than HIV underpinned this decision.

Chemist Joe Martin, who had set-up Roche's virology department in the early 1980s, remembers, 'Management told us to drop everything else, I guess about 80% of the virology team were working on or were even dedicated to this project.' It was clear that the input of both chemists and biologist, both located in the same building, would be essential. The first task of the chemistry group, headed by Joe, was to review all molecules to identify possible targets that would allow preventing the virus either from entering the cell or from reproducing. One problem when developing a drug is to find an area for attack that is as specific as possible. If a sequence of events is targeted that can be found in aspects of human biology, then healthy cells will be attacked along with the targeted ones, leading to high levels of toxicity.

Information about the structure and function of HIV protease was far from complete when the inhibitor programme began in 1986. The virology team in Welwyn had little prior experience with protease biochemistry, although there was considerable experience in Welwyn in related areas. Some clues could be obtained from a study of similar viruses in birds and Ian Duncan, a senior virologist at Welwyn, was able to suggest potential cleavage sites, including one that was particularly unusual.

It was the unusual one that caught the imagination of the scientists. From Ian's perspective, the enzyme responsible for splitting the viral proteins up into building blocks for a new virus seemed a good starting point, but he felt that he needed input from a colleague to assess biological aspects. Scientists from all backgrounds had been discussing their work on HIV all the time, and from their internal networking they knew that biologist Noel Roberts had worked for the past 12 years on the biochemistry and inhibition of proteases other than HIV. Noel was invited to join the team to advise and participate on that aspect of the work.

Noel recalls, 'I started by investigating the literature and did some thinking and then gave my thoughts to management. In my view it was essential to get the

The protease had been provisionally classified as an aspartic protease on the basis of an Asp-Thr-Gly amino acid motif in its sequence but this was not confirmed and there was a problem in that all previous aspartic proteases contained two such motifs and this contained only one. The possibility of the enzyme being formed from two identical subunits was proposed and later confirmed by x-ray crystallography.

The cleavage site specificity of the enzyme was also unknown, i.e. between which amino acids did the enzyme cleave the *gag* and *pol* proteins? One of the cleavage sites suggested by Ian Duncan was the unusual cleavage between the amino acid pairs Phe-Pro and Tyr-Pro. (The cleavage sites that Ian Duncan speculatively proposed were later confirmed by researchers in Roche Basle directed by Jan Mous.)

They had no HIV protease in a test tube to inhibit (no one had achieved that at the time), there was no assay to test for the inhibition of the enzyme once they got it, and no test for the inhibition of whole HIV replication (a special high containment laboratory would have been required to work with whole HIV and Welwyn did not have such a facility at that time).

enzyme into the test tube so we could start working on it.' He observed that the unusual cleavage sites, between Phe and Try-Pro, were unique for HIV and similar virus proteases, and that no human proteases, including the mechanistically similar human aspartic proteases, could make such cleavages. Thus, an inhibitor of HIV designed using chemistry based on the amino acids Phe-Pro should be able to produce an inhibitor of HIV protease which would not inhibit the human proteases. This was important as unwanted inhibition of human proteases could result in drug toxicities.

Thus the strategy was set. However, it was largely based on hypothesis, and on the belief that they would be able to achieve a number of significant scientific challenges. When the teams presented to the Hoffman La Roche Senior Research Management Team in October 1986, the project was fully approved. The timing of the programme was very tight and required simultaneous working on several aspects at once, each group working on the assumption that all the other groups would be successful. The programme that was agreed to in November 1986 read as follows:

1. Clone and express enzyme (protease) and demonstrate cleavage of Phe-Pro in a peptide (short piece of protein) substrate (mid-1987).
2. Purify enzyme; develop a rapid assay; achieve a potent and selective inhibitor (mid-1988).
3. Demonstrate antiviral activity (end 1988).
4. Select a drug candidate (end 1990).

After that a method for the large scale production of the compound would need to be found and clinical trials would be the final testbed for the quality of the drug.

TACKLING THE CHALLENGES

'In 83 the virus had been completely unknown and by 89 it was probably the best understood virus in the world. To be part of this activity was exciting, to make headway even more so.'

To take their investigations further they needed the enzyme. But as it was not possible at the time to grow HIV to get the enzyme – not least because no one

Attempts to clone and express the HIV protease in a bacterium (E coli) using molecular biology techniques were pursued simultaneously by Jan Mous in Basle and by Mary Graves and her group in Nutley; Noel Roberts with help from peptide chemist Raj Handa, set about devising an assay to first detect the activity of the protease and then to assay its inhibition; Ian Duncan established a collaboration with St Mary's Hospital Paddington which had the facilities to set-up an antiviral assay using HIV and Joe Martin and his chemistry team started to make at first relatively simple compounds which could provide the basis for an inhibitor.

Employing some very old chemistry from the 1930s, Noel showed that proline (the Pro part of Phe-Pro) at the end of a peptide would react with a compound called isatin to give a blue colour, but while in the middle of the peptide it would not. Thus, if a peptide were made with a Phe-Pro bond in the middle and this were then cleaved by HIV protease a blue colour could be formed with isatin and the resultant smaller peptide. Soon, bacterial cultures potentially containing genetically engineered HIV protease were coming from the Basle and Nutley labs. In September 1987 a bacterial lysate (broken-up bacteria) added to a Phe-Pro containing peptide, incubated and then reacted with isatin turned blue. They had active HIV protease in the test tube! This assay then needed further refinement to make it both sensitive and quantitative so that they could use it to assay for HIV protease inhibition with the compounds Joe's team were already making. That took about another two months.

The concept of transition-state analogues is that short peptides containing a stable dipeptide mimetics should bind competitively to the active site of the protease, thus preventing the natural substrates (*gag* and *gag-pol* polyproteins) access to the active site of the enzyme and therefore from being processed. The use of crystal structures of enzymes, with and without inhibitors bound in the active site, had been used successfully to aid the design of enzyme inhibitors in other therapeutic areas. Unfortunately, at this early stage there were no crystal structures of HIV protease. Therefore, to assist in their search for novel structures that may bind in the active site of the HIV enzyme, the team began studies to produce crystals of the protein and determining wanted to get anywhere near large quantities of live HIV – they would have to synthesize it by getting bacteria to produce it, which was a complicated process in which both Basle and Nutley were involved. After the cloning of the HIV protease had been achieved successfully, an assay was needed to prove firstly the activity of the enzyme and then the effectiveness of inhibition.

Noel decided to try to devise a colorimetric assay for the protease, i.e. one in which a colour change in the test tube would indicate the presence of the active enzyme. That would enable rapid assessment of results at least semi-quantitatively, by eye. Noel remembered about his first breakthrough, 'Between Christmas and New Year 1986 I spent three days in the lab, when it was nice and quiet and no phone would ring. It was then that I first managed to observe the formation of a blue colour in the test tube which could be used to detect the presence of the enzyme.' By November 1987 they had a working assay (test) that allowed visual assessment which meant that they could tell within a few hours whether a compound was inhibiting or not. But even nine months before Noel got the assay working Joe had developed compounds based on the link identified, and the first proteinase inhibitors had been synthesized as early as spring 1987.

When working on compounds, past experience came in handy again. Roche had applied a process, called Transition State Mimetics (TSM), before. What this means is making a chemical compound which looks to the target protease to be like molecules that it usually binds to and cleaves but which cannot be cleaved. Thus the mimetic (inhibitor) binds to the enzyme and gets stuck there – 'the wrong key in the right lock'. The challenge was to find a key that would fit the HIV protease without fitting other locks, leading to toxic side effects. In the search for such a key, the computer-based modelling tool developed by the Physics Methods Department at Roche Welwyn was of great help.

A systematic approach to lead generation and lead optimization was adopted. Some of the structures were inhibitive, but not all of them were selective, meaning that they would interfere with other processes too, leading to undesired side effects.

its three-dimensional structure. Meanwhile, homology modelling of the HIV protease active site was initiated using computer graphics which had been developed in the Physics Methods Department at Roche Welwyn. The use of homology modelling enabled the team to look at a three-dimensional structure of the enzyme, from all angles, but also to dock structures of potential inhibitors into the putative structure of HIV protease. This is an extension of the early concept of the 'lock and key' approach to the design of enzyme inhibitors.

In the lead generation process a series of transition-state mimetics was prepared and incorporated into small peptide-like molecules and evaluated as inhibitors of HIV protease. Very rapidly, a range of molecules from different structural classes were identified that had modest inhibitory activity. One of these which was of particular interest because of its novelty and small size (a tripeptide analogue) was considered a lead structure.

The next step was to begin the lead optimization phase. First, six key structural features were identified in the lead structure; each of these were considered essential for activity. Next, each of the six key elements was modified separately keeping the other five constant. Thus, in this first round of optimization a number of preferred structural fragments at each of the six critical sites in the lead structure was identified. The next phase of lead optimization was to assemble individual molecules each containing permutations of all of the best fragments into individual molecules. It was very satisfying to find that the contribution of each of the

A systematic process of chemical modification to the lead Phe-Pro mimetic structure was guided by assaying the potency of the compounds to inhibit HIV protease and their activity against whole HIV. Potent inhibitors were rapidly achieved and, to a large degree, potency against the enzyme was accompanied by potency against the virus. Potency as an antiviral in the test tube is only part way to identifying a drug candidate. The compound must also have an acceptable pharmacokinetic profile (i.e. if you take it by mouth does it get to the parts of the body where it needs to act in sufficient concentrations to be effective), and it needs to have low (ideally no) toxicity. Two or three potential development compounds had been identified by the autumn of 1989.

To get to this point the team had synthesized about 250 compounds; normally they would have expected to have made thousands. From the decision to commence the project to this point it had taken the team only about three years though Joe points out, 'At that time is was incredibly fast and we were even three months ahead of schedule but today things can be done even quicker, mainly due to advances in technology.'

Patenting, of course, was a critical activity, but it also presented some difficult decisions. A patent can be filed immediately after the discovery has been made, but this sets the clock ticking. Alternatively, one can delay filing which will give a longer protection period after marketing. Also, the longer patent filing can be delayed, the stronger the patent can be made by inclusion of additional examples. The downside of delaying is that the competition might file a patent first, which means they would have sole rights to the invented compounds. As competition was fierce in this field, a patent was filed in 1988, covering the genetic aspects of the Roche inhibitors, but the team's preferred compound was specifically claimed in a new patent filed in December 1989.

During the entire research phase less than 10 g of material had been available, with most of the in vitro studies having been completed with no more than 25 mg.

optimized fragments was additive when incorporated into a final molecule. We then had a number of compounds that were very potent inhibitors of the HIV protease. This was the first step towards finding a medicine to inhibit HIV infection.

The next stage involved evaluation for antiviral activity in a cell-based assay that had been set up in collaboration with scientists at St Mary's Hospital, Paddington, London. Again, it was very gratifying to find that the very potent inhibitors of the HIV protease display excellent activity in the antiviral assay. Furthermore, there was a good Structure–Activity Relationship (SAR), that is, the level of activity in the antiviral assay followed in parallel the potencies in the enzyme assay. This was another major advance in the project. Next, it was important to assess the compounds for selectivity and hence potential toxicity. Since there were no animal models available to assess the toxicity of these inhibitors the team took a different approach to assess the toxicity potential. Collaboration was established with Prof John Kay, an expert on mammalian aspartic proteases, at the University of Cardiff. Prof Kay measured the potency of the optimized compounds against a panel of important human aspartic proteases, which gave the Welwyn group a measure of the toxicity potential of their inhibitors. Yet again, they were delighted to find that their potential development candidates were totally selective for the viral enzyme. Thus, none of the compounds inhibited any of the key enzymes in Prof Kay's panel of important human enzymes.

The next step was to select one of the compounds to be the development candidate. A key step was to determine whether any of these compounds had sufficient oral bioavailability to enable the molecule to be taken in tablet form and achieve adequate levels of substance in the blood to be an effective anti-HIV agent. A number of studies were carried out in rats, dogs and monkeys from which it was concluded that these compounds did achieve adequate blood levels to be an effective drug. At this point the compound whose code number was Ro 31-8959 was considered to be the likely development candidate.

DEVELOPMENT – FROM TEST TUBE TO MASS PRODUCTION

Noel recalls, 'In autumn 1989 we had two or three components but one seemed to work best, it was more potent than the others. The problem with that compound, Ro 31-8959, was that it was the chemically most difficult to produce. We had a meeting, myself, Joe, Ian Duncan, David Clough (director of research who had given the project unlimited support throughout) and Peter Machin, director of chemistry. Intuitively we all wanted to go for the most difficult one, but it was really for Peter to decide whether it could be produced on a large scale. Most of the building blocks were able to be purchased or readily prepared, but the decahydroisoquinoline moiety that replaced the proline residue found in the substrate was extremely difficult to make.'

Even though the synthetic tractability was not proven at that time and, on the contrary, it was expected to be rather difficult if not impossible, nevertheless, and despite the fact that only one out of ten drugs that enter development makes it to market, Peter felt quite confident that they would be able to produce the compound in the quantities required and the decision was made to follow gut feelings. The compound, later to become known as saquinavir, was handed over from the research team to an International Project Team (IPT). The IPT was responsible for the development of the compound into a product and also for taking that product to market. The stages involved were: pre-clinical development and formulation, toxicity studies in animals, evaluation in healthy volunteers (Phase I), clinical studies (Phase II and Phase III), registration and marketing (see also Appendix II).

In 1990 experts in chemical process research and production chemistry found themselves confronted with the difficult task of producing the complex molecule on an industrial scale. The elements of the molecule had to be assembled in a specific order to afford the correct molecular structure. Only one out of 64 possible scenarios was wanted, which meant that ways of detecting the one desired outcome were needed. Dieter Krimmer, a development chemist based in Basle, had the task to develop a viable synthetic process that could produce saquinavir on a much larger scale than had previously been undertaken. At the time many competitors knew the compound and its structure, but all of them had declared that it would be impossible to manufacture the compound on production scale and at an acceptable cost to be profitable. If choosing the Phe-Pro mimetic as the core of inhibitors had already been considered very risky, developing a production process was now seen as an outstandingly difficult challenge.

At the same time, other companies such as Merck and Abbott had much larger teams working on similar products. Abbott had chosen to focus on symmetrical inhibitors, whereas Merck and SB were working on renin-like molecules. In fact, Roche had looked at these options as well but had, in the end, decided to focus on protease inhibition based on the more difficult but potentially more selective Phe-Pro moiety. Separately, a group of scientists in Roche at the Nutley site in New Jersey were studying TAT antagonists as an approach to HIV therapy. Both project teams identified development candidates at approximately the same time but because the protease inhibitor had a higher chance of success the decision was made to concentrate on that approach.

The challenge facing the development chemist is not simply a matter of producing material on a larger scale, but also to improve the synthesis to be more efficient by reducing the number of steps in the process. The initial synthetic route deployed in the research phase involved 26 steps, but by the time early clinical studies were being initiated, batches of 30 kg of bulk material were being prepared using a process that had been improved to involve just 17 steps. Another advantage arising from the shortened synthesis was that the time required to produce a batch of saquinavir was reduced by a third, from 15 months to 10 months.

In the early phases of research and development, the physical characteristics of the active substance does not affect the outcome of experimental studies, but by the time large scale manufacture is reached the final product has to be made available in a physical form that is suitable for the preparation of capsules and/or tablets. The physical characteristics of early batches of saquinavir were such that it was very difficult to fill capsules needed to conduct the early clinical studies. Fortunately, the problem was easily overcome and in 1991 when the production process had been optimized the final compound was obtained as a free-flowing crystalline powder.

CLINICAL TRIALS AND INTRODUCTION

Another challenge was to determine the right dose. The question was, how much needs to be given to ensure that the patient receives enough of the drug for it to be active, but not so much of the drug for the patient to experience unacceptable levels of side effects. Phase I clinical trials were undertaken with healthy volunteers, and took place in 1990.

Following the completion of Phases II and III, a daily dose of three times 600 mg was recommended, and Invirase, as the product based on saquinavir was called, was brought to market in 1995, creating the first of a new class of HIV drug.

The fact that Roche was in the process of creating a new class of HIV drug had also put the company into the limelight early in what was a whole new ball game in the pharmaceutical industry. One of the first groups hit by the HIV epidemic was the gay community. The gay community had established advocacy networks and lobbying experience, and soon began to focus on HIV. HIV treatment advocacy groups began to gain strength, their intention being to reduce the negative stigma associated with HIV, to initiate public awareness to halt the spread of the virus through education about safe-sex practices, and to pressure pharmaceutical companies and regulatory authorities for early access to life-saving medications. Initially, there was a lot of anger. The advocates were literally fighting for their lives, and there was not an established basis for communications between the advocates and the industry. As a result, there were often public displays of anger. All of the drug companies involved in HIV in the early days experienced such action, as did the regulatory authorities and leading HIV physicians.

There was considerable public pressure on Roche to make its new drug available before all clinical trials had been completed. After first hints on the development of a new class of drug had been published in 1993, demands were made to make saquinavir freely available to HIV sufferers by allowing them to participate in Compassionate Use Programmes. Compassionate Use Programmes pushed companies outside their comfort zone, as these programmes required that companies make their drugs available before clinical studies had been completed and evaluated, while at the same time maintaining full responsibility for the

In the Phase II clinical trials the drug was given to HIV-infected individuals, providing the first indications for the product's efficacy. Phase II involved double-blind studies with a total of 200 patients in the UK, France and Italy. The results were good; the number of CD4 cells (the cells of the immune system, which HIV destroys) increased. It seemed to work even better in combination with AZT (the first anti-HIV drug available for clinical use which inhibited another enzyme in the virus, reverse transcriptase). A further study took place in the US with 300 trial participants, exploring three different drug combinations. Finally, in Phase III, which began in the US in 1994, the aim was to detect clinical improvements as well as changes in surrogate HIV markers. In this study 978 patients were involved who were given either saquinavir, or Hivid (another AIDS drug from the first class of compounds – the reverse transcriptase inhibitors) or both. A second part of Phase III began in August 1994 in 200 centres in 24 countries around the world with 3500 patients (the largest combination drug study ever to be carried out in the HIV area). In this study triple drug therapy for HIV was used for the first time. This is now the treatment norm. Side effects were detected in less than 4%, indicating very low levels of toxicity. The Phase III studies showed that Invirase significantly improved the patients' clinical status by delaying the progression of AIDS and improving survival.

consequences. In addition, the usage of the drug in such programmes tends to be less well controlled and monitored than in clinical trials. Compassionate Use Programmes often include patients with more advanced stage of HIV who may suffer more acutely from adverse drug reactions. Roche was initially cautious in agreeing to such a programme. In 1993 AIDS activists had demanded that a different HIV drug Roche had been working on, based on TAT inhibition, should be released. However, Roche had refused – and later clinical trials revealed unacceptable levels of toxicity in the drug, which eventually led to the discontinuation of development of the TAT inhibitor. However, in the case of saquinavir, Roche agreed to set-up a Compassionate Use Programme ahead of approval, and the programme got under way in July 1995. By the end of August 1996 some 12,000 patients had been included.

Thanks to the close cooperation of the teams at Roche with various authorities in relevant countries from an early stage, approval of the drug was more rapid than could normally have been expected. The NDA (New Drug Application) Dossier delivered to the Food and Drug Administration (FDA) on 31st August 1995, consisting of 600 volumes and 160,000 pages, was approved in record time. Approved in the US in December 1995, by the end of 1996 the drug had been approved in North and South America, Australia and several countries in Europe and Asia.

Recognition
1995
• Roche International Research Prize
• Prix Galien (UK)
1997
• Prix Galien (Spain)
• Prix Galien (Portugal)
• SMR Drug Discovery Award
• Innovation Award (Pharmazeutische Zeitung)
1999
• International Prix Galien
• PhRMA Discovers Award (USA)

QUESTIONS

1. Drug development normally takes up to 15 years; Invirase was developed much faster. What enabled the speedy and successful execution of the project?
2. Given the situation in 1996, how would you have taken this part of the company forward?

Additional information on AIDS can be found:

> http://www.medicalfutures.co.uk/

Comment: This is the website of *Medical Futures*, a venture aimed at promoting innovation amongst healthcare professionals and facilitating the successful commercialization of these innovations. Medical Futures operates through three main channels: innovative events, a high-quality magazine and database-driven websites

> http://www.aidsmeds.com/

Comment: This website, run by people infected with HIV, offers up-to-date information on treatment, developments, readings, conferences, etc.

APPENDIX I: TEAM MEMBERS

Chemistry

JA Martin	AC Freeman	WC Spurden	MP Gunn
BK Handa	RA Hopkins	S Redshaw	JH Merrett
C Kay	KEB Parkes	JC Gilbert	IR Johns
RW Lambert			

Biology

NA Roberts	IB Duncan
AV Broadhurst	JC Craig
AJ Ritchie	L Whittaker

Virology (Roche, Basle)

J Mous

Molecular Biology (Roche, Nutley)

M Graves

Virology (MRC Collaborative Centre)

AS Tyms
DL Taylor

X-Ray Crystallography (Roche, Nutley)

B Graves

Biochemistry (University of Cardiff)

J Kay
AD Richards

Pharmacokinetics

SL Malcolm
AF Clarke
A James

Molecular Modelling

WA Thomas
A Kroehn

APPENDIX II: DRUG DISCOVERY VALUE CHAIN

10–15 years from exploratory to launch

NOTES ON CHAPTER 14

[1] Primarily based on the *Oxford Dictionary* and the *Encyclopaedia Britannica*.

15 The Effects of Industry and Cultural Context

The concerns and issues in the Roche case study seem somewhat different from those of the earlier case studies. The BBC case study the issues were about internal selling of an idea, about collaboration and, to a certain degree, considering a multinational audience. The ihavemoved.com story was about branding and strategic flexibility. The Lotus Elise and the Quattro were about more traditional new product development-related issues such as prototyping, internal and external collaboration, processes and market research. Most of the above are under the control or at least strong influence of the people within the organization. Many of the influences in the development of saquinavir – industry regulations, pressure groups – were external and mostly outside the influence of the people within the organization. Understanding the context at four levels – national, industry, company and project – is an important part of innovation success. As we have already looked at aspects of company context in Chapter 6, this chapter will focus on the project, industry and national level.

WHY THINK ABOUT CONTEXT?

In recent years, people have become increasingly aware of the importance of the context in which individual products are developed as an element that should be considered in shaping the design and development process. There are a wide range of factors that can – not necessarily will – have an influence on a product's design and development process.

The terms 'design process' and 'new product development process' often assume generic applicability to a very wide range of product: tangible and intangible, large and small, involving all sorts of different skills and types of design. While I agree that the basic components of the design management and development process will be applicable for most situations, there are also aspects that require different approaches and tools, depending on the product in question. In his book, Baxter (1995: p143) compares four products along different dimensions (Table 15.1).

And, from a design perspective, these are more or less the same types of projects, i.e. most of them will require primarily product design. Having said that, the first two will also involve packaging design, the last interior and engineering design – I am sure we could find other design types too. But that is not the main point. The main point is that these projects vary considerably in terms of their requirements, in terms of what is needed for them to be completed successfully. And success here means primarily on budget and on time. (See also Chapter 25 for a discussion on success and failure.) It is important to understand the differences as it is advisable to adjust approaches, tools and techniques to the particular situation in question. For example, consensus decisions are considered to play an important role in the successful completion of a project. This is great – but while in the case of the screwdriver (again looking at Table 15.1) consensus can be achieved between all members of the team it would be more difficult for the printer and certainly impossible for the Chrysler. This might seem fairly obvious, but illustrates the issue that it is not possible to take a tool or 'golden rule' and apply it slavishly, regardless of the specific context.

Table 15.1 Different Types of Products (Ulrich and Eppinger 1993) (Reprinted by permission of McGraw-Hill Companies. From Product Design by Baxter, M., Copyright 1995 by the McGraw-Hill Companies)

Company	Stanley	Hewlett Packard	Chrysler	Boeing
Product	Jobmaster power screwdriver	DeskJet 5000 printer	Concorde automobile	777 aeroplane
No. of unique parts	3	35	10,000	130,000
Development time	1 year	1.5 year	3.5 year	4.5 years
Development team	3 people	100 people	850 people	6800 people
Development costs	$150,000	$50,000	$1 billion	$3 billion
Sales price	$30	$365	$19,000	$130 million
Annual production	100,000	1.5 million	250,000	50
Sales lifetime	4 years	43 years	6 years	30 years
Development costs/ lifetime sales	1.2%	3%	3.5%	1.5%

UNDERSTANDING CONSTRAINTS

One reason why understanding the specific context is important is that out of the context arise constraints. So in order to define its response to a particular innovation task, an organization needs to understand (a) the context and (b) the resulting constraints. The relationship between these three is shown in Figure 15.1.

Every project will face some constraints, some very obvious (e.g. a given budget), some less so, and they may become apparent only later in the process. Constraints arising from the use of a certain material or its characteristics often fall into the last category. It seems obvious that the development team should want to be aware of as many constraints at the outset as possible, but it does not seem that many organizations take the time upfront to investigate the specific context and related constraints. However, unless conscious decisions are made to address constraints, they can become an impediment to the best possible execution of a project. Constraints can be related not only to the organizational response, but also to the task itself. An example of a constraint related to the task could be the existence of a dominant design – limiting the choice of technology – and we come back to that in the section on industry context. An example of a constraint related to the organizational response might be the skills or technologies readily available in-house.[1]

While a brief generally defines the objective of a project, reference to constraints is more often than not limited to financial and time aspects. But there are generally many more constraints, implicit in the brief and arising from the company's skills and knowledge, structure and processes, competitive and market position. The organization has to take these constraints into consideration when deciding on how to approach a development task. Interestingly, it is the innovators who find ways around constraints and sometimes redefine industry norms in the process.

Figure 15.1 Development Task in Context, and Organizational Response (von Stamm 1999)

Hence, constraints need careful consideration as to whether or how their impact might be minimized or even neutralized, e.g. by changing the dominant design or employing additional skills. Generally a trade-off will be required. For example, if to get a better product you want to change the machinery involved in production you have to invest additional money. If you put more people on a project you might be able to complete it in a shorter time span – but it will be more expensive. Changing the dominant design for a product might grant tremendous income – if it is successful in replacing the existing dominant design, but will cause tremendous losses if it does not.

A reference to constraints in the context of product development can be found in Goel and Pirolli (1992). Their research into the structure of design problem spaces has identified a number of features that are overt in design task environments. They state that, 'The constraints on design task environments are generally of two types: (a) nomological, and (b) social, political, legal, economic, and so on. The latter consist of rules and conventions and are always negotiable. The former consist of natural laws and are never negotiable. However, the laws of natural law vastly undermine design solutions.'

It might be true that legal and economic constraints are negotiable in principle, but it is doubtful if the range of actual negotiability is wide. For example, safety regulations for a high-speed train will not be relaxed just because they pose a significant constraint on the development of a new train. Each product development takes place in a specific context, and there are constraints related to that context.

Gause and Weinberg (1989) refer to a constraint as 'a mandatory condition'. They continue, 'In order for the final design solution to be accepted, every constraint must be satisfied.' They perceive a constraint to be part of the specification that has to be adhered to, but I consider constraints to provide the initial boundaries for a project. While some constraints are truly unmoveable (e.g. government regulations), it generally depends on the parties involved in the development whether they seek to overcome them, or operate within their boundaries. In other words, an organization needs, first, to identify the constraints and, secondly, it needs to establish whether or not a constraint can be changed and, if it can be changed, what the costs and benefits are.

Taking a closer look at the interaction between design constraints and the complexity inherent in the design task (contextual complexity) suggests that high levels of complexity tend to be associated with 'design as technical problem solving', whereas low contextual complexity and few design constraints tend to be associated with 'design as self-expression' (Figure 15.2).

However, projects may have elements of both types of design, and a key issue in the management of design is to balance the claims of both. For example, a combination of high contextual complexity and few design constraints will

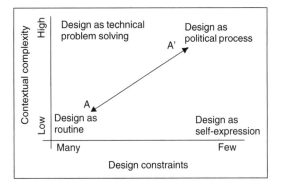

Figure 15.2 Contextual Complexity and Design Activity (based on Boisot *et al.* 1995)

require intense negotiation between the stakeholders involved, i.e. the further up the curve A-A' a project is located, the more political the negotiation process becomes and designers will find themselves confronting and negotiating with 'silent designers' (see the section on design in Chapter 1).

The distinction between design as self-expression and design as technical problem solving is made in a similar way by Crawford (1994) – albeit in a different context.[2] His concept, shown in Figure 15.3, bears some resemblance to Figure 15.2 and relating the two one could say that the 'engineer/chemist' represents 'design as technical problem solving' and 'painter/composer' represents 'design as self-expression'.

When a product is fairly new, there are likely to be only a few constraints in terms of standards and regulations. However, over time dominant designs emerge that constrain an organization's choice of technology and design, while at the same time reducing complexity. As the number of constraints on choice of technology increases, a shift takes place from a focus on solving technical problems to a focus on product features and aesthetics.

The point is, an organization should aim to match the complexity of the task and the complexity of its response. The complexity of organizational response is seen to be reflected by the degree to which cooperation and coordination are facilitated. Looking at existing research for a suggestion on how best to achieve this, one insight is that highly innovative or complex projects are more likely to be successful when conducted within a matrix structure, whereas incremental innovations can be addressed within a functionally oriented structure. Two extremes of the spectrum are represented by a functional structure on the one hand, and a matrix structure on the other.

One indication useful for determining the most appropriate choice of organizational response can be found in the 'Law of Requisite Variety' (Ross Ashby, 1964). This law states that if a problem is to be solved, the variety of the response must be equal to or greater than the variety of the problem, i.e. the complexity of a response must at least match the complexity of the problem. The line where contextual complexity equals complexity of organizational response, the Line of Requisite Variety, represents an optimal match between the complexity of a given problem and that of the response.

If a company is below the Line of Requisite Variety, it does not – or cannot – use its competencies to its full potential; if a company is above the line, the problem addressed is likely to be addressed in an inadequate way. Positioned either above or below the line the company has two choices:

Above the line:

1.   Enhance organizational response capacity to match design task complexity (either by developing competencies internally or by bringing in outside expertise).

Figure 15.3 Types of Creativity (Crawford 1994) (Reprinted by permission of McGraw-Hill Companies. From New Product Management by Crawford, C.M., Copyright 1994 by the McGraw-Hill Companies)

2. Reduce the complexity of the design task (by breaking the system down into subsystems, i.e. by devising components that can be looked at separately).

Below the line:

1. Work on products with higher complexity (i.e. of an untapped potential for adding value).
2. Reduce internal skill base (i.e. outsource less complex tasks).

Examples of products that are above the line are those that have failed to meet their performance requirements – technical or otherwise – such as the early version of the British tilting train, the Advanced Passenger Train (APT). Examples of overemphasizing the technical or design aspect of the task could be a Japanese electronic consumer product that has more features than anyone would want to use (over-engineered product), and of overemphasizing the aesthetic aspects of the task could be a building by the Spanish architect Ricardo Bofill such as the airport in Barcelona, which looks very good but is highly non-functional (over-designed product).

In other words, being on this line would mean that a company applies just the right structure, competencies and resources necessary to deal with a given task. So the relationship between the task complexity and the organizational response could be illustrated as shown in Figure 15.4.

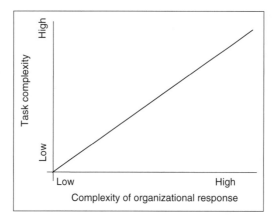

Figure 15.4 Task Complexity and Organizational Response (von Stamm 1999)

One issue with innovative projects, though, is that levels of complexity and uncertainty are often not well understood at the outset when the project structure and the key players are chosen.

CONTEXTUAL FACTORS AT THE INDUSTRY LEVEL

While the discussion above referred primarily to the project level, there are also contextual factors at the industry level that are worth considering. We take a brief look at the following:

- Professional dominance
- Speed of change
- Related to the above, product life-cycles
- Norms and industry standards
- The degree of globalization

In addition, we look at the role of different types of design in different industries.

PROFESSIONAL DOMINANCE

Different industries are dominated by different professional backgrounds. For example, fast moving consumer goods and foods tend to be dominated by marketers, electronic consumer goods by engineers, and pharmaceuticals by researchers and scientists. Why is it important to be aware of that? Let's say that you are an organization that has its roots in science, with scientists' values dominating the company culture. According to some interviews I conducted, scientists tend to view collaboration as a sign of incompetence. If this is the case, how likely are we to get high-quality internal and external collaboration? And given that collaboration is a cornerstone of innovation, it is important to be aware of potential internal resistance, and the underlying reasons for it.

SPEED OF CHANGE

A critical influence is the frequency at which new products are brought to market. Think about the computer industry with products introduced today being out of date tomorrow – and Moore's law about computing power doubling every 18 months – whereas the car industry experiences much longer product life-cycles. Short product life-cycles require different structures, processes and approach than long cycles. To me it seems that aesthetic aspects fall by the wayside of short-lived, technology-driven products such as computers. Is the success of the new Apple due to its technological superiority or its different, appealing design?

But increased speed is not only observed with regards to individual product introduction rates. It seems that more generally the pace of change in business is increasing, requiring organizations to respond to it and adapt. Changes can be induced from within an industry, but they are more likely than not triggered by an event outside. Again, participants in the anniversary celebrations of the Innovation Exchange named 'unexpected competition from outside their own industry' as one of the major challenges of the future. The internet has been enabled by computer technology – but think about the industries on which it has had an impact: retailing, banking, and so forth. So it is not only about bringing products to market faster, it is also about addressing, responding to and countering changes in the wider industry environment quickly.

One word of caution, though. Managers often seem to be so caught up in the desire to bring products to market as quickly as possible that shortcuts are taken. But taking shortcuts, particularly during the early stages of a project can have time consuming and costly consequences later on. As Aristotle said, 'Understanding the problem is half the solution.' So managers urging project teams to go straight into developing solutions would be better advised to ask the team to verify first that the problem thought to be the issue is indeed the problem for which a solution should be sought. Speed not haste is the motto.

LIFE-CYCLES AND INDUSTRY NORMS

Product and industry life-cycle have already been referred to above, but I'd like to look at them in a bit more detail. They are important for two reasons. First, they determine on what aspect of a product an organization focuses its effort to compete successfully, e.g. technology or features, product or process. Secondly, they influence the number of players within an industry. At the birth of a new product category or industry, there will only be a few players. If the new category is profitable, more players are likely to enter the scene. With increased competition prices decline, often leading to a phase of mergers and acquisitions, i.e. a reduction in the number of players (see Figure 15.5).

Demands on product development will change over the five stages of a product's life-cycle (development, introduction, growth, maturity, decline). With the maturation of the product, a better understanding of customer's

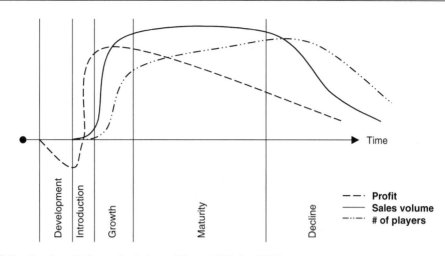

Figure 15.5 Product Life-cycle (adapted from Wright 1998)

requirements and an associated shift from product to process innovation demands on product development change and different skill sets are required. This is as true for the overall skill mix in general as for the design skills in particular. But not only that, as Henke et al. (1993) state, 'As the product moves through its life-cycle, fewer functional areas tend to be involved on a continuous basis.'

The Sony Walkman may serve as an illustration of design skill requirements changing over time. In the early phases the miniaturization of the technology was the major concern, i.e. developing components small but powerful enough to satisfy both the space constraint and quality of sound. Hence, the main focus was on engineering design and technical aspects of the product. At a later stage, when Sony modified the product to capture different market segments – a Walkman for different activities such as jogging, a waterproof one, one for different customer segments, i.e. for children, and so on – industrial design or even graphic design (packing) became most important.

A further phenomenon of a product's life-cycle is the emergence of a dominant design. A dominant design is a single architecture that establishes dominance in a product class. It reduces uncertainty, permits firms to design standardized and interchangeable parts and to optimize organizational processes for volume and efficiency. However, at the same time it also limits the number of choices a company can make in pursuing the development of a particular product. As a consequence of the reduction in uncertainty and a better understanding of the technology, which are characteristic of the emergence of a dominant design, organizational standards, systems and managerial practices evolve.

But the very fact that makes the development of products easier and allows for continuous incremental improvements can be an obstacle to creativity, radical innovations, and openness to change. Because organizational structures, processes and procedures are established and people have become used to certain working methods and being able to rely on their existing knowledge, there can be a tendency to continue working in old ways despite the context having changed.

We have talked about the fact that the emergence of a dominant design causes a shift from a focus on solving technical problems to a focus on product features and aesthetics. Similarly, Tushman and Anderson (1986) describe a shift from radical to incremental innovations over the course of a product's life-cycle. This shift is generally driven by a change in market dynamics, whereby the basis for competition shifts from product innovation to product improvement and differentiation, implying a stronger focus on product features and styling.

A further shift associated with a product's life-cycle briefly mentioned above is that from a focus on product innovation to a focus on process innovation. Tidd et al. (1997) comment on the fact that different stages of a product's life-cycle are associated with different foci for innovation. While early phases are seen to be characterized by rapid and frequent product innovation and an emphasis on variety, later stages are more likely to be characterized by a fairly stable product concept and a stronger emphasis on process innovation.

Similar to products, industries go through life-cycles too and the number of players competing in any industry generally depends on the stage of its life-cycle. Think about cars. In the beginning, there were few who believed in the future for the car, it was a product for the rich and famous. With time, more and more competitors entered the market, unit cost came down, and with advancements in other areas (production lines, etc.), the number of cars on the road began to increase. And now, about a century later, we have just been through a phase of consolidation, the latest being the merger of Daimler and Chrysler. An example of a new industry opening up is the world wide web.

Industry norms and standards I would also consider here. While not all of them are binding, adhering to them is often seen as minimum requirement from the customer's point of view. You may be familiar with the concepts of 'qualifier' and 'order winner'. The former refers to a criterion that the minimum requirements that have to be fulfilled in order for consumers to consider the product at all, the latter refers to characteristics that sway the consumer's decision in favour of a particular product. Adhering to industry standards and norms is generally considered to be a 'qualifier'. For example, a survey undertaken by the London Business School in 1996 (Temple and von Stamm 1996) showed that the two most important reasons for introducing ISO 9000 were (1) company reputation, and (2) customer requirement.

GLOBALIZATION

We have already talked about globalization and its implication for innovation in Chapter 4. With increasingly instantaneous exchange of information and falling trade barriers, organizations need to look beyond their own national boundaries to understand what is going on in their industry. Even products that were formerly perceived to be tied to national boundaries, such as perhaps cement, have to compete on an increasingly international basis. So while there are still products that are designed for and bought in a local market, the internet and travelling make it increasingly likely that the number of products to which

> **No more local goods?**
>
> On the contrary, products will be sold across countries *because* of their local association: potatoes from Jersey, maple syrup from the east coast of the US, white consumer goods from Germany. Why else do most products have a label declaring where the product has been made?

such conditions apply will shrink. Competition comes not only from within the own national boundaries, it can come from any other country around the globe. Even for perishable products such as fruit, butter and milk. Makes me wonder what kind of processes these products go through to arrive in our shops looking fresh... In terms of product development, it means primarily that for gathering market intelligence companies need to cast their net wider.

TYPES OF DESIGN AND TYPES OF INDUSTRIES

The four aspects above – professional dominance, speed of change, life-cycle and industry norms, and degree of globalization – will vary from industry to industry. Another aspect that varies from industry to industry is the kind of design services that are typically used. We briefly look at different types of design likely to be most used or most appropriate in the following:

- fast moving consumer goods
- white consumer goods
- investment goods
- luxury goods
- pharmaceutical products
- services
- non-profit and government organizations

FAST MOVING CONSUMER GOODS

Fast moving consumer goods, packaged consumer goods, and foods will most likely have significant input from packaging and brand design. More recently, structural packaging has gained popularity, and often means that the packaging is becoming part of the product offering, e.g. pump-sprays being used instead of the chemical, environmentally harmful versions. Products are sold based on the strength of their individual brand – often consumers don't even know which company is behind the product. Or would you necessarily know who is behind Bounty, Ariel or Pear's Soap? The success of such products is generally quite sensitive to the advertising spend. Such products are purchased frequently, and repeat purchase generally depends on the quality of the previous experience.

WHITE CONSUMER GOODS

In terms of design, white consumer goods will require input primarily from engineering and industrial design. Bought less frequently, they rely more on the reputation of the manufacturing company. Quality and reliability are traits for which many a consumer is willing to pay a premium. However, it also seems that these products are often particularly technology driven which can mean that design aspects – usability, aesthetics, sometimes even functionality, may suffer. Think about washing machines with endless programmes no one ever uses, or the confusing number of buttons of a remote control. However, companies that can combine great technology and great ergonomic and aesthetical design, such as Apple or BMW, are on to a winner.[3]

INVESTMENT GOODS

Even more so than with white consumer goods, investment goods rely on the quality of the engineering design, and company reputation is even more important. Solutions are often bespoke and one-off (plant and machinery). Here 'how it looks' is even more frequently compromised for technical capability and functionality. Managers in such companies often underestimate the contribution design can make to functionality, and user friendliness.

LUXURY GOODS

I have listed this category separately, even though you can find top-of-the-range products as a subsegment in most of the other categories too. This is probably the category where the aesthetics, quality and brand name are most important. The brand name is often that of the designer behind the luxury brand/company – think about fashion houses. Succession and institutionalization of the brand name can be difficult challenges facing such organizations. Products are bought not only for what they are, but perhaps even more importantly, what they stand for. It is often the lifestyle represented by the product that customers acquire. People are willing to pay a premium to be seen to be part of the club. I sometimes wonder whether it is perceived rather than actually quality than persuades people to buy... It is interesting to note that the association you buy with a product seems to become more and more important.

PHARMACEUTICALS

Again, I feel this merits a separate category as specific conditions apply here: long development lead-times, high R&D expenditure, the reality of patent implications. Many products are dependent on being subscribed by doctors, which means that the end-user and 'purchasing unit'. (e.g. the doctor) are different. This has implications for marketing and advertising. Unlike prescription drugs, over-the-counter (OTC) products rely increasingly on graphic and packaging designers to help sell their products. The quality and success of the product depends primarily on the quality of the R&D staff. At least in prescription drugs design (by designers) plays a very limited role. Having said that, if the drug is administered through a device as is the case with asthma inhalers, involving industrial designers can be of huge advantage.

SERVICE PROVIDERS

Here people often think that design is not so important – but have you tried to fill in any forms of insurance companies or banks? How many times have you despaired at nonsensical questions or bad layout? It is here that graphic design plays an important role and can make a huge difference to the perceived quality of the service.

NON-PROFIT ORGANIZATION (INCLUDING CHARITIES AND GOVERNMENT)

Design here takes probably mainly the shape of graphic design (publications, posters, etc.) and architecture. One difference I can think of is that such organizations need to ensure more than others that any design reflects 'political correctness', or is aligned with and representative of what the organization stands for. If Greenpeace were to use highly glossy brochures it would make their arguments less credible. I would like to emphasize the 'even more so', as all good design should support the image and value of the organization it represents.

CONTEXTUAL FACTORS – THE NATIONAL LEVEL

There are certain aspects of the wider national environment that can influence an organization's approach to design and development such as:

Economic and legislative conditions

- The overall economic conditions, i.e. boom or bust, tax and investment policy (e.g. government policy towards subsidies.

- Legislation, including patenting laws, environmental as well as health and safety regulations.

- Business-specific conditions such as company law and structure of company ownership.

Cultural differences

- National characteristics, preferences and values (culture), e.g. focus on design and aesthetics in countries such as Italy, focus on engineering and quality in Germany, focus on natural materials in Scandinavian countries, and so on.

- Attitude towards environmental issues, i.e. recycling of packaging is the responsibility of the manufacturer (in Germany), penalties on not separating rubbish (Denmark), speed restrictions in many countries, etc.

- Cultural differences at the company and departmental levels.

These aspects will be explored in more detail below.

ECONOMIC AND LEGISLATIVE CONDITIONS

To illustrate the point, Table 15.2 compares the wider political and economic environment in the UK and France. These differences impact, for example, on investment decisions and the availability of public funding for projects 'of national interest'. This means that if a project is considered to be of national importance, such as the high-speed trains, significant amounts of money are made available to pursue the idea. The risk and uncertainty associated with innovative projects are accepted – and financed – for the greater good.

But the influence of governments can come in various shapes and sizes. Not only does the attitude towards investment and subsidies have an influence, there are also regulations and legislation that can have a profound impact. Take, for example, health and safety regulations. They impact on various aspects of the design and development of new products: they can impact the choice of material, on thickness of glass for windows, fire-resistant quality of upholstery material, what materials are usable in conjunction with food, and so on. Such restrictions can act as a damper for innovation as many organizations might be reluctant to follow the lengthy and expensive testing procedures that are necessary to get a new material or technology approved. For example, to have a new and different disc joint for shaft couplings in cars approved the company would have to go through crash tests and procedures before it would be acceptable to a car manufacturer (see the GKN case study in Chapter 20).

Some of these contextual issues might be known at the outset, others will arise during the course of the development. Needless to say, to avoid costly changes later on, it is important to be aware of what might be applicable to the product in question at the outset of a development process. This is especially important for innovative products where parts are new may even need approval.

But, particularly for large scale projects, governmental influence can go beyond this. Let me give you another example from the Eurostar, the high-speed train connecting the capitals of the UK, France and Belgium. One critical

Table 15.2 Differences in the Wider Economic Environment (based on Kemp 1993)

UK	France
Conservative government	Socialist government
Hands-off approach to industry	National hi-tech projects
Let the market decide	Mixed industries
Privatization	Joint state–industry projects
Competition for capital projects	National champions

determinant during the set-up phase of the project was the involvement of the governments. As the tunnel project was seen to be highly prestigious, not least because it was a milestone in engineering history, the governments of both France and the UK were determined that 'their' companies should have an involvement not only in the development of the tunnel, but also the train that would run through it. They therefore applied pressure on the initially competing consortia from UK and France to get together and submit a joint proposal. When a bit later the Belgian government decided that Brussels too should be linked into the high-speed train network, it was more or less self-explanatory that Belgian companies would join the consortium. In the end the manufacturing consortia, calling itself the Trans Manche Super Train Group (TMSTG), consisted of ten companies, four each from the UK and France and two from Belgium. It seems hardly accidental that the split more or less reflects the split of the financial backing for the project: UK and France had a share of 44% each, Belgium 12%. This split not only applied to the engineering task, it was also applied to the design task, resulting in the British design consultancy, Jones Garrard, being asked to design the nose of the train and the driver's cab, the French designer, Roger Tallon, ADSA, being responsible for the interior and the exterior, and the Belgian designer for the toilets, overhead luggage racks and the seats. It is not difficult to imagine that the multi-company, multinational set-up had far-reaching consequences for the management and execution of the project, as well as the results.

You may think, well, does it? But, thinking about it, for the successful completion of any project cooperation between all parties involved is essential. Successful cooperation does not generally come easy, but in this particular situation it is made more difficult because the partners did not come together on their own accord. The individual companies forming TSMTG had not been selected primarily based on what they would have to contribute to the team, but because they had been part of the originally competing consortia. It was not 'what skills do we need and who has them', but 'that is who we have, who can do what'. Admittedly, the original consortium had been assembled to represent all skills required – but of course that meant that individual tasks could be performed by either a French or a British company. So a way needed to be found to split the workload that was acceptable to all. Again, the financial backing was used to decide what percentage share should be carried out by each country. As a consequence, tasks were allocated not only on expertise, but also to fulfil the quota. For the manufacture this meant that some parts were dual sourced, i.e. produced on two different sites. For example, half of the main transformers were manufactured in Stafford, UK, and half in St Ouen near Paris.

Even though the split of the workload according to the financial involvement was very fair, it also caused additional costs due to transporting components back and forth across the three countries. One example of components being shipped around several manufacturing sites was the Inverter Module, which is part of the Motor Bloc. Its odyssey is shown in Figure 15.6.

On top of that they had to overcome language barriers, and cope with geographical dispersion; which brings us to the last point, the cultural context.

CULTURAL CONTEXT

Culture is an important factor to consider. But what is culture? Kroeber and Kluckhohn (1952) give the following definition: 'Culture consists of patterns, explicit and implicit of and for behaviour acquired and transmitted by symbols, constituting the distinctive achievement of human groups, including their embodiment in artefacts. The essential core of culture consists of traditional (i.e. historically derived and selected) ideas and especially their attached values. Culture systems may, on the one hand, be considered as products of action, on the other, as conditioning elements of future action.'

Figure 15.6   Odyssey of the Inverter Module (von Stamm 1999)

In understanding the concept of culture, three aspects of this definition are of particular importance: (a) that some of the cultural patterns are implicit; (b) that those patterns have evolved over time (historically derived); and (c) that these patterns influence future behaviour. What it actually means is that people have developed patterns of behaviour that are based on their experience and influenced by their environment. This in turn means two things: first, to someone within a country, within its culture, particular traits might no longer be obvious. He or she is so used to them that certain values are built into products without questioning – that's the way they've always done it. At the national level one might want to think of engineering-driven solutions in Germany, with an emphasis on quality and durability, design-driven solutions in Italy, and so on. This means that when people go out to buy a product these often implicit values are the 'qualifiers' according to which products are selected for closer consideration. And, as such aspects are implicitly expected, they may not be raised as an issue in traditional market research – it is so obvious that no one will mention it. Similar values exist at the company level. If not acknowledged and understood, they can prove to be major obstacles to innovation.

Secondly, more often than not, people will approach a task in the way that they are accustomed to without investigating alternative approaches. Generally, alternatives are only then considered when the normally followed approaches fail. If that is true for cultural behaviour at the national level, it is likely to be equally true at the company level. This is also pointed out by Adler (1986), 'Our ways of thinking, feeling, and behaving as human beings are neither random nor haphazard but are profoundly influenced by our cultural heritage. [...] For years people have thought that organizations were beyond the influence of culture and that they were only determined by technology and task. Today we know that work is not simply a mechanistic outgrowth of either technology or task. At every level, culture profoundly influences organizational behaviour.'

It seems that organizations still have to address three issues: (a) they have to acknowledge that there actually are some cultural differences between people of different nationalities; (b) they further need to be aware that cultural differences can exist between companies of the same national background; and (c) they have to move away from assuming that one way is superior to the other. Instead, they should focus on finding ways that combine the strengths of each culture, taking advantage of the diversity. Hence, it is important to understand that there is no 'right' and no 'wrong', just different approaches, and each approach will have its merits and problems.

Within cultural differences, differences in language deserve particular mentioning. 'Language differences' here refers to the fact that different groups of people tend to use different vocabularies. Such groups of people can be defined by national or geographical boundaries, by social boundaries, by company boundaries, or even departmental boundaries. Or even worse, people with different background may have different meanings and associations with certain words – which are not necessarily shared by others who nevertheless use the same words. This can make people believe that they have established a shared understanding while they actually talk about different things. You may want to have another look at Figure 3.2 in Chapter 3. The acknowledgment of the existence of such differences is important as ignoring them can lead to costly mistakes. Language is also important in another context, corporate headquarters must ensure that a consistent and clear message is presented throughout its global operation. To quote Patrick Sim, Vice President of Nortel's Supply Chain Materials Management, as saying, 'Everyone, no matter who they are globally, must get the same information and get it in a consistent fashion' (in Zuckerman 2001).

But, as indicated above, it is not only cultural differences at the national level that have an impact. Cultural differences at the company and departmental level are of equal importance.

DEPARTMENTAL AND PROFESSIONAL LEVEL

Research has been undertaken into cultural differences between a variety of departments: between designers on the one hand and engineers and scientists on the other (Cross 1993; Dormer 1993), between designers and managers (Walker 1990), between marketing and R&D personnel (Griffin and Hauser 1996), as well as between marketing and engineering (Workman 1995). Any inherent differences have been reinforced over time through training and exposure to other likeminded people.

For example, Biemans (1993, in Ulijn et al. 2000) lists common mutual misperceptions of engineers and marketers: 'The latter believe that scientists/engineers have no sense of time, costs, service, or competitive advantage. They hide in the lab and continue developing a product without strategic planning, holding standardization and technology sacrosanct, and expecting the client to adapt. The marketers are, in the eyes of the scientists/engineers, aggressive, demanding, and unrealistic. They want everything NOW, want to deliver a product before it is ready, are always in a hurry and impatient, or cannot decide what they want. As a result, they promise more than they can guarantee, often change the specifications because they have no sense of technology, have no trust in scientists/engineers, and are not interested in their problems. Finally, scientists/engineers think that marketers focus on unrealistic targets.'

An interviewee from the Innovation Exchange research pointed out that in their experience, 'Scientists may understand the rationale for collaboration but in their hearts would not buy into it. To scientists collaboration is a sign of weakness.' For global innovation, for which collaboration is paramount, such an attitude can provide a significant obstacle.

COMPANY AND NATIONAL LEVELS

There is little doubt that each organization has its own unique style. Procter & Gamble and Unilever may both be in the FMCG business, but each has a quite different set of values and behaviours. Compatibility of company culture is an important aspect for successful inter-company collaboration, be it on a project basis, through joint ventures, mergers or acquisitions.

An additional layer of complexity is added when a company operates in more than one country in which case managers have to understand and manage the interface between their own and the host countries culture. As Ulijn et al. (2000) point out, 'When a multinational firm, such as Philips, operates in the United States, it is accepted almost as an U.S. firm since it is loosely related to the individualistic U.S. society where interaction is explicit, low context, and monochronic. On the other hand, to be successful in Japan, Philips should behave as a Japanese firm, where national culture and corporate culture overlap in a tight, collectivistic society where interaction is implicit, high context, and polychronic. High context cultures use informal implicit ways of communication, while low context cultures need to state messages explicitly in written text.'

And perhaps most significant are differences at the national level. Hofstede (1980, 1991) has written extensively on the issue of national differences. The five dimensions of culture he has introduced (power distance, collectivism versus individualism, femininity versus masculinity, uncertainty avoidance, and long-term versus short-term orientation) are used widely to understand and explain differences between cultures. For example, most Western countries are individualistic cultures, whereas consensus and group-oriented behaviour can be found in East Asian countries.

These cultural differences are reflected in how meetings are run, what form of communication is acceptable, and, especially important in the context of new product development, how relationships and collaboration are approached. Ulijn et al. (2000) cite Weggeman (1989) and Nonaka and Takeuchi (1995), who suggest that Japan pursues an innovation strategy quite different to the West. Japanese learn implicitly through oral communication, rather than explicit by written instructions. He also points out that other dimensions such as uncertainty avoidance and power distance, loose/tight individualistic/collectivistic and implicit and explicit might affect the innovative capacity of a firm, and poses the question, 'How important are uncertainty avoidance and power distance to the innovative capacity of a firm?'

When asked whether he would carry out a multinational project again, Daniel Brun, the representative of SNCF (the French railway company) on the International Project Group said, 'I would say, probably not, it's very time consuming. Trying to reconcile what I'd call Latin culture and British culture is still very difficult' (Evamy 1994). It also seems that this was the most underestimated challenge. While the differences in project management styles and design preferences were most obvious, there were also differences regarding the judgement of who the customer would be, and the wider economic environment.

Let me give you some examples from the Eurostar of the consequences resulting from differences in national culture, and a lack of understanding them.

Project management

An aspect not fully anticipated by participants – at least not initially – was the fact that each country had a different approach to project management. Differences of approach showed in the tendering process, and even more so in expectations of how the relationship between railway and manufacturer would be managed. While SNFC was used to taking a very active role in the design process, BR was used to giving a design specification to the manufacturer and seeing him, again, more or less, once the product is delivered.[4] Some of the differences between BR and SNCF are shown in Table 15.3.

Meetings

The French and British had also quite differing views on the meaning and conduct of meetings. The French would have a series of informal meetings, sounding out options and then go into a meeting where a decision would be reached without too much further discussion. The British, however, would expect to share information and facts during the meeting, have a discussion to elaborate on different options and views, and then make a decision based on the preceding discussion. The two expectations could not be more opposing. As a result, participants were confused and actual decision making took a long time.

Different design taste

Even though there might have been an element of national pride, there were certainly real cultural differences in taste. Bob Illingworth, BR's representative on the International Project Group, commented that, 'The talk about regional differences wasn't all bullshit. There were big differences in taste' (in Evamy 1994). An illustration of the 'cultural differences' in design taste might be the market testing of the seat for the Eurostar. Both the French and Belgian designer suggested a seat for the Eurostar. The two models were then market tested. Without knowing which designer had designed which seat, the French preferred the seat designed by the French designer, the Belgians preferred the one designed by the Belgian designer. Despite all the talk about internationalization or even globalization of consumer taste, and despite the fact that the European market is becoming more and more integrated, there seem to be differences in national taste that cannot be denied.

Industry journalist Michael Evamy (1994) commented, 'An excess of widely diverging advice on the design, colours and finishes in the train has left its mark. Cultural divides between the three railways were wider than anyone anticipated. The resulting entity is a frenzy of old, new, cool, warm, kitsch and hi-tech; it's all there, and the disappointment is all the greater after the excitement of the highly individual external styling.' Hence, the attempt

Table 15.3 Differences between SNCF and BR (based on Kemp 1993)

SNCF	BR
Is the design authority	Is customer, supplier is responsible for design
Approval of drawings	Design scrutiny
Loose contracts	Strict legal contracts
Established contacts are important	Lowest bid wins
Informal contacts to resolve problems	Disputes resolved by the contract
International technological leadership	—

to combine design input from three countries into a unified, well-balanced whole led to an amalgamation of design tastes, reflecting in a compromise at the lowest common denominator rather than a combination of best designs.

The customer

Finally, there also seem to have been differing views as to which customer (end-user) the Eurostar would be serving and whose marketing information was more trustworthy. Tony Howard, who was BR's Deputy Head of Design at the time said, 'The French were very good on engineering. I think we brought a commercial realism to the project. We were ahead in our knowledge of the commercial market of the future. BR had split up into sectors, so we were already tailoring the interiors of Intercity trains to be very different from, say, regional trains in North Wales' (in Evamy 1994). However, Roger Tallon, who had a different view, said, 'SNCF have been carrying out qualitative studies of their client's expectations since 1973. BR, on the other hand, have been practising a marketing of "conviction", which varies according to changes in personnel or situation.'

In the end the layout of the interior was very closely modelled on the TGV. However, the Eurostar serves a different customer profile, i.e. the Eurostar has far more leisure travellers than the TGV, and problems arose from a lack of luggage space. During the summer season, problems became so severe that the railways had to employ extra staff to administer luggage storage, and eventually had to take out some seats to provide additional luggage space.

Of course, there are many more areas where cultural differences exist – for example, another is how companies measure corporate success. But I think these examples from the Eurostar case study make clear how important it is to understand and acknowledge national differences.

I'd like to finish by referring back to the anecdote from the Eurostar case study about the pink-frosted lampshades in the first class carriages. Each side thought it was the other country's taste that had influenced the decision, while no one seemed to be happy with it. If that happens when coordinating tastes between three countries, and all of them European, what would happen to a global product?

NOTES ON CHAPTER 15

[1] This assumes that the organization is unable or unwilling to buy-in additional expertise.

[2] Crawford developed these categories when discussing idea and concept generation and identifying different types of creativity. He argues that research has identified two types of creativity (artistic creativity and scientific creativity), and that both are required to develop new products.

[3] Though, of course, it is debatable whether BMW belongs into this category or, rather, to the category of luxury goods.

[4] In this context, it is quite interesting that the English word 'scrutiny' was until 1993 translated with the French word 'approbation' (approval).

16 Informal Networks and the Management of Knowledge

Another part in the jigsaw that makes an innovative organization are informal networks. It is about knowing who to go to when you need a particular bit of information or a particular skill, who can do a particular job for you – or who is the right person to influence decision makers. Such informal networks played an important role in the Roche case study – but also in others. In the BBC case study it was Mike Milne's web-based discussion groups that helped to find people with the right skills and attitude. In the Black & Decker case it was Lawrie Cunningham knowing that Nigel Robson would take the design task and turn it into something really exciting.

In this chapter we will look at the role of informal networks for innovation, and the way managers attempt to formalize such information networks, namely what is generally known as knowledge management.

INFORMAL NETWORKS

The reason why informal networks are so important for innovative projects is that it is often not possible to identify what kind of skills will be needed in the course of the project at the outset. Therefore, being able to find the right skills if and when required can be essential.

There is one issue with informal networks: they are 'owned' by individuals, and when these individuals move on so does their knowledge. In Chapter 13 we mentioned the negative implications downsizing and restructuring have for innovation, exactly for that reason. In the past informal networks have been severely disrupted when round after round of downsizing and restructuring has taken out layers of middle management – those people who often know who knows what in the organization – and has allowed experts to leave – those who know what. People close to retirement with a vast body of tacit knowledge acquired over the working life, and those who can easily find new jobs elsewhere, specialists and experts are the ones most likely to take up redundancy and early retirement offers, leaving gaping holes in informal knowledge networks.

Only slowly managers come to realize the value of informal networks, and the consequences of destroying them. One consequence of a non-functional informal network can be the hiring of external expertise, even though the skills required might readily be available in-house (Hodgson 1999). As managers have become increasingly aware of the value of such informal networks, many organizations are now seeking to put infrastructure in place that aids the capture of such knowledge. Expert databases are one way of capturing people's areas of expertise. Hodgson (1999) has identified the following advantages of such databases:

- Elimination of rework and duplication of effort by linking together individuals working in similar areas
- A reduction in cycle time and costs through quicker resolution of problems
- Increased transfer of best practices

BOX 16.1   What Managers Should Ask When Setting Up an Experts Database (reproduced from (Hodgson 1999))

- What is the purpose of the database?
- How will experts be identified and selected?
- Will inclusion be voluntary?
- What are the responsibilities of the experts who are listed?
- What information will be included in the expert's profile?
- What keyword list/thesaurus will be used to standardize expertise descriptions?
- Will profile information undergo a review process?
- What security and access controls will be needed?
- How will data be maintained, by whom, and how often?

However, she also points out that managers establishing such a database must be clear about its purpose. Is it an experts database or a skills database that is needed? A list of other questions to be asked before starting to set up an experts database are shown in Box 16.1. Hodgson describes an experts database as selective, assuming that some people have more knowledge than others, due to their education and or experience. Such a database is used to create networks and linkages between different parts of the organization. She also suggests that expert databases can facilitate the elicitation and sharing of tacit knowledge.[1]

A skills database on the other hand is more inclusive and can provide information on just about anyone in the organization. Hodgson suggests that such a database would generally be used by the human resources department to identify personnel for project teams of particular job placements.

In my view, the problem with the expert database is who actually identifies the experts. While Hodgson suggest five possible avenues (see Box 16.2), I would argue that it is sometimes the most unlikely people who have some relevant experience, and this may only be known by a few. Another reason for being more inclusive, especially in the context of innovation, is that you may not be aware what kinds of skills you may need for an innovative project. Giving people the opportunity to provide insides into skills and expertise, areas of interest and involvement in past projects (possibly even outside work) will ensure that all that employees have to offer can be harnessed. However, this means that the database can be quite large, which makes it necessary to have search facilities that are easy to use. The last section of this chapter, 'The management of knowledge', gives the example of BP, which has successfully introduced a knowledge management database. Before we go into deeper into why the management of knowledge is important, and what companies can do about it, let us have a brief look what 'knowledge' actually means.

BOX 16.2   How to Select Experts (reproduced from (based on Hodgson 1999))

Peer recommendation
Experts are identified by their peers.

Management recommendation
Based on the assumption that management has insights into their staff's areas of expertise through annual reviews etc.

Awards recognition
Identifying individuals that have received awards, e.g. for innovation or quality improvements.

▶

Publications

Internal and external publications such as articles, patents, internal reports.

Self-nomination

Can help to ensure that an important person is not missed but assumes that everyone would be confident enough to put themselves forward.

WHAT IS KNOWLEDGE?

We can know more than we can tell.

Michael Polanyi (1966)

There is often confusion about what the terms data, information and knowledge and knowledge management mean, and how they are different from one another. Data is basically the raw material, the facts and figures, without any categorization or analysis. For the latter three, Quintas *et al.* (1997) provide the following definitions:

- Information is organized facts and data

- Knowledge consists of truths and beliefs, perspectives and concepts, judgement and expectations, methodologies and know-how (Gurteen suggest a much simpler definition of knowledge: 'Is that it is about know-how and know-why'[2])

- Knowledge management is the process of continually managing knowledge of all kinds to meet existing and emerging needs, to identify and exploit existing and acquired knowledge assets and to develop new opportunities

So knowledge is distinguished from information and data in that an interpretation is applied to it. This also means that knowledge is something that is developed by individuals, and that the quality of the knowledge depends on that individual's insights and expertise. Nonaka (1991) comments, 'Creating new knowledge is not simply a matter of processing objective information. Rather, it depends on tapping the tacit and often highly subjective insights, intuitions, and hunches of employees. The means of making use of such knowledge are often soft – taking the form of slogans, metaphors, and symbols – but they are indispensible for continuous innovation.'

He distinguishes two different types of knowledge, tacit and explicit. He describes explicit knowledge as follows, 'Explicit knowledge is formal and systematic. For this reason it can be easily communicated and shared, in product specifications or a scientific formula or a compute program. Tacit knowledge, on the other hand, is not separable from the individual who holds it, it is very personal.' Nonaka comments 'It is hard to formalize and, therefore, difficult to communicate to others. Tacit knowledge has an important cognitive dimension. It consists of mental models, beliefs, and perspectives so ingrained that we take them for granted, and therefore cannot easily articulate them.' He suggests that the ability to tap into tacit knowledge is one that characterizes what he calls 'knowledge creating' companies. The four patterns of knowledge creation Nonaka identifies are described in Box 16.3.

BOX 16.3   Nonaka's Four Basic Patterns for Creating Knowledge

- Tacit to tacit – socialization (person to person – because their knowledge never becomes explicit, it cannot easily be leveraged by the organization as a whole)

▶

- Explicit to explicit – combination (combining existing pieces of knowledge which does not really extend the company's existing knowledge base)

- Tacit to explicit – articulation (learning and sharing it with a group)

- Explicit to tacit – internalization (new knowledge becomes part of thinking pattern)

He considers figurative language and symbolism (e.g. metaphors) to be the most powerful tools for converting tacit knowledge into explicit knowledge as they provide a clear sense of direction.

The ability to access tacit knowledge is very important – but there are also problems associated with it, as Quintas et al. (1997) point out, 'Lots of what employees know (their tacit knowledge) reflects the past that we are trying to escape.' This means that existing knowledge can often hold innovation back. If people are too aware of constraints, of what is possible and what is not – or rather, what they consider to be possible or not, based on their previous experience – they might miss great opportunities to innovate. It is those who believe that the impossible is possible, despite of what everyone is telling them, who are the great innovators.

THE IMPORTANCE OF KNOWLEDGE MANAGEMENT

Lots of innovations depend on knowledge which has long been known but not applied to the current problem.

Quintas et al. *(1997)*

Minimizing the impact of the destruction informal networks through redundancies and retirement is one reason why managers engage in knowledge management. But there are other reasons while organizations striving to become more innovative should consider a formal knowledge management process. Innovation happens when making new connections, connections that have not existed before – applying laser technology to fix eye problems or using microwaves to heat food.

In his report on the Second Comparative Study of Knowledge Creation Conference, held June 1998 in St Gallen, Switzerland, Rumizen (1998) uses a Unilever case study as an illustration of the fact that 'Many organisations are beginning to recognize the need to manage knowledge assets to meet business needs.' A summary of the Unilever case study is shown in Box 16.4.

BOX 16.4   The Unilever Case Study (based on Rumizen 1998)

Unilever have realized that making its knowledge asset fully productive is one of the preconditions for fulfilling their corporate purpose, as well as avoiding the repeating of mistakes. They have identified four stages of organizational development in the management of knowledge:

1.   Sharing – improve sharing of knowledge and best practices which often involves the changing of cultural norms and creating social networks to create an open mindset.

▶

2. Leveraging – emphasize ways in which knowledge can be made more productive, including releasing experts from the routine work of re-answering frequently asked questions, and identifying ways of gaining new revenue streams from knowledge-related services and products.

3. Creating knowledge – gain new knowledge from genuine insight, creativity and the ability to recombine existing sets of knowledge in new ways. This requires a tolerance for failure, time for reflection, high levels of trust and organizational mechanisms for the cross-fertilization of different knowledge cores and ideas.

4. Competing with knowledge – examining the knowledge potential of an organization or business unit to uncover an opportunity to reposition the business in terms of competitive capability or customer/consumer value proposition.

Solving the problems and meeting the opportunities in each of these stages involves three convergent elements:

1. Knowledge processes – including identification, acquisition, mapping, storing, accessing, distributing, leveraging and using knowledge.

2. Technology enablers – including information systems, document retrieval, groupware, corporate intranet, knowledge-based systems, etc.

3. Organizational alignment – leadership is a critical part of alignment, together with rewards, roles, mindset, structure and openness.

THE MANAGEMENT OF KNOWLEDGE

The capture of 'who knows what' has become one important aspect of knowledge management. Another aspect is to store and make available any information on past and current projects, and in a way idea management[3] can be classed as another aspect of knowledge management. In fact, I would suggest that all major stages of new product development should be covered in a company's approach towards knowledge management:

● Idea management (from idea generation to idea selection)
● Development and review
● Commercialization and monitoring

I will explain briefly what I mean and why I believe it is important.

IDEA MANAGEMENT

Idea management involves the storage of ideas generated in focused sessions, as well as those coming through suggestion schemes. Keeping track of ideas, what happens to them, why a certain idea is selected, and why others are rejected can provide a powerful trail that helps understand an organization's innovation projectory. Keeping information on ideas that have been rejected as well as those that have been selected is important for two reasons. First, when the same or similar idea comes up again it can be checked why it has been rejected previously, and whether the reasons for rejection are still valid. The other is that ideas that do not fit within an organization's innovation strategy might still be great ideas, which means it should be investigated whether they can be sold off. The earlier example of the Xerox lab comes to mind, which generated so many significant inventions but where there were no mechanisms in place that allowed Xerox to capture their value.

DEVELOPMENT AND REVIEW

Once ideas have been chosen for development, again there is great value in tracking their progress. What went right and what went wrong during the development, and why? What lessons can be learned and how can they be fed back into future projects? It is at this stage that the experts or skills database comes in handy. Who has been working on similar projects, who has the right skills? Quick access to such information at any time during the project can save a lot of time and money (particularly if it helps to avoid buying in outside experts). Finally, while most organizations are getting better at generating data and information on projects due to the use of stage-gate process (though often this is not stored in a systematic and easily accessible way), it seems true that most organizations could increase their learning by undertaking 'post mortems' of those ideas that have not made it to market.

COMMERCIALIZATION AND MONITORING

But even once the product has been introduced to market, the learning is not over. What is the reception in the market, how does the product or service perform? Is there anything to be learned from competitors' reactions? Are sales or market shares targets met? And so on.

Despite powerful arguments for the use of knowledge management, many organizations struggle with it. Systems are put in place, but are not used. The most frequently used arguments as to why companies are not engaging more in the active management of their knowledge asset is lack of time. However, my question would be, is it not more time consuming *not* to manage knowledge, repeat mistakes, and spend time and money on finding the right skills if and when needed?

However, there are also some challenges for the database-based management of knowledge. Table 16.1 lists the three major ones, and suggests some further challenges.

Table 16.1 Knowledge Management – Challenges and Possible Solutions

• How to ensure consistency of the quality of information put into the system	• Provide guidelines what kind of data is to be entered, provide glossaries or thesaurus
	• Train people to use the database; one company asks people to sign a 'code of conduct'
• How to keep information up to date and relevant	• Ensure that time is scheduled for maintenance and upkeep tasks
	• Appoint a dedicated database manager
• How to make sure that learnings and insights are fed back into future projects	• Schedule consultation of database during the early stages of a project's development
	• Close projects properly, i.e. a review of activities and issues should be undertaken

Box 16.5 summarizes an interview and an article with John Browne, CEO of British Petroleum, both published a few years ago in the *Harvard Business Review* (Anonymous 1997; Prokesch 1997).

BOX 16.5   BP's Approach to Knowledge Management (extracted from Prokesch 1997)

John Browne, CEO of BP explains, 'The aim of this computer network is to allow people to work cooperatively and share knowledge quickly and easily regardless of time, distance, and organizational boundaries.'

The network consists of a large number of high-specification personal computers (including video conferencing capability, electronic blackboards, scanners, faxes, and groupware) that allow their users to work virtually, and access the company's rich database of information.

In addition BP has established an intranet on which everyone within BP can create his or her own home page which serves a number of purposes:

- Functional experts describe the experience they have to offer

- The sharing of technical data on a wide range of subjects

- The sharing of contacts

- Information about programs and processes available for technical areas relevant to oil extraction and refinement

- Space for discussions of topical issues such as how to manage the millennium bug

- Dedicated sites for each technology discipline

- Sites for the general managers of all the business units in BP Exploration and Production (BPX), listing their current projects and performance agendas

The realization that working virtually would require new behaviours meant that about one-third of the $12 million spent on the pilot programme in 1995 went to behavioural scientists.

Interesting also that signing up to the network was voluntary. Browne commented, 'After about six months, we suddenly found out that a lot of people in other groups were asking, "How do we get one?" Some people were bootlegging and buying the stuff on their own.'

In the year following the pilot Browne made virtual networking available to everyone in BP, however, they had to pay for it out of their own budgets. No one seemed to mind which means that today people from the most disparate parts of the world can work together.

But the network is not restricted to people inside BP, collaborative partners such as for example Shell in the Gulf of Mexico can join the virtual team too.

Browne states that some of the benefits of the virtual team network are quite easy to measure:

- A big drop in the person hours needed to solve problems as a result of improved interactions between land-based drilling engineers and offshore rig crews

▶

- A decrease in the number of helicopter trips to offshore oil platforms

- The avoidance of a refinery shutdown because technical experts at another location could examine a corrosion problem remotely

- A reduction in rework during construction projects because designers, fabricators, construction workers, and operations people could collaborate more effectively

BP estimates that the virtual team network produced at least $30 million in value in its first year alone.

READING SUGGESTIONS

Nonaka, Ikujiro and Takeuchi, Hirotaka (1995) *The Knowledge Creating Company.* Oxford: Oxford University Press

Comment: Classic on this subject

Polanyi, M. (1983) *The Tacit Dimension.* Gloucester, MA: Peter Smith

Comment: Might want to go back to the origins of the concept of tacit knowledge. By the way, his notion of tacit knowledge is that it is impossible to illicit, that this is what it is by its very nature

SOME USEFUL WEBSITES

www.knowledgeassociates.com.

Comment: Provides some useful articles and other information on their website, and are also organizers of a conference on knowledge creation

NOTES ON CHAPTER 16

[1] Tacit knowledge is knowledge that exists in people's heads and that is difficult to codify, i.e. make accessible for other people. It is most likely to be shared and passed on through 'learning on the job' and observation. See also the section in this chapter 'What is knowledge?'

[2] Brackets inserted by author.

[3] Idea management and suggestion schemes will be discussed in more detail in Chapter 22.

17 Innovation for the Environment

CASE STUDY 6: PLASWOOD BY DUMFRIES RECYCLING

Plastics recycling and recyclate is good for the environment and good for business. Recycled material is a largely untapped resource. It is an additional resource stream waiting to be exploited by industry and an opportunity which many businesses are currently missing out on.

Rt Hon Michael Meacher MP, Minister for the Environment during a conference on recycled plastics, London, 6 March 2000

INVEST OR SELL?

British Polythene Industries PLC, of which Dumfries Plastic Recycling (DPR) is a 100%-owned subsidiary, have always placed strong emphasis on recycling. In fact, in 1999 about

> Approximately 60% of total plastic waste is packaging which typically has a 'life' of less than 23 months.

25% of the company's £452 million turnover come from recycled products, £5 m of which are contributed by the products manufactured and sold through DPR. Cameron McLatchie, Chairman and Chief Executive, declares on the company website, 'As the leading manufacturer of Polythene Film Products in the UK we accept that we have a responsibility to manufacture products which meet recognized environmental criteria, and to produce them in a way that fully meets our social commitments.' With its business being in the manufacturing and selling of polythene products – primarily thin materials such as films, plastic bags and wrapping materials – McLatchie had recognized early on the need to recycle plastic.

In the early 1990s bpi produced about 400,000 tones of polyethylene a year, and it was felt that it should be possible to make some use of the wastage generated in the process. In addition, there had been enquiries from their customers about recyclability of PE products, most of which have a very short lifespan. It was also anticipated that legislation would be introduced to enforce recycling on a wider scale – and being able to make use of recycled material would put bpi in a competitive position.

Over the past 5–10 years the company had invested significantly in its recycling facilities – about £15–20 million in the past five years alone – but so far returns on investment had not been quite as expected. The reasons were manifold. Government regulation had not panned out the way it had been anticipated and the government's expectations of the market regulating prices had not happened – and were not likely to either with existing legislation. Instead of encouraging recycling-related industries to be established in the UK, British interpretation of EU legislation (EU Directive on Packaging and Packaging Waste) which states that in 2001 50% of packaging waste has to be recovered, resulted in much of the 'raw material' being exported to the Far East.

> **From bpi's 1999 Annual Report and Accounts**
>
> Despite years of experience in the recycling of post-consumer waste films, we have yet to see an acceptable return for this activity. The current system of producer responsibility may indeed be delivering compliance with packaging regulations at the lowest cost for retailers and packer fillers, but it has done nothing to improve the infrastructure for recycling of genuine post-use waste polyethylene film in the UK. This has a direct bearing on our post-use retail waste film plant at Heanor which is currently operating at a loss. Our agricultural film recycling plant at Dumfries survives on waste film sourced from Eire, the Channel Islands and mainland Europe, all of which subsidize local collection of material for recycling. In the UK, farmers cry out for help with their waste polyethylene films, but so far all we have is some marginal help for a pilot collection scheme in Wales. There is clearly a discontinuity in the government's thinking in this area.

The idea of recycling plastic was not new, but previously manufacturing processes had been restricted to the use of reasonably clean recycled plastic. A high percentage of

> Contamination refers to labels on plastic bottles, soil and other waste on agricultural films.

recycled plastic was highly contaminated, requiring extensive and costly washing procedures. Backed by strong senior management support, a team of bpi engineers, led by David Butler, Operations Director of bpi.recycled products, started to work on developing processes that would allow processing of stronger contaminated materials, and to identify new applications for such a material. The company's efforts, combining two previously separate technologies of washing dirty, low-grade plastic waste and recycling it, resulted in a material called 'Plaswood' which could be manufactured into multi-purpose plastic blocks. The material was used to develop a range of replacement products for items made previously from timber, metal or concrete such as fence posts, benches and pollards. In 1995 Dumfries Recycling Ltd was set-up to manufacture and sell Plaswood products.

At present there were some conflicting indicators. On the one hand, the overall cost structure as defined by legislation and 'raw material' prices meant that parts of the recycling division operated at a loss. On the other hand, there were the company's firm commitment to recycling, consumers increasing environmental consciousness and their interest in products made from recycled materials, and requests by users of PE products for environmentally friendly solutions for the disposal of plastics.

PLASTIC RECYCLING IN THE UK

Recycling: to reclaim a product after its primary use, for the manufacture of either the same or another product.

UK's Producer Responsibility Obligations (Packaging Waste) Regulations passed by the House of Commons, March 1997

Worldwide production of plastic materials has gone up annually from about 5 million tonnes in the 1950s to about 80 million tonnes in 1997, of which 3.5 million are consumed in the UK. As most plastic products have a fairly short lifespan they contribute hugely to waste disposal problems. Out of the approximately 2.8 million tonnes of plastic waste generated in the UK in 2000, about 60% or

> The legislation defines packaging as 'All products made of any materials of any nature to be used for the containment, protection, handling, delivery and presentation of goods from raw materials to processed goods from the producer to the user or the consumer.'

1.7 million tonnes are packaging waste. With landfill being the primary means of disposing of plastic waste, this is a major problem.

In an attempt to address increasing environmental concerns and the increasing shortage of landfill sites, the European Union had introduced a directive in 1994 that requested each member to put systems in place to recover 50–60% of all packaging waste by 2001 (94/62 EC). The minimum quota for each type of packaging material was set at 15%. How countries would achieve the target was left entirely up to them.

It is important to distinguish between 'recovery' and 'recycling'. Recycling is one method of recovery, others being incineration and what is called feedstock recovery, i.e. returning packaging to its original raw material or components as long as it would involve diverting the waste from landfill. These targets were incorporated into UK legislation on packaging in 1997. With waste from plastic packaging amounting to around 1.7 million tonnes in 2000 it meant that 255,000 tonnes of the total amount to be recovered (850,000) would have to be mechanically recycled into new products. For 2001 the anticipated volume of plastic actually recycled lay between 150,000 to 180,000 tonnes, well short of the target.

Plastic Recycling and Recovery Methods

- *Mechanical recycling* by producing new finished plastic products (melting and moulding, manufacturing regranulate)

- *Feedstock recycling* by breaking polymers down into their constituent monomers which in turn can be used again in refineries or petrochemical and chemical production

- *Incineration* with energy recovery, where plastics can be burnt to release electricity or heat

The UK is concentrating on mechanical recycling.

Who recycles and how much?

Raw material manufacturer
e.g. a manufacturer of sheet steel to be made into packaging   6%

Converter
e.g. a manufacturer of steel cans for the food industry   9%

Packer/filler
e.g. a company filling cans with food   37%

Seller
e.g. a retailer selling canned goods to their customers who throw away the cans   48%

(Companies generating less that 50 tonnes of packaging waste per year are exempt.)

Products made from recycled plastic

Polyethylene bin liners and carrier bags; refuse sacks; bottles; water and sewer pipes; flooring; fibre-fill duvets; audio, video and compact disc cassette cases; fencing and garden furniture; office accessories; seed trays and building insulation board. It is possible to buy scissors and knives with handles of recycled plastic. Recycled plastics are also used in multi-layer containers for fabric softeners, engine oil and paint. Even fleece clothes, e.g. jackets, hats and gloves, are made up of recycled PET bottles.

The UK legislation introduced a system of Packaging Recovery Notes (PRNs) which shares costs of recovery between producers of the raw material, converters, users and sellers, each part of the chain has an obligation to recover. Andrew Green, MD of bpi.recycled products explains that the PRN system is, 'Based on the legislation a compliance scheme has developed. It is like a non-profit making club, in the end it is the club's responsibility to ensure recycling. Members pay the club, thereby buying off their organization's obligation. The club outsources recycling to companies such as bpi.' This means that a company does not necessarily undertake any of the recycling itself, it just needs to show proof – by purchasing PRNs – that a certain amount of packaging waste has been recycled. PRNs are sold by companies (reprocessors) which turn recycled materials back into raw materials or

In establishing their recovery responsibility companies can *discount* the following:
• Packaging that is thrown away
• Packaging that is exported
• Packaging that has been used before
• Packaging a company does not legally own
• Production residues (from production process)

new products. However, Green also points out that at present the scheme is not working very well, the main reason being that the value of PRNs is very low. This means that a company taking on other organizations' obligations to recycle by selling PRNs can only realize small incomes, while on the other hand, the process of recycling is expensive and finding markets for products made of recycled plastic is not easy. Green indicated that a company would have to charge about £150 per tonne to make recycling financially viable – the price realized per PRN per tonne of material was £45–55 and £45–60 in October and November 2001, respectively.

There are several aspects of the plastic industry that make the recycling less straightforward than one might expect:

UK estimates of post-use recycling plastic in 97	
Polyethylene (PE) film	66,000 t
Polyethylene (PE) other	10,000 t
Polypropylene (PP)	20,000 t
Polystyrene (PS)	5000 t
Expanded polystyrene (EPS)	2500 t
Acrylonitrile butadiene styrene (ABS)	2000 t
Acrylics	1200 t
Polyvinyl chloride (PVC)	10,000 t
Polyester (PET)	3000 t
TOTAL	119,700 t

• There are about 50 different family groups of plastics, with hundreds of different varieties; the number of different plastics makes sorting complicated and requirements for successful recycling vary

• Methods have yet to be developed to process different types of plastic together

• Most post-use plastic is contaminated, e.g. by labels, soil, etc., and cleaning can be difficult and costly

• Plastics are light in weight which means that transport costs for waste plastic to a recycling centre are relatively high

• Quality of recycled plastic is never as good as virgin material and also more variable

• Virgin material is about £400–600 per tonne for polyethylene, recycled polyethylene costs about £300–500 per tonne

In addition, less packaging than anticipated has been used, resulting in a lower UK obligation to recycle (see Box 17.1).

BOX 17.1   UK Obligation to Recycle Plastic at 15% of Packaging Volume Predicted Versus Actual

Year	1997	1998	1999	2000	2001
Predicted	45	119	170	231	272
Actual		90	125	178	240

But there were also other factors causing problems. During a conference in London in March 2000, Keith Stenning, Group Resources Director of bpi, criticized current legislation, stating that, 'PRN funding has now reduced to a level which will only support the simplest of recycling processes. Regulations have merely sustained activity through the last plastic price cycle without significantly increasing the infrastructure of capacity in the UK.' He further referred to a study that concluded that there would be no ecological benefit in plastic packaging recycling rates above 15%, and urged greater focus on energy and feedstock recovery options, adding: 'If we are to sustain plastic recycling programmes in a free market environment we need markets and applications which can realize beneficial use at an affordable cost. If the packaging chain can not or will not support the costs of current recycling routes within the UK, and significant waste holders opt to export waste, then this not only puts the UK recycler at commercial risk but also cuts off his waste resources. Does the answer lie in low cost third world economies becoming the recycling partners of developed economies? I cannot believe that this was the intention of the global drive towards sustainability.'

While bpi has a number of competitors within the UK, the biggest threat comes from the Far East – both for the picking up of the 'raw material' (e.g. plastic waste) and supplying products which would in the UK be made out

> Today almost all carrier bags come from the Far East, and at a very good price, but most of them are made from virgin material.

of recycled material such as plastic bags (albeit that plastic bags from China tend to be made from virgin material). Andrew explains, 'The Far East seems to have an almost unlimited demand for waste plastic which keeps the price of waste artificially high. It pays to ship plastic waste over there because of the vast number of empty containers that travel back – so transportation costs are not an issue. Once over there they have lots of cheap labour they can throw at segregating the waste.' bpi used to get plastic from Sainsbury which charged them £150/t to collect it, but now it ships all its plastic recycling to the Far East. The plastic sent to China tends to be recycled into plastic pellets that are used for rigid products such as the casing of electronic consumer goods. As a consequence of the competition from the Far East, a number of plastic washing plants all over Europe have closed down in recent years.

Another distinction is important: scrap and post-use plastic. The former is 'process scrap' from industry, which is easy to recycle as the ingredients are known, and it is clean as it has not entered the waste stream. Many companies working with recycled plastic concentrate on this – and

> A lot of other companies make pellets from rigid products, under the government scheme they were getting PRNs for what they had been doing all along anyway.

have done so before legislation was introduced. It is generally recycled in-house or with a local processor. Post-use plastic, on the other hand, is defined as 'plastic material arising from products which have undergone a first full service life prior to being reclaimed'. This plastic waste requires collecting, sorting and, in most cases, cleaning, which means it is more difficult and costly to recycle. In 1997 bpi recycled about 14,000 tonnes of post-use packaging and about 34,000 tonnes of process scrap.

One of the flaws of the existing system is that it does not differentiate between different sources for recycling plastics. While processing scrap plastic is comparatively straightforward and easy, the tricky bit is working with post-use plastic. It can cost about £200 per tonne to have the recyclable material delivered to the factory alone – in

> A neighbouring plant was filling containers with plastic material and having to pay for its removal. bpi offered to take it off their hands and save them the container charges – but they were not interested unless bpi would pay them for it.

comparison, the cost for other recyclable materials such as paper, glass or steel is around £20 per tonne. The problem here is that people see post-use plastic as raw material and price it accordingly. In addition, one does not get 100% return out of the material that arrives at the plant. For example, at Dumfries Plastic Recycling they get about 40% PE out of 100% delivered material. This is due partly to the fact that not all of the material delivered is usable, partly because the contamination (a) is 'dead' weight and (b) incurs costs, as the material needs to be cleaned before it can be processed.

Other companies focus more on bottles from the domestic waste stream, which are relatively easy to separate, but machinery is expensive. Bottles tend also to be contaminated by paper, and different plastics are used in the production of plastic bottles, which means that it is generally necessary to sort bottles by type of plastic. To avoid problems arising from the mixing of different types of plastic, Germany has introduced legislation that attempts to prevent mixing at the source.

One final distinction is that between rigid and flexible plastic. Rigid plastic has the advantage that it tends to be easier to segregate and clean, and many domestic or consumer rigid plastic packaging contains an identification marking. David Butler Operations Director, Refuse & Recycling, bpi

- Approximately 40% of local authorities in the UK now have plastic bottle recycling schemes

- There are more than 3757 plastic bottle collection banks on 2660 sites across Britain and plastic bottles are collected from more than 2.7 m households

- In 1995 50% of plastic bottles collected came from kerbside collections compared with 40% in 1994

- About 95% of plastic bottles in household waste are made from PE, PVC, PET

Recycled Products explains, 'As long as products are rigid they can be sorted. For example, US grain sorters are good for sorting different coloured pellets. There are also machines that can identify different plastics. But at present there are no machines for sorting films, it tends to go all over the place.' Plastic film, even if it were marked, remains a problem as it tends to be mixed with other waste. At present, the only working plant in the UK for processing recycled plastic film is bpi's plant in Dumfries.

BACKGROUND TO BRITISH POLYTHENE INDUSTRIES

Between 1983 and 1997 British Polythene Industries had grown significantly. As David Butler, Operations Director of bpi.recycled products recalls, 'In 1987 we consisted of five to six small companies. By the late 90s, after we had completed a number of mergers and acquisitions, we had grown to 50.' The expansion of the company had started with the acquisition of Anaplast Limited by Scott & Robertson in 1987, after which its current Chairman Cameron McLatchie joined the board, which was also when the company became its current name, bpi. This was followed by further important steps:

- Purchase of PCL Recycling in 1986
- Acquisition of Visqueen from ICI in 1988 – more than doubling group size
- Merger with Alida Holdings in 1989 – moving into the retail sector
- Acquisition of Brithene Bridgewater from Courtaulds in 1991 – expanding the stretchfilm sector
- In 1992 acquisition of Novathene Films from BP – expanding the collation shrink sector
- Acquisition of Parkside Flexible Packaging in 1995 – moving into the high-quality flexible packaging sector
- Acquisition of polythene film business of Wavin and Low and Bonar – establishing significant presence on the continent and market leadership in silage stretchwrap

In 1999 bpi was the largest producer of polythene products in Europe, generating a turnover of £452 m and £27.5 m operating profit (before employee share scheme), with just under 4000 employees. The group is now split into seven strategic businesses:

- *Recycled Products*   Manufacture and sale of recycled products including refuse sacks, construction films; recycling of post-consumer waste (~19% of group turnover)

- *Industrial Products*   Manufacture and sale of heavy-duty sacks and pallet covers for the fertilizer, chemical, animal feed, construction and horticulture markets (~18% of group turnover)

- *Stretchfilms*   Manufacture and sale of film on the reel products including hand and machine pallet stretchwrap, silage stretchwrap and agricultural and horticultural sheeting (~16% of group turnover)

- *Films*   Manufacture and sale of collation shrinkfilm, converter, lamination and overwrap films (14% of group turnover)

- *Packaging Services*   Provision of services for a range of polythene-related products through manufacturing, converting and merchanting operations; products include polythene film and bags, pallet stretchwrap, paper sacks and tape (~13% of group turnover)

- *Consumer Packaging*   Manufacture and sale of polythene and paper bags for the food, petcare and consumer markets (~12% of group turnover)

- *Belgium*   Manufacture and sale in Europe of printed films, industrial stretch films and silage stretchwrap and agricultural sheeting (8% of group turnover)

McLatchie, Chairman since 1987, had always felt strongly about the company's obligation to recycle. Since 1995 the company had invested £16m in state-of-the-art recycling and film extrusion technology and, as stated on the company website, 'We remain at the forefront of innovative and environmentally responsible high-performance products.' However, David points out, 'It seems that we have made a lot of long-term investments and are taking a long-term view, but of course the city does not like that and they were seen to be weak and a takeover target.' The website further contains a statement on bpi's environmental policy: 'I consider it important that we let you know in a clear and concise manner the environmental Policy of British Polythene Industries Plc.' (See also Box 17.2.)

BOX 17.2   bpi's Environmental Policy

We will ensure that:

- *all* our products will be manufactured to conform in every respect to prevailing government environmental standards
- *we will* seek to minimize the use of non-renewable raw materials
- *our products* will be manufactured from materials which are capable of being recycled
- *recycled products* will be offered where they can be demonstrated to be fit for purpose
- *we will* provide, wherever practicable, the facilities for the collection and *recycling* of polythene film products
- *we will* be a responsible employer and a good neighbour
- *we will* manage our operations and processes in a way which respects and protects the environment
- *our operations will* conform to current legislation
- *we will* be in the forefront of developing new environmentally responsible initiatives, where it is economical and practical to do so

In 1999 the company discharged its recovery obligations on paper through the national compliance scheme, but plastic recycling obligations were met through its own resources. Seven sites were accredited by the Environment Agency, which meant that they could sell PRNs to generate additional income. However, while the legislation on packaging waste recovery had originally been thought to give this aspect of the business a significant boost, the company had to learn to the contrary at its cost.

> To be allowed to issue PRNs bpi had to be accredited, by the Environment Agency for England and the Scottish Environmental Protection Agency in Scotland. Through accrediting companies the government maintains a certain degree of control and can collect the data necessary to prove to the EU that they are fulfilling the UK's post-use packaging recycling commitment.

Deteriorating prices of PRNs and cheaper processing in the Far East meant two things. First, volume throughput was likely to go down, and secondly, access to suitable waste would become increasingly difficult.

While the Annual Report 1999 still mentioned seven sites dedicated to the recycling business, 2001 saw the closure of two, partly due to difficult circumstances in the recycling industry – competition from the Far East – and partly to consolidate bpi's recycling efforts. In addition, one of the five sites has been reassigned to the production of high-quality refuse sacks made from virgin material (see Appendix II for the use of the remaining four sites).

The competition from the Far East is particularly felt in the market for carrier bags – and this is true for the retail as well as the recycling side. Whereas bpi used to have a business recycling bags from stores, that part of the company was closed down in June 2000 as supermarkets preferred to ship their waste plastic east; Sainsbury, formerly a customer of bpi, being one of them. As David explains, 'To ship a 24-tonne container from the UK to Hong Kong costs about $500; to ship 1 tonne back costs $150. Once the container gets to China the contents get dumped into the streets of small villages where the villagers sort the plastic by hand. Polyethylene goes to one village, polypropylene to another. The people sort it by colour and degrees of contamination (paper, etc.). Labels and other paper-based contaminations are then cut out by hand and used as fuel. The plastic is then hand-stuffed into the extruders – something that would be forbidden for safety reasons here. The pellets resulting from this process can then be blown into good film.' He continued, 'Our Chairman Cameron McLatchie has tried to explain it to the government and other interest parties how short-sighted it all is – but no one wants to listen. So the UK allows massive exports of recyclable plastic. Ireland, on the other hand, is much stricter. Its exports to Dumfries are the exception and allowed only because Ireland does not have its own film recycling plant.'

bpi Product Range from Recycled Plastic

Rigid products

- Geoblock ('porous' pavement system)
- Plaswood (fencing, street furniture, signposts, garden furniture, marine use, playground furniture)
- Reblocks (traffic bollards)
- Pallets
- Cable ducting

Flexible products

- Envirolope (genuinely recycled envelopes)
- Carrier bags
- Waste sacks
- Collation and transit packaging (shrinkfilm and pallet stretchfilm)
- Tissue overwrap (for toilet paper)
- Mailing film
- Multibags (crisps and snack food)
- Refuse sacks and bin liners
- Kerbside collection sacks
- Polly Teen (educational scheme for primary school children developed by bpi)

DUMFRIES PLASTIC RECYCLING

The Dumfries plant is now solely dependent on imported agricultural plastic waste from subsidized collection schemes in Southern Ireland and Continental Europe. As yet there is no sign of any Government support for a Farm Plastic Recycling Programme in the UK.

bpi Annual Report 1999

In 1995 bpi spent £5 million to set-up Dumfries Plastic Recycling as a subsidiary to manufacture and sell rigid products made of Plaswood. Between 1992 and 1995 bpi had produced Plaswood on the company's site in Stroud, Gloucestershire. Dumfries had been chosen for its closeness to Ireland, a major source of its 'raw material', post-use agricultural film. But there were other favourable conditions: the process of recycling plastic needs an abundance of water – and the site was right next to

> Plaswood, a substitute for wood, concrete and metal, is made from 100% recycled polyethylene. It is produced in a wide variety of shapes, lengths and colours, and can be customized to match clients' requirements. It is extremely durable, rot proof, maintenance and splinter free. Applications include children's play areas, harbour decking, park fencing and floating pontoons.

the River Nith; the previous owner of the plant had been trying to sell it off for quite some time and was therefore willing to negotiate the price; and finally, some grants were available.

When bpi first entertained the idea of producing rigid products from post-use plastic waste, they had hoped to be able to sink large amounts of recycled material in the process. However, they soon enough found out that it would not work like that. To arrive at a 'raw material' that is suitable for the production of rigid products, the recyclate going into the process had to be homogenous

> A competitor of DPR had recently gone bankrupt mainly because they did not understand the importance of segregation and that one could only achieve good results from recycling if materials are separated; otherwise the resulting material is too inconsistent and not unsuitable for producing film.

with its characteristics known, otherwise the outcome would be too variable both in terms of quality and performance. They found that only certain plastics were suitable – and segregation is a costly and labour-intensive process.

Interest in the new material was extremely slow to pick up. When they re-assessed the market after about one year, they decided that they would need something that people could see which would help them to understand the benefits of the material – and they needed something that would bring in money quickly. In 1993/94 they decided to build a set of street furniture: a park bench, a picnic table (adult and junior) and a backless bench. These were some very basic products, but people reacted positively saying, 'Now I see what you were talking about.' Kim also remembers, 'The street nameplates introduced in 1995 were our first big hit, not least because people did not need much imagination to see how that would work.'

While bpi have invested a lot in recycling technology, they tend not to spend on R&D. Andrew explains, 'We are doing very little R&D in this area. Some of the machinery manufacturers and raw material suppliers are doing a lot but this will not continue if the commercial viability of recycling continues to be very poor.' However, DPR have developed processes that allow for the recycling of lower grade plastic waste than other companies are using. When asked whether they did some research before going into the production of rigid products Andrew answers, 'Very little research was done before developing the process. We embarked on it primarily because we were looking for a product that would accommodate lower grade waste than was necessary for making film. The technical and market strategy was developed in conjunction with a Dutch manufacturer of similar products with whom we began a licensing agreement some 10 years ago. The agreement ended about five years ago although we continue to work together and continue to buy product from them. The Dutch effectively sold us their process technology in return for a royalty on the products we make and sell.'

The end of the collaboration agreement with the Dutch company and the decision to specialize in the recycling of agricultural film were the trigger for setting up DPR. After

> In agricultural stretchfilm about 58–60% of the 'ingredients' are sand, soil and water.

David, who had been charged with preparing the plant for the production, had remodelled the plant it was capable of producing 5000 tonnes per year of pellets from post-use agricultural stretchfilm. However, as bpi.recycled products Managing Director Andrew Green remembers, while they had been part of the plant in Stroud, 'There was no real allocation of costs.' Once they had moved production to Dumfries this became all too obvious, the washing plant lost money from day one. Only recently had it started to make a small contribution. In fact, DPR came under serious review about four years ago, and the question was asked, do we really need to be in Plaswood? Strongly influenced by the company's commitment to the environment it was decided to continue production – but that product prices would have to start reflecting true production costs. Kim remembers, 'When Andrew took over and realized how much money they were losing, one of the first things he did was to put up the price for our products by 30%. It was quite remarkable, we explained to our customers that the reason for the price increase was the need to cover cost – rather than to increase our profits – and we lost hardly any of them.' Another reason customers stayed with them was that their products were of a quality superior to competitors' products.

Coming to talk about competition, there was agreement that there was in fact quite little – at least in terms of similar products made from recycled plastic. David comments, 'There is not much competition, certainly not for street furniture. One company is making flat panels for pigsties but that's a niche market. There are a few companies on the continent, one in the Netherlands and two in Italy, the latter also making furniture from recycled plastic but only on a small scale. As transport costs are quite high, there is not much cross-border trade. On the other hand, for flexible recycled plastic products, such as refuse sacks, there is horrendous competition.'

With 45 employees DPR processes about 60,000 tonnes of polythene a year, about half of which is post-use plastic. After the recyclate has been washed it is 'reduced in size' – which means it is shredded – and then melted in an extruder. In the extrusion process the liquid plastic is pressurized into moulds. Once the material has cooled down in water, it is pushed out by compressed air. David points out, 'Make sure that you don't stand in the way when it is pushed out, it is like a torpedo!' It is important to give sufficient time to the cooling process. Again David explains, 'The outer skin has to be "frozen" before the product can be taken out of its form; it must be kept in its mould until the outside is sufficiently hard, otherwise the product will disintegrate.'

Over the years the Plaswood product range had expanded continuously. Asked about where product ideas come from David comments, 'They come from within the organization as well as from our customers. We also scan the market for existing products and ask whether making them from Plaswood would bring any advantages to the consumer.' Kim Williamson, Sales Manager, adds, 'We are working very closely with our customers, for

> Waitrose is a very enlightened company, they have 'bags for life' which customers buy, use until they are worn out and can then exchange for a new 'bag for life'; the worn out bags get collected and come back to Dumfries who then produce Plaswood products with them which in turn go back to Waitrose which use them either for their shops or donate them.

example Safeway and Waitrose. We supply Waitrose with all their car park requirements and also take their old plastic bags back – it is a win–win situation.' Kim continues, 'It is important to be reactive to customer needs – and listen. It is also important to keep the sales team informed and provide them with the latest insights, knowledge and developments. We at Dumfries aim to give very good service and delivery. My philosophy is, get in front of customers as much as you can. Honesty is very important too. Say if you believe something does or does not work.

You have to know the product inside out so you don't make promises that cannot be delivered. For example, if the customer requires something for which Plaswood is not the ideal solution, we do not hesitate to recommend a combination with other materials.' About 75% of products sold are off-the-shelf solutions, 25% are bespoke to customer requirements.

bpi's products from recycled materials are sold predominantly into the following markets: the building industry, local authority and private waste contractors, as well as catering and janitorial. However, most of these markets are interested in flexible rather than rigid products. DPR's main customers tend to be local authorities. In fact, the four top accounts are with local authorities, and about 40% of DPR's business is conducted with its four major customers. 'Keeping in constant contact with the local authorities is very important,' says Kim. 'Our sales staff contact all local authorities with the latest product info, etc. about twice a year. In fact we conduct much of our sales activity over the phone. Persistency, and the fact that our organization has been around for some time, delivering high-quality products and good service, had led several local authorities to start specifying products made from recycled materials in their tender documents. Of course they cannot request our products but it is a step in the right direction.'

The material characteristics – maintenance free, non-rotting, resisting vandalism, immune to infestation by insects and salt water resistance – make it ideal for the outdoor/marine environment. Hence the product focus is on outdoor furniture – benches, bollards, street signs – and other outdoor products such as children's play environments, fencing and decking products for wet environments (band revetments, floating pontoons, fendering, etc.). DPR also supply people/companies with 'raw material' for them to do their own furniture.

The team at Dumfries are keen to identify new applications and product ideas for Plaswood material. One recent move was to add different colours. Kim comments, 'Orig-

> **Fancy a Sturdy Kung Fu Partner?**
>
> Dummies, traditionally made from wood, are an important part in Kung Fu training. When Simon Brooker, dedicated Kung Fu disciple, wanted to acquire his own he ran into unexpected difficulties: price, quality and size were not encouraging. Having heard about Plaswood he approached DPR who were, while initially sceptical, happy to help. Assuming that more people were struggling with traditional wooden training dummies, he set-up his own company, Immortal Creations, now selling four variations.

inally all of our products were black. Since we have developed brown Plaswood in addition to the black, the market for fencing has taken off.' They have just started the production of some Plaswood products in brighter colours such as yellow, green, red and blue, which gives the customer more choice and makes them particularly attractive for playgrounds and nurseries. Early in 2001 DPR introduced a new product called Post Saver. Post Saver is a boot of recycled plastic lined with bitumen which can be heat-shrunk onto a wooden post which means that the part of the post that is underground is protected and hence less likely to rot. Environmental concerns had motivated the product, as previously posts had to be treated with a highly toxic wood preservative containing copper chrome and arsenic.

While this was all very exciting, and DPR had just finished a record quarter, there were some concerns. Plaswood was not a cheap material, neither was production, so consequently nor were any products made of it. In fact, while they were much easier to maintain and of longer durability (expected lifetime is a minimum of 50 years), they would sell at about the same retail price as hardwood. In addition, despite the advantages, many customers would still prefer wood to plastic, and Kim points out, 'One of our biggest challenges is how to change the consumer's perception of our product.' Andrew points out that 'Manufacturing cost for the products would have to come down by 50–70% to make them commercially viable. To achieve that we would need to increase throughput considerably.' DPR had plans to recycle 10,000 tonnes of plastic by 2006. 'But,' Andrew asks, 'would there be sufficient customers for our products?' On top of that recent checks had revealed that the washing plant in Dumfries had lost between £500 k and £1 million between 1994 and 2000.

QUESTIONS

1.   Putting yourself in Andrew's shoes, what decisions would you take regarding Dumfries Plastic Recycling?
2.   What are factors underpinning success for 'green' products?
3.   Discuss the difference between 'green' and 'sustainable'?

APPENDIX I: ALTERNATIVES TO RECYCLING

(Source: bpi website)

1. BIODEGRADABLE PLASTIC

Biodegradability is an exciting and potentially very useful technology used in the correct applications. However, until EC standards are set any manufacturer of biodegradable products can make untrue and misleading claims about their products. This means that some degradable products may be marketed for use in inappropriate applications. Currently, biodegradability is suitable for products which will be composted, not for products going to landfill or being recycled where the effects of biodegradability on the recyclate are unknown. Biodegradability is expensive. Environmentally it is acceptable in some specific applications but at present it is generally undesirable.

2. CALL FOR INCINERATION

Incineration might be an alternative to landfill, but there is some public resistance against it; it is a question of education. Arguments for and aspects of incineration include:

*   Is safe and clean; modern plants control emissions by the installation of devices such as acid gas scrubbers, bad filters and electrostatic precipitators

*   A minimum temperature of 850°C is needed

*   Incineration converts nearly all carbon to CO_2, while in landfill under normal conditions methane is predominantly formed; methane gas contributes to the greenhouse effect 30 times more than CO_2

*   Incineration of municipal solid waste (MSW), i.e. domestic refuse, drastically reduces the volume of waste by up to 90%

*   Plastics have a calorific value greater than coal, make up 7% by weight of MSW, and produce 50% of all energy produced during incineration, making plastic a vital component of MSW (Switzerland, Denmark and Sweden rely heavily on energy recovery from waste)

*   Plastic waste can also be used to manufacture high calorific fuel pellets, termed Refuse-Derived Fuel; RDF can be transported and stored and are used to generate heat for industrial processes

APPENDIX II: RECYCLING AT bpi

The six recycling related sites and their activities are:

Dumfries	Washing plant; production of rigid products from recycled plastic. 100% is post-use
Stockton	Refuse sack plant; processing about 12,000 t/year of refuse sacks; selling mainly to the NHS; the plant process bpi scrap; bpi own the site

Heanor	Used to be part of bpi retail; recycling has taken over half of the site since January 2001; this plant too is scrap based, scrap here comes from inside bpi as well as outside; the washing plant at Heanor has been mothballed
Stroud	Production of flat sacks for local authorities; part of company since 1987; also scrap based, some stems from Dumfries and more is bought from other companies within the UK
Rhymney	Production of building films from 100% recycled plastic about 60% of which is post-use
Witney	Production of building dampproof course from 100% recycled plastic about 80% of which is post-use

18 Green Design – Clean Environment or Clean Conscience?

Companies can minimize environmental impact by reviewing and adapting their corporate and marketing operations policies and strategies, and their management styles and training to integrate environmental expertise.

Dermody and Hammer-Lloyd (1995)

Pressures on companies to become more environmentally conscious come from two sides. First, there are increasingly tougher environmental regulations introduced by governments, and second, consumers are becoming more environmentally aware. While consumers would not necessarily want to pay a higher price, all else being equal they'd rather buy an environmentally responsible product. But is not only external pressures that motivate managers to look into 'greener' development, it is also about positioning the company as responsible and proactive – and the insight that environmentally conscious development makes business sense.

In this chapter we make the argument for increased environmental consciousness, take a closer look at what environmentally friendly actually means, introduce the concept of natural capitalism, and conclude with some suggestions on the designer's role in making environmentally responsible products a reality.

> **Organic – great idea, but. . .**
>
> You may recall that Iceland, the producer of frozen foods, announced a few years ago that all their products would be based on organic ingredients, at prices that would match non-organic foods. Their decision was driven by consumer demand and, I am sure, extensive consumer research that indicated that such a policy should significantly increase the demand for their products. However, after they had introduced their 'all organic' policy, consumers behaved differently from what they had expected, production cost did not decrease at the rate anticipated, and as a result Iceland had to reconsider its position.

THE ARGUMENT FOR ENVIRONMENTALLY RESPONSIBLE DESIGN

Unprecedented consumption of natural resources, an increasing pollution, desertification, ozone depletion, acid precipitation, global warming, and loss of habitats and species diversity.

Dermody and Hammer-Lloyd (1995)

With an ever growing world population and decreasing natural resources, but also caused by more and more obvious signs of environmental problems – piles of rubbish and toxic waste (see Box 18.1), dying trees, extinction of already rare breeds of animals and plants, global warming – there is an increasing concern with the impact of our consumer society on our environment.

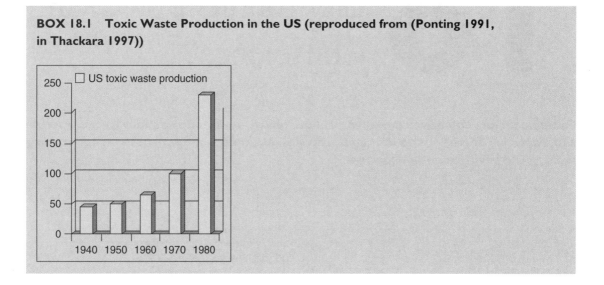

BOX 18.1   Toxic Waste Production in the US (reproduced from (Ponting 1991, in Thackara 1997))

To achieve global ecological sustainability, the environmental impact of products and services has to be reduced by Factor X. Biologists Ehrlich and Ehrlich (in Magnusson 2001) have proposed the following formula:

Total environmental impact(I) = Population(P) × Capital stock per person or affluence(A)
× Environmental damage done by particular technologies(T)

Building on the premise that the earth has a limited capacity to carry environmental impacts, sustainability can only be achieved if the negative environmental impacts worldwide are less or equal to, the earth's capacity. Needless to say that, today, our consumption and demands exceed capacity, the world's population keeps growing, and affluence is continuing to grow, particularly in developing countries. As it seems difficult to control population growth, and particularly the developing countries need to be allowed to increase their affluence, one important lever to balance demand and capacity is to minimize the environmental damage done. The specific factor which describes these reductions is also known as Factor X. Depending on the assumptions made about the earth's capacity and future population and consumption, Factor X is estimated to lie between four and 50.

Just think about the amount of waste produced from each shopping trip. Unpacking after one trip to the supermarket generally fills the rubbish bin easily with plastic bags, containers and cardboard items. As usual there is a debate as to who should address the problem, the consumer or the producer. In Germany, for example, regulation has been introduced that placed the responsibility for disposal of packaging firmly with the providers of goods. This means that consumers can leave all superfluous packaging material at the shop or supermarket.

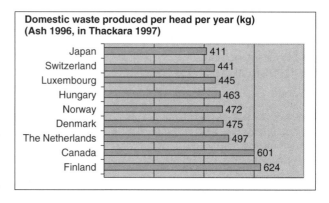

And as the managers of shops and supermarkets do not like to end up with piles of cardboard and other packaging materials, and carry the cost for their disposal, they in turn put pressure on the suppliers to cut down on the packaging. In Denmark waste segregation laws are very strict, and people have to pay penalties if they are found to put rubbish in the wrong containers. In both cases, the consequence seems to have been some reduction in waste.

More and more regulations and legislation is being passed to encourage – or force – organizations to consider the environmental impact of their activities both at production and usage level. However, there is always a fierce battle between industry and government as to how strict regulations should be, and how quickly they are to be implemented. Industry generally argues that improving environmental performance would add costs, endangering jobs and putting them at a disadvantage in international competition. However, much of this is based on assumptions, and companies that have embraced sustainability have actually experienced great benefits, in terms of cost, profit, market share and reputation. Some examples will follow later in this chapter. So most of the time, compromises need to be reached, generally leading to a dilution of the original intentions and the stretching of time frames. However, it seems that leading firms take initiative in talking to government and defining the rules. This, of course, has not only the advantage of being seen to be proactive, but with it comes the benefit of being able to influence what kind of regulations and legislation are being put into place.

Still, much activity in this area has been driven by government, and even more so the European Union, where particularly the Dutch government with its eco-design initiatives has been pushing the frontiers.[1] However, nations' view on the importance and urgency of responding to the environmental challenges varies. Lewis et al. (2001) state that 'In Australia, environmental protection is still viewed by some (vocal) parts of industry as just another potential burden that will increase costs and reduce profits. In the European context (and to a great extent in the USA and Japan), regulations and policies to increase environmental protection appear to have become a new stimulus for innovation and to have led companies to identify new business opportunities.' They name companies such as Xerox, Electrolux, Bosch, BMW, Philips, Volvo, AEG and Wilkahn as leaders in this area. These companies have invested heavily in new processes, systems, production technologies and design methods in the search for dramatic reductions in the environmental impacts of their products. Lewis et al. have found that companies invest in reducing their environmental impact because they:

- want to position themselves as market leaders and innovators
- do not want future surprises (they want to anticipate the changing regulatory and market context, rather than to react to changes as they are upon them)
- recognize the emergence of a new business paradigm and a new competitive terrain
- desire to act responsibly (to have a clear conscience on the part of directors)
- desire to influence the direction of regulations and legislation (in partnership with government and to secure their investment)
- desire to strengthen technical competence and develop new areas of technical competency
- want to change or improve the market image of the whole company

WHAT ARE ENVIRONMENTALLY RESPONSIBLE PRODUCTS?

Because our problems are caused by industry and the solutions must be found by industry, environmentalists have got to roll their sleeves up and get stuck into working with industry.

Elkington and Burke (1989)

So there are a number of good reasons why leading companies engage in environmental issues. But what exactly is an environmentally responsible product?

One of the results of an increased environmental consciousness is that more and more companies start to use terms that indicate 'environmentally friendliness' in their marketing and product literature. Therein lies a problem: anyone can describe their products in whichever way they see fit. OK, within limits, but many of the claims made on promotional literature and packaging are difficult for the consumer to check, leading to confusion. In response to this problem, and to provide consumers with some guidance, labels such as the 'green point' (Europe-wide), the Blue Angel (in Germany), the Soil Association (UK) or the Forest Stewartship Council have emerged. But even labels require a certain degree of education, and not all of them are backed by legislation or clear definitions. For a less knowledgeable consumer it remains difficult to differentiate between empty logos and labels that are backed by official schemes. For example, while the Soil Association and the Forest Stewartship Council stand for specific products, the Blue Angel can be associated with all kinds of product and so the consumer does not quite get as much information and help.

Take, for example, organic food. There are so many products on the market that claim to be produced organically – which makes the consumer feel good, but if asked, how many consumers would actually be able to respond what 'organically produced' means?[2] Having just recently looked it up on the government's website (www.food.gov.uk) myself, I now know that organic food should be produced under the following conditions:

- no fertilizers (unless approved for organic production)
- no pesticides (unless approved for organic production)
- the land has been farmed organically for a minimum of two years

An inspector has to verify the above, and the labels of organic produce need to state the certifying body that has issued the certification. The code number, and name or trade mark of the certification body may also be shown. As there may be some problems obtaining all ingredients required for a product from organic origins, manufacturers of organic food are allowed to use up to 5% non-organic ingredients. While this is certainly a start, there still seem to be some loopholes that can be exploited by those who jump onto the bandwagon purely for financial, rather than for financial and ethical, reasons. How many people would know which institution or organization is qualified to certify organic food and which one is not?

Casting the net wider than food, what does it generally mean, 'an environmentally responsible product'? A whole host of terms are used, and I would suggest that people are not quite sure what they actually mean, and what the differences are – see Box 18.2 for a list of the most common buzzwords. Is 'environmental design' better than 'green design'? What is the difference between a socially responsible design and ecologically oriented design? I would suggest leaving terminology to one side, and looking at what actually characterizes an environmentally responsible product instead. Many organizations claim to follow an environmentally responsible philosophy. But is it really environmentally friendly to buy softener in plastic pouches – instead of bottles? Is the question not rather, do we need this additional product at all (which, by the way, was developed out of by-products from the washing powder production)? Is it environmentally responsible to buy pencils that are made from plastic cups? Would it not be better not to produce these plastic cups in the first place? There are a whole host of products out there that are appealing at our 'green' conscience – but that really are do just that, make us feel better – not help the environment. When Honda's president Nobuhiko Kawamoto stated in 1992 that making cars more environmentally friendly was the most important challenge facing manufacturers, he followed the statement with specific action: in August the same year Honda withdrew from motor racing to focus more on environmental aspects of development (in Lamming 1993).

BOX 18.2   Palette of Buzzwords

- Eco-design
- Sustainable design
- Design for sustainability (DfS)
- Design for the environment (DfE)
- Green design
- Dematerialization
- Life-cycle design

Companies that are serious about protecting the environment go beyond glossy annual report statements. For example, Dermody and Hammer-Lloyd (1995) highlight the following as noteworthy from Procter & Gamble's environmental quality policy:

- they assess the environmental impact of their products following the cradle to grave concept (see below)
- they have set themselves the goal of exceeding environmental laws and regulations
- they subscribe to a continual assessment to meet environmental goals

However, the fact is there are hardly any products that are truly good for the environment. All products take up resources, use energy produce waste that has to be processed, leaving a 'footprint'. Lewis et al. state, 'Every product we make and use contributes to environmental degradation in many different ways. It has an "ecological footprint" that extends well beyond national boundaries and long after a product has been used and discarded.' So the best companies can do is to ensure minimum impact of their products. One way of achieving it is to consider all inputs and outputs, stage by stage of a product's life-cycle.

The 'cradle to grave' approach mentioned above is one tool that facilitates this (Box 18.3). It encourages companies to consider the environmental impact of a product from its conception to its disposal, looking at a number of different possible areas of impact. Only when a product is looked at over the period of its useful life can the true environmental impact be assessed.

BOX 18.3   Cradle to Grave Matrix (Used in the Assessment for Eco-labelling Schemes)

Product Life-cycle / Environmental fields	Pre-production	Production	Distribution (incl. packaging)	Use	Disposal
Waste relevance					
Soil pollution and degradation					
Water contamination					
Air contamination					
Noise					
Consumption of energy					
Consumption of natural resources					
Effects on ecosystems					

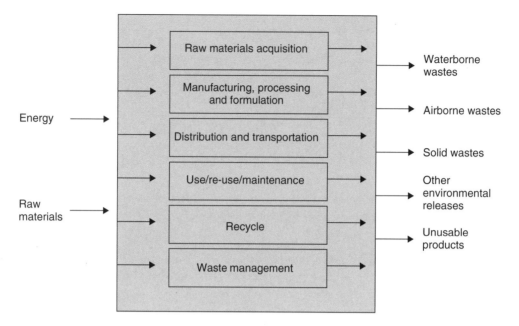

Figure 18.1 Product System from a Life-cycle Perspective (SETAC 1992, in Lewis *et al.* 2001) (reproduced by permission of Greenleaf Publishing)

A different representation of the same idea is shown in Figure 18.1. With the environmental impact in mind, it suggests considering the input demands as well as the outputs at each stage of a product's life-cycle.

The following list of questions by Burall (1996) helps to minimize the environmental impact over a product's life-cycle:

- Consider from the outset what the ideal life might be for the proposed product: calculate data cradle to grave (minimum packaging, energy efficient, using renewable resources)

- Ensure that the product will be easy to use and repair, and that product manuals encourage repair

- Increase the 'service intensity' of the product

- Avoid trendy designs that encourage early product replacement (designed to last, fulfilling real needs)

- Design to facilitate upgrading (e.g. modular components)

- Consider from the outset how the product is to be disassembled (minimum non-reusable waste)

- Check that any fixing methods and finishes do not inhibit recycling

- Ensure that plastic components carry permanent identification of materials

- Avoid toxic materials

- Optimize high-turnover goods (e.g. food) for low transport intensity (using local resources)

- Investigate setting up a destination for recycled elements in advance

- Ensure that materials do not create hazard on disposal

Figure 18.2   Eco-Wheel Diagram (reproduced from (van Hemel 1995, in Thackara 1997))

However, when there are some different options none of the above is too helpful for assessing different types of environmental impact relative to one another. Is it more damaging to use more energy during consumption or use more non-renewable resources? A tool that might provide some help with the comparison of different options is the Eco-wheel developed by van Hemel (1995) (Figure 18.2). By mapping different options on the spider diagram, it helps managers identify the option with the least environmental impact. However, the challenge remains to define the scales in a way that allows a sensible comparison of the different axes of the spider diagram.

NATURAL CAPITALISM VERSUS 'GREEN DESIGN'

When we talked about Factor X earlier in this chapter, what was really referred to was sustainable development. Sustainable development goes beyond environmental responsibility. It is not about developing products that use a bit less energy or are easier to recycle. It is about developing products in ways that will not deprive

> **Taking responsibility for future generations**
>
> One Indian tribe measures its decisions against their impact on the people seven generations hence.

future generations. A similar is notion is expressed in the definition by the Bruntland Commission (the world commission on environment and development) in 1997: 'Sustainability is about meeting the needs of the present without compromising the ability of future generations to meet their own needs.' The implication is that for development to be sustainable, it must take account not just of economic factors, but also of environmental and social factors, and must assess long-term consequences of actions as well as short-term results (in MacKenzie 1997).

To achieve the step from environmentally responsible to sustainable, a previously omitted factor has to be integrated: costing the impact on the environment. Lovins et al. (2001) state, 'The reason that companies (and governments) are so prodigal with ecosystem services is that the value of those services doesn't appear on the business balance sheet. But that is a staggering omission. The economy, after all, is embedded in the environment. Recent calculations published by the journal *Nature* conservatively estimated the value of all the earth's ecosystem services to be at least £33 trillion a year. That is close to the gross world product, and it implies a capitalized book value on the order of half a quadrillion dollars. What is more, for most of these services there is no known substitute at any price, and we cannot live without them.'

'Costing the earth', and taking this cost into consideration when pricing projects, would make many a project that is undertaken today unrealistic, even irresponsible. Think about nuclear energy. The costing of nuclear power stations has never included the cost for the storage and impact of nuclear waste, or of the decommissioning of nuclear power plants. Had this been the case, nuclear power would never have been able to compete with solar or wind energy, and if the money that has gone into the research and development of nuclear energy had gone into alternative energies, effectiveness and efficiency of wind and solar energy could have been improved sufficiently to make them a viable alternative. However, the field of nuclear power was pursued not only to provide new sources of energy. Political and military considerations will have played their part in these decisions.

Lovins et al. suggest a new approach called 'natural capitalism'. This approach would help to protect the biosphere, but also improve profits and competitiveness. It is no good trying to try to persuade managers to adopt a different approach for ecological reasons only. Lovins et al. emphasize – and have ample convincing examples – that natural capitalism is good for both the environment *and* business. They have identified four steps in the journey towards natural capitalism:

1.   *Dramatically increase the productivity of natural resources*   This is achieved primarily by reducing waste through changes in the product design and production processes. In their experience, companies that pursue such options have increased yield 10 or even 100 times. With such efficiency improvements, the initial investment required pays for itself in short periods of time. Looking at the wider system (systems approach), and all aspects of a product's life-cycle can provide the insights necessary to achieve such reductions.

Example: Interface Corporation (based on Lovins et al. 2001)

When designing a new carpet factory in Shanghai, interface engineer Jan Schilham realized that two simple design changes could reduce power requirements from 95 horsepower to just seven, while costing less and without requiring any new technology. His approach was to use fatter pipes, causing less friction and hence less pumping energy. Traditional costing would have looked at the cost of the fatter pipes and decided against them as they are more expensive than thinner ones. Schilham took a systemic approach, looking at the system and costs over the product's life-cycle. The second insight was to make the pipes short and straight. This was achieved by positioning the pipes first and then positioning the other equipment. This did not affect the workflow, all it did was improve the energy efficiency of the entire system. One of the reasons that no one had looked at it this way before is that the pipes seem to be the least important part of the system, so they were considered last. However, the systems approach requires all aspects

> of the system to be considered at the outset, hence allowing optimizing of the *system* rather than any one aspect.

2. *Shift to biologically inspired production models* Aim to eliminate waste by trying to achieve closed-loop systems as seen in nature, e.g. compost; if the closed-loop system does not work for a single product, perhaps the waste from one product can be used as input for another. This approach can reduce a company's materials' requirements by up to 90%.

Example: Interface Corporation (based on Lovins et al. 2001)

Interface have developed a new material called Solenium that not only lasts four times longer and requires 40% less material than ordinary carpets, it can also be remanufactured into an identical new product. It is also free of chlorine and other toxic materials, can be cleaned with water and does not grow mildew. The chairman of the company has an interesting definition of waste: any measurable input that does not produce customer value and all inputs until they prove otherwise. The zero-waste approach led to an increase in revenue of $200 million while resource requirements remained constant. $67 million of the revenue increase were as a direct result of reduced landfill charges (down 60%).

---

3. *Move to a solutions-based business model* Shift from an emphasis on sales of goods to sales of services. Example: agricultural chemical producer who sells weed-free fields instead of bags of chemicals, hence ensuring that a minimum rather than a maximum of chemicals are used – it is in the interest of the manufacturer to use as little as possible, rather than to sell as much as possible.

Example: Interface Corporation (based on Lovins et al. 2001)

Realizing that people want to use and see carpets but not necessarily own them has led Interface to sell the service of providing carpeted floors, rather than carpets. Monthly inspections identify and replace tiles that are worn out. This leads to a 35-fold reduction in the flow of materials needed to maintain a carpet-covered floor.

---

4. *Re-invest in natural capital* As the costs arising from deteriorating ecosystems rise, businesses need to invest in renewable resources. Companies face direct costs from the consequences of deteriorating ecosystems, resulting in climate changes, e.g. high winds and floods. Lovins *et al.* mention the example of the deforestation in China's Yangtze basin in 1998, which triggered floods that killed 3700 people, dislocated 223 million, and destroyed 60 million acres of cropland. The total costs of the disaster amounted to £30 billion, forced a logging moratorium, and it required a $12 billion crash programme of reforestation.

Example: California Rice Industry Association (based on Lovins et al. 2001)

Companies are increasing efforts to live with nature rather than against it. Rather than focusing on a single product, the Association has discovered the value of diversity. Instead of burning the rice fields they allow

150,000–200,000 acres of the Sacramento valley rice fields to flood after harvest. This not only creates seasonable wetland which is ecologically valuable, but creates other benefits such as the replenishment of the groundwater and improved fertility. Through the flooding, the straw that was previously burned (polluting the air) has increased silica content, which means that its resistance to insects has improved, meaning it can profitably be sold as a construction material.

THE ROLE OF THE DESIGNER

Lovins *et al.* give impressive evidence that considering the environment makes commercial sense. In the previous section we looked at several tools and questions that help assess a product's environmental impact. The question is,

Interestingly, but not surprisingly, much of the writing on environmentally responsible product can be found in the design literature.

who should take responsibility for ensuring the minimum environmental impact of products? Of course, senior management buy-in and leadership are essential. Life-cycle consideration and a systems approach will be new to many organizations, and such a significant departure from how things have been done in the past cannot happen without top management support. However, at the project level environmental considerations need a champion too. Designers – industrial designers, design engineers, packaging designers, and so on – are well positioned to take up such a role. MacKenzie (1997) comments, 'For many years, designers have been asserting their influence and demonstrating the power of design. The new demands on designing for minimum ecological impact will provide an ideal platform from which designers can justify their claims and acknowledge their responsibility. Why should so much responsibility fall to the designer? Design is one part of a holistic process, which involves a wide range of other skills. However, design is a pivotal part of the process.' And Lewis *et al.* point out, 'The designer, as the principal determinant or creator of the product itself, has a direct influence on the amount of damage which will occur at each state in the process.' It is also designers who manipulate consumption indirectly as influencers of trends and fashions.

Toys are a great (negative!) example. How many toys are created as a fashion, to last for but a season, to be thrown away as soon as batteries run out or the next toy comes along. How many clothes are designed to last one season instead of a lifetime? Who would like to buy one high-quality suit rather than two or three cheap ones, even though they will last only a fraction of the time? Of course, it is not just the designers who need to reconsider looking at their output with sustainability in mind. Consumers, all of us, will have to rethink our values and priorities if we are serious about handing the planet to the next generation in a healthy and liveable state. Sounds dramatic? People joke about selling fresh air – people joked about selling fresh water less than a century ago. Just something to keep in mind.

Designers have knowledge about the characteristics of materials, they can influence the number of different materials used, they influence the number of components, they are involved in the design of systems, and so on. Lewis *et al.* have in fact identified nine major environmental problems that designers should keep in mind when making their choices:

- global warming
- ozone depletion
- reduced biodiversity
- resource depletion
- water pollution
- air pollution

Figure 18.3 A Framework for Achieving Green Design (Burall 1992) (reproduced by permission of Design Council; copyright Paul Burall)

- land degradation
- solid waste
- acidification

Burall (1992) suggests a framework for achieving what he then called 'green design' which mirrors the questions introduced earlier in this chapter summarizing aspects that designers should consider in the design and development of environmentally conscious products into four categories (see Figure 18.3).

All the above are influenced through product design. Lewis *et al.* suggest that one way of sharing responsibility for ensuring that products are based on sustainability principals is to write environmental/sustainability criteria into the design brief (see Box 18.4).

BOX 18.4 The Design Brief (reproduced from (Lewis *et al.*))

Introduction

- Define the aim of the (design) project
- List specific objectives

General requirements

- Define primary function of the product
- State the durability requirements
- List aesthetic considerations

▶

- Define ergonomic requirements
- List the safety requirements and issues
- Outline the required performance and quality

Environmental objectives

- List specific strategies relating to materials, efficiency, recovery at end of life, and so on
- Include quantitative targets where relevant (e.g. 'use 50% recycled materials')

Production requirements

- Specific manufacturing requirements or limitations
- Include any objectives or targets (e.g. minimize components to streamline assembly process)

Regulation and standards

- List any mandatory regulations, standards or codes of practice relevant to the product

Cost

- Specify limits on cost of production to ensure that the product is competitive

It is also important to point out that it is not only the product design that needs to be considered. Process design, and in fact business design, as we have seen in the case of the Interface Corporation, need to be considered too.

And one final comment; many organizations are wondering where to concentrate their innovation efforts and what selection criteria to establish for choosing concepts to be taken forward. Focusing on ideas that combine a minimization of environmental impact and maximization of cost efficiency might provide a viable framework. Such products not only provide extra value for the consumer; positioning yourself at the forefront of environmental consciousness and thinking can also become a differentiating factor for your organization.

READING SUGGESTIONS

Hawken, Paul, Amory and Lovins, L. Hunter (1999) *Natural Capitalism: The Next Industrial Revolution* London: Earthscan

Comment: If you want to read one book on the subject, this is the one

Papanek, V. (1991) *Design for the Real World*. 2nd edn. London: Thames & Hudson

Comment: When the first edition came out in 1971 it was well ahead of its time in terms of highlighting the social and ethical responsibility of design and designers. Should be required reading for all designers, and gives ammunition to those who want to argue for better and more responsible design. You may also want to look at his (1995) 'sequel', *The Green Imperative: Ecology and Ethics in Design and Architecture*. London: Thames & Hudson

Charter, Martin and Tischener Ursula (eds) (2001) *Sustainable Solutions*. Sheffield, UK: Greenleaf Publishing

Comment: Addressing the need for suitable management structures and practical tools to address increasing environmental concerns, the book addresses the following: (1) issues of business sustainability, (2) methodologies and approaches toward organizing and developing more sustainable products and services, (3) a collection of global case studies, (4) a list of literature, resources and addresses of useful organizations

Lewis, Helen. Gertsakis; John, Grant; Tim, Morelli, Nicola and Sweatman, Andrew (2001) *Design + Environment – A Global Guide to Designing Greener Products*. Sheffield, UK: Greenleaf Publishing

Comment: This book is very 'hands-on', reviewing many tools, comparing the use of recycled and non-recycled raw materials, listing hazardous materials, etc. It also reviews specific design areas such as packaging, clothing and textiles, furniture and electronic and electrical products

MacKenzie, D. (1997) *Green Design, Design for the Environment*. 2nd edn. London, UK: Laurence King Publishing

Comment: MacKenzie starts her book by explaining the designer's contribution to creating products that are more environmentally responsible, provides some background for creating the urgency, and then looks at how 'green design' should be reflected in different design disciplines (architecture and interior design, product design, packaging design, print and graphic design, and textile design)

SOME USEFUL WEBSITES

http://themes.eea.eu.int/showpage.php/improvement/management? pg = 40, 494

Comment: From the website of the European Environment Agency (www.eea.eu) you can download a guide on Life Cycle Assessment (LCA), including information on methods, terminology, history and other information sources

http://grn.com

Comment: On this website by the Global Recycling Network you can find company directories, process, publications and news about recycling

http://www.ends.co.uk/

Comment: Environmental Data Services Ltd (ENDS) is an independent publisher which has served environmental professionals since 1978

http://www.emcentre.com

Comment: Founded in 1996, Environmental Management Centre (EMC) has positioned itself as a niche player both in India as well as in international environmental management consultancy. It lists a number of case studies across industry sectors which you can access from http://www.emcentre.com/unepweb/tec-case/

NOTES ON CHAPTER 18

[1] For a brief summary of the Dutch eco-design initiative, see http://www.emcentre.com/unepweb/tec-case/links/ promise.htm.

[2] You may want to read more on 'What organic really means': visit www.food.gov.uk.

19 A Note on Intellectual Property Rights (IPR)

The basic Bell patents for the telephone were defended in court and the survival of Bell Telephone was ensured by a few crude notes made by Bell on the back of an envelope which (luckily) had been properly signed, witnessed and dated.

http://www.quantumbooks.com/Creativity.html

As innovation is often risky and costly, most companies are quite keen to protect their innovations for as long as possible through patents and other forms of intellectual rights protection. How important, and how effective, the protection of intellectual property is will vary from industry to industry. In the pharmaceutical industry, where research and development costs are immense, patents play an important role in paying for future R&D activities. The exclusivity for the duration of the protection also allows companies to charge a premium, which tends to get eroded once 'generics' come onto the market. This makes timing quite critical: registering a patent too early means that the company is losing out on profits; if the team waits too long with the registration there is a danger that a competitor might get a registration first. This conflict was alluded to in the Roche case study.

On the other hand, there are people who believe that making intellectual property freely available can be greatly beneficial. During a recent workshop at the leading-edge innovation consultancy IDEO, one of their staff commented, 'We believe that ideas are free. It is what you do with them that creates the value.' I also found it quite interesting to hear CD sales went up during the period when music titles could be copied freely – at the same rate as the downloads – just to drop again when downloading became prohibited.

This chapter provides an overview of different types of IPR protection, summarizes the general requirements and process for patenting, comments on filing patents internationally, takes a brief look at issues around patenting in the pharmaceutical industry, and comments on some recent changes to design rights.[1]

TYPES OF INTELLECTUAL PROPERTY RIGHTS

There are a number of different ways of protecting intellectual property, applicable in different contexts and for different types of products. Below we review the following:

- Patents
- Copyright
- Designs
- Trade marks
- Know-how

PATENTS

While a patent gives it owner the legal right for the exclusive use of an invention for up to 20 years, its main purpose tends to be to prevent others from using it – or at least using it without consent.

To qualify for patent application, the following criteria need to be fulfilled (from the UK Patents Act of 1977 and the related European Patent Convention):

- The invention must be new, i.e. it must not have been disclosed by the inventor(s) prior to filing the application – we explore this issue in a bit more detail later

- It involves an inventive step which means it is not blatantly obvious

- It can be described in an enabling fashion (so that others can reproduce the invention)

- It is capable of industrial application

- Is not specifically excluded from patent protection (see sections below)

Patent law specifically provides that the following subject matters as such are not patentable inventions:

- A discovery, scientific theory or mathematical method

- A literary, dramatic, musical or artistic work or any other aesthetic creation

- A scheme, rule or method for performing a mental act, playing a game or doing business, or a program for a computer

- The presentation of information

Patent law further provides that a patent shall not be granted:

- For an invention the publication or exploitation of which would be generally expected to encourage offensive, immoral or anti-social behaviour

- For any variety of animal or plant or any essentially biological process for the production of animals or plants, not being a microbiological process or the product of such a process

THE PATENTING PROCESS

The patenting process is time consuming and somewhat costly: it can take in excess of two years from filing the initial application to granting the patent, and cost around £25,000. Figure 19.1 illustrates the process, cost and time lines.

FILING PATENTS INTERNATIONALLY

The filing and recognition of patents is truly international – in January 2000 the Paris Convention for the Protection of Intellectual Property of 1883 (revised and updated many times) had 157 signatory nations. While there are some national differences, most processes and procedures share a large degree of communality. As a rule of thumb, you have to ensure for patent protection in those countries in which you would like to see your patent protected, and in most countries patent laws would expect you to commercially exploit your patent within three years.

Figure 19.1   Patenting Procedures

WHERE THE US PATENT LAW DIFFERS

There are actually some differences in patenting law between Europe and the US. While an invention is considered non-patentable if it has been disclosed in public before the patent is filed in Europe and most other parts of the world, the US patent law allows for one year to lapse between the first public disclosure and the filing of the patent application.

Related to this is the other main difference: the importance of the filing date for priority. Unlike in other countries where the critical moment for deciding who owns a patent is decided the moment a patent is filed – 'first-to-file' system – the US operates a 'first-to-invent' system. If someone can prove that they have made the invention before the person who has filed the patent application, they may be entitled to that patent after all. This means that keeping dated, signed and countersigned records of any documentation or drawings that could prove that you have been the first to come up with a particular invention is critical. For example, research scientists should be encouraged to keep laboratory notebooks documenting their work, whereby they have to ensure the signing, dating, peer scrutiny and countersigning.

However, there are further details to be aware of, concerning the conception – 'the complete performance of the mental part of the inventive act', and the reduction to practice – 'when a working model is made and a practical utility demonstrated'. The filing of a patent application is considered to be the point when an invention is reduced to practice. If there is a conflict about who has come up with the invention first ('interference' in legal terms), the rules shown in the following box apply.

The person who can prove the earlier date of conception and reduction to practice wins.

Party A conception first   reduction first
Party B   conception second   reduction second
A wins

However, if A can prove conception before B but reduction to practice occurs after B, then A will have to prove 'reasonable diligence' in reducing the invention to practice. 'Reasonable diligence' generally requires 'reasonably continuous activity'.

Party A conception first diligence   reduction second
Party B conception second   diligence   reduction first
A wins

Party A conception first insufficient diligence   reduction second
Party B conception second   diligence   reduction first
B wins

PATENTING AND THE PHARMACEUTICAL INDUSTRY

If patent protection is important in most industries, it is critical to the pharmaceutical industry. Nowadays it can easily take £100–200 million in R&D investment to bring a new drug containing a New Chemical Entity (NCE) to the marketplace – and not every NCE is a blockbuster. To get one blockbuster pharmaceutical companies have to develop thousands of compounds and materials, most of which will get discarded before they reach the market. Even drugs that make it successfully into the market often fail to generate return on investment. Escalating development costs and stricter regulatory and safety demands have led to the shortening of the period from bringing a product to market to the expiry of the patent. For example, recent estimates of the Centre for Medicines Research suggest that the effective patent life in the UK (from market introduction to patent expiry) is on average only about eight years. It is very much due to decreasing returns even from successfully introduced drugs that has led to a drop in annually introduced NCEs from 90 in 1969 to less than 40 in 1989. Legislation in the US and Japan (1994 and 1988, respectively) has been changed to address this issue, and it is now possible to extend the period of protection. Similar legislation has also been introduced in Europe, where pharmaceutical companies can apply for a Supplementary Protection Certificate (SPC), which provides a maximum of 15 years' legal protection, counting from the first marketing authorization in the European Union.

COPYRIGHT

Whereas a patent protects an idea, copyright protects the way in which the idea is expressed. So you cannot copyright an idea, only its expression. Typical candidates for copyright are books, musical compositions, artwork, illustrations, films, records, broadcasts and typographical arrangements, including computer software. Copyright laws prevent other people from copying or exploiting the originator's work without permission. It is a weaker but wider form of protection than patent. Infringement has to involve proven copying of a substantial part of the work. Unlike patenting, copyright applies automatically, which means it is quicker and cheaper. Once the material is created, it is protected. However, it is still worth registering to ensure protection in some circumstances, especially in the US. The owner of the copyright tends to be the originator, though when the work has been undertaken as part of an employment, the employer will be the owner. For literary works the copyright will generally continue for 70 years after the author's death. For other works the time span of protection is different, and the rules of ownership are more complex.

DESIGNS

REGISTERED

Registered design rights become relevant when the novelty lies in the appearance rather than the new idea or principle itself. A registered design gives the owner exclusive rights to a certain appearance of a certain article. This means he or she can stop anyone else from making, using and selling a product of the same design without permission. This kind of protection generally applies to commercial objects with a unique or aesthetic appearance. To achieve the status of 'registered design' the originator has to submit drawings or photographs showing the item to the Designs Registry. The main costs associated with obtaining a registered design are the initial filing costs. Upon registration the design is initially protected for five years, with the possibility of extending, five years at a time, up to 25 years.

UNREGISTERED

Besides the registered design rights, there are also unregistered design rights. These are not directly associated with appearance, but protect internal and external features. However, they only give protection against the copying of the features, e.g. the brand name, the company logo, the physical design of computer chip or architectural drawings. Design right exists automatically, you do not need to apply for it. However, to prove that you are the originator it is advisable to sign and date the original drawings and/or prototypes and keep them in a safe place. While design right can be relied upon in the United Kingdom, overseas protection is not necessarily guaranteed unless further protection is sought.

RECENT CHANGES

Towards the end of 2001 a new European Directive was implemented bringing a number of important changes to Design Registration law. The six key changes to the law are:

1. Instead of the article bearing the design it will be the design that is protected. In the past, the protection of a pattern would be linked to the particular object for which is was registered, if the pattern was to be applied to a different object or material a separate registration would be required, e.g. if the original registration was for a cup, a new registration would have been required for bed linen or a table to which the same patterns would be applied. Since the change it is the pattern that is protected, independent of the product to which it is applied. This means that graphic symbols, such as desktop icons, can now be registered.

2. Whereas there was previously a minimum number of units (50) that had to be produced before a design could be registered, the change allows the registration of unique products, e.g. a sculpture or any handicraft item. This enables the artist to keep control of licensing arrangements.

3. Whereas previously the entire object had to be registered – it had to have an 'independent life of its own' – now any visible part of a product can be registered. For example, you can now register the lid of a pot, be it applied to a teapot, a sugar bowl or a biscuit tin.

4. Previously the application for a registered design would be checked against existing UK registrations. Now a disclosure in any other country in the world would similarly cause an application to fail on the grounds of lack of novelty. So if the designer of a particular piece of period jewellery sought registration, he or she might be refused because such a piece exists in a museum somewhere in the world.

5.   The rules for what is classified as 'novel' have been tightened up. Registration is refused if the object in question evokes a *déjà vu* in the eyes of an 'informed user'. The informed user will not be a design expert, but someone familiar with the object in question, e.g. a waitress would comment on the degree of familiarity with a new cup design.

6.   Whereas before only designs that had not previously been disclosed could be registered, now designers have a 12-month 'grace period'. In the past, many a designer only realized the value of his or her design when it became a success in the market – by which time it was too late to register it. However, designers should be aware that if someone discloses the same or similar design, which this someone has created independently, first then the designer will have lost his or her opportunity to register the design.

TRADE MARKS

Trade marks can be registered or unregistered. Registered marks afford better legal protection. Registered trade marks are the only intellectual property right which can exist indefinitely – provided the mark is used and periodic renewal fees are paid whereas copyright and patents which expire after a given time. A trade mark is a sign, name or symbol that distinguishes one product or services from similar competitive products or services. Good trade marks seem to share in common that they are easily pronounceable (if they are words), memorable and pleasing to the eye. One example of a trade mark is the Coca-Cola bottle. A trade mark could be anything from the design of a label to the shape of a product's packaging, or even the sound or smell of a particular product. Having a registered trade mark means that no one but the registered owner or someone with his or her consent can use the image or shape for their product – which can be extremely valuable in maintaining a market leader position. Trade marks like patents are territorial, i.e. you have to apply for them in the country or group of countries in which you want to use them. You usually have a grace period after the first country filing to register in other countries as well.

KNOW-HOW

'Know-how', sometimes also referred to as 'confidential information' or 'trade secret', is a fairly new type of intellectual property protection. Unlike other international property rights, it is not based on a statutory scheme, but is rooted in case or judge-made law. Any process, technique, formula, information, device, design or even client list can be a trade secret as long as it is not generally known (i.e. a secret) and represents a competitive business advantage. You do not need to do much to secure a trade secret, generally you would only need to proof that you have done everything to ensure confidentiality (e.g. have employees or other people who come in contact with the trade secret sign confidentiality agreements). The problem with trade secrets is that they are only protective while the information is secret. If the secret information is made public by legitimate means, e.g. reverse engineering, disassembly or chemical analysis, there is no way to protect it. It is only when the secret has been obtained illegitimately, e.g. though industrial espionage, that protection might be enforceable.

READING SUGGESTIONS

Bouchoux, Deborah E. (2001) *Protecting Your Company's Intellectual Property: A Practical Guide to Trademarks, Copyrights, Patents and Trade Secrets.* New York: Amacom

Comment: This is a detailed look at how to protect the four key areas of 'intellectual property': trade marks, copyrights, patents and trade secrets (including customer lists, marketing plans, and other in-house documents). Written for a general business reader, the book shows that intellectual property is often a company's most valuable asset

SOME USEFUL WEBSITES

http://www.cipa.org.uk/info_ip_pros/briefing_2.html

Comment: For information and questions around patents in the UK, the website of the Chartered Institute
              of Patent Agents (CIPA), the professional and examining body for patent agents (also known as
              patent attorneys) is the right one for you. The web address for the UK patent office is
              http://www.patent.gov.uk/ and for the US patent and trademark office it is http://www.uspto.gov/

http://www.derwent.com/patentfaq/process.html

Comment: This is the website of Thomson Derwent, part of the Thomson Corporation, which provides
              patent and scientific information

http://www.dyson.com/inventors/inventors.asp

Comment: This website includes information on why patents are important, how to obtain a patent, the
              cost of obtaining a patent as well as useful contacts for inventors

NOTES ON CHAPTER 19

[1] The content of this chapter is based on the following sources:

http://www.medicalfutures.co.uk/

http://www.cipa.org.uk/info-ip-pros/briefing-2.html

http://www.derwent.com/patentfaq/process.html

http://crct.oyster.co.uk/pat_matt/pat_req1.html

http://www.designcouncil.org/design/content/fact.jsp?contentID =09009e0d8003e9d8

Legal matters, software and the patent trap, Innovation Business, issue 2, publication by the Natwest & The Royal
Scottish Bank p 5.

E. Bobrow, *Complete Idiot's Guide to New Product Development* (1997) New York: Alpha Books, pp211–233.

20 Innovation in Large Organizations

CASE STUDY 7: GKN – LIGHT COMPOSITE DISC JOINT

DECISIONS, DECISIONS

To spin or not to spin, that was the question senior management of GKN's Automotive Driveline Division (GKN ADD) was facing in October 2001. Over the past decade a product – the Light Composite Disc Joint (LCD) – had been developed internally which was innovative, offering a number of customer benefits. But there were two main reasons why GKN was hesitant to embark on full commercialization within the Group: the first was that there was not widespread confidence that sales would be of a scale acceptable to GKN; and secondly, it was felt that the product was not close enough to its core.

Dr Andrew Pollard, GKN ADD's project champion who had been involved in its development since the early 1990s, had spent about one year developing a business plan which had recently managed to attract the interest of two investor consortia, one based in London, one in the Midlands. Particularly the London-based one was very keen to proceed. In the business plan the concept of Spinning-Composites Ltd, as the business was to be called, read as follows:

> Spinning-Composites Ltd is a spinout operation from GKN plc with the aim of exploiting composite shaft and coupling technologies developed in GKN's Automotive Driveshaft Research and Development centre. Confidence in the potential of the new business is underlined by GKN's commitment to invest and retain an equity stake. In particular, Spinning will produce and market the GKN Light Composite Disc Joint (LCD), an innovative new kind of shaft coupling that has been awarded Millennium Product status by the Design Council in the UK. Spinning is being established to exploit the identified business potential for industrial and non-automotive driveshafts, which is non-core business for GKN Automotive Driveline Division.

Since the original decision that the only way forward for the LCD would be to spin it out, GKN had started to review its policy towards 'non-core' business concepts. But had the success in attracting investors put some doubts into the minds of GKN ADD senior management as to whether a spin-off would be the best solution? Might there be a solution internally to take the business forward after all? Andrew Pollard was wondering what would be decided.

- In the automotive business it is essential to be a global player and to provide consistent products wherever they are produced – which means engineering standardization of materials/components/processes/suppliers is a big issue

- GKN has 38% of world driveshaft production worth about £1.7 bn; a further 31% is done in-house by car manufacturers, but many of them license GKN products. GKN have worked on convincing car manufacturers that they have more in-depth knowledge and expertise in driveshaft development than anyone else in the world; have recently acquired in-house production of driveshafts from Fiat, Opel, Nissan

- Due to size of operation and complexity of customer relationships (global, etc.) the management structure is complex and heavily focused on standard CVJ product

- R&D is aligned closely to products

HOW THE PROJECT HAD STARTED

In the late 1980s, GKN had started an initiative to investigate the use of composite materials as a replacement for the metal used for its core products, shafts and joints that transmit power from a car's gearbox to its wheels. Composite materials offered some potential advantages in the area of Noise, Vibration, and Harshness (NVH), particularly for longitudinal propeller shafts that are used in rear-wheel drive vehicles. In addition, lighter components would also aid car manufacturers in their quest to improve the fuel efficiency of their cars.

Though the main focus of the efforts was to develop shafts made of composite materials, applications for the joints were considered too. In the late 1980s, Wolfgang Löbel of GKN Löhr & Bromkamp (LBO) in Germany, a producer of Constant Velocity Joints (CVJs), developed a constant velocity joint made from composite materials, later to be known as the light composite joint disc. The new product concept was aimed at enabling a much lighter form of CVJ for automotive propeller shafts. Although metal CVJs are very effective at transmitting power through big misalignment angles (e.g. when a car's wheels are turned), they are rather complex and heavy. A small scale development had been progressed in Germany before the project was transferred for further development and the identification of applications of the product within the automotive sector to GKN Technology (GKNT), GKN ADD's R&D facility in the UK, in 1991.

Even in the early 1990s, ADD had a very globally integrated structure, so everyone could find out what other people in his or her area of interest were working on. Andrew, who had joined the company in 1986 with a degree in mechanical engineering, and who had since developed an expertise in composite products, had already heard about the concept through the company grapevine, and was keen to take it forward. Between 1991 and 1996

> The LCD is an innovative lightweight and flexible coupling suitable for use in power-transmitting driveshafts, and delivers a range of technically exciting competitive advantages. It comprises a composite of glass fibre in an epoxy matrix, with controlled orientations of glass fibres throughout the laminated structure of the disc.

the project was part of the regular development programme for automotive couplings in GKN's R&D facility in Wolverhampton in the UK.

As technical questions (product design, materials, process, performance) were answered, the focus of the development programme moved to the commercial potential of the LCD for automotive applications. Although the total potential automotive market for this type of product was estimated around four million units per annum, the manufacturing investment required to achieve low enough costs and win a significant share of this market were prohibitive in relation to the expected commercial return. In 1996, it was decided to stop the development programme for automotive applications.

Those involved in the development of the LCD remained fascinated by its extraordinary performance within a particular sector of technical coupling requirements. Additional avenues were found more or less by accident. LBO was at that time also selling their CVJ products for non-automotive applications. Wolfgang Löbel believed that the LCD might help to solve application problems that they were suffering due to overheating and maintenance needs of CVJ used in wind turbine driveshafts. However, there was one problem, company rules said that GKN Technology could not talk to customers directly – not even to GKN business units outside Automotive Engineering, for that matter. Determined not to let company rules get in the way, Andrew worked with the GKN design engineers in the German driveshaft business, the engineer from the German company in turn talked to the GKN people in Denmark, who then spoke to the potential customer, the producer of wind turbines.

The Danish GKN engineer succeeded in persuading the Danish wind turbine producer to test the disc, which was a great step towards moving the project forward. But trying the new product required a leap of faith: imagine offering to replace a hefty, somewhat complicated assembly of steel parts weighing 20 kg with an extremely thin 390 gram 'plastic' disc! The response from the wind turbine manufacturer, though, was positive and, although accessing this additional market still meant the LCD business was trivial in GKN terms, Andrew got the green light for further development. This was due not least to the fact that LBO had considerable political power within the GKN organization, were interested in finding an improved replacement for the CVJ joint used in wind turbines at the time, and were ready to invest £60–70,000 in the tooling and testing of the LCD.

HISTORY OF GKN

Under its current name GKN had started trading at the beginning of the 20th century when three companies got together: John Guest whose ancestor had started iron smelting in Wales in 1767, Arthur Keen who had started a bolt company in the 1860s, and John Sutton Nettlefolds, specializing in woodscrews, wire and metal rods. Soon after that the company added forging, rolling and stamping to its portfolio. The company rode on the increased demands for automobiles in the first half of the last century, complementing its existing expertise in the 1960s through acquisitions. In the late 1960s GKN expanded its operations into Germany by acquiring a stake in Uni-Cardan AG, maker of constant velocity joints (CVJ). International expansion continued during the 1970s with business acquisitions in Australia, US and France.

In the 1980s GKN diversified its service operations and strengthened its automotive business through further acquisitions while disposing of most of its interests in steel. It was also in the late 1980s that GKN acquired a stake in Westland, a UK helicopter maker (bought outright in 1994). When Hong Kong-born Sir C.K. Chow took over as Chief Executive in 1996, he found a GKN that looked, as the *Economist* described, 'More like an Asian mini-conglomerate than a textbook firm focused on a core business.' In the 1997 Annual report Chow wrote, 'We redefined our corporate values earlier this year. GKN's traditional values, to which we have a firm and continuing commitment, relate to our dedication to our customers, respect for and development of our people, and a sense

> In 1999 GKN had three main business lines:
>
> 1. *Automotive* including automotive driveline, powder metallurgy, auto components, off-highway vehicle systems; 51% of business or £2394 m in 99
>
> 2. *Aerospace* including aerospace structures and helicopters; 31% of business or £1439 m in 99
>
> 3. *Industrial services* including Chep (pallets, etc.), Cleanaway (waste disposal), Meineke (exhaust replacement chain in US) 17% of business or £810 m in 99

of responsibility towards the communities in which we operate and the environment in which we all live. To these we have added a commitment to fostering entrepreneurship and innovation. We encourage our people to create wealth by being innovative and resourceful in meeting the needs of our customers. We want them to be commercially agile and to manage risk carefully. We also want to create an environment which allows them to perform at a high speed.'

The drive towards entrepreneurship and innovation was reflected in a three-horizon approach. The aim of Sir C.K. Chow, to transform the old-established UK engineering company into an innovative, fast growing leader in its chosen markets, resulted in the divestment of the Industrial Services business in August 2001. With consolidation achieved, GKN also revised its approach to innovation. GKN's top management decided that Horizon 3 projects should no longer be pursued, but that increased emphasis should be placed on Horizon 1 and Horizon 2 developments (perhaps including the LCD coupling) that related to the core automotive and aerospace businesses.

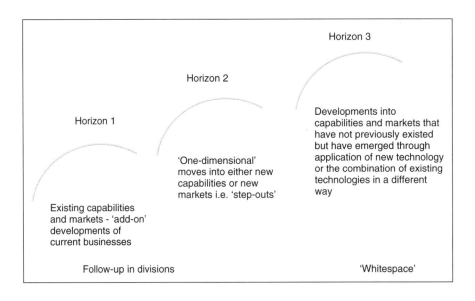

FULL STEAM AHEAD

In September 1997, after LBO committed funds for further development of the LCD, Ian Leadbetter, Engineering Director GKN Automotive Driveline (ADD), agreed that to enable the project to move forwards, Andrew should be allowed to communicate directly with Dansk Uni-Cardan, the Danish GKN company that supplied to the wind turbine producer. Until this point, the communication and product engineering chain ran from GKN Technology through ADD Engineering to the Engineering Department in LBO (one of the ADD business units), and back down through the Aftermarket Operations (AMO) organization to Dansk Uni-Cardan.

Andrew spent 1998/99 communicating to other AMO companies within GKN, to explore other potential application areas for the LCD coupling, as it was thought that GKN AMO would be the customer-facing unit – and they were quite enthusiastic about it. Andrew was pulling strings wherever he could, which meant working to get the helicopter division interested, and (successfully) applying for a 'Millennium Product' award. Receiving the award was particularly helpful in protecting the project internally. In

In 1998 Ian was succeeded by Graeme Walford, who in turn left GKN in August 2001. (He was replaced in November 2001 by Al Deane, previously responsible for engineering in the USA.) While not convinced personally, Graeme was fairly supportive of the project and gave advice and inputs to the ADD Financial Director between April and August 2001.

the meantime, Dansk Uni-Cardan were successfully winning new business for the application of the LCD in wind turbines, while AMO UK were making inroads into motorsport applications. All these activities led Andrew to feel that he was successfully sowing the seeds to a viable business.

There was a small structural change to GKN Automotive in January 1999, which was helpful to Andrew's project. The AMO companies had previously operated as quite independent national units, mainly after sales services and the distribution of spares, and reporting at the divisional (GKN Automotive) level. In 1999, they were formed as a business unit within ADD. This made it more legitimate to cultivate direct links between GKN Technology and the AMO companies.

Relevant parts of GKN structure, after January 1999

A significant problem arose in late 1999 when Graeme Walford made organizational changes within ADD Engineering, which resulted in Andrew reporting to a different director. The new R&D director was adamant that only projects directly relevant to automotive were to be continued; all others had to be wound up.

END OR BEGINNING?

In early 2000 there was a whole host of arguments as to why the project should be discontinued, not only the lack of relevance to automotive:

- The manufacturing process had nothing in common with existing ADD operations

- A product aspiring to sales of £5 m was seen to be too much of a niche product in an organization with total sales approaching £2000 m

> Andrew recalls, 'All in all, I was generally able to persuade people that it was a worthwhile project. But those I could not persuade made things quite difficult for me.'

- It was seen to represent a distraction to ADD management time

- Drawing on resources that could be used better to support existing business

- The organization was not set up to cater for start-up businesses

In short, the LCD was not able to meet company criteria and did not fit into any of the existing GKN boxes. It seemed that in an organization set-up for maximizing returns from existing products and delivering against set customer expectations, the culture was such that, as someone put it, 'It would crush anything that is in its wake.'

Andrew realized that if he could not come up with an alternative solution, the project would soon be officially stopped. Explaining his determination, he said 'In R&D about 95% of the work you do disappears without trace so, if you hit something, you really want to pursue it; it is about making something real out of an idea.' Another personnel change did not help much either: in December 2000, AMO got a new CEO who was supportive of the project in principle, but felt that AMO's business was about sales, not manufacture of a technical product.

One aspect of the strategy for GKN set out by Sir C.K. Chow, though, was very much to Andrew's advantage: the drive to increase innovation. In 1999 GKN had set up an Innovation & Learning Group (ILG) that was responsible for coordinating and stimulating innovation and learning activities from a central level, and one aim was to identify potential new lines of business. After finding out about it and developing his case, Andrew emailed Jenny Smith (Manager, Innovation & Learning) of the ILG. She recalls, 'Andrew felt that what he was doing was not quite strategic enough and that if he was released from his "normal" activities he could do more. I could tell he felt quite strongly about it.' She raised the issue with Marcus Beresford, the Chairman of the ILG and an Executive Director of GKN plc, and it was decided that this project might serve as a good example for what GKN wanted to achieve with its drive for entrepreneurship in the organization. They felt that it would be a good project to trial processes and concepts they planned to develop for the incubation of new businesses.

In October 2000 the GKN Plc board decided that Andrew should be given the mandate to develop a business plan to spin off the LCD business as an independent company. He was taken out of line reporting and given six months to find, finance and launch as an independent business. The assignment was signed off by two of the company's board directors, Marcus Beresford – his responsibilities included the ILG – and Ian Griffiths, the board member responsible for GKN Automotive. Andrew made sure the announcement would be made publicly as he knew that top management's officially declared support would be instrumental in securing the help and input from other people within the organization. In addition, KPMG were hired in January 2001 to act as independent advisers to Andrew – rather than GKN – to help develop a viable business plan and add credibility with external investors.

THE BUSINESS PLAN

To validate the idea, Jenny also asked Andrew to present to the St John's Innovation Centre near Cambridge. The St John's Centre is linked to Cambridge University Science Park, and its aim is to encourage and help incubate new businesses; the Centre works with about 400 businesses per year. Financially, the centre is backed by the university and draws additional funds from leasing space in its buildings outside Cambridge. The presentation in July 2000 went very well, and Walter Herriot, its director, recalls, 'The business plan Andrew brought was pretty good. It was clear that Andrew was well motivated, intelligent and had a business background. He was mature in age as well – as opposed to most other people who come here to present their business plan. This meant that his

St John's College is an educational charity and has set up the St John's Innovation Centre Ltd to:

- Enable the College to maximize the return on its investment by the efficient professional management of the Park

- Provide a supportive environment for tenant businesses by providing quality, cost-effective services

- Provide an environment in which technology transfer and innovation are promoted to assist small and medium-sized business at a local, national and international level business plan was much higher up in the chain of probability. His proposal required much less input than most others.'

According to Walter Herriot, the majority of spinouts did not come from universities, as widely believed, but from within companies. Discussions with Walter emphasized the importance of clarifying IPR issues. In the case of the LCD, this was complicated by the fact that some patents were registered in the name of the German inventor – and that in fact German patenting laws were different.

The development of the business plan took Andrew up to April 2001, somewhat beyond the target completion date of March 2001. As he recalls: 'They realized that it was not a straightforward process, but that I was getting somewhere so they continued to support me.' The plan also set out a need for commercial expertise and input; whilst Andrew had all technical expertise necessary to make a success of the business, it was obvious that additional management and business skills would be needed. Investment was needed to procure tooling to produce a full product range of the LCD coupling, to carry out tests on the prototype couplings to obtain data needed to publish specifications, to improve some of the production processes and to undertake commercialization.

It was reckoned that the LCD had potential to be applied to a wide range of industries. Industrial driveshafts are used in a huge range of applications, typically to transfer power between motors, gearboxes and loads. Some applications, for example, are the driveshafts between gearbox and generator in a wind turbine, fan driveshafts in cooling towers, pump driveshafts, rail traction driveshafts, marine driveshafts, cranes, escalators, etc. The overall potential world market for flexible couplings needed for such driveshafts was estimated to be $1.1–$1.4 billion. Unlike automotive applications (dominated by couplings capable of working at big angles), the industrial market is dominated by couplings optimized for small angles. The real uncertainty was how big a share of this market might be taken by the LCD, particularly considering that in many industries lengthy testing is required before a component's safety and reliability is accepted. There were also two other companies, both based in the USA, that could be considered competitors in using composites to produce flexible driveshaft couplings, but none in Europe.

FINDING INVESTORS

After finishing his business plan, Andrew started campaigning to investors in May 2001; all in all he gave over 20 presentations. KPMG had contacts with investors, but Andrew was also fairly proactive in identifying possible parties. He went to a few DTI events and made contact with Investor Champions, a network of Business Angels. Through Investor Champions he did a presentation in July 2001 on-site at GKN Technology to about 12 participants who had enquired about the business plan. Rather than being venture capital funds or companies, this group was made up predominantly by individuals of means. A few followed up further and Andrew continued discussions with one particular individual around whom a consortium based in the Midlands developed.

He also went to the British Venture Capital Association website and did a search to find VCs who might have an interest in similar products/businesses. The names of the individuals identified he passed on to KPMG, who then wrote a letter introducing the idea. About one-third of the 20 parties approached requested the business plan, and one contact led indirectly to a London-based consortium.

By September 2001 Andrew and some senior members from GKN had several conversations with the two interested consortia. However, while the initial interest had been very positive, both consortia now wanted to renegotiate the venture's structure, and requested that the new company should be given the freedom to pursue automotive applications of not only the disk, but also other products based on the composite, to exploit the technical know-how that would be transferred to the new company.

QUESTIONS

1. What would your decision regarding the LCD have been and why?

2. What are alternative approaches to dealing with highly innovative or marginal products within large, established organizations?

APPENDIX I: MANUFACTURING FLOW FOR THE CDJ

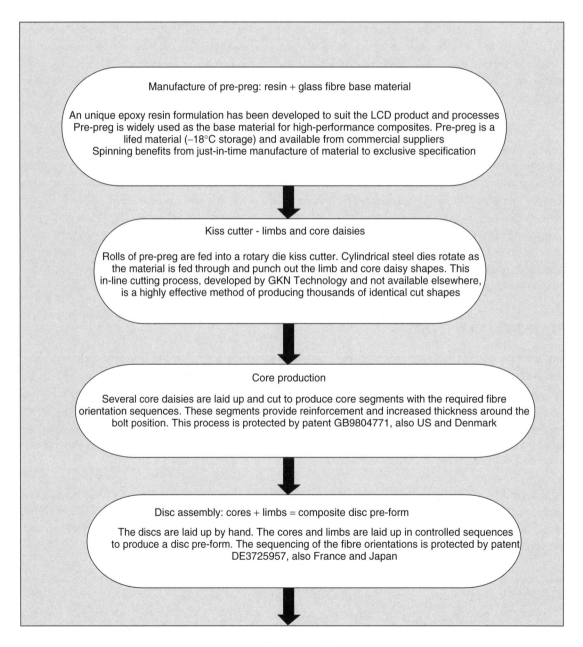

Manufacture of pre-preg: resin + glass fibre base material

An unique epoxy resin formulation has been developed to suit the LCD product and processes
Pre-preg is widely used as the base material for high-performance composites. Pre-preg is a lifed material (−18°C storage) and available from commercial suppliers
Spinning benefits from just-in-time manufacture of material to exclusive specification

Kiss cutter - limbs and core daisies

Rolls of pre-preg are fed into a rotary die kiss cutter. Cylindrical steel dies rotate as the material is fed through and punch out the limb and core daisy shapes. This in-line cutting process, developed by GKN Technology and not available elsewhere, is a highly effective method of producing thousands of identical cut shapes

Core production

Several core daisies are laid up and cut to produce core segments with the required fibre orientation sequences. These segments provide reinforcement and increased thickness around the bolt position. This process is protected by patent GB9804771, also US and Denmark

Disc assembly: cores + limbs = composite disc pre-form

The discs are laid up by hand. The cores and limbs are laid up in controlled sequences to produce a disc pre-form. The sequencing of the fibre orientations is protected by patent DE3725957, also France and Japan

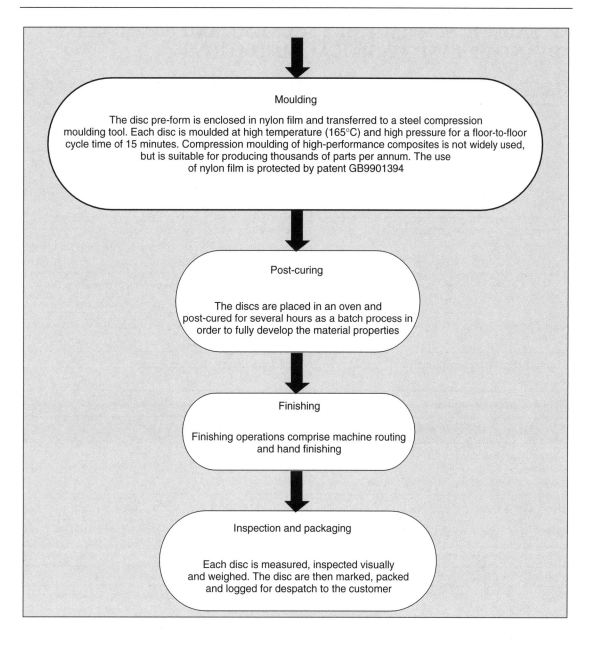

Moulding

The disc pre-form is enclosed in nylon film and transferred to a steel compression moulding tool. Each disc is moulded at high temperature (165°C) and high pressure for a floor-to-floor cycle time of 15 minutes. Compression moulding of high-performance composites is not widely used, but is suitable for producing thousands of parts per annum. The use of nylon film is protected by patent GB9901394

Post-curing

The discs are placed in an oven and post-cured for several hours as a batch process in order to fully develop the material properties

Finishing

Finishing operations comprise machine routing and hand finishing

Inspection and packaging

Each disc is measured, inspected visually and weighed. The disc are then marked, packed and logged for despatch to the customer

APPENDIX II: SUMMARY OF TECHNICAL AND COMMERCIAL ADVANTAGES AND TECHNICAL LIMITATIONS

LCD joints – technical competitive advantages	
High operating efficiency, joints run cool	Key for wind turbines, motorsport – any application where high power is sustained for long periods or absolutely minimum energy losses desired
Low axial stiffness	Minimizes force transmission between connected systems; can be important for gearboxes, noise and vibration transmission
Low weight, low inertia, no backlash	Low weight is often desirable. Can be extremely important for high acceleration systems, e.g. positioning servo drives
Good tolerance of angular misalignment	Better than most alternatives, e.g. steel disc couplings typically restricted to 0.75° continuous angle
Good tolerance of harsh environments	e.g. humidity, temperature, salt water, ozone, oils – all of which can cause problems for other coupling types
Non-conductive, non-magnetic, radar transparent	Electrical isolation is often important
No wear, maintenance free	Major advantage over gear couplings
LCD joints – commercial competitive advantages	
Comprehensive patent cover	Appendix C
Exclusive, vertically integrated m/t process	Section 7
Resin system exclusive to GKN	With m/t process, prevents product copying
GKN brand and driveshaft know-how	
LCD joints – technical limitations	
Restricted axial load capacity	Consequence of low axial stiffness
Torsionally still, no torsional damping	In common with gear couplings and laminated steel couplings, but torsional compliance and damping can be important for a significant share of the market
Can't accept radial misalignment as a single coupling	Some (low speed) coupling types can, but in mitigation the thinness of the disc enables very short spacer couplings which is important for a significant range of applications, e.g. rail

21 How to Infuse Innovation?

In a way, much of the GKN case study is about how large organizations approach innovation. What structures and processes could they use to infuse organization, and are different kinds of processes needed for incremental versus radical innovation? Should venture capital be sought? The following two chapters address these issues.

In this chapter, we review two aspects of infusing innovation into organizations: first, idea generation and suggestion schemes; secondly, different possible organizational structures for infusing innovation. The chapter concludes with a few considerations about the differences between incremental and radical innovation, and their implications.

IDEA MANAGEMENT

The issue of idea management, already mentioned in Chapter 16, will be investigated here in more depth, looking at three aspects:

- Idea generation
- Idea selection
- Managing 'unsuitable' ideas

IDEA GENERATION

Based on the insights that great ideas can come from anywhere within the organization, most companies operate idea suggestion schemes. Getting these right, however, is quite critical for making them a success. Many companies are reporting a paradox around idea generation: they report that they get more ideas than they can cope with while at the same time lamenting that the ideas they have are not enough. It is all less paradoxical when understanding that the ideas companies get through suggestion schemes are plenty, but not exciting enough. Managers are often frustrated with the quality of ideas generated through suggestion schemes. Some feel that employees will only come forward with great ideas when suitable financial rewards are given. However, there is quite some controversy about the effectiveness of financial rewards in eliciting innovative ideas, and the consensus seem to shift towards the view that financial rewards do not make a difference, and that in fact they might even have a negative effect. However, recognition of some kind is essential, otherwise people feel ignored and undervalued. Many employees will be motivated by public recognition through awards and ceremonies, others by being able to put up a certificate in their office. It might be a good idea to have a number of different possibilities available to cater for different tastes and preferences.

A second issue around idea generation is that of managing feedback and communication. It is important to provide timely and satisfactory feedback on all ideas submitted, otherwise people get frustrated, feel undervalued and are not likely to offer any further insights and ideas. There is a second issue around the volume of ideas coming through the system. There is the danger of allowing too many projects to start, as the initial resource requirements tend to be quite low. This can give a false sense of security and lead to problems when the project needs to be scaled up. It is therefore important to have mechanisms in place that allow consideration of the entire product portfolio, the identification of project that best complement existing activities, and the termination of projects that fail to meet set criteria.

A very powerful method for dealing with large numbers of ideas is to group them into themes. This has several advantages. First, it makes it possible to tell every single person that has submitted an idea that their idea has contributed to and has flown forward into something, i.e. every person feels that they were able to make a contribution. Secondly, theming ideas provides managers with some 'hotspots', i.e. it helps identify areas where there seems to be an opportunity for new product or service offerings. And the third point is, even if none of the many ideas that feed into a theme is the right one, the theme itself provides a starting point for developing ideas that will be stronger than any of the original ones.

The third comment relates to the incremental/radical issue. Suggestion schemes tend to be great for the former but bad for the latter. This is partly due to the way such suggestion schemes operate. Ideas tend to be reviewed either by a small team of people, or by peers who have an expertise relevant to the suggestion made. This is fine for incremental innovations, but less likely to work for radical innovations for the following reasons:

- If the idea is really radical it may be difficult to describe into the standard submission form

- If something is really new existing expertise is more likely to cause a rejection – 'we have tried this before', 'I know that it does not work because...'

- Radical ideas tend to need room to grow and develop, they tend to change shape and scope

- Selling radical ideas requires persuasion and explanation, neither is easily done on a single sheet of paper

But generating just incremental innovations need not be a bad thing. Even small improvements or changes can result in significant cost savings (though *not* new income streams). As cost cutting seems to be an issue with most companies most of the time, suggestion schemes are a valuable source for identifying cost savings opportunities. In their book *Corporate Creativity*, Robinson and Stern (1997) give many great examples of how small changes have resulted in big cost savings. The following one is from American Airlines. A cabin crew had noticed that most people (72%) do not eat the olive in their salad. Big deal, one might say. But when knowing that the salad is costed based on the number of different items included, it starts to make a bit more sense: four different items cost 60 cents, whereas five different items were priced at 80 cent. Serving the salad without the olive saved the airlines around $500,000 per year. So the fact that idea suggestion schemes generate incremental rather than radical ideas does not mean that they cannot generate great financial savings.

Box 21.1 shows the example of the very successful idea suggestion scheme run by the University of Arizona. All people need to know fits onto one page: a focus and clear evaluation criteria, what information is required when submitting an idea, how, when and by whom suggestions will be reviewed and taken forward, and assurance that senior managers support the scheme.

BOX 21.1   The University of Arizona Employee Suggestion Program

PURPOSE

Bright Ideas! is a University-wide program designed to encourage all employees of the University of Arizona community to contribute innovative suggestions that can enhance campus life and working conditions.

Suggestions should be creative and should benefit the University by:

- improving the quality of working conditions and campus life;
- eliminating inefficiencies, waste or duplication;
- saving money, resources or time;
- streamlining administrative procedures and operating methods; and
- increasing safety, promoting health, or improving morale.

Suggestions must be realistic, cite a specific area for improvement, include a brief analysis of the intended results, and recommendations for potential implementation strategies.

Bright Ideas! will be reviewed by a committee made up of various University employees from all over the UA campus.

HOW DO I SUBMIT MY *BRIGHT IDEA*?

Any UA faculty, staff, or student employee—or group of employees—may submit a suggestion at any time. Suggestions made be submitted <u>on-line</u>, via e-mail, campus mail, or fax by using a suggestion form and including all pertinent information outlined below.

Suggestions should include:

- A description of the problem to be addressed or the area to be improved;
- A detailed description of the solution; and
- An analysis of the benefits to the University.

The Suggestion Coordinator will immediately acknowledge, in writing, the receipt of each suggestion. The suggestion is encoded to ensure anonymity and then forwarded to the *Bright Ideas*! Suggestion Team. Each *Bright Ideas*! suggestion will be reviewed at the Team's bimonthly meetings.

The Suggestion Team will submit results and recommendations of appropriate ideas to the Program Sponsors. Ideas that are more appropriately dealt with at the college or unit level will be referred to a suitable individual for further evaluation and action.

Bright Ideas! will be awarded and recognized upon implementation. The Suggestion Team will present employees with cash awards, plaques, or other great gifts for meritorious *Bright Ideas!*

THE *BRIGHT IDEAS!* TEAM

The following individuals are the current team members. They represent a wide cross-section of the University community; faculty, staff, students and appointed personnel.

▶

[This is followed by a list of names and telephone numbers and the names of the program sponsors, in this case the Senior Vice President for Business Affairs and the Associate Vice President for Administrative Services.]

(http://w3.arizona.edu/%7Ebright/index.html)

If a suggestion scheme does not work, one of the following might be the reason:

- *Political games* – decisions for which ideas to take forward are based on personal preference, nepotism or budgetary considerations rather than clear selection criteria and merit of the ideas

- *Overload* – the flood of ideas has been underestimated and resource to manage and assess incoming ideas are insufficient, leading to people not being kept up to date with progress, which in turn destroys positive energy and trust

- *Lack of sincerity* – if the scheme has been in place 'because everyone does it' instead of the true belief that it creates value, and if managers are not really interested at all in the ideas brought forward

- *'Illiteracy'* – the inability to express (from the person submitting the idea) or understand (by the person reading the suggestion), particularly if the idea is more radical or 'off the wall'

Having said earlier that suggestion schemes tend to produce incremental rather than radical ideas, there are also ways to set up schemes as to be more conducive to the submission of more radical ideas. An example of such a scheme that seems to work quite well is given in Box 21.2.

BOX 21.2   Innovation Fund (von Stamm 2001)

The underlying principle is, 'no risk, no money'. This is a significant change in our culture and in the first year about 30% of applications emphasized the low or no risk factor of the idea – we rejected them for that particular reason to make sure people understood that we were truly looking for different, more risky projects. The fund is non-bureaucratic. Initially all that is needed is to fill in a two-page form, available either as hard copy or on the intranet, which will be turned around in two days. We have some set criteria – known by everyone – against which the suggestions are evaluated:

- Business and strategic fit
- Substantial potential benefit to business – BIG
- Not business as usual, think high risk
- Needs to have a senior business sponsor
- Potential substantial technology capability acquisition

Other things we are looking for are:

- Commitment, enthusiasm, vision (use virtual groups, wide range of backgrounds, etc.)
- Client/customer involvement (think early about realization and implementation)
- Supplier support/participation

▶

The funding process involves four stages:

1. Enrolment (that's when senior business person's support is required)
2. Concept – concept development (what support would be needed to get to market)
3. Demonstration
4. Pilot

From stage 4 onwards, 50% of cost are to be carried by a business unit, i.e. there is tapered funding – but these rules are not written in stone, people can jump to any stage. All suggestions are stored electronically; the database is not available internally yet but will be. We have also plans to publish projects that have won awards on our website.

Finally, suggestion schemes are only one way to generate ideas. Best practice companies combine continuous idea generation through suggestion schemes with 'bursts of idea generation', for example through focused brainstorming sessions. Such sessions are more likely to generate some radical ideas, but the most likely source for radical ideas remains the individual. Building on an article by Prather and Turrell (2002), Table 21.1 provides a comparison of 'continuous' and 'bursts'.

Table 21.1 Idea Generation – Continuous versus Bursts (building on Prather and Turrell 2002) (Reprinted by permission of Harvard Business Review. From 'Spark innovation through emphatic design' by Leonard, D. and Rayport, J.F. November-December, 1997. Copyright @ 1997 by the Harvard Business School Publishing Corporation; all rights reserved)

	Employee suggestion system	Creative problem-solving workshop
Use when...	To involve all employees On a particular problem from a wide range of perspectives	Known problem, particularly difficult
Potential number of participants	Limited only by the number of people who have access to the system	Small group of people Diversity and lateral thinking are important
Type of ideas generated	Tactical rather than strategic Usually easy to implement Tend to be of incremental rather than radical nature Cost saving rather than new business	More strategic than tactical Implementation often more difficult and time consuming Of radical rather than incremental nature New business rather than cost saving
For success, this is required...	Visible and continued top management support Clear and easily understood structures and procedures for input as well as selection Sufficient resources to manage suggestions	Strong team leader Problem is real, important, no easy solution, specific, requires action Needs dedicated time for the team (the authors suggest two days) Benefits from experienced facilitator

IDEA SELECTION

Once ideas have been generated the next challenge is, which ones to select? This is often seen as a greater challenge than the generation of ideas. The Innovation Trend Survey conducted by the Confederation of British Industry (CBI), published in February 2001, came to the same conclusion, 'Idea generation may not be a problem for most, but how effective are companies in picking up these ideas, recognizing their worth and turning them into innovations?'

Looking at the company's overall product portfolio is one way, and we have discussed this in Chapter 3. The 'Buyer Utility Map' (see Box 21.3) developed by Kim and Mauborgne (2000) is a variation on the theme of portfolio management. They suggest looking at the different stages of the buyer experience cycle and a number of product aspects that create value to customers. Existing products can be mapped onto the matrix, giving an indication of the fields that are already addressed through existing products. The managers can then decide which of the 'open windows' they might want to address with their new developments. Used this way the matrix can be used as starting point for idea development. However, it can also be used to map existing ideas, identify where hotspots are, and check that against existing offerings. A great way of ensuring that development efforts are focused on satisfying a new or different need, rather than being 'yet another one of these'.

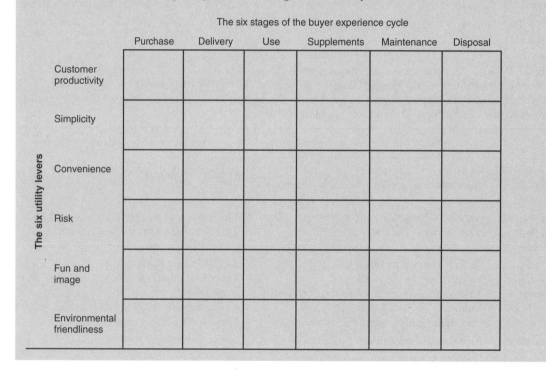

BOX 21.3   The Buyer Utility Map (Kim and Mauborgne 2000) (Reprinted by permission of Harvard Business Review. From 'Knowing a winning buisness idea when you see one' by Kim, C.W. and Mauborgne, R. September–October, 2000. Copyright 2000 by the Harvard Business School Publishing Corporation; all rights reserved)

Kim and Mauborgne give Starbucks as an example of a company that has used a different lever at the same stage (offering fun and image instead of competing on prices), whereas Dell is an example of a company that has used the same utility lever in a new stage (competing via distribution rather than faster computers). Finally, there is of course the option of using a new lever in a new stage. Here the authors give the Alto lightbulb developed by electronics giant Philips as an example (offering environmental friendliness and convenience at the disposal stage).[1]

MANAGING 'UNSUITABLE' IDEAS

Not all ideas collected are of immediate value. In the previous section we looked at ways of identifying the right ideas. However, there might be great value in those that were not selected. In Chapter 16 we have already suggested that there is value in storing unused ideas in a meaningful way in a database. Making most of those is an art that not many organizations have discovered yet. There are a number of options:

- Ideas can be revisited periodically to see whether their applicability or the reasons for rejection have changed

- Ideas can be sold off to parts of the company or other organizations that are closer aligned to the concept

- New ideas can be checked against the database to see whether something similar has been tried before, what the result was, and why

- Even if individual ideas might be difficult to realize, a theme might be emerging that is worth pursuing

In addition, there might be cases where a product has been developed, be it through skunkworks or regular project work, that does no longer seem to fit with corporate objectives – as in the GKN case study. The question is, what to do with ideas that have great potential but do not really fit with what we are doing? One way is to set up a separate business unit and/or spin it out. Table 21.2 provides managers with a check list of questions for each stage of the development process that will help to make and execute the critical decision whether or not to spin.

Some best practice for idea management includes:

- *Scan high and low* – involving customers as well as suppliers; using suggestion schemes as well as bursts of idea generation

- *Provide focus for idea generation* – which can be cutting cost; the identification high risk/high reward projects; a particular topic or for a particular part of the business

- *Be clear about the innovation ambition* – e.g. how radical should the suggestions be, how closely do they need to fit with existing business; are you really interested in taking forward something that is outside your organization's core?

- *Offer a clear structure* – a simple process, information requirements, time lines, etc.

- *Start with lots of ideas and encourage experimentation but narrow down quickly* – select an idea and create lots of variations around that particular idea rather than develop loads and loads of ideas

> 'A lot of trial and error goes into making things look effortless.'
> Bill Moggridge, IDEO, in the *Financial Times*, 30 July 2002

- *Summarize and combine* – to reduce the total number of ideas you may want to group them together under emerging themes; these themes can also be used to start focused idea generation sessions

- *Make submission of ideas easy and provide good support* – don't ask for complete business plans

- *Ensure that rejections are not taken personally* – people need to know why ideas are selected or rejected, which means that the selection criteria are known by everyone in the organization

- *Manage and store* all *ideas* – provide mechanisms that allow the most value to be got out of your pool of ideas, whether it is by using them yourself or selling them off (at whatever stage of their development), and be prepared to sell off those ideas that do not fit with your corporate strategy

Table 21.2 Challenges and Considerations for Spinouts (Lord, Mandel and Wagner 2002) (Reprinted by permission of Harvard Business Review. From 'Spinning out a Star' by Lord, M.D., Mandel, S.W. and Wager, J.D. January, 2002. Copyright 2002 by the Harvard Business School Publishing Corporation; all rights reserved)

Stage	Key challenge	Critical consideration	Recommendation
Conception	The decision: why and when to spinout (or not)	Is spinout really the right strategic choice? Or should we develop internally, form partnerships, license, sell, or simply cut the programme? What is the best way to maximize value creation?	Make sure the spinout has a sound strategic logic behind it. Ensure that it is not driven by short-term financial gimmicks and that it is indeed a non-core asset with a solid case as a standalone business
Gestation	The team: leadership and championing	Who will lead and champion the nascent venture? Should the leader come from outside or inside the corporate parent? Which key managerial and technical people should go with the spinout and which should stay with the parent?	Initially, a leader from the ranks of the parent company may best be able to navigate the process; later, increased external leadership likely will be required or negotiated, especially as the spinout's independence grows
	The strategy: focus and purpose	What will be the specific strategic scope and direction of the spinout? What are its vision, mission, goals, and objectives, especially *vis-à-vis* the parent?	The spinout should have a clear understanding of what it is and what it will do, reduce future tension and conflicts with the parent by defining its focus and boundaries upfront
	The organization: creating internal autonomy	Is it necessary to create internal legal, financial, and organizational autonomy for the spinout as a prelude to its eventual separation from the parent, and if so, how?	Create a legally separate subsidiary or affiliate with its own management, organization, and books. Minimize complex parent–offspring ties
Separation	Alliances: attracting and negotiating with outside partners	Who should we pursue as partners? How can we convince them to join? How can the parent and spinout best tackle the three-way negotiations?	Gather outside partners to validate and accelerate the separation process Remember that spinout partners don't want to be entangled in complex or subordinate relationships with the parent
	Funding: attracting and negotiating with outside investors	Who should we pursue as investors? How much should we sell and at what prices? Again, how can the parent and spinout best tackle the three-way negotiations?	As with partners, outside investors should be brought in to validate the merits of the venture and to accelerate the separation process. But investors need to know that they are on a clear and level playing field when investing in the spinout, not one skewed by entanglements with the parent
	Freedom: achieving true independence	What should be the nature of the relationship between parent and offspring? How can the spinout be free to chart its own course while still allowing the parent to recoup its investment?	The parent should drop to a minority stake and should not dominate the spinout's management or board. Any remaining umbilical ties should probably be severed so that dealings between the parent and the spinout stay at arm's length

STRUCTURES FOR INNOVATION

Under this heading there are probably two main issues that need to be discussed. The first is what kind of structure companies use to infuse innovation; the second is what kind of innovation they are hoping to achieve through the chosen structure. Not always do companies proceed to ask the second question, which can lead to problems. Let us start with looking at the different structures that companies use to infuse innovation.

There are a number of different ways in which organizations can approach innovation, as insights from an Innovation Workshop held July 2002 illustrate (see Box 21.4). However, there are possibly three main starting points companies use:

- The innovation champion (standalone)
- The dedicated innovation team (bolt-on)
- The central innovation department with 'ambassadors' (infusion)

Each approach has its merits and issues – and which choice a company makes will generally depend upon their specific circumstances. It also seems that it has an impact at what stage in the innovation journey the company is.

BOX 21.4 Different Approaches for Starting Innovation (http@//iexchange.london. edu (based on Innovation Exchange Workshop July 2002))

(1) Company A: as a result of his original work remit becoming redundant Stephen decided to redefine his job description. Building on the premise that the organization needed to address IP issues he and James started an innovation group, for which they gained the support of the new MD. One of the main strategies of making it happen and gathering support was to always say 'not a problem, we can do that (for you)'. The initiative has been very successful and is gathering momentum.

(2) Company B: at group level an innovation champion was put in place, supported by a top-level steering group. The main aim of the initiative was to generate Horizon 3 ideas and business concepts; with tightening economic conditions the decision was made to dissolve the steering group and delegate responsibility for innovation back to individual divisions. Discussions are taking place whether there are benefits to the centre taking a stronger role again.

(3) Company C: innovation has been identified as a key driver to future business success though the company had already successfully introduced innovations in the past. An innovation team was set up to investigate how best to set up and support a corporate venturing unit, and fill the newly introduced product development process with life.

(4) Company D: this situation is slightly different. The team Tim represented is not directly involved in the generation of ideas but the facilitation of it through D's Innovation Lab enabling the people of the business to do their own 'innovation' as part of their every day work. Thus 'innovative ideas' are not thrust upon them from 'innovation teams' with all the associated issues of lack of commitment, time and resource.

INNOVATION CHAMPION

The innovation champion tends to be a bit of a lone fighter, often tasked with infusing innovation into an organization single-handedly. Such a position tends to come with a wide remit and lots of freedom – but generally little authority.

As one champion explained, 'At present I feel I am just adding to people's workload. I can only ask people to do things, not tell them – but then, people are generally very cooperative. We have very good people, but they don't (yet) understand the value and role of innovation so it's often hard work.'

The individuals, generally very enthusiastic and highly committed to their course, tend to report into a senior manager – which seems to indicate that it is a top management priority. However, at times it feels as if establishing the position of an innovation champion is somewhat of a token gesture. One is seen to be doing something – but the belief that things will really change is quite limited.

The question is also, what happens when the individual leaves or is moved on. It seems that one of two things can happen: either the position disappears, or a team is put in its place. If the former is the case, the organization goes 'back to normal' – the attempt of infusing innovation has failed. In the latter, management has realized both the value of innovation and that a lone fighter – depending on the size of the organization of course – cannot by him- or herself turn attitudes and behaviours of an entire organization around. More often than not, nothing. It does not seem to happen that there is a series of individual innovation champions.

However, having said all that, if a company is really serious about infusing innovation into their organization and the innovation champion has authority as well as responsibility, he or she can actually make a real difference. This seems to have been the case in one of the participating companies where the innovation champion explained, 'I get visible support from the top and everyone knows I am acting on their behalf.' But it should also be pointed out that behind this champion is not one senior manager but an entire group of senior executives: 'Members of the innovation and learning group are all senior people and come from the different divisions, so the initiative is recognized as being high profile – and spans across the entire organization.'

And one last comment on champions. The literature generally highlights the importance of a champion or strong project leader in order for projects – innovation or otherwise – to be successful. This literature tends to refer to new product development and the individual project level, not necessarily to a company-wide initiative. However, looking at the list of desirable attributes for project leaders, taken from *Project Management*, by Harvey Maylor (1996) (see Box 3.2, Chapter 3), this is true for larger projects too – as long as the two balances are kept:

- No responsibility without authority
- No authority without accountability

DEDICATED INNOVATION TEAM

A different approach is the setting up of a separate innovation team. This tends to be driven by the insight that innovation requires a different culture from that of day-to-day business, but that establishing an innovation culture may take too long – or that change in the overall company culture does not seem desirable.

In this situation, responsibility for innovation is delegated to the innovation team – whereby it has to be said that the kind of innovation an organization is looking for when setting up a separate, dedicated innovation team tends to be radical rather than incremental. Incremental and 'day-to-day' stuff happens within the existing business – though people can interpret the fact that a dedicated innovation team exists as releasing them from any responsibility to think 'innovation'. We will come back to the differing requirements of radical and incremental innovation in the last section of this chapter.

The reaction of the rest of the organization to the establishment of an innovation team is often mixed – at all levels. Such teams often encounter great scepticism from people in the parent organization, who do not believe that they could actually have an impact. And even though top management tends to subscribe nominally to such teams, real belief is often lacking.

A very important consideration when setting up an independent innovation team is what mechanisms to develop to bind the group back into the main organization, and how to ensure that there remains sufficient common ground to avoid any NIH syndrome when transferring concepts back from the innovation team into the main organization. Communication, establishment of a mutual understanding of what each part of the organization can contribute to the whole, and constant exchange between the two parts of the organization are key in preventing the innovation team from becoming 'too independent'.

The way in which one member company of the Innovation Exchange has structured the innovation team seems be a very good approach for addressing such issues. The small team is made up of a number of dedicated full-time staff from different functions of the business – not necessarily innovation experts, but people who are excited by the idea, open-minded and creative. These are joined by (a) a number of part-time people who spend the other half of the time in their 'normal' jobs in the main organization, and (b) secondees from the main organization who spend 1–2 years with the team. In this way, a continuous flow of communication is ensured, which brings with it insights into what is happening in the group, and it might even spark an interest of people within the company for wanting to join the group.

A challenge for innovation teams is to remember that they have been set up to be different, and must therefore resist the development of stifling processes and procedures.

CENTRAL INNOVATION DEPARTMENT AND INNOVATION AMBASSADORS

The third approach combines a very senior team or individual (depending on company size) at central level with a team of 'innovation ambassadors'.[2] The role of the central team/individual is to coordinate innovation activities across the entire organization, evaluate and select projects, resource projects and monitor their progress, often beyond launch.

The innovation ambassador(s), while being part of the centre, will work alongside local teams and provide them with expertise, a company-wide perspective and company best practice. His or her role means that these people tend to be quite a senior, more often than not with a track record for innovation. This seems to be the approach preferred by multinational innovative companies, as it allows them to achieve a balance between 'central and local'.

Interesting, too, is the difference in the selection criteria for people on the innovation team versus innovation ambassadors. Where characteristics for the first included 'very young', 'fresh perspective', 'not caught up in company traditions', characteristics for the latter are focused more around 'experience and expertise', 'track record' and 'good company knowledge'. But looking at the purpose behind each approach might help explain the differences. A separate innovation team tends to *generate and explore ideas* that are radically different, whereas the innovation ambassador is brought in to help with the *implementation of ideas* and concepts.

This approach to infusing innovation is also quite different from the innovation champion, where innovation is seen to be an additional burden; the innovation ambassadors are an additional resource. And as the innovation ambassador tends to work alongside the local team, rather than spreading his or her wisdom from the lofty heights of headquarters, he or she tends to become accepted as a part of the team and a welcome extra pair of hands.

While each company needs to identify its particular needs around innovation and develop an approach to innovation that is specific and suitable to its context, there are some insights they might be useful for any of the three options, as well as different contexts.

- *Establishing credibility* – while support from the top is generally important, it is equally important that the people driving innovation have credibility and clout within the organization

- *Create urgent need for innovation* – innovation has to be seen as necessity, not a nicety; this might involve creating a 'crisis' or making the need explicit in any other way (e.g. future growth predictions, collapse of the product pipeline, competitor action, profit warnings)

- *Top-level sponsorship* – is critical, but note that the most appropriate and effective sponsor might not necessarily the most senior one; look for a sponsor who can influence others, make funds available, has credibility with others etc.

- *Generate small successes* – it might be necessary to 'prove' the success of an innovation team/initiative before being able to secure funds; 'liberating' funds to create these initial successes might be required; it is also important to pick the time for talking about the innovation initiative and successes, people need to want to listen – better to be asked about it than trying to do a 'hard sell'

- *Work with volunteers* – when starting a drive for innovation, working with people who want to be involved and who are enthusiastic is more likely to lead to success; if people are 'press ganged' into innovation services, they will do the minimum, not go the extra mile as often required; it might also help to make being involved in innovation something special: make involvement difficult but not impossible, people like a challenge

- *The right skill mix* – while volunteers are great, it is also important that they have the right skills and the right mix of skills; you need innovators as well as adaptors (see Kirton, Chapter 10)

- *Mix new and old blood* – involve people who are new to the organization as they are not infected by 'the way we do things around here' and hence can challenge assumptions and habits; at the same time you want people around who know the organization inside out and can explain why things are done a certain way and more importantly, how things work

- *Understand different needs* – understand different needs and what people might want to get out of innovation; this can be caused by differences in either national or departmental cultures

- *Clarify risk* – make sure people on the team are aware that it is a 'fire escape job' – though management should also make sure that there is a safety net for people to return into other jobs in the organization

- *Find ways of ringfencing innovation budgets* – if times get tough and resources are scarce, don't necessarily stop the innovative project, ask people whether they can liberate resources somewhere else

- *Adjust HR* – make sure innovation is integrated into people's performance measures; make sure it is not seen as a an overhead, separated from day-to-day business

- *Fun* – make it fun, it not only attracts people and makes them want to be part of it, it makes risk more acceptable

- *Space as symbol* – you may want to dedicate some space to the innovation activities, it is a visible commitment and focal point for those who want to contribute (see also Chapter 27)

INCREMENTAL VERSUS RADICAL – WHAT'S THE DIFFERENCE?

Most organizations would probably argue that they are quite good at incremental innovation – idea generation as well as implementation. Where companies seem to struggle more is radical innovation, and again, this applies to idea generation as well as implementation. However, there are probably not too many organizations that use different processes, depending which type of innovation they pursue. We have pointed out above that some approaches to infusing innovation are more likely to generate radical innovation than others. So why is it important to make the distinction, and what are differences in requirements for each kind? In their valuable book *Radical Innovation*, Leifer *et al.* (2000) provide some great insights as to why so many organizations struggle with radical innovation. They provide a comparison of conditions and facts for each type of innovation (see Table 21.3), from which it becomes crystal clear that these two different types cannot be approached in the same way.

The important point is, incremental and radical innovation require very different business conditions, skills, structures and processes. So if most organizations aim to achieve the two different types through the same systems and processes, it is not surprising that it does not lead to the desired results. Managers who are serious about radical innovation should set up separate structures, with different process, time frames and evaluation criteria. There are a number of options, and the innovation team introduced above can be one of them. Other distinct approaches are:

- *Internal venturing* – tends to be opportunistic; new companies are created internally and are wholly owned initially; possibility of spinout or spinin

> Two-thirds of the US top 100 companies are thought to be either using or thinking of using corporate venturing as a means of finding new customers, new markets and new technologies.
>
> CBI (2002)

- *Venture incubators* – as opposed to internal venturing, a separate unit is set up with the aim to create new business; new companies are seeded internally with a spinoff or spinin as options; examples are BT Brightstar or the P&G Ventures Group[3]

- *External venturing* – equity is purchased in external companies; can also be explored through joint ventures; often leading to acquisition; Intel Capital or Novartis' Bioventures are examples hereof. You may also want to refer to the TTP case study in Chapter 29

However, even when setting up a separate venture unit, it is still important that there is some unique link and contribution from parent to venture unit, be it synergies in R&D, distribution or existing industry relationships. If a project is completely outside the competencies of the parent organization, the question is why it should be linked at all (see also Table 21.2, 'Challenges and considerations for spinouts'). There are powerful examples that external venturing can be extremely profitable. For example, in 1999 Intel's external venture unit contributed 15% of company profits – though managers should be aware that many more radical innovations will take at least five years before starting to pay back.

Table 21.3 Incremental versus Radical Innovation (building on Leifer *et al.* 2000) (Adapted and reprinted by permission of Harvard Business School Press. From Radical Innovation – How Mature Companies Can Outsmart Upstarts by Liefer, R., McDermot, C.M., Colarelli, O'Conner, G., Peters, L.S., Rice, M. and Veryzer, R.W., Boston, MA 2000 by Daniel Goleman; all rights reserved)

	Incremental	Radical
Time frame	Short term – six to 24 months	Long term – usually ten years plus
Development trajectory	Step after step from conception to commercialization, high levels of certainty	Discontinuous, iterative, set-backs, lacking information, high levels of uncertainty
Idea generation and opportunity recognition	Continuous stream of incremental improvements readily available and tend to come up through systematic idea development or suggestion schemes; idea fully formed at outset; critical events large anticipated	Ideas often pop up unexpectedly, and from unexpected sources; it is important to have structure in place to allow the ideas to surface; slack tends to be required; focus and purpose might change over the course of the development
Process	Formal, established, generally with stages and gates	A formal, structured process might hinder rather than help, companies complain about large ideas becoming small
Business case	A complete business case can be produced at the outset, customer reaction can be anticipated	The business case evolves throughout the development, and might change; predicting customer reaction is difficult
Players	Can be assigned to a cross-functional team with clearly assigned and understood roles; skill emphasis is on making things happen (Kirton's adaptor)[1]	Skill areas required will evolve during the development, key players may come and go; finding the right skills often relies on informal networks; flexibility, persistence and willingness to experiment are required (Kirton's innovator)
Development structure[2]	Typically, a cross-functional team operates within an existing business unit	Tends to originate in R&D but could start anywhere in the organization; tends to be driven by the determination of one individual who pursues it wherever he or she is
Resource and skill requirements	All skills and competencies necessary tend to be within the project team; resource allocation follows a standardized process	It is difficult to predict skill and competence requirements; additional expertise from outside might be required; informal networks are important and flexibility is required
Operating unit involvement	Operating units are involved from the beginning	Involving operating units too early can again lead to great ideas becoming small

[1]See reference to Kirton's work in Chapter 10.
[2]Please see also Table 3.2 in Chapter 3.

READING SUGGESTIONS

Leifer, R., McDermott, C.M., Colarelli O'Conner, G., Peters, L.S., Rice, M. and Veryzer, R.W. (2000) *Radical Innovation – How Mature Companies can Outsmart Upstarts*. Boston, MA: Harvard Business School Press

Comment: Focusing on issues around how to implement and nurture radical innovation – extremely useful book for those interested in radical innovation in particular

Robinson, A.G. and Stern, S. (1997) *Corporate Creativity – How Innovation and Improvement Actually Happen*. San Francisco: Berrett-Koehler Publishing

Comment: In their book, the authors advocate the view that financial rewards are actually counterproductive. Full of examples and case studies

SOME USEFUL WEBSITES

http://www.imaginatik.com

Comment: Imaginatik is one of the leading companies providing software-based solutions for idea generation and management. Their website provides a number of useful links, articles, and other information

http://radicalinnovationgroup.com

Comment: This website has been set up by the authors of *Radical Innovation*; it provides insights and information on radical innovation

NOTES ON CHAPTER 21

[1] In their article 'Knowing a winning business idea when you see one', the authors offer two further tools: the 'price corridor of the mass', which helps managers to identify the pricing level with the maximum number of customers and 'the business model guide', which offers guidance in assessing the company's ability to delivery the new idea at the optimum price (*Harvard Business Review*, September–October 2000).

[2] This kind of approach was pioneered by Nestlé.

[3] The latter has been written up by Dean Whitney as a Harvard Business School case study (1997, No. 9–897–088).

Venturing Beyond Company Boundaries

In the previous chapter, we looked at different approaches for infusing innovation into an organization. All options explored rely entirely on internal funding. However, as in the GKN case study, external funding can play an important part in making innovation happen. After providing a brief overview of the spectrum through which innovation can happen, and some background to the subject of venture capital, in this chapter we address the following questions:

- What are venture capitalists looking for and what to remember when negotiating with venture capitalists?
- What are other sources of external funding?

AVENUES FOR ACHIEVING INNOVATION

For existing organizations there are a number of different avenues for pursuing innovation. Most traditional, and undertaken by every but the most stagnant organization, is what is traditionally referred to as new product development. This involves continuous or discontinuous development activities, generally of incremental nature – variations on a theme – and most companies will have processes and structures in place to accomplish this.

Many companies have decided that incremental improvements are no longer enough to ensure survival into the future. This comes with two realizations. First, it tends to be small start-up companies that are good at radical innovation, leading to realization number two; it does not seem easy to pursue more radical departures from the existing through established organizational structures and processes. This is why many managers have tried to encourage entrepreneurial behaviour within their organizations. Dollinger (1999) describes what is also known as *intrapreneurship* as follows:

- Entrepreneurship within an existing business

- The development within a corporation of internal markets, or autonomous or semi-autonomous business units, which produces products, services or technologies in a unique way

- An opportunity for corporate managers to take initiative and try new ideas

- An internal corporate venture

He argues that intrapreneurship gives corporations the ability and opportunity to experiment in the market. However, while the theory sounds easy, the practice is much more difficult to achieve within existing structures for the following reasons:

- Corporate bureaucracy
- Internal product competition
- Competing demand for resources

Table 22.1   Different Avenues to Innovation

Category	Outcome/ aim	Financed through	Initial location	Type of innovation anticipated	Learning	Main concern
Traditional new product development	Improved or new products	Regular budgets within functions	On-site, within departments	Incremental, in line with existing business	Low	Unsuitable for generating radical innovation
Internal venture unit	New products or new businesses, can lead to spinout	Ringfenced budget within existing business	On- or off-site	Incremental or radical, within our outside existing business	Potentially high	Can a distinctly different culture be maintained? Is it relevant to existing business?
External venture unit or business incubator	New businesses, intention often to sell off	Investment fund set up by parent company, often with contributions from external investors/ investor groups	Off-site	Radical, within or outside existing business	Potentially high	If too far removed, can investment be justified?
External venturing	New businesses, intention to spinin	Investment by parent company in external businesses	Off-site	Any, most likely radical	Potentially high	Can the new venture successfully be integrated into existing business?
Mergers and acquisitions	Integrated into existing business	Investment by parent company	Off-site	Any	Potentially high	Can the new venture successfully be integrated into existing business?

- Resistance to change
- Absence of internal venture capitalists for guidance
- Employees' lack of ownership reduces commitment
- Corporate environment not as free for a creative as an entrepreneurial environment

This is why many organizations are trying to develop different vehicles that allow people to 'think outside the box', and find 'new themes'. A number of different approaches are possible:

- Internal venture unit
- External venture unit or business incubator
- External venturing

In addition to the three options listed above, there is the traditional new product development, as well as mergers and acquisitions. All five approaches are compared across a number of criteria in Table 22.1.

For companies that are aiming to simulate a competitive funding environment for new business ideas, it is helpful to understand how the venture capital industry operates. This will be the subject of the rest of this chapter.

THE VENTURE CAPITAL INDUSTRY

Venture capital is money provided by professionals who invest alongside management in young, rapidly growing companies that have the potential to develop into significant economic contributors. Venture capital is an important source of equity for start-up companies.

http://www.indiainfoline.com/bisc/veca/

The concept of venture capital is not a new one, in fact, it probably existed before banking: an entrepreneur seeking finance to realize his (as generally 'his' it was) venture, promising the lender a share of the gains in return. A famous example from the 15th century is Christopher Columbus, who first asked the King of Portugal to fund the voyage to discover a new route to India in return for the use of this new route for the lucrative spice trade. When the Portuguese king refused he tried the Queen of Spain, who was more agreeable. In the old days, getting access to funding depended on who you knew and whose ear you had. Today, while personal connections are still important, there is an established industry for bringing entrepreneurs and investors together.

This industry started to take shape after the Second World War with the American Research and Development Corporation and J.H. Whitney & Co., both founded in 1946, leading the way. From what was probably considered to be an eccentric's fancy in the 1940s and 1950s, an asset class developed that today is considered mainstream. In 1998 the capital committed by venture firms in the US amounted to $25 bn, and venture capital has become an important source of funding for start-up companies. Companies such as Digital Equipment Corporation, Apple, Federal Express, Compaq, Sun Microsystems, Intel, Microsoft and Genentech are all examples of companies that received venture capital in the early stages of their development. Many of the venture capital firms are privately owned, but the money can come from a number of different sources:

- Private and public pension funds, currently about 50% with the remainder split between the following:
- Endowment funds
- Foundations
- Corporations
- Wealthy individuals
- Venture capitalists

While the money can come from a variety of different sources, venture capitalists tend to have the following in common, they:

- Finance new and rapidly growing companies
- Purchase equity securities
- Assist in the development of new products or services

- Add value to the company through active participation
- Take higher risks with the expectation of higher rewards
- Have a long-term orientation (return is expected in 5–7 years)

FINDING VENTURE CAPITAL

Whether someone is trying to sell a new business idea within an organization, or externally, to venture capitalists, the considerations and concerns will be more or less the same. The first step is to develop a business plan. The resulting document should include information about the product or concept and the management team, a marketing plan, cash flow predictions and, of course, finance requirements. As venture capitalists tend to go through a large number of proposals – venture capitalist Arthur Rock (1992) reports that he looks at about 300 business plans a year – they have to be clear, concise and to the point. It is also interesting to note that Rock invests in about one or two per year, with about half of his investment meeting performance expectations.

One problem when seeking venture capital is to find the venture capitalist who is actually in a position to make a fair judgement of the proposal. In Chapter 1 we talked about the problems of selling something that does not exist. If you are trying to sell a new pharmaceutical device to someone who is an expert in farming equipment, he or she will have difficulties assessing the potential of your idea. This is the reason why over the recent past, more and more venture capital funds have started to focus their investment activities on areas where the evaluators of business plan have a certain expertise. The investment fund set up by two people from the case study company The Technology Partnership is one example (see Chapter 29).

Purcell suggests that there are ten vital questions potential investors ask:

1.   Is there a need – or is this a technology looking for a problem?

2.   Is the proposed solution compelling – enough to overcome people's inertia?

3.   Is the potential market large enough?

4.   Has the company the potential to become the major player?

5.   Has the competition been assessed properly – and does the entrepreneur understand where future competition might come from?

6.   It is easier to expand from a niche than to enter a major market head on – though if it is a niche market, is it big enough to be of interest?

7.   What are the anticipated routes to market – have sufficient allowances been made for customer acquisition costs?

8.   Is there a strong management team – does the team have the right skill mix, balance, energy and drive?

9.   Does the revenue model stack up – what influences the breakeven point, are key assumptions valid?

10.   How does the cash flow look – how long can the company survive?

While all ten questions need to be answered positively, there is one that seems to be key in influencing a go/no-go decision: is there a strong management team? Rock elaborates on this point when commenting about what criteria he uses when assessing business proposals. He says, 'Good ideas and good products are a dime a dozen. Good execution and good management – in a word, good *people* – are rare.' Therefore, when talking to entrepreneurs his questions very much revolve about people issues, including:

- Who do you know?
- Who do you admire?
- What is your track record?
- What mistakes have you made and what have you learned?
- Who are they planning to recruit and how?
- What are your motivation, energy and commitment?

He also tries to assess whether the entrepreneur is driven by the desire to make their business a success or only in making 'a fast buck', and whether they are realistic in assessing potential problems, and have thought about possible solutions. And finally, he seeks to understand what the person's attitude towards him as an investor is.

So it will be a combination of the merit of the idea proposed and the quality of the entrepreneur, and his or her team that will influence an investment decision. However, having said that, there are also external aspects that will influence an investment decision. First, an investor's decisions can be influenced by who else is showing an interest in the business proposition. It can end up in a vicious circle where the entrepreneur finds that several potential investors say, 'If you find someone else who is willing to invest, we might consider investing too.' It is also a reflection of the fact that a fair proportion of the venture capital industry is quite conservative in the investment decisions.

Secondly, the general economic conditions also influence an entrepreneur's likelihood of obtaining funding as well as the structure of the deal. Supply and demand will determine price. If there is plenty of investment money around it will be easier to get access to finance and to negotiate a deal that favours the entrepreneur. A shortage of venture capital money can mean that he or she has to give up a larger share of the business than in times when cash flow is ample. The structure of the deal will also depend upon how desperately an entrepreneur needs money. If economic conditions are tight investors also tend to stick with safer investments – which generally means less innovative.

Finally, what is considered to be 'flavour of the month' will also have an influence on the investment decision. For a while everything that was a dotcom received funding. Many investors were getting careless in the attempt to get a stake in the booming market for e-commerce. After the crash in spring 2000 no one with a dotcom idea, however clever and promising, could find an investor.

Interestingly, for corporate investors some additional rules apply. A study by the American venture capital firm VentureOne observed interesting investment rules for large corporations. If the investment resulted in a strategic advantages such as access to technologies, products or markets large corporations were willing to double what professional venture capitalists would be willing to pay for a given ownership position in a company. It is worth noting that, though many venture capitalists take a minority stake, they often increase their powers by negotiating blocking rights on certain critical decisions.

For the investor the investment cycle tends to involve the following steps:

- *Generating a deal flow* – building up a portfolio of investment opportunities that are attractive to the investor

- *Due diligence* – industry term that means assuring that everything possible is done to avoid mistakes, i.e. checking the qualitative as well as the quantitative aspects of a business plan, including the checking of references and background of the management team

Table 22.2   Instruments of Finance (based on http://www.indiainfoline.com)

Instrument	Issues
Loan	Clean vs. secured Interest bearing vs. non-interest bearing Convertible vs. one with features (warrants) 1st charge, 2nd charge Loan vs. loan stock Maturity
Preference shares	Redeemable (conditions under Company Act) Participating Par value Nominal shares
Warrants	Exercise price, expiry period
Common shares	New or vendor shares Par value Partially paid shares
Options	Exercise price, expiry period, call, put

- *Investment valuation* – calculation of future revenue streams and anticipated profitability, prediction of the future value of the business, identification of preferred ownership structure to maximize return on investment

- *Pricing and structuring the deal* – negotiating the financial instruments (see Table 22.2) and the pricing with the entrepreneur

- *Value addition and monitoring* – this is where the venture capitalist – as opposed to a bank – can add value: he or she can advise, bring in some extra expertise and experience

- *Exit* – the exit strategy will have been agreed in the initial investment agreement and can take a variety of forms, the entrepreneur might buy back the stake, find a different investor to take up the stake, or put the company through an initial public offering

Venture capitalists are one source of funding for entrepreneurs, and probably the one that most seek in the first instance. However, there are other avenues which will briefly be explored below.

OTHER SOURCES OF EXTERNAL FUNDING

Rather than approaching individual venture capitalists for finance, entrepreneurs can investigate the following avenues:

- Business angels
- Venture capital trusts
- Corporate venturing

BUSINESS ANGELS

In addition to venture capitalists, there are also private investors who invest directly in small companies or start-ups in return for a share of the equity. Quite frequently these investors, often referred to as 'business angels', also join the company's board to provide managerial expertise and other insights to the management team. They tend to bring industry experience as well as independent funds to the party. They are more likely than venture capitalists to invest at the very outset, sometimes even in the development of a product concept. They might be as excited about the idea as the entrepreneur, and driven as much by the desire to realize the idea as to achieve a positive return on their investment. The presence of a business angel on an entrepreneur's management team can also have a positive influence on the assessment by venture capitalists at a later stage.

VENTURE CAPITAL TRUSTS

More and more trusts tend to specialize in certain industries or technologies, and also have set selection criteria. The process tends to be more formalized as with individuals, in fact, the type of investment they can make is regulated. The fact that such trusts underlie legislation means that they can offer tax incentives to private investors. After the initial fundraising, the shares of such funds are quoted on the stock exchange, and can be found in the listing of financial broadsheets such as the *Financial Times*.

CORPORATE VENTURING

In corporate venturing a non-financial corporation makes money available for investment in other companies, either directly or through a venture fund that is set up as subsidiary. Usually, the investments are in line with the company's strategy, and the idea is to gain access to a particular technology or market, or to obtain other benefits that enhance the investing company's competitive position. The fact that the difference in objective between corporation (strategic benefit) and venture capitalist (make money) leads to different pricing strategies has already been mentioned above.

If a corporation engages in venture capital activities, it is important to ensure that people with appropriate skills are in charge of such programmes. Running a venture capital fund and understanding issues in small and start-up companies requires a different skill set from running a mature company.

An example of a corporate venturing programme is that of Apple Computers. Established in 1986, the objective was twofold: to earn high financial return, and to support the development of Macintosh software. The structure – compensation mechanisms, decision criteria, operating procedures – were modelled on those of venture capital firms and funding decisions were made to maximize financial returns. Though the programme delivered an Internal Rate of Return (IRR) of 90%, it did little to improve the position of Macintosh (http://www.indiainfoline.com/bisc/veca/).

Besides being a potent route to new revenues, diversification and flexibility, corporate venturing is also one way of experimenting with radical innovation without threatening the core business – unless, of course, too much money is lost in the process.

READING SUGGESTIONS

Hill, Bill E. and Power, Dee (2001) *Inside Secrets to Venture Capital*. Chichester, UK: John Wiley & Sons

Comment: To quote a reader's review from amazon.com: 'A complete guide to venture capital covering all aspects from understanding what venture capital is, to writing the business plan to negotiations, written in an easy to understand, practical manner'

Lerner, Josh (2001) *Venture Capital and Private Equity: A Casebook.* Chichester, UK: John Wiley & Sons

Comment: In its four modules, the book looks at the following issues: (1) how are private equity funds raised and structured, (2) what are the interactions between private equity investors and entrepreneurs, (3) how do private equity investors exit their investments, (4) a review of the key ideas developed in the volume

Camp, Justin J. (2002) *Venture Capital Due Diligence: A Guide to Making Smart Investment Choices and Increasing Your Portfolio Returns.* Chichester, UK: John Wiley & Sons

Comment: Takes the reader through all aspects of due diligence in venture capital

SOME USEFUL WEBSITES

www.bvca.co.uk

Comment: On the website of the British Venture Capitalist Association, you will find information on private equity and venture capital in the UK, sources of funds and professional advice, as well as a number of publications, information on research and other relevant material

http://www.nvca.org/def.html

Comment: On the website of the US-based National Venture Capital Association you will find information and articles on and around the venture capital industry, as well as some useful links to related websites. The association is also involved in research in this area

www.firsttuesday.com

Comment: First Tuesday cities hold monthly events, such as: the *OOOClassic* event, which traditionally brings together the full range of a city's membership on the first Tuesday of the month; *OOOThought Leadership* events, which bring together leading experts to brainstorm on issues in the technology sector; or *OOOWireless Wednesday* events, which are focused on the wireless segment of the telecom sector

23 Innovation in Financial Services

CASE STUDY 8: SHARED APPRECIATION MORTGAGE – BANK OF SCOTLAND

The UK housing market is thought to have an aggregate value of about £1200 bn, greater than the combined value of the UK's stock and bond market.

Financial Times *14th November 1996*

Financial Times *14ᵗʰ November 1996*

THE IDEA – RATIONALE AND GETTING BUY-IN

'There must be a way of giving investors access to one of the largest asset pools there is, the housing market,' thought Craig Corn, working at Merrill Lynch at the time as a Director in structured finance. The UK housing market was dominated by owner occupation, with private rental playing only a small role. This meant that for many households a large proportion – in some cases well over 100% – of their net wealth was tied up in a single illiquid asset. The housing mortgage, which plays an essential role in financing housing purchase, does nothing to help householders reduce or diversify their risks. At the same time, commercial investment in residential property was very limited, discouraged by the cost of managing rented property and the difficulties of getting repossession of the asset. Pulling these thoughts together, Craig was convinced there should be some value in designing a financial device that would somehow open up the enormous asset pool and give homeowners an opportunity to leverage their asset. What if one could find a way of linking an investment to a real mortgage? An alternative option would have been to have call options – but he felt that they would be more difficult to understand – and the mortgage market was not so tightly regulated. The seed for what was to become the Shared Appreciation Mortgage was sown.

	Owner occupied	Private rented	Housing association rented	Public rented	Total
1960	7.0	5.2		4.4	16.6
1970	9.6	3.8		5.9	19.2
1975	10.6	3.1		6.2	19.9
1980	11.7	2.4	0.4	6.5	20.9
1985	13.2	2.3	0.5	5.8	21.8
1990	15.1	2.1	0.7	5.0	22.9
1995	15.9	2.4	1.0	4.5	23.8

Stock of dwelling by tenure in the UK (in millions)
Department of the Environment

When Merrill Lynch's management felt that, while quite exciting, such a product would not fit into their existing product portfolio, Craig decided to look for takers of his idea elsewhere. When the Swiss Banking Corporation (SBC), one of the companies he approached, were immediately interested, he decided to move there. Once at SBC he was looking for people to join his team, in particular for a person who would have knowledge of the UK mortgage and capital markets. David Garner, who had previously been with a building society and had joined SBC in late autumn 1995, fitted the bill perfectly. Over the next months David and Craig worked on putting the product together and seeking legal opinion. Quite soon the idea emerged that homeowners could perhaps give up a share in the appreciation of their property in return for a fixed-term, low-interest mortgage. The second part of the equation would be an investment vehicle that gave investors access to the shared appreciation in return for their investment, which would be paid by homeowners.

Competitive products at the time

Common Home Income Plan: allows people over 69 to remortgage up to £30,000 of capital from their homes and buy an annuity; part of the income from that is used to repay the loan, set at a fixed rate for the rest of the borrower's life, and part is paid as income to the person concerned. But the income is limited. A woman of 75 would receive only around £1240 a year or £1400 if a non-taxpayer.

Home Reversion Scheme: involves selling all or part of the property at a discount to its full value in return for a cash lump sum (or, in some cases, annuity) and rent-free occupancy for life. Upon death, the buyer becomes owner or part-owner. The price paid depends on how long the buyer waits for the property – and that will depend on how long the owner lives. A 70-year old selling his entire property would get 40% of its value now; an 85-year old would get 55%. The rest is kept by the provider because it might have to wait many years for the home to be sold.

While it was important to secure support from SBC, having an investment bank willing to take the idea forward would not be sufficient, a mortgage lender would be needed to market and manage the mortgages. As Craig and David were looking for a mainstream, respected lender with a solid reputation, they started talking to building societies. But they also talked to the retail-oriented banks. Amongst these was the Bank of Scotland, which was not only highly reputable but also considered to be innovative. They had been the first to introduce pension-backed lending stabilizers and special status lending. As John Lloyd, Director of Sales, Mortgages commented later, 'We are amongst the top 10 lenders, but are nevertheless thinking of ourselves as a niche player. We are not competing solely on price but on product differentiation and quality of service. We want to be known as an innovative and specialist lender.'

Corporate Statement (from BoS Report & Accounts 99)

The Bank of Scotland Group aims:

- To meet customers' needs by providing friendly, prompt, professional and imaginative service

- To deliver a range of distinctive financial products and services throughout the United Kingdom and internationally

- To train, develop, inform, encourage and respect staff so that they can perform an effective and fulfilling role

- To maintain its reputation for integrity and stability

- To make a particular contribution to the cultural and economic prosperity in the local communities in which it operates

- The achievement of these aims will result in long-term growth in profits and dividends for the benefits of its proprietors

Craig's first contact at the Bank of Scotland in February 1996 was Willie Donald, who had recently joined the bank as Director of Sales. Willie immediately took to the idea and decided to go right to the top to George Mitchell, Divisional Chief Executive of Personal Banking via George While, Head of Mortgages, knowing that management was always willing to listen to new ideas. They too liked the idea, and George Mitchell felt that such a product could enhance their reputation as an innovator in the mortgage market. For the same reason he felt it would be a good idea to put the concept to the main board, who after some consideration gave their approval in principle in June 1996. Sanctioning from the top was important for another reason; they had been working on a new product for about the past year, and it was clear that the bank would not be able to resource and support both projects. John Lloyd, who had been with the bank for a long time, was on the project team and succeeded Willie later in the role of Director of Sales. He commented, 'Had Craig approached me at the time I would probably have said no. The current business was being very successful with high levels of growth and I would have feared that resourcing/servicing might become an issue.'

GETTING STARTED

The SBC and the Bank of Scotland reached agreement to cooperate quite quickly with broadbased letters of intent being signed at the outset. After that the Bank of Scotland set up a team for the development and implementation of the product. When George Mitchell thought about who should work alongside Willie to take the concept further, Neil Forrest came to mind. Neil had been with the bank for about 7–8 years, and needed a new challenge. With his expertise in securitization, mainly purchasing MBS notes for BoS, he would complement Willie well, who had just successfully completed the introduction of the Personal Choice Mortgage. Neil remembers, 'I came from structured financing into retail, which meant that I could ask "stupid" questions which challenged everyone and made them think.' He continued, 'Within our small group Craig and Willie were the visionaries, they would dream things up, many of which would not work – but that did not matter. We all got to know each other very well in the process. David Garner and myself were more on the technical side, translating their ideas into something realizable.'

After Neil joined the team in March 1996 they spent about 4–5 months going down what Neil now describes as a blind alley. 'But,' he continues, 'We learned many lessons from it that were very useful later on. And despite having spent quite some time going down the wrong track the top management still had the vision and belief in the product so we got another try.' The first version of the product had not involved securitization. One reason was that securitization had a bad reputation – one only did it if one could not afford direct financing. Another that the interest rate swaps originally suggested would have meant that the bank would have retained a substantial taxation risk, which they did not like. By the time SBC suggested securitization again, the Bank's executive was quite excited about the retail product, and so decided to give the go ahead.

Once the concept was finalized, Neil and Willie presented to the senior management team, just in time for a board meeting in September 1996 where the product was approved. After that, Neil and Willie sat down together to decide who should be on the implementation team, but asked George White to actually nominate the people. Neil recalls, 'Initially people had to be told to show up to the first meeting, but when they found out about the product they got quite excited about it and really wanted to be involved. Everyone was clear about what we were trying to achieve, we might have had plenty of arguments along the way, but in the end everyone did what was necessary to make the product happen.' The implementation team, also referred to as steering group, was pretty senior, consisting of:

- Willie Donald and Neil Forrest, responsible for the product
- Ian Dickson and John Lloyd, sales

- John Trouten, customer care
- Dave Smith, process area
- Three people from systems

Meetings were held on a weekly basis, with interim meetings taking place if and when required. Gary Gordon, Manager, Operations at the time, joined the team after their first meeting in early October 1996. Meeting notes were copied to all heads of functions and regular progress reports were given to the board. In addition to the implementation team, a second team was dedicated to developing the processes surrounding SAM (Shared Appreciation Mortgage), as the product was called.

Throughout the development, confidentiality and timing were a concern. To ensure that as little as possible about the product would be known before the launch, the development area within the Bank of Scotland was declared restricted access. At the same time, there was agreement that informing all relevant audiences simultaneously – staff, intermediaries, branches, financial advisors, etc. – would be very important. During the first steering group meeting, 25th September 1996, the launch date was set for 4th November 1996.

PRODUCT AND MARKETS

Once the concept had been signed off, the team quickly decided to focus on two different types of interest rates only. John said, 'Two interest rates were sufficient for the launch as we were trying to keep things as simple as possible given some of the product features were complicated enough to communicate as it was. In fact, initially we asked that applicants seek advice from a financial advisor or a solicitor to ensure they really understood what they were signing. Applications that came without the input of a financial advisor were sent back. On the insistence from the executive, we also included sentences to make sure the customer really knew in return for a low interest rate they would forego some of the future appreciation in their property in both the approval in principal and the formal offer letters.'

Bank of Scotland SAM Product Criteria

- Lifetime fixed interest of either 5.75% or 0%

- Shared appreciation levels depending on choice of interest rate

- 5.75% interest rate – maximum loan to value is 75%, the shared appreciation level is equal in proportion to the percentage loan to value (1:1)

- 0% interest rate – maximum loan to value is 25%, the shared appreciation level is three times the loan to value (3:1)

- Purchase or remortgage – repayment method interest only

- Properties without existing mortgages accepted

- Minimum/maximum valuation £60,000/£500,000 (higher values may be considered on an individual basis)

- Minimum/maximum loan is £15,000/£375,000 (higher values may be considered on an individual basis)

- Arrangement fee of £500 which can be added to the loan

- No maximum term

- No maximum age

- Partial redemptions – minimum £10,000

- Early repayment fee if the mortgage is redeemed within the first three years: 5.75% SAM – 3 months gross interest, 0% SAM – 1.5% of loan

- Termination charge – administration fee of £300, plus the cost of the sale valuation to establish the level of appreciation

Strongly influenced by sales' point of view, the two scenarios chosen were (a) a 0% mortgage where the borrower could borrow up to 25% of the value of the property and would give up future appreciation worth three times the percentage borrowed (i.e. a maximum of 75%), and (b) a 5.75% mortgage – which was very competitive at the time – whereby the homeowner could borrow up to 75% of the property value, foregoing future appreciation at a rate of 1:1. Any improvements on the house would be discounted from the appreciation calculations; to calculate this, homeowners would have to inform the bank in advance of any major improvements made to the home. As the product was designed with specific customers in mind, people who would want either to remortgage or raise capital, they were expecting to get a customer profile of asset rich, cash poor. They were also expecting to see lots of old people, who needed to top up their pension, interested in the product. For that reason, consultations with Help The Aged and SAGA had taken place throughout development. Neil commented, 'We did not market test but rather relied on input from our sales people and other experts.'

For the investor side the product would work as follows: the 5.75% SAMs would be securitized into fixed-rate notes with a coupon of about 55% of the 10-year gilt yield. The zero-interest SAMs would be securitized into floating-rate notes with a coupon of about 60% of three month Libor. According to SBC's marketing literature, 'Trading in the familiar form of Eurobonds, SAMs offer all the benefits of involvement in residential property, with some protection from downside property exposure.' Coupon payments to

	Equities	Government bonds	Residential property
Return	15.1%	7.5%	8.4%
Volatility	20.4%	11.3%	4.9%
		SBC Warburg Dillon Reed	

investors would be made on a quarterly basis, and would consist of a fixed or floating element plus a supplemental interest element to reflect price gains for SAMs terminated that quarter; in addition, debt would be amortized each quarter as the number of underlying homes in any SAMs pool would become smaller. Willie Donald commented, 'The step-up coupons were designed to offer some attraction to investors who were buying something without a fixed maturity; but we were calculating on the basis that it would amortize after 25 years.' The issuer had the option to sweep up the paper should the note size outstanding fall below 20% of the original total, or if a withholding tax were imposed.

With SAMs being like equity but less risky, it was thought that they should be attractive to pension funds. A SAM would be long term and earnings linked, rather than being linked to the RPI. Craig felt that the product could enable pension funds to manage their long-term liability and improve earning power. In *Euromoney* December 1996, Craig commented on potential takers for the bonds, 'Pension funds should be interested, because historically house prices have not only outperformed inflation, but matched increases in earnings. Most pension fund liabilities are earnings linked. Property funds should certainly be interested. And there's enough equity in the bonds to encourage some equity investors as well, although the mortgages are being sold on the basis that stock markets have historically outperformed house prices.'

Main features of SAMs

- Asset diversification into a significant asset class
- Upside exposure to a superior performing asset on a risk-adjusted basis
- Asset/liability matching by means of an excellent wage inflation hedge
- A legally efficient and cost-effective means to enter the owner-occupied residential property market
- Joint economic interest to preserve the value of the home
- Greater diversification than direct investment
- Extra value derived from a 'portfolio of options' effect
- Direct support of and investment in the local housing market

---

The Bank of Scotland would be taking no interest in the loans; 100% of debt and equity would go to bondholders, with the Bank of Scotland receiving a fee. SBC released one issue per company. A separate book ID on the BoS system would enable tracking of transactions between companies. The money from the mortgages coming into the Bank of Scotland would get cleared on a monthly/weekly basis to SBC. At the time, SBC was one of the few financial institutions that had a triple A rating, the highest. It effectively stated that the likelihood of default was very slim. (At launch all SAM notes were AAA rated.) In the absence of a suitable model, initial pricing for the bonds was based largely on SBC's research, which incidentally also indicated high levels of interest from investors in the SAM bonds.

To keep funds associated with the SAMs separate from its main books, the Bank of Scotland set up an independent company for each SAM, with the Bank of Scotland acting as an agent for the BoS SAM (legal charges were in the name of the BoS SAM rather than the BoS). For the Scottish SAMs special arrangements were needed: a special service vehicle company was set up which originated both rated and zero SAM; the two books were sold to SAM 3 and 4. The company was not involved in the securitization, but sold to one of the English companies which then securitized the assets.

TRIALS AND TRIBULATIONS

During development and implementation, the team had to be aware of a number of acts and regulations. For example, they needed to ensure that the offering would not be in conflict with the Betting Act. Then there was the risk that, while interest might be legally enforceable, the appreciation aspect was not likely to be. Many of these issues had been identified during the first session, where the team had a brainstorming session about what things could go potentially wrong. While many of the possible problem scenarios were familiar from previous projects and the team had the bank's new product development process and internal check lists as reference points, for example the Critical Sheet for Actual Lending, there were a number of issues no one had encountered before.

During their second meeting in early October, the IT people alerted the implementation team to the fact that Unisys, one of the bank's IT systems on which all accounts would be domiciled, and through which all transactions were managed and recorded, would only accept loans up to 50 years, no longer. With the SAM set up as an open-ended mortgage – until death (or sale) – this was potentially a problem. But this was not the only IT-related challenge. Unisys would not accept an interest rate of 0%. The suggestion to run SAM with 0.0001% interest, which would have meant that no statement would be issued, was not acceptable, as it would still have had an impact on the account. With a separate company for each of the SAMs there was a concern that processing, which was done overnight, might overrun, particularly at the end of the month. The decision to upgrade processing capacity was made quickly. Setting up a standalone system for mortgages on Unisys had the advantage that they would not be affecting the mainframe, and would avoid any loss of time and interference with priorities.

The team was aware that, due to the fact that the SAM would be externally securitized, they would have to design the infrastructure for SAM in such a way that would make it distinct from BoS with a clear and separate audit trail. Normally, most documents would be microfilmed, and only some key documents would be kept. But this was seen not to be sufficient for SAMs; they would have to satisfy external auditing requirements; this drove decisions on what kind of documentation would be required and for setting up separate companies. They even chose a special colour for the folders so they would be easily identifiable.

With appreciation being calculated on the difference between the initial valuation and exit valuation, valuations were an important issue. Countrywide was appointed to administer the panel of valuers who would provide all valuations.

During the team meeting on the 9th October, it was decided to launch on the 11th of November and announce the launch in the *Sunday Times* on the 4th November 1996 – the team was quite positive that this would be front-page news.

MARKET INTRODUCTION AND REACTION

The deal represents the first chance for many institutions to gain access to the £850 bn pool of UK housing equity, rather than the housing debt market.

Euroweek *6th February 1996*

It would make sense for individuals to own less housing, and for institutional investors, such as pension funds and insurers, to own more (they now own almost none).

Economist *17th January 1997*

As no similar product had existed before George White decided to inform many of BoS's large intermediaries directly about the product. As the magazine *Euromoney* pointed out in their article of December 1996, 'It isn't like anything the capital markets have seen before.' The article continues by quoting Craig Corn: 'It's a convertible bond wrapped up in a securitisation vehicle; it's a property-linked bond; it's an equity securitisation; it's a mortgage-backed security; it's equity in retail housing; if I had to pick one bond which it was like, I'd say it was most like an index-linked gilt, linked to house prices instead of inflation.'

The team also made sure that marketing material would be available to intermediaries ahead of the launch. Several other steps were taken in preparation of the launch: people were nominated to man the phones within the bank's mortgage area on the day of the press release, which was a Sunday; more people had to be added when it turned out that telephone calls would last up to 45 minutes – rather than the 2–3 minutes normally spent on customer enquiry calls. A memo was sent out requiring all enquiries to be forwarded to the dedicated team within the mortgage area. The board was also kept fully informed, and had asked that nothing be released that had not been approved by them.

By the time the product was launched – which was actually before contracts with SBC Warburg had been finalized or terms and conditions had also been copy written – the bank was already receiving around 2000 phone calls per day, the majority of callers being interested in the 0% option. The interest had been stirred prematurely by a press leak in a Sunday paper on the 20th of October, which had put additional pressure on the team to launch – and which had meant that by the time the product was launched, the bank had already a database with about 2500 individuals who had requested information on the product. Demand far outstripped what the team had anticipated, and by the second week of December they had run out of brochures. The first two tranches were launched in England with the first moneys drawn on the 31st of December 1996. The team at the Bank of Scotland was quite keen to keep the momentum going and launch the following tranches as quickly as possible.

But not only were the borrowers keen on the new product, most of the press wrote enthusiastically, and the Warburg[1] first issue was, in fact, oversubscribed. For the 5.75% option, the BoS SAM 1, bonds worth £27.2 m were issued, for the 0% option, the BoS SAM 2, bonds worth £105.6 m. However, pension funds were not amongst the takers.

> **From Internal BoS Memo to All Sections**
>
> All enquiries should be diverted to the business development teams who have been briefed and have in-depth details of the product. As far as existing customers are concerned they should be transferred to the SAM implementation team, who will respond as follows:
>
> 'SAM is a new product and concept and at the present time there is a limited amount of funds available for this. Consequently it is not available for existing customers but it is our intention to review this after 6 months once we have had some experience of the likely demand and availability of funding which is provided through issuing Eurobonds. I would also mention that in the event this does become available to you, any transfer will involve a full remortgage with all the costs associated with this such as legal costs, valuation and arrangement fees given the mortgage is only available through a separate subsidiary of the Bank which has its own documentation.'

AFTER THE INITIAL ENTHUSIASM

Shared appreciation mortgages, a way of selling part of a property while continuing to live in it, are temporarily off the market after demand from borrowers outstripped the supply of money from the bonds market. Demand for the bonds has dried up after £750 m worth from the Bank of Scotland plus a first launch of bonds from Barclays, which offered a SAM briefly this year.

Financial Times *11th July 1998*

While the bank's new product had caused great interest from borrowers, after just having lived through the problems of the pension funds, intermediaries were much more sceptical. As the bank received many calls from borrowers who felt quite strongly that they were quite capable of making decisions without legal advice, the bank decided to relax its requirement for applications to come through intermediaries. To their surprise, applicants were also more often than not asset rich as well as cash rich, and they received several requests for what Willie Donald termed 'jumbos', huge properties. They also received calls from homebuilders building retirement homes who were enquiring on behalf of their customers, a group that had not been anticipated. In addition, the age profile was different from what had been anticipated; applicants tended to be in their fifties and sixties rather than seventies, and they found that many Muslims were interested in the 0% option.

With interest from borrowers unabated, investor interest began to slacken after the first two issues. The bank had been keen to maintain the momentum, but SAMs 3 and 4 could not be launched until securitization of SAMs 1 and 2 had been completed because of limited warehouse

> But how interested will investors be in the securitization of an asset with no track record because it has not existed before.
>
> *Euromoney* December 96

funding lines. Also, due to the different legal system in Scotland, introduction of the product had to be delayed, and it was not until mid-February 1997, with financial crises looming in Asia and Russia, that the SAM was introduced in the bank's home country. This coincided with the launch of tranches 3 and 4. While the emphasis had originally been on the innovativeness of the product and the great potential of the housing market at the time, the following tranches tried to present the SAM as an established product that was there to stay.

Tranches 3 and 4 took much longer to place, and tranches 5 and 6 had to be taken up by SBC Warburg itself, despite the fact that, based on Halifax house price indices, it could be expected that BoS SAM1 would have a return of 4.3% and BoS SAM2 a return of 4.4% against an overall increase

> Craig Corn in *Euroweek* 18th July 1997: 'We have been educating investors about a whole new asset class. This deal is a hybrid, and the job has been to find the part of an institution which will buy it.'

of 3.4% in the UK as a whole. During the preparations for the issue of SAMs 5 and 6, SBC Warburg went through the merger with UBS, and while the team at the Bank of Scotland was hoping SBC Warburg/UBS would find a way to interest investors in the product, in the end, they had to take the product off the market. Within the bank Neil, as Director of Product Development, was given the remit by top management to pursue the idea for a further year, and to expand the product development department.

COMPETITORS' REACTION

While applauding the ingenuity of the project, rival bankers said many hurdles needed to be overcome before the bonds could see the light of day. Some structuring issues were within the compass of SBC Warburg, such as coming up with a model that would convince investors they could accurately predict the rate at which mortgage holders paid off the loans – a crucial component of measuring return on asset-backed securities.

Euroweek *15th November 1996*

Corn predicted that some of the UK's top 10 lenders would launch rival products in the second half of the year with a view to securitization in 1998.

Euroweek *18th July 1997*

In March 1998, after the Bank of Scotland had taken their product off the market, Barclays Capital launched their first securitization of shared appreciation mortgages with a 98 m triple-A rated zero coupon bond. The Millshaw SAMs No 1 Ltd issued a 55-year deal that was backed by 3253 first charge mortgages that Barclays had signed up between May and July 1998. These loans had a maximum loan to value ratio (LTV) of 25%. Like BoS SAMS 2, 4 and 6 no interest was charged, but once borrowers sold their house, paid off the mortgage or died, they would have to surrender a share in the appreciation of the value of the property, calculated as three times the LTV. While progress was slow, Barclays found that institutions were buying the bonds for their high returns. If real property inflation ran at 2%, slightly below its long-term average of 2.2%, and retail inflation were 2.5%, Millshaw would yield 7.8%, around 330 bp over gilts. Barclays expected that any significant growth would only come with familiarity and that a retail bid for the assets could eventually play a part in making this theoretically persuasive market a reality.

QUESTIONS

1. What would your advice have been to both the Bank of Scotland and UBS Warburg after the issue of SAMs 3 and 4?
2. Do you consider the product to be a success or failure (a) from the BoS perspective, (b) from UBS Warburg's perspective, and why?

APPENDIX I: ADDITIONAL INFORMATION

*   The time available to applicants to accept a mortgage offer set at 14 days, three months was normal; they decided to cut it to maintain a tight control of the money going out, as there were only certain funds available for each phase

*   After acceptance, borrowers had six weeks to draw the funds; normally they could do that any time – for the same reason as above

*   Allocation was on a first come, first served basis

*   For normal mortgages they have a 60% conversion rate (from offer to being drawn); for SAM they had a 95% conversion rate; disagreement with valuations was the only reason that led people to withdraw

*   Borrowers were expected to meet all valuation costs (at outset, in between in case of home improvements, etc.)

*   No proof of income was required for the 5.75% mortgage, as applicants had to go through intermediaries who were expected to be able to judge whether the people were creditworthy or not; the requirement was not reinstated even when the intermediaries were no longer required

*   No life cover was required for the 0% option; for the 5.75% option it had initially been required but was later waived

*   The APR for the 0% was 8.6% and 8.9% for the 5.75%

*   It was not possible to add dependants onto the mortgage

*   Borrowers were required to undertake any major repairs before the initial evaluation

*   If people wanted to make improvements to their property, they had to inform the BoS beforehand; valuers, paid for by the borrowers, would assess what percentage of future appreciation would be due to the improvement so it could be deduced on exit

NOTES ON CHAPTER 23

[1] Warburg merged with UBS in 1998.

24 Innovation in the Service Industry

The case study of the Shared Appreciation Mortgage is an example of innovation in the service industry. It also provides some interesting insights into innovative organizations' perspective on what constitutes 'success or failure'. This chapter takes a closer look at particularities of the service industry, the role of design in developing services, and compares factors that underlie successful service development. Issues around success and failure in new product development and innovation in general are addressed in Chapter 25.

PARTICULARITIES ABOUT THE SERVICE INDUSTRY

Let us start with a couple of observations before we look at the particularities of the service industry. First, increasingly the boundary between tangible and intangible products gets blurred. For many products, it becomes increasingly difficult to say whether it is a service or product. Think about any form of leasing (a service) versus buying the product, for example, cars. Is a programme providing internet access a product or a service? Is the selling of 'weed-free fields' referred to in Chapter 18 a product or service? The second observation is that services tend to be much more profitable than products. Blumberg (1989) reported that services obtain margins of 15–25% before tax, whereas products can demand only 7–11%. Not least for this reason, more and more companies are either trying to tie in products with services, or switch to selling services all together. Interestingly, many of the examples for companies that have switched from products to services have been motivated by sustainability arguments (e.g. the company that offers the service of keeping your floor covered instead of selling carpets (see Chapter 18). Another reason is pointed out by Terrill and Middlebrook (1996), who state that 'When a product is offered in conjunction with a service it is often the service that adds value, not the product.'

But how is 'service' defined? Johne and Storey (1998) provide a number of definitions that might be useful:

- *Service product* – the predominantly intangible core attributes which customers purchase

- *Product development/innovation* – the development (or improvement) of tangible or service products

- *New product development* (NPD) – the development of tangible products which are new to the supplier. Sometimes NPD is expanded to include new service development (see below)

- *New service development* (NSD) – the development of service products which are new to the supplier

- *Offer development* – the development, by the supplier, of core product (or service) attributes, plus the development of the processes by which the product is evaluated, purchased and consumed

Many of the considerations for new product development and innovation are the same, whether the end result is tangible (i.e. a product) or intangible (i.e. a service). The usefulness of a formalized development process, the early involvement of all parties involved throughout the development, and the need for senior management to signal clear support for development and innovation activity, to name but a few. Given the aforementioned, I found it quite interesting that an article published in 1997 (Sundbo 1997) describes the innovation process in the service industry generally as an 'unsystematic search-and-learning process', while it seems that most companies engaged in the development of tangible products have formalized product development processes by now. The description of the process for developing new processes by Terrill and Middlebrooks (in Kuczmarski and Associates 1995) does not look very different from that for the development of tangible products (see Box 24.1).

BOX 24.1   New Service Development Process (in Kuczmarski & Associates 1995) (reproduced by permission of Kuczmarski & Associates Inc.)

1. Problem description

   2. Idea creation

      3. Concept definition

         4. Analysis and screening

            5. Concept design

               6. Delivery and operations test

                  7. Broad market testing

                     8. Infrastructure scale-up

                        9. Introduction and launch

                          10. Post-launch check-up

However, there are also aspects of services and service development that are different and which need to be understood to innovate successfully. Most of the differences arise from the fact that services tend to be intangible by nature, but the exploration below is broken down under the following headings:

- consequences of the intangibility of services
- 'manufacture' and delivery happen simultaneously
- difficult to protect
- easy to innovate

CONSEQUENCES OF THE INTANGIBILITY OF SERVICES

The most obvious difference between a tangible product and a service is that the latter is intangible. This means that you cannot look at or touch a service and that it is difficult to assess before a purchasing decision is made. At a basic level, service innovations might be easier to understand, e.g. internet banking means that you conduct all your banking activities on the computer, instead of going into the bank or posting letters. However, the real test comes in the experience, when actually using the online service. No description of the product is likely to point out the problems of establishing a connection, problems with setting up transfers to accounts that are held at a different bank, or the problems one can have in speaking to a real person to discuss a problem. A friend from Germany just reported that his bank would only allow 'either or', i.e. he would either have to do *all* his transactions via the internet, or all the traditional way. As he spends time travelling for longer periods, which means that access to the internet cannot always be guaranteed, subscribing to the internet services is not really an option for him.

The fact that by the time that you are able to assess the quality of the service you have already paid for it means that reputation and word of mouth are of critical importance. Reputational issues were a major consideration for the Bank of Scotland in the development of their innovative product. Senior management were quite adamant that everything possible should be done to ensure that purchasers of the Shared Appreciation Mortgage would be absolutely clear about the conditions and implications of entering into such a mortgage agreement. This was the reason why a dedicated, well-trained team was set-up to answer questions about the new product, and why applicants were initially asked to seek professional advice before submitting their mortgage applications.

'MANUFACTURE' AND DELIVERY HAPPEN SIMULTANEOUSLY

Because the product is consumed upon delivery there is no manufacturing as such, and ergo no possibility to 'manufacture' in advance and put into inventory. Unlike with tangible products where quality controls can be built in at several stages during the manufacturing and delivery process, if there is a lapse in quality for intangible products, the customer is probably the first one to notice. As a consequence, the medium through which the service is delivered – be it an IT system or people – are critical for the quality of a service, as well as for its consistency.

On the subject of IT systems, it seems that many organizations, are introducing new and expansive IT systems under the umbrella of improving customer services. However, anyone who has tried to get through a system of option after option after option in automated telephone answering systems will be aware that most of these systems have little to do with customer service, and are implemented for cost reasons only. My own recent experience with the provider of financial services for the lease purchase of a car is an example of how 'improvements' of IT systems can backfire significantly if not designed and executed carefully (see Box 24.2).

BOX 24.2   Experiencing Service Quality...

Contact from financial service provider	Response by customer
Letter of 16th May 02 informing customers about a new computer system, asserting that the customer does not need to take any action; electronically generated signature by 'A'	No action taken
Letter of 19th June 02 informing customer that 'due to lack of funds in your account your bank has been unable to make your last payment...' electronically generated signature by 'B'	Upon return from a holiday 2nd July the customer telephoned the financial service provider, after checking that the account in question had been in credit throughout the period in question. A flash of inspiration led the customer to ask what account details were used which resulted in the insight that an account that had been used for the first months of the contract, back in late 1998, had been used; correct account details were given. Spoke to E

▶

Letter dated 1st July informing the customer that the bank had rejected the request for the second time; electronically generated signature by 'B'	No action as the customer assumed that phone call and computer-generated letter had crossed
Letter dated 4th July asking me to provide correct bank details signed by 'C'	Customer received and sent letter 8th July AND spoke to 'C' 8th July ca 10.00 confirming AGAIN the correct bank details
Letter dated 11th July signed by 'D' acknowledging my letter of 8th July	No action taken – though the customer was quite annoyed as it is yet another computer-generated letter referring to the correspondence as 'complaint'. . .
Letter dated 11th July electronically signed by 'B' informing me again that they were unable to draw from customer's account, setting an additional charge	Received and called 15th July, spoke to 'E' again giving current bank details. Customer requested a return call to confirm that problems had been resolved. No such call came
	Customer called again 18th July and requested to speak to the most senior person; explained the situation again and was yet again promised that problems had been sorted out
Letter dated 19th July, identical computer-generated letter electronically signed by 'B'	Received 25th July, 12.00; customer asked to be put through to 'B' and was told 'B' does not take customer calls, spoke to 'F' instead; customer (!) suggested that if they had used the wrong bank details they might also have sent a letter notifying the bank of the changed arrangements to the wrong address; 'F' was very helpful and seemed, again, to be able to sort out the problem and promised that the customer would get no more computer-generated letters
Letter dated 26th July, signed by 'A' informing the customer that a new account had been set up	No action taken
Two identical letters dated 31st July, electronically signed by 'B' requesting that the customer should call him	Upon receiving the letter 5th August the customer attempted to call 'B' (although of course the customer had previously been told that 'B' does not talk to customers); after several attempts and time spent in waiting loops the customer gave and wrote letter including a summary of all above correspondence
Letter dated 7th August, signed by 'G', apologizing	Customer called 20th August upon returning from travels abroad, spoke to 'H' and confirmed that the company should continue with direct debit until all instalments were paid; 'H' agreed to call should there be a problem (there was only one outstanding)

▶

	Customer called 6th September when she found that her account had been drawn on twice; 'I' explained that they were the penultimate and last payment but that due to the problems in drawing from the account in June there was still one payment outstanding; customer decided to sent cheque the same day to sever all relations with that company, the cheque was drawn from account 12th September
Two identical letters dated 23rd September electronically signed by 'B' stating 'We refer to the arrangement for payment of the arrears on your account. The promised payment has not been made and we therefore require immediate payment. If full payment of the arrears or contact, is not receive within 10 days, legal proceedings may be taken by this company without further notice'	Customer writes rather angry letter to the financial service (. . .) provider with copies to the British Consumer Association, the CEO of the car manufacturer associated with the financial service provider, and the MD of the UK branch of the financial service provider
Telephone call from the personal assistant of the car manufacturer's CEO, as well as from the PA of the MD of the UK company of the financial service provider	Customer demands letter to acknowledge that all claims had been deleted from her account; letter received 1st November 2002, signed by the MD of the UK company

Frustration caused by IT systems seems to be common in financial services – it seems the same everywhere. From personal experience, I also know that complaining about bad service is one thing, actually doing something about it is something entirely different. How many people are dissatisfied with their banking arrangements but stay with their existing supplier – out of convenience, rather than conviction. The highly successful launch of Egg shows that there are tremendous opportunities for service quality improvements.

DIFFICULT TO PROTECT

Unlike tangible products, which are often built around complex technologies or formulae that can be patented, services are very difficult to protect. It is literally impossible to patent services or service components, and not only that, it is generally very easy for a competitor to copy and improve existing offerings (Naslund 1986). Having investigated innovation in the banking industry, Naslund explained that 'In my project several respondents suggested this fact [that service innovations are easy to imitate] as a reason for the low number of innovations in banks. A bank that innovates will not receive much of the profit from the process because competitors quickly imitate the new product.' Many service providers are therefore attempting to develop new offerings in secrecy – as was the case for the Shared Appreciation Mortgage. While the product was under development, the bank tried to ensure that only a few people knew about the development, and were also quite selective about which customers and intermediaries to involve. Herein lays a conflict. On the one hand, innovative services are difficult to understand unless they are explained in detail, and preferably experienced, and a lack of customer involvement can lead to services being designed based on assumptions rather than real needs. On the other hand, secrecy is important to prevent competitors from introducing the same or a similar product first, and hence stealing the thunder. The aim of the Bank of Scotland was to be first to market, to be seen as innovator, and to create a level of bind-in customers that would help them to establish a market leader position. Interestingly, though, once the product was on the market the bank would have been quite keen for competitors to take up the product to help create a market, particularly for the bonds that were issues to securitize the mortgages. Unfortunately, while customers were very keen to take up the product, the interest amongst investors was insufficient to create an effective market for the bonds.

However, having said that services are easy to copy, it should be pointed out that it is the 'what' that is easy to copy. The 'how' is often more difficult to replicate. If a service provider can establish an innovation in the marketplace through delivering a high-quality service, a competitor might be able to offer the same service, but if customers are satisfied with existing services levels they are not very likely to switch to a different provider. Providing superior service levels through training and building expertise can be as effective in fending off competitors as are patents.

EASY TO INNOVATE

The fact that new service development is quite inexpensive – no R&D expenditure to speak of, nor any investment requirements for plant and machinery – means that anyone can come up with a new service proposition. While it is frequently pointed out that it is easy to innovate in a service context, the fact that much of the success of establishing a new service in the market depends upon reputation and trust means that the 'coming up with ideas' is the easy part, but implementation can be quite difficult, and often depends upon an established and trusted brand underwriting the new offering. For Craig Corn, the ideator of the Shared Appreciation Mortgage, the reputation of the Bank of Scotland as an innovator was an important selection criterion. He was looking for a bank that would have a high level of credibility in bringing an innovation to market, which customers would trust and believe that the bank would fulfil their promises.

As with the development of tangible products, there are certain organizational characteristics that support innovation, whereas others hinder the flow and realization of innovations. In their research into innovation in the banking industry, Johne and Harborne (1985) found that banks are traditionally characterized by tight, bureaucratic structures involving high levels of standardization, formalization, centralization and limited flexibility and specialization. They saw this as one of the reasons as to why there is little real innovation in the banking industry. This argument is supported by further insights from their study, which indicate that those banks that were innovating successfully where characterized by flexible operating structures.

Terrill and Middlebrooks (1996) propose that there are five possible angles to service innovation:

1.   Positioning innovation
2.   Process innovation
3.   Service offering innovation
4.   People innovation
5.   Communications innovation

Using the first angle, positioning innovation, they propose to develop a unique positioning that differentiates the product or company from existing offerings. Restaurant chains offering a particular service or offering are one example. Think about Starbucks coffee, which has changed the fast and cheap caffeine intake into a lifestyle experience for which they charge a substantial premium.

With the second angle, process innovation, they refer to the removal or addition of a process step to improve the customer experience. Being able to use credit cards at petrol stations is an example. However, this option is less likely to be sustainable than the first.

The third angle, service offering innovation, encompasses three options: first, the creation of a unique set of benefits of features by bundling or repackaging existing offerings; secondly, the adding of new benefits to an existing service; and thirdly, the creation of a totally new service offering. As an example they quote garages that offer a service that includes lifetime oil changes, thereby locking customers into future servicing and creating real switching costs.

The fourth angle, people innovation, is based on the concept of increasing or decreasing the discretion individuals have to improve a customer's service experience and provide individualized services. Walt Disney's messages to their theme park employees is, it is up to you to exceed customer expectations.

And finally, with communications innovation Terrill and Middlebrook refer to the branding of a service offering or the use of a unique communication approach to differentiate a service. The example the authors give is that of consulting firm CSC/Index, which branded their approach to cost reduction 'reengineering', and created awareness through articles, books and seminars.

Part of successful service innovation is the ability to identify the right customer segment. Kennedy (2001) points out that effective service innovation can generate top-line revenue growth, as well as bottom-line profits. He argues that, to realize this, the following are essential:

- Understanding customer value creation
- Targeting high-value customer segments
- Choosing the correct customer interaction model
- Creative pricing
- Understanding cash flow

He emphasizes that his research showed that 'Selling to the wrong customers, poor retention, failure to deliver value, and delivering service to customers who do not appreciate it destroyed value.' I was impressed when a service provider suggested that the value of changes and innovations should be assessed to determine whether it was introduced to serve and please the customer – or the company.

However, I found it interesting that de Brentani (2001) concluded from her research that realizing radical innovation can be quite difficult for service companies. She explains that, 'For new industrial services, moving into fields that are unrelated to the firms known capabilities and resource can be particularly problematic. Especially for highly intangible professional or expert services – where customers use the firm's reputation and past experience as a proxy when evaluating the new service itself – a low level of synergy with the company's known capabilities can have a detrimental effect. Conversely, new products involving adaptations, refinements and enhancements of existing products and/or service delivery systems often achieve a higher level of success because they leverage the unique resources and skills of the firm.'

And finally, it is noteworthy that Johne and Storey (1998) found from their review of the literature that 'Leading edge new service development practice seeks to marry organizational aspiration with the aspirations of individuals.' It confirms the importance of the project leader, and his or her enthusiasm to drive the project forward. We will find in the case study on The Technology Partnership, presented in Chapter 29, that the practice of following individuals' interest and passion has also proved a great contributor to the success of the company.

DESIGN AND SERVICE DEVELOPMENT

Hollins and Hollins (1991) start their book *Total Design* with the following:

Services are products

Products need to be designed

Design is a process

This process must be organized

This organization is the job of management

While there is an increasing awareness among managers of the contribution design can make to the success and impact of tangible products, the realization that design can play an equal part in the successful design and development of services is less common. However, the involvement of designers can improve the experience of many services significantly. For most services there is a tangible component – be it forms to fill in when applying for mortgages or insurance policies, be it a computer interface or the physical environment at a hairdresser's or an advertising agency. Design can help to make the experience as smooth and easy as possible, and all things being equal – as they often are with services – people will be more likely to fill in a form they understand immediately, than one where they have to spend hours finding out what exactly is required, or go to a website that is easy to navigate than waste a lot of time searching around different pages.

Increasing competitiveness, as in the financial services industry, for example, should also motivate managers to consider all levers they can pull to differentiate their product.

SERVICE DEVELOPMENT – WHAT DRIVES SUCCESS?

Given the particularities of the service industry, there are a number of considerations managers should keep in mind to maximize their chances of success. The first is to involve customers as early as possible, and to attempt to get as close to prototyping as possible. A study conducted by Martin and Horne (1995) suggests that increasing direct customer participation in the development process in general, and the use of information about the customer at specific stages, increases the potential for success. But even though there seem to be great benefits to be gained from involving customers, Gadrey *et al.* (1994) point out that, at least in their research in the early 1990s, the service firms were not very efficient in establishing and using external networks, or involving customers in the innovation process.

Often, it might even be feasible to engage customers as development partners. This is a way of ensuring that there is a real market for the new service. However, it is worth taking a closer look at what kind of customer is participating in the development. If the service is innovative, it is advisable to involve early adopters and those who are known to be open to new ideas and risk taking, rather than a group of customers who are known to be laggards and highly risk averse.

As it is the 'how', not the 'what', that makes it difficult to copy services, the second consideration is that particular attention needs to be paid to the quality of the service delivery, be it through IT systems or people. This is why internal and external communication, as well as advanced training and customer education, are essential. In fact, in her research into innovation in the financial service industry, de Brentani (1989) found that ineffective communication between the different parts of the service organization caused major problems. Insufficient external communication, particularly for radical innovations, can lead to unrealistic or false expectations of the customer, which in turn will have negative implications for the acceptance of the new service. This is again something that the Bank of Scotland took very seriously during the development of its innovative product. And if it is indeed the 'how' that makes a difference, it is also critical to keep service delivery in mind throughout the design and development process. This is also where design – interface design, the design of forms and brochures, etc. – can make a significant difference.

The third consideration concerns the development process. De Brentani found that successful service innovations have the following in common:

- They address a specific market need, e.g. close contact with and intimate knowledge of customers' needs and operations

- They followed a formal upfront process as well as a formal and detailed launch process, which includes test marketing, front-line training and internal marketing, developing a formal promotion and launch plan

- They were exploring corporate synergies and building on frontline expertise; corporate synergies refer to fit with managerial skills and preferences, expertise and human resource capabilities, delivery and behind the scenes competences, marketing and financial resources and frontline expertise, the extent to which the new service uses high-level expert/professional resources in performing judgemental tasks during service delivery

In addition, she found that, particularly for radical service innovation, an internal innovation environment (e.g. effective new service development culture and management) is critical. Table 24.1 shows the aspects investigated and their potency in explaining success or failure in incremental and radical service innovation.

Table 24.1 Success Factors – Incremental and Radical Service Innovation Compared (de Brentani 2001) (reproduced by permission of Blackwell Publishing)

	Incremental	Discontinuous
Market/need fit	XXXX	XX
NSD: planned launch	XXX	+
Front-line expertise	XX	X
Corporate synergy	XX	X
NSD: culture and management	X	XXXX
NSD: formal upfront process	+	Ns
Improved service experience	+	Ns
Standardized service	+	Ns
Service complexity/cost	Ns	Ns
Service quality evidence	Ns	X
Competition	Ns	Ns
Market potential	Ns	Ns

XXXX < 0.0001; XXX < 0.001, XX < 0.01 X $< 0.05 +< 0.10$; Ns – not significant

READING SUGGESTIONS

Zeithaml, Valerie and Bitner, Mary (2000) *Services Marketing*. New York: McGraw-Hill International

Comment: Dedicated to enabling the reader to understand issues in service development, including customer expectations and behaviours, the development process, service delivery and pricing

Hollins, Gillian and Hollins, Bill (1991) *Total Design, Managing the Design Process in the Service Sector*. London: Pitman

Comment: Even though the book is dedicated to the service industry, much of the reading covers ground that is equally relevant to the development of tangible products

SOME USEFUL WEBSITES

http://www.green-alliance.org.uk/Programmes ServiceInnovation.htm

Comment: Service innovation is essentially the transformation from product- to service-based enterprises. This new business model has the potential to significantly reduce material resource use and environmental impacts. The shift changes incentive structures, from maximizing the volume of product sold to deriving profit from resource efficiency

http://www.csfi.demon.co.uk/

Comment: This is the website of the Centre for the Study of Financial Innovation, which is an independent London-based think-tank, funded by the world's top banks. It explores the future of the financial services industry. They have an active agenda of meetings, seminars and research projects which are of wide interest to all who work in, or use, the financial markets. Their contact details are: 18 Curzon Street, London W1Y 7AD, United Kingdom. Tel: +44(0)171 493 0173, Fax: +44 (0)171 493 0190

25 Definitions of Success and Failure: Measuring for Innovation

Many people might consider the Shared Appreciation Mortgage to be a failure as it did not stick in the marketplace. Interestingly, though, both the Bank of Scotland and UBS Warburg rejected the idea that the development had been a failure. Both companies emphasized the valuable learning and insights that the experience had provided them with. While it is also true that neither organization lost any money, which might have influenced their assessment on success or failure, such an attitude is characteristic of innovative organizations. Innovative organizations will not try to brush 'failures' under the carpet, but will look at them carefully with the aim of extracting as much learning as possible. We shall also explore other reasons why failure isn't always such a bad thing.

However, it is of course the aim of any organization to minimize the failure rate, and this is why will start this chapter by taking a closer look factors known to influence success or failure in new product (and service) introductions.

WHAT UNDERPINS SUCCESS AND CAUSES FAILURE?

Despite more than 30 years of research into the design and development process of products, the issues surrounding success and failure remain much the same. The importance of the early stages is constantly emphasized, because mistakes made at this stage prove costly and time consuming later on. While there are some suggestions in the existing literature as to what can be done to improve this part of the development process (market research, careful screening), the issue is not dealt with sufficiently, and the same loop is experienced time and again.

In their review of the literature on success and failure in new product development, Balachandra and Friar (1997) comment that, 'The review shows first that even with a conservative approach to listing significant factors, the list is very long. Second, comparing the factors across studies demonstrates that different authors have found that the magnitude of significance and the direction of influence vary. Third, given the differences in context, the meaning of similar factors may also vary.'

While the individual factors identified underlying success and failure in new product development may vary considerably, overall the factors underlying success and failure seem to have remained the same over the past 30 years. Suggestions on best practice published by Karger (1960) are not very different from those published by Cooper and Kleinschmidt (1996). As early as 1957, Carter and Williams identified good people at all levels, a willingness to take on new knowledge and sharing of knowledge, and cost consciousness as factors underlying successful product development. Consequent studies analysing product failure have generally identified the mismatch between product offering and market need as the main culprit.

When do Products Fail? (Hollins and Hollins 1991)

Basing their figures on findings of various researchers, Hollins and Hollins (1991) have found that project tend to fail at the following stages:

Ideas	Product design specification	Concept	Production	Selling	Success
100%	20.6%	17.5%	17.0%	12.25	4.75

Urban and Hauser (1993) have contemplated the reasons for failure, and suggest some safeguards against those most commonly observed (see Table 25.1).

Table 25.1 New Product Failures and Safeguards (reproduced from (Urban and Hauser 1993))

Failure reason	Elaboration	Suggested safeguard
Major shifts in technology	'Blind-sided' by radical change in technology; stayed with old technology too long	Monitor new technologies; look for new benefits they can produce continuing education for R&D; have a contingency plan for shifts
Changes in customers' tastes	Substantial shift in customer preference before product achieves market penetration	Frequent monitoring and updating of customer preferences in the design, testing and launch phases
Changes in environment constraints	Drastic change in some key factor such as economic conditions or material costs	Analysis of environmental constraints in opportunity identification; monitoring in testing and launch; adaptability in design
Poor repeat purchase or no diffusion of sales	Customers buy the product in the beginning, but sales never reach potential	Trial and repeat, and diffusion measured in design phase and monitored in testing and launch; product designed to deliver real benefits; advertising matched to product's benefits delivery
Poor after sales service	Product complex or not reliable and service not delivered	Service considered as an explicit designed in benefit; monitored in testing and launch
Insufficient return on investment	Poor profit relative to investment	Careful selection of markets, forecasting of demand, design of product for low-cost production; value maps facilitate profit maximization

▶

Table 25.1 (*continued*)

Failure reason	Elaboration	Suggested safeguard
Lack of coordination in functions	R&D develops a product that does not meet customer needs; marketing identifies benefits that cannot be delivered; design changes make production difficult	New product process is used to coordinate marketing, R&D, engineering and production; the input from the customer drives the design
Organizational problems	Conflicts between marketing, R&D and production; inadequate communication of key aspects of design and marketing	Careful attention to communication and explicit programmes to coordinate with quality design programmes; management involvement and review at various stages of the process; careful go/no-go decisions with objective criteria
Market too small	Insufficient demand for this type of product	Market is defined and rough potential estimated in opportunity identification; demand forecasts in design and in testing
Poor match for the company	Company capabilities do not match the requirements for producing and marketing the product	In opportunity identification the company's capabilities are matched to the strategic plan; this is then tested in pre-launch, pre-test and test markets
Not new/not different	A poor idea that really offers nothing new to the customer; the technology mat be new, but the benefit to the customer is not evident	Creative and systematic idea generation in opportunity identification; product designed with a focus on the customer; product and position tested before launch
No real benefits	Product does not offer better performance *vis-à-vis* customer needs; under investment in core technologies	In design, a strategic benefit position is identified and the product engineered to deliver these benefits; R&D designs real product performance improvements; product test with customer assure adequate benefit delivery
Poor positioning vs. competition	Perceived benefits from the product are dominated by a mix of competitive products; low value	The use of perceptual mapping, value mapping, and preference analysis identifies gaps in the market relative to competitive products
Inadequate support from the channel of distribution	Products fail to generated expected channel support; demonstrations not provided if needed; product not available to customers; after purchase service not available	The channel is considered in opportunity identification; service delivery is part of the product design; the channel reaction is monitored in testing and in launch

Table 25.1 (*continued*)

Failure reason	Elaboration	Suggested safeguard
Forecasting error	Excess production due to overestimation of sales; opportunities are lost because of underestimation of sales and low production and marketing	Systematic methods in design, pre-test. And testing phases of the process improve earlier forecasts as the product and marketing strategy near completion
Poor timing	Enter too late in market; cycle time too long; miss window of technology or market opportunity	Design process to get to market fast; monitor changes; trade-off risks of go or delay
Competitive response	Competitors respond quickly before the product can achieve a success in the market; price and promotion; competitors copy design and improve it	Strategic positioning *vis-à-vis* competition; consideration of competitive response in design, pricing, and marketing plans; 'what-if' scenarios; monitoring of test and launch; move aggressively to establish first in market advantages

Looking on the other hand, at factors which support success, Barclay (1992a) provides a still valid summary – perhaps not surprisingly, all five aspects represent good current management practice:

1. An open mind and professional management
2. A good market knowledge and strategy
3. A unique and superior product that meets customers needs and wants
4. Good communication and coordination
5. Proficiency in technological activities

Much of the same is reflected in other reviews of the literature (e.g. Craig and Hart 1992; Balachandra and Friar 1997). There is generally also a great emphasis on the importance of top management commitment (Booz Allen Hamilton 1982; McGrath 1996). However, all these ingredients seem fairly obvious, and for me the question is, this knowledge has been around for a while, and best practice is generally known – why does it still not happen?

> **Variations between Incremental and Radical Innovation**
>
> De Brentani (2001) has identified a number of variations in success factors for incremental innovation on the one hand, and radical or discontinuous innovation on the other. Demonstrated product superiority is likely to play a key role in the success of *discontinuous innovation*, because these incorporate new technologies which often solve previously unsolved problems or handle customer concerns in completely different, more effective, ways. For *incremental* improvements or adaptations, an overwhelming product superiority is much less likely to be achieved and, in the case of services – due to their intangible, conceptual, nature – is even more difficult to effectively demonstrate.

It seems that insufficient analysis of the task and an underestimation of change, or a preconceived idea about what the task would be like, can be a major influence on blinding companies to potential problems and issues at the outset. Unexpected events are in the nature of innovative projects, but to build in slack for accommodating such events, an awareness of potential problems areas and the overall level of innovation needs to be understood at the outset. Research (von Stamm 1999) found that what tends to get in the way of a realistic assessment at the outset are two things: habits and assumptions. We take a closer look at both.

Habits are accustomed ways of doing things, and the problem with habits is that we tend to be unaware what our habits are, and how much they drive our behaviour. Most people in most situations will approach a new task building on what has worked in the past. Not many projects start with a reflection and questioning of whether the task has been understood sufficiently, and the identification of aspects that are different from what had been done before.

The literature attributes such behaviour – approaching a new problem with established mindsets and procedures – to human nature. For example, looking at developments of new concepts in science, Bohm and Peat (1991) observe that there is a general tendency of people to 'Become accustomed to using their tacit skills and knowledge in subliminal and unconscious ways; there is a tendency of the mind to hold on to them and to try to go on working in old ways within new contexts.' They continue, 'Scientists attempt to press on by putting "new wine in old bottles". But why should this be? It involves a psychological factor, the mind's strong tendency to cling to what it finds familiar and to defend itself against what threatens seriously to disturb its overall balance and equilibrium. Unless the perceived rewards are very great, the mind will not willingly explore its infrastructure of ideas but will prefer to continue in more familiar ways. One way of defending the subliminal structure of ideas is to overemphasize the separation between a particular problem and other areas.'

Basically, what they are suggesting is that existing knowledge and existing approaches can get in the way of the creation of new knowledge and approaches. This observation has not only been made in the context of science. In the context of new product development, Leonard-Barton (1992) has made a similar observation. She argues that the source of strength of an organization – its knowledge base or as she calls it, 'core capabilities' – can also act as a barrier to the development of future strength. Because core capabilities are part of what an organization has known to work and what it takes for granted, they dictate how projects are approached. She concludes that, 'Because core capabilities are a collection of knowledge sets, they are distributed and are being constantly enhanced from multiple sources. (. . .) They are not easy to change because they include a pervasive dimension of values, and as Weick (1979) points out, "managers unwittingly collude" to avoid actions that challenge accepted models of behaviour.'

In his book *Science of the Artificial*, Simon (1992) uses the concept of 'bounded rationality' to explain such behaviour. He argues that problems are often too complex to be solved within the time available. As a result, humans tend to rely on patterns of behaviour that were successful in the past. These patterns are only reviewed if problems are encountered – or someone questions them.

Moving on to the subject of assumptions, we find that Schein (1992) argues that beliefs and assumptions form the core of an organization's culture. Many projects run into problems because existing assumptions have not been challenged. These assumptions, which were either explicitly or implicitly understood, influenced choices, decisions and actions throughout the development process. Assumptions are needed at the beginning of any project, because not all the necessary knowledge and information is available at the outset – which is of course particularly true for innovative projects. However, these assumptions need to be acknowledged and decisions taken on the basis of assumptions being recognized as such.

The consequence of habits and assumptions is illustrated in Figure 25.1.

You may want to refer back to Box 1.1 in Chapter 1, where insights from Guy Claxton's (1997) book *Hare Brain Tortoise Mind* are summarized. His insights help to understand different modes of responding to a situation and how people's unconscious exerts an influence in the classification of a new situation. The framework introduced in the following section suggests a way of eliciting habits and assumptions at the outset of a development process.

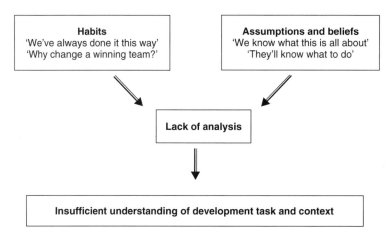

Figure 25.1   Consequences of Habits and Assumptions (von Stamm 1999)

THE COMPLEXITY FRAMEWORK[1]

The framework is designed to aid members of an organization in understanding any particular new development task in its specific context, to elicit potential problem areas and constraints, and to help them design the organizational response to a specific development task. It does so by requiring its user (a) to evaluate the requirements of the new development task against the eight elements, and (b) to assess the current status quo of the organizational context, again, against the eight elements, and with the particular requirements of the task in mind. It should bring out present knowledge levels as well as implicit habits and assumptions, whereby the former and latter are closely linked.

Eight common elements are identified as having an impact on a development task:

- Time frame
- Technology
- Skills
- Financial resources
- Participants
- Processes
- Cultural aspects
- Customer and markets

Besides understanding product-related aspects, it is further important to understand the organizational context in which the development takes place. We have discussed the implication of context and constraints in Chapter 15. Each of the eight elements contributes to the overall level of complexity of a development task. The specific context in which the development takes place will have considerable influence on the assessment. Therefore, the development team needs to look at (a) the requirements of the new development task, and (b) its own starting position, i.e. the current knowledge base, company processes and procedures, typical approaches and preferences, and so on.

TIME FRAME

Ulrich and Eppinger (1995) comment on time pressure in new product development: 'Any one of the difficulties [in product development] would be easily manageable by itself given plenty of time, but product development decisions must usually be made quickly and without complete information.' Time pressure not only requires decisions to be made based on assumptions rather than facts, but it can also force an organization to develop components of a product in parallel (McGrath 1996). This in turn will necessitate careful planning and close cooperation of all parties involved.

The time constraint under which a product is developed will also have a considerable influence on the approach an organization takes. The tighter the time frame, the more likely it is that an organization will try to fall back on existing components, solutions and concepts, thereby often neglecting the fact that the new problem task requires a different approach and a different solution (Bohm and Peat 1991). Along similar lines, Amabile (1998) points out that 'organizations routinely kill creativity with fake deadlines or impossible tight ones'.

Tight time frames have also become more of an issue in recent years, not least owing to the debate on 'time to market' and the need to shorten development cycles which was strengthened by an influential article by Bower and Hout (1988). They state that high-tech products that come to market late, but on budget, earn 33% less profit over five years, whereas products coming out on time being 50% over budget decrease company profit by only 4%. The views on the impact of reduced development times differ. Kuczmarski (1988) suggests that unrealistically short time frames, introduced as a consequence of the 'race to market', have become more of a problem in new product development. More recent publications also caution and point out that the trade-off between speed and quality needs careful consideration (e.g. Cohen et al. 1996; Calantone et al. 1997). Cutting corners to achieve shorter development times is found to be negatively related to product success. Contrary to a commonly held view, it is not always true that a speedy market entry secures financial success. Cooper (1994), for example, points out that it is more important to bring out the right product than to bring out a product at the right time.

The importance of timing is likely to vary from product to product. The race to bring products to market as quickly as possible is particularly obvious for rapidly changing markets such as computers and mobile telephones. Here new product features and improved performance can render existing products obsolete, and promote the establishment of a new market leader.

Generally, a tight time frame, particularly when externally motivated, acts as a constraint. However, a lack of understanding of the complexities arising from the other elements of the framework can lead an organization to agree to a particular time frame – because it is assumed to be realistic (see Table 25.2).

TECHNOLOGY

Technology-related issues were found to arise from two aspects: (a) the interdependencies, between components or between a product and the wider system of which it is part; and (b) the degree of innovation which, by nature, is

Table 25.2 Constraints – Time Frame

Constraint	Implication
Externally or internally imposed time frame (e.g. competitor has announced timing for the introduction of a similar product; being part of a system; product introduction required for company's survival)	Restricts the ability to experiment and explore different options Increases the likelihood that an organization will rely on existing and proven designs and technologies

associated with corresponding levels of uncertainty (Smith and Reinertsen 1995). Both Adler (1992) and Fujimoto *et al.* (1991) have found a link between high levels of innovation and uncertainty and the need for interactive integration mechanisms.

For example, if a project is developed in the traditional, sequential fashion, interdependencies between components can result in the need for substantial reworking of components that have been developed during earlier stages. Thus, a high level of interdependency leads to an increased need for coordination and integration. Holt (1987) suggests that, in cases where the degree of innovation is high, there will also be an increased requirement for slack (in terms of time and human resource) to accommodate unforeseen events. The useful translation of this insight faces two problems: (a) an organization would have to be aware of the degree of innovation inherent in the development task – which does not seem to have been the case is any of the three case studies; and (b) pressures on companies to bring products to market in ever shorter cycles make it less likely that companies will accommodate this need.

A constraint related to technology is the existence of a dominant design. Unless an organization can be certain that its new concept would be capable of replacing the existing dominant design, it is not likely to take the significant risk. Having to adhere to an existing dominant design can pose a considerable constraint. At the same time, the existence of a dominant design permits a firm to design standardized and interchangeable parts and to optimize organizational processes for volume and efficiency, hence reducing complexity. Though complexity is reduced, so are the number of choices an organization can pursue in achieving a particular development task (Utterback 1994).

Company internal standards – resulting from the company's plant and equipment, knowledge of technology, structures and procedures, or a combination of these – can also act as a constraint.[2] This type of constraint is most difficult to deal with because it is not explicit and, hence, often not perceived as a constraint. If an existing procedure or internal company standard hinders rather than aids the development effort, Leonard-Barton (1992) would describe this as a 'core rigidity'.

Beyond industry and company standards and dominant designs, there are also government regulations, for example on environmental or health and safety issues, which can act as constraints. Finally, Tidd *et al.* (1997) point out that whether or not a product is part of a system is an important factor. If the product to be developed is part of a larger system, this can act as a constraint. Consider the Eurostar; the high-speed train is part of not one but four different railway systems, and many parts of that system are non-changeable, such as the signalling systems, track widths and platform heights. While these were changeable in principle, in reality it had to be accepted that they were not only non-changeable but also different from country to country. This inevitably had constraining consequences for the design and development of the train. Constraints related to 'technology' are listed in Table 25.3.

SKILLS

The greater the range of skills required to complete the task, the greater the need for coordination and cooperation. However, it is also important to look at potential changes in the skill mix as compared with previous projects, i.e. it is important to understand where and how demands on skills have changed. In some cases, it might be necessary to consider bringing in external resources.

Changes in the mix of design skills will also differ at different stages of a product's life-cycle. We referred earlier to the example of the Sony Walkman, where skills required changed over the product's life-cycle.

Table 25.3 Constraints – Technology

Constraint	Implication
Dominant design	Restrict the choice of design and technology High risk is attached in deviating from the dominant design
Industry standards	Restrict the choice of design and technology
Company internal standards	Restrict the choice of design and technology Can prevent experimentation with different approaches and technologies
Government regulations (environment, health and safety)	Restrict the choice of design and technology Changes in regulation may require redesign of existing components
Being part of a system	Restrict the choice of design and technology

The skills available within the company and, even more specifically, skills available for each individual project, will also influence the approach.[3] It might be that, owing to the number of projects undertaken at any one time, the most appropriate people are not available to the project. Also, while it is important to have people with relevant experience on the project to avoid a replication of existing knowledge, such people are also more likely to refer back to concepts and approaches that were useful to them. This can lead to problems of a 'fixed mindset'.

A further issue is that the problem might be seen through one function's particular 'glasses', i.e. issues relating to that function's area of expertise might be highlighted while others remain unexplored. Constraints related to the 'skill' element are listed in Table 25.4.

FINANCIAL RESOURCES

A very obvious constraint which needs little explanation is financial resource. While most project ideas can be realized technically, it is often a question of whether or not the cost can be justified. Most companies have guidelines regarding the pay-back period of their investments, and apply these during the project selection process (see Table 25.5).

Table 25.4 Constraints – Skills

Constraint	Implication
Skills available within the company	Company finances and politics will influence the freedom to bring in external expertise; company politics can also decide over who is involved in the project (prestige projects tend to get the best people)
Skills available to the project	Due to other projects the most appropriate skills may not be available to the project
Existing knowledge base	May prevent a critical assessment of a new task

Table 25.5   Constraints – Financial Resources

Constraint	Implication
Budget	If financial resources are not available even the most congenial idea cannot be realized There is a technical solution to most problems but the result may not justify the investment

PARTICIPANTS

Today, alliances, joint ventures and supply-chain issues mean that it is common for more than one company to be involved in the process of designing and developing a new product (see also Chapter 13). The greater the number of participants, the greater the need for coordination and integration. The same is true for a single-company project, where the varying interests and needs of the different departments involved need to be coordinated and integrated. As the number of participants increases, more politics get involved. The more complex a project, the greater the need for arbitration – you may want to refer back to the reference to work by Fujimoto in Chapter 3 (the section on 'project leader'). The need for cooperation and coordination may decrease with increasing familiarity between the various parties involved. One might compare this with someone learning a foreign language: the more the language is practised and experienced in the national context, the greater the understanding of the meaning and use of words.

For multi-company projects and geographically dispersed organizations, the distance between sites is also an issue to be considered. Even additional expenses and time requirements for both travel and negotiations are a factor, and are not entirely mitigated by today's technology (teleconferencing, email, networked computers, etc.). If a joint venture or other form of partnership is chosen, it might be necessary to break down the workload so that each of the partners gets a 'fair share'. This can lead to the work being shared according to each partners' financial involvement rather than each partners' expertise and knowledge. For constraints related to 'participants', see Table 25.6.

PROCESSES

Unless the implications of a particular organizational or manufacturing process for the development process are understood, the project is likely to suffer. Barclay and Lunt (1987) argue that a holistic approach that considers issues

Table 25.6   Constraints – Participants

Constraint	Implication
Distance between partners	The distance between partners can act as constraint on the communication flow
Split the workload	If more than one company is involved, each partner will expect a 'fair' share of the work, whereby the 'fair' share might not be equivalent to the distribution of expertise but is often related to the financial backing by the companies involved
Partners (externally) imposed	Particularly in international projects the choice of partner might be externally influenced, e.g. by government; in national multi-company projects headquarters or other institutions of power might influence the choice
Politics	As the number of participants increases politics between differing interests are likely to impact on speed and efficiency

Table 25.7   Constraints – Processes

Constraint	Implication
Existing plant and machinery	Unless financial resources are available to alter existing plant and machinery, they can significantly constrain the choice of materials and technology
Existing organizational processes and procedures	The implications of a change need to be understood, i.e. how does the new process require the 'ways we do things around here' to change

of finances, technology, people and management, is important when investigating the introduction of new processes. The constraints related to organizational and manufacturing processes are closely inter-linked with other elements of the framework such as financial resources, skills and culture (see Table 25.7).

CULTURAL ASPECTS

Where different cultures are involved, cooperation and coordination need to be planned more carefully. Cultural differences exist between companies of different national background between different companies, and even between different departments within an organization. The literature on design management and product development comments on cultural and language differences between several different functions such as between designers on the one hand, and engineers and scientists on the other, between designers and managers, between marketing and R&D personnel, as well as between marketing and engineering. This has also been discussed in Chapter 15.

At company level, each party involved will have developed its own rules and procedures that are likely to differ from those of partner companies. Time and effort will be required to establish a shared understanding and find mutually agreeable solutions. Company culture will also have a profound influence on how people interact, what values they have – and not least what habits and assumptions they share. While this thesis has identified the crucial influence of company culture it will remain the challenge of future research to investigate its influence on contextual complexity further.

At the national level, differences might be found in design taste and also in the wider economic environment, i.e. differences in the relationship between state and industry. Finally, in a cross-border project the need to converse in two or more languages can be a major constraint. Either interpreters are needed, which can prove difficult if technical vocabulary is required, or only people with a command of the languages in question are used on the project. This can result in a compromise on expertise (see Table 25.8).

CUSTOMER AND MARKETS

Important factors here are the existing customer base and a company's reputation. While it is not suggested that a company is restricted to its existing customer base, the way the company is perceived by its customers (i.e. its reputation) needs to be taken into consideration. A whole body of literature is concerned with brand extension (see Table 25.9).

Table 25.8   Constraints – Culture

Constraint	Implication
Language	The need to share a language might restrict the choice of people working on the project If different cultures (national as well as company or departmental) are involved, more time and effort has to be spent on ensuring shared understanding (objectives, procedures, etc.)
Different procedures and systems	Can slow a project down owing to the need to 'translate' between different systems; alternatively investment might be required to ensure compatibility
Habits and assumptions	Can influence, for example, the realistic assessment a new task, how people interact and how decisions are made

Table 25.9   Constraints – Customers and Markets

Constraint	Implication
A company's reputation	How a company and its product are perceived by its markets and customers can be a constraint on the kind of product and the pricing strategy
Regulations	Regulations in different markets can also impact on the choices an organization can make, this aspects has the most severe impact on technology

OVERCOMING CONSTRAINTS

While constraints can have a significant, impeding impact on a product's design and development process, few of them are insurmountable. However, to overcome a constraint an organization needs to be aware of its existence. Meaning, for example, a team has to be aware of a lack of time to ask for more resources, or a team needs to be aware that it is lacking a certain skill essential for completing the task to take steps to redress the problem. Once there is an awareness, the people responsible can then make a conscious choice and decide whether or not a trade-off should be made. Interviewees from the research underlying the development of the framework felt strongly that most of the above would not have been possible without the determination and foresight of an individual or small group of people who pursued their goals in spite of obstacles, and against the conviction of others.

THE FRAMEWORK

The assessment of a project for each of the eight elements has to be based on the company-specific context. To gain a better understanding of the development task, the project team should first look at the requirements of the new project along the dimensions of the eight elements of the framework, and then consider the company-specific context in which the task is to be executed.

The importance of the company's specific context in association with the management of innovation is emphasized by Tidd et al. (1997). They suggest that, 'Innovation management is about learning to find the most appropriate solution to the problem (…), and doing so in the ways best suited for particular circumstances in which the organization finds itself.' This is an important point, as what seems simple to one organization may be complicated to another. Table 25.10 summarizes the eight elements and their sub-categories, what they refer to, and suggests a scale for their assessment. The aim of the framework is not to provide an instrument for exact measurement of objective complexity, but to elicit the levels of complexity as they apply within an organization's specific context.

To do this, the project team will have to ask itself how the new development task compares with its existing position, previous projects and past knowledge. Asking about the conduct of previous projects and comparing this with the plans for the execution of the new development task will help people understand more about 'the way we do things around here'. Consideration of past knowledge is a critical point. As has been pointed out before, it can

Table 25.10 Components of Contextual Complexity (von Stamm 1999)

Element	What it refers to	Scale
Time frame	In comparison with projects of similar scope	Long/short
Technology		
Interdependencies	Can arise from (a) interdependencies between different components and (b) being part of a wider system (e.g. trains, computers)	Few/many
Degree of innovation	The percentage of new components; the level of technological uncertainty is generally related to the degree of innovation	Low/high
Skills		
Level	Number of different skills required	Low/high
Mix	In comparison with previous projects	Same/different
Financial resources	The degree to which financial resources are available to the project	Ample/tight
Participants		
Number	Number of departments and/or companies involved in the design and development process	Few/many
Proximity	Proximity of sites (departments and/or companies)	Close/far
Familiarity	Familiarity of parties involved, i.e. have they worked together before, both at the individual and company level	Intimate/none
Processes		
Familiarity	The degree to which an organization – and more specifically, the part of the organization that is to develop the new product – is familiar with (a) organizational processes and (b) manufacturing processes	Familiar/unfamiliar
Appropriateness	The degree to which the processes chosen are appropriate for: (a) the task at hand and (b) the organization's context	Appropriate/inappropriate
Cultures	Number of different cultures involved (cultural differences can arise between departments, companies and/or nations)	Few/many
Customers and markets		
Familiarity	Whether the product is aimed at an existing or a new audience	Same/different
Reputations	The degree to which the product reflects the existing reputation of the organization, e.g. the degree to which the new product has credibility with the customer	Established/has to be built

obstruct a clear assessment of the development task. It is essential to establish which part of existing knowledge is beneficial to the project and which aspect may be an obstacle.

To use the framework for a project, the template shown in Figure 25.2 is useful. The template has been filled in for the comparison of an imagined product to facilitate the discussion. Such a comparison not only highlights where differences have to be understood, but also where the gap between present and future is greatest.

In the example given, the time frame is tighter than for previous projects, but at the same time, more financial resources are available. This would mean that the organization might be able to allocate more resources to the project to compensate for the tighter schedule. The framework suggests how trade-offs can be made – which Ulrich and Eppinger (1995) consider to be an essential part of the new product development process.

The example also suggests unfamiliarity with the chosen manufacturing processes, which generate a cross-check into whether the degree of unfamiliarity is reflected in the assessment of the 'skill' element. Using the proposed framework is not a one-step approach, but an iterative process that can be continued throughout the design and development process.

The framework aids in the correct assessment of any particular new development task. It might also provide an organization with knowledge about itself, and facilitate insight into its habits and assumptions. In eliciting these, an organization can make an educated choice as to whether its present methods are still appropriate for the future, or whether its 'core capabilities' are in danger of turning into 'core rigidities' (Leonard-Barton 1992).

Figure 25.2 Template for the Application of the Proposed Framework

IS FAILURE REALLY FAILURE?

I like fiascos because they are the only moments when there is a flash of light that can help you see where the border between success and failure is. It is a precious experience in the development of new products. Our most beautiful fiasco was the Philippe Starck Hot Bertaa kettle. I did not realize that we had gone too far. Inside the kettle was some complicated but very intelligent engineering that prevented stream from escaping when the water was being poured. On the prototypes it worked well but when we produced thousands and thousands and thousands it did not work so well. The kettle was very much criticized. But it was never a stupid project. We just went too far. There were so many positives, not least the courage of the designer. He wasn't playing a joke on the customers. He just felt the need to experiment. Our customers seem happy to take risks with us, probably because they realize that we are always sincere. They like walking the borderline with us. Customers are much more progressive than marketing people, distributors or retailers believe. Society is much more exciting than just a target market. A target market is a cage where people try to put society. It bears no relation to what people feel and want.

Alessi (in Wylie 2001)

Three of the big secrets of innovation are embedded in the above story, to innovate you need to take risks, to innovate you need to experiment, and to innovate you need to accept or even love failure. The story also shows that innovations can be valuable for different reasons. It is not only immediate and significant success in the market – though that is of course the main reason companies innovate. But even if the success in the marketplace is not as big as desired, there may still be benefits:

- *Increased market share* – in the fight against competition, increased market share can actually be as valuable as large profits

- *Learning experience* – the Bank of Scotland and UBS Warburg valued the experience of developing the Shared Appreciation Mortgage, as it provided them with valuable insights and learnings

- *New expertise* – through working on the recycling products, bpi developed a number of new skills that position them well to take advantage of future emission and recycling regulations

- *Enhanced reputation* – innovation specialist IDEO develop products to illustrate and demonstrate their innovation capability

In their research into new service development, Storey and Kelly (2001) found that companies were undertaking new service development for the following reasons:

•	To increase profit	88%	•	To develop distribution	14%
•	To increase sales	53%	•	To improve an existing product	12%
•	To increase revenue	40%	•	To improve the product range	12%
•	To satisfy customer needs	35%	•	To respond to regulation	9%
•	To develop new markets	26%	•	To improve customer satisfaction	7%
•	To address a new customer segment	23%	•	To improve the image	7%
•	To fill a gap in the market	23%	•	To reduce costs	7%
•	To improve the strategic position	19%	•	To increase market share	5%

WHY FAILURE CAN BE A GOOD THING

Before moving on to measuring innovation success, I would like to share Petroski's (1997) view on failure, as he puts a different spin on it, saying 'We actually want certain things to fail and break, for otherwise we would be frustrated in their use and possibly even harmed by their existence.' He illustrates his argument with examples of products that are actually designed to fail, drawing on nature as well as manufacturing. Think what would happen if eggs did not break – there would be no reproduction. Other examples of products that are deliberately designed to fail – albeit under desired conditions – are sprinkler systems and fuses. And sometimes I would actually wish that the peanut bags served on aircrafts were more disposed towards failure as, more often than not, the contents of the crafty little bags end up in my drink or on the floor, rather than in my stomach.

MEASURING SUCCESS

As more and more companies see innovation at the heart of their growth strategy, it is not surprising that more and more companies also seek to identify ways to measure the impact of their innovation activity. The critical questions are, what to measure and how? Before summarizing the insights by Thomas D. Kuczmarski, who has addressed just these questions in his article 'Five fatal flaws of innovation metrics' (2001), I would like to share a few observations. It is generally the view that 'what gets measured gets done'. This is mostly true, and clear and widely known measures can help employees to focus their efforts and make sure that resources are used most effectively. However, there are also the cynics who say, 'what gets measured gets fiddled'. If employees are rewarded based on the number of new products that are brought to market, they might invent all sorts of minor product changes, packaging changes, simple changes in colours, etc. to fulfil their quota. This does not make sense, clutters up the product portfolio and can even confuse the customer. A similar effect can be observed with suggestion schemes, where teams or departments are asked to provide a certain number of suggestions in a certain period of time.

In his article, Kuczmarski (2001) identified five problems with innovation measures, and suggests that if these are addressed, measuring innovation should become both easier and more successful. The five 'flaws' he has identified are:

1. *Too many metrics* – most likely this is caused by addition lots of new measures to already existing performance measures. This can lead to either everyone being confused as to what is really important, and people giving up on measurement, or the measuring in itself becomes and end in itself, rather than the means to an end. He suggests a three-step process: (1) identify what is essential and what the reason for measuring is; (2) decide on how to measure; and (3) ensure that they link together and actually provide you with useful insights into what affects your success. To avoid a problem arising from too many metrics, he advises establishing a thorough planning and review processes, starting with 'One metric per use and per screening criteria/operating function, and then expand this system by developing subsets as appropriate. Part of this process should include review against existing and emerging needs to identify measures that are no longer relevant.'

2. *Too focused on outcome* – expectations that innovation activities result in concrete outcomes each and every time can cause projects that, while not having led to a specific new product or service themselves, have provided springboards for other projects or product platforms are considered as failures. He suggests that viewing innovation as a continuous activity and process that does not go in a straight line can help to overcome the problem. He sees this as a problem of attitude and perspective. He quotes the example of Chrysler's K-Car, which was considered to be less successful than its individual parts such as the basic frame, structure, and design. Related to the outcome focus is the expectation of immediate financial results. While the aim of innovating is of course to improve the long-term financial performance of an organization, it might be necessary to allow different time frames to realize the benefits. His antidote for problem number two is

to 'Develop innovation platforms to serve as the springboards for spawning groups of ideas that will generate new products and services.'

3. *Too infrequent* – he considers this to be indirectly related to the absence of a clearly defined innovation programme or an outlook that is based on finances only. The innovation programme should constantly seek to identify customer needs and develop solutions for them. To overcome the problem, he suggests setting up cross-functional teams, as they help to ensure that the innovation agenda is for the best of the entire organization, rather than following the interests of just one or two departments.

4. *Too focused on cutting costs* – in Kuczmarski's view, customer-focused innovation is very likely to lead to cost cutting, whereas cost-cutting exercises hardly ever lead to exciting innovations. To overcome problems arising from a cost-cutting mentality, he suggests focusing on customer needs and product quality.

5. *Too focused on the past* – while I am not sure that I agree with the headline chosen for this last point, I certainly agree with the message. Kuczmarski argues that many of the reporting systems associated with measuring are used to 'identify the guilty and punish the innocent', and continues to say that only a change in attitude can overcome this problem. His suggested antidote is leadership that emphasizes the value of experimentation and learning, and rewards rather than punishes failure.

In their article on how to evaluate and measure firm performance, Kaplan and Norton (1992) introduce the concept of a 'Balanced Scorecard'. The aim of using the Balanced Scorecard is to provide a set of measures that balances different needs and benefits. The four areas that are covered by the Balanced Scorecard are (a) financial, (b) customer, (c) internal business process and (d) learning and growth. Success measures found in the context of new product development and innovation have been identified by Hultink and Robben (1996) and Kuczmarski (2001), respectively (see Tables 25.11 and 25.12).

Table 25.11 Performance Indicators (Hultink and Robben 1996) (reproduced by Permission of John Wiley & Sons)

Measurement level and performance indicator	Time perspective	
	Short term	Long term
Firm		
Percent of sales by new products	X	X
Market acceptance		
Customer acceptance	X	X
Customer satisfaction	X	X
Met revenue goals		X
Met market share goals		X
Met unit sales goals		X
Product level		
Launched on time	X	
Product performance level	X	X
Met quality guidelines	X	X
Financial		
Attain margin goals		X
Attain profitability goals		X
IRR/ROI		X

Table 25.12　Innovation Measures (Kuczmarski 2001) (Copyright 1998 American Society for Quality; Reprinted with Permission)

Measure	Explanation
Financial: return on innovation investment (ROI)	Total net profit from innovation is divided by R&D costs, plus incremental production costs, plus initial commercialization costs
Strategic: brand innovation quotient	Number of customers who view the brand as innovative divided by the total number of potential customers
Strategic: innovation loyalty	Number of repeat purchasers divided by total number of purchasers; For instance, for frequently purchased items or impulse purchase-type items, the innovation loyalty number might include the number of repeat purchases made before switching to a competitor as well as just the total number of repeat purchases
Operational: pipeline process flow	Measures the number of products at every stage of development

Interestingly, Kuczmarski suggests ROI as a valid measure for innovation, though he mentions 'too focused on outcome' and 'too focused on cost cutting' as possible problems arising from innovation measures and measuring. In my view, ROI can encourage both, as the following story, shared through the American Innovation Network (www.thinksmart.com), illustrates. Innovation Network founder Joyce Wycoff quotes Robert D. Shelton, Vice President with the former Arthur D. Little consulting firm who includes ROI in his list of symptoms of an anemic internal market for creativity and innovation and illustrates the point through the following imaginary conversation:

Manager:　I think we should invest in innovation.

VP:　What's the ROI?

Manager:　Uh. . . I don't know but I'll see if I can find out.

Actually, this isn't a conversation at all. It's a one-act play. The Manager is trying to be an innovation champion but doesn't have the confidence, and perhaps the understanding, necessary to sell the concept. The VP is using the ROI sledgehammer to avoid making a decision and possibly a mistake. Imagine another version:

Manager:　I think we need to deepen our capability to innovate. We have very few new products in the pipeline and our revenue from new products and services has dropped dramatically in the past few years.

VP:　What's the ROI on innovation?

Manager:　I'm not sure that's the right question. Here's some different questions we might ask:

- At our present rate of new product and service development, where will we be in five years? Is that good enough and where do we think our competition might be?
- How much new business do we need to generate and how are we going to do that? What resources and capabilities do we need to develop to generate that new business?
- What new business or technology might actually put us out of business? Where might that come from?

- If we looked at ourselves through the eyes of our competitors, what would we do to put us out of business?

VP: So what should we do to address some of these questions?

To conclude this chapter I would like to draw on Brenner (1994), who reports how and why the company Air Products measures their innovation success. He argues that, to get value from the measuring process and use it to gain valuable insights for future innovation programmes, the question is not only what measures to use, but also which products to track. He reasons that 'Attention must be paid to definitions, relevance to the businesses, consensus-building, analysis techniques, and communication mechanisms.' He believes that data gathered in such a way over a period of time can provide insights for future innovation programmes. He reports that the 'Monitoring of new product sales at Air Products has resulted in significant actionable conclusions regarding the impact, life cycles, and returns from the innovation programs.'

It actually starts with selecting products to be tracked. Air Products use the following criteria to define 'new products':

1. A threshold sales level of $100,000/ year to start the tracking period – this avoids confusing the picture with products that are short-lived or superseded quickly by follow-up versions
2. Products are 'new' for five years – once measurement starts, products are considered to be new for five years. They found that it actually takes about five years to get an accurate picture of the success of a product. This is likely to vary from industry to industry
3. New product sales can be the result of a number of different internal or external sources, for example, new products or processes coming out of their own R&D department, or product lines established through acquisition

They emphasized that the definitions evolved over a period of time as the company strived to develop criteria that would be stable over time, be relevant to both current and envisioned business activities, and allow benchmarking against with similar companies. They found that collecting information on the source and type of the new product, as well as the sales per year the company has identified the following benefits from their data collection:

- It provides meaningful input for senior management decisions
- They are able to quantify the impact of new products on the corporation's growth
- The gain insights into trends, product life-cycles, and returns from product investments

In their annual reporting they consider the following:

- Total new product sales in dollars as well as percentage of the corporation's overall sales

- Dollar and percentage change in new product sales (year to year as well as cumulative)

- The number of new products introduced in past year (new as defined above)

- It emphasizes highlights – recent introductions, largest, superior performance, Highlights of new products: introduced in last year

- Growth rate analyses and projections (mostly by trend)

Some lessons they have learned over the course of their experience since 1980 are:

- Significant actionable conclusions from new product tracking are unlikely until five years after starting. If the commitment for this long-term effort cannot be made, it is probably not worth beginning

- Real data must be used—the new product sales must be the same data that financial and business managers recognize as sales
- The data should be collected with the participation of the business organizations that 'own' the products and the sales and performance that result from them. The analyses that are performed should be structured to be helpful to the operation of these businesses
- The new product's definition should be consistent across the corporation and relevant to the company's businesses, but some flexibility is always necessary for exceptional cases

READING SUGGESTIONS

Ambler, Tim, (2000) *Marketing and the Bottom Line*. London: Pearson Education

Comment: The entire book is concerned with metrics albeit primarily from the marketing perspective. The book summarizes a 30-month research project into marketing metrics, carried out by London Business School, sponsored by the Marketing Council, the Marketing Society, the Institute of Practitioners in Advertising, the Sales Promotions Consultants Association and London Business School

NOTES ON CHAPTER 25

[1] The Complexity Framework was developed by Bettina von Stamm as part of her doctoral thesis, 'The impact of context and complexity in new product development' (1999).

[2] Here is a link to the 'culture' element. According to Schein (1992), culture is 'The pattern of basic assumptions that a given group has invented, discovered, or developed in learning to cope with its problems of external adaptations and internal integration, and that have worked well enough to be considered valid, and therefore, to be taught to new members as the correct way to perceive, think, and feel in relations to these problems', i.e. it defines the 'way we do things around here'.

[3] On this subject, Tidd *et al.* (1997) have commented, 'We have shown how firms are inevitably constrained by their choice of innovation strategies by their accumulated skills.'

26 Building for Innovation

CASE STUDY 9: JOHN McASLAN & PARTNERS

BACKGROUND

We always insist in having a look at a client's existing buildings and examining the client's company culture, we consider this standard good practice.

Andrew Hapgood, John McAslan & Partners

After having spent some time with the Richard Rogers Partnership in the early 1980s, John McAslan, born in Glasgow in 1954, set up his practice in 1984, originally with partner Jamie Troughton, who left the company in 1996. He has always had a particular concern for history, which has led his studio into rehabilitation and adaptive projects for classic Modernist icons such as the Peter Jones store in London and Wright's extraordinary campus at Florida Southern College. He comments on his office,[1] 'Working with the past is second nature to the practice, but our central concern is a timeless one: insistence on the proper use of materials and the creative use of space and form. We seek to make an honest, accessible modern architecture for the twenty-first century, rooted in the past but looking to the future.'

Today, John McAslan & Partners has 50 staff based primarily in its Notting Hill office, but also its Manchester and Milan studios. The company operates in the UK and overseas, often in association with local executive architects who assist in statutory procedures and documentation and management. The practice has a number of units specializing in landscape, interiors, industrial design, computer visualizations and model building.

JMP has undertaken a wide range of projects from commercial and operational projects for international clients such as the Yapi Kredi Bank's operations centre near Istanbul, Turkey (completed in 1998) and Max Mara's headquarters and distribution facilities in Reggio Emilia, Italy (completed in 2002), to projects for the educational sector such as the new performance and teaching facilities for the Welsh College of Music and Drama in Cardiff, transportation schemes, for example the newly completed Jubilee Line Extension stations at Canning Town and Stratford, and residential projects, and redevelopment of existing buildings, including the adaptation, restoration and extension to 78 Derngate, designed by Charles Rennie Mackintosh in 1916–1919 and the on-site remodelling of the Royal Academy of Music in London's Regents Park within the shell of a Grade I listed 1822 villa designed by John Nash.

THE ROLE OF THE BUILT ENVIRONMENT

Whereas there was a time where most organizations would have been happy to move into speculatively built, readily available office space, today there is an increasing number of companies that are keen to ensure that there is a close fit between the way they operate and the physical work space environment. Part of the reason for McAslan's success is that in their work the company places strong emphasis on ensuring that its architecture is closely aligned to what a company stands for.

> A strong minded client can be both good and bad, depending on the level of insight and 'expertise'.
>
> *Andrew Hapgood*

Three examples from McAslan's work show how companies are trying to gain most benefits from their built environment and use it to communicate messages about their organization and culture.

HELPING TO CREATE A NEW CULTURE – THE OPERATIONAL CENTRE FOR THE YAPI KREDI BANK IN ISTANBUL

The new operational centre with its open streets and courtyards communicates national culture – and that the company cares. When investing into office space managers should always remember that happy people are more productive.

John McAslan

When the Yapi Kredi Bank, one of the leading banks in Turkey, produced the brief for the invited competition in 1993 they requested that the design should address the following issues:

- *Geography of site* – 23 hectares on a sloping site with differences of 40 metres, located on an earthquake faultline

- *Expandability* – to accommodate anticipated growth, initially 45,000 m²

- *Environmentally friendly* – consume as little energy as possible

- *Influence workplace culture* – facilitate exchange and 'bumping into each other' of people from different departments

Considerable time was spent in understanding and clarifying the brief. Though delighted with winning the competition, Andrew Hapgood, lead architect acknowledged, 'It was quite a brave decision of the bank to go for UK-based architect!' To address the challenges, McAslan worked with a multidisciplinary team based in London and Istanbul, liaising very closely with a proactive client representative who participated fully in the project. In fact, in addition to frequent meetings and Andrew's presence in Istanbul for much of the time, for the detailed design stage the entire consultant team moved out to Turkey for six months, working closely with a local architectural practice. Throughout the project a number of independent consultants, including specialist engineers, façade engineers, landscape architects, security consultants, construction specialists and artists, were involved (see Appendix I for main participants). An engineering studio was asked to test the design and structure through computer modelling, physical models, drawings and calculations. As Andrew Hapgood recalls, 'The main problem was to overcome technical challenges within an achievable and acceptable standard of construction. One thing the project has highlighted is the importance of fostering a positive atmosphere within the design team as well as the contractor and client.'

The result was a modular molecular plan of usable office floorplates linked by a three-dimensional circulation network of bridges, stairs, ramps and lifts. This had many benefits; it allowed for future growth and expansion that would not look like an 'add-on'; and it meant that buildings could be moulded into the ascending hill, an integrated structural approach to earthquake resistance.

The fact that the centre was erected on a greenfield site, with limited access to infrastructure, meant that to a large degree the centre had to be self-sufficient in the provision of water, power, as well as the management of waste. The result was an integrated service system designed to maximize the potential of the limited resources available on site. The structure they chose minimized exposed surface, with external and internal shading preventing exposure to direct sunlight, thereby reducing requirements for extensive air conditioning. The semi-public street areas linking the modular buildings act as climate balancers for the air-conditioned office spaces, utilizing waste heat and 'cooling' to optimize energy use. The irrigation system currently in place is intended to eventually become redundant as native plants take over and the self-sustaining ecosystem is re-established, as it was in classical pre-goat times.

The bank was designed in response to the bank's company culture, and their desire to change its workflows and patterns. With their new operations centre, the bank wanted to bring together some previously independent administrative functions and, whilst they wanted to allow each function to retain its own identity, they wanted to facilitate a new culture of collaboration between all functions. McAslan's team engaged in detailed discussions with members of Yapi Bank's groups, not only to understand their current ways of working but also to develop an architecture that would facilitate the introduction and development of new ways of working.

Addressing the need for both connectedness and independence, McAslan, picking up on the oriental theme of street bazaars, developed a system of modular units that are linked by internal streets and walkways. And, according to Andrew, 'The streets are what really matters and facilitate the exchange and contact between departments. Here you find all the communal activities: moving and arriving, eating and drinking, chatting and meeting.' Each street is designed and landscaped differently, offering variety and helping orientation within and around the building. That the streets became a synonym for the

> Perhaps the greatest compliment Yapi Kredi pays to its host country, however, is not to be condescending. The design does not pilfer local motifs or assume a fake vernacular or a needless grandiosity. Instead, it honours, with modesty, certain traditional responses to conditions in that part of the world that the modern architect would be wise to learn. The house of the family of Yapi Kredi is a harmonious one.
>
> Architectural Record (*March* 1999)

company's new culture is illustrated by John McAslan's comment, 'On some occasions Burhan Karacam, President of Yapi Kredi Bank, could actually be found with his secretary, sitting in one of the streets, working away.'

The ten courtyard office buildings are linked by covered courtyards and walkways that imitate the traditional Ottoman marketplaces.

The bank was pleased with the result: 'The Operations Centre Complex undertakes an enormous mission in transforming the efficiency of our Bank to an extraordinary level,' said Karacam. And as the Bank felt 'Operations Centre Complex' did not do the centre justice, they renamed it 'Information Age Banking Base'.

MAX MARA'S HQ IN REGGIO EMILIA – LOCAL GROUNDEDNESS AND CORPORATE VISION

Within the fashion industry, there is a belief that because you are able to innovate, you must destroy what has come before and that innovation is entirely about change. Max Mara stands alone in their belief that, in fashion, 'good designer style is closer to architecture, instilling a culture of working towards the permanent'. As a company, Max Mara look for the 'well designed' incorporating a close and strong element of functionality. At the same time, our working method is aimed at creating tools for human beings to reinforce their identity and not to overcome their personality.

Luigi Maramotti in an interview with Andrew Hapgood, spring 2001

The roots of Max Mara's roots go back to the middle of the last century when in 1951 Achille Maramotti presented his first Italian-styled *prêt-à-porter* collection under the name Max Mara. Quite a daring step at a time when fashion was dictated by Paris and dressmakers' ateliers. By the late 1970s Maramotti had brought together a number of autonomous companies under the name Max Mara, producing a range of different collections and styles for the working woman. Today Max Mara consists of six design and production companies, has its own distribution company which supplies to over 1000 Max Mara stores worldwide, and employs some 2700 people. With the commissioning of a new headquarters for Max Mara the current generation of Maramottis running the company, Luigi and Ignazio, wanted to achieve the following:

- Provide a physical and emotional anchor point for the organization

- Be a focal point and representation of the company's values and beliefs

- Continue its commitment to the region (in the Po Valley in Pianura Padana, northern Italy)

- Demonstrate its belonging to the region through a design that would respect and integrate into the existing landscape

John McAslan remembers, 'One aspect that was very close to the Maramottis' heart was that the building looked as if it belonged to the land.' On their choice of McAslan & Partners, who had teamed up again with the American landscape architect Peter Walker, as a result of an invited design competition between three architects Luigi Maramotti commented, 'The McAslan/Walker team had the greatest sense of a belonging to the land. The team's response provided a more urbanistic than architectonic approach at the competition stages, together with an integration with the site which set the scheme apart from the others. JMP Studio submitted a conceptual design that had fully interpreted our brief with a great understanding of the importance of integration with the landscape. The project was chosen also for its coherence and clear vision of the relationship between buildings, functions and people.'

The 42,000 m² headquarters facility was to be located on a 30 hectare agricultural site just south of Milan. The brief consisted of offices for each of Max Mara's companies as well as showrooms and a 15,000 m² distribution warehouse located in an ecological park setting. Andrew Hapgood describes their approach, 'Each of the principal buildings are individually expressed in a distinctive modernist architectural vocabulary of concrete, steel, brick and glass.'

While the company did not have much experience in preparing an architectural brief they felt that cultural aspects would have to be an important element. As the chairman Luigi Maramotti felt strongly about the importance of company as well as regional culture, Andrew was invited to spend two weeks with the company observing. Andrew commented, 'It is difficult to provide a brief that conveys that.' This echoed McAslan's emphasis on culture and Andrew recalls, 'We began working with each of the companies in the group to

understand their differences as well as their parts of common identity.' The challenge was not dissimilar to the one McAslan had been facing with the Yapi Bank and again modularity offered opportunity for both diversity and communality. The 18 by 18 metre pavilion buildings provided a sense of individuality while the overarching design, based on a grid that echoed the irrigation systems characteristic for the region, provided the connectivity and unity of a whole. While each company had its own office space, other components such as the showroom, the warehouse and the spacious staff restaurant with its panoramic views were shared.

Andrew comments of the main components of the complex, 'The three principal elements in the development were each designed to a highly specific brief. The offices and studios can be seen as the heart of the operation. The three linked blocks which house them are highly flexible in form, a mix of cellular and open-plan space which eschews dated ideas of rank and hierarchy. While offices look out to semi-public external spaces, with courtyards which echo the squares of nearby Reggio Emilia, the first floor design studios form a sanctum where the ideas which drive the business emerge. Lofty and generously day-lit, these spaces, where new designs are drawn up and specimen garments assembled, have a gravitas and intensity. In contrast, the showroom block is Max Mara's window on the world, where its products face the scrutiny of the customer. Simple but refined, this building makes no attempt at superfluous display but offer a series of clear and flexible spaces in which the products speak for themselves to retail trade buyers. The great warehouse finally, with its sophisticated mechanized racking and storage system, is the first part of the scheme to be completed and is, on one level, frankly and unapologetically industrial in its aesthetic, a place of constant movement, served by an endless succession of vehicles. Nonetheless this building has not been identified as a place apart. Putting the restaurant there, which services the entire site, removes any sense of isolation with most staff visiting the building daily.'

Company internal considerations were only one part of the equation; ensuring that their buildings would correspond with the surrounding landscape was essential to the chairman. High quality, simplicity and connectedness were sought inside and out. Andrew explains, 'The buildings on the site are elements within an overall landscape which extends into the "groves" of parking, and which gives the development its essential unity. Like the traditional city, this is a place of constant movement, interaction and human contact. From the autostrada to the individual workspace, it is connected by a landscape designed to encourage easy circulation and a sense of constant activity. The squares, avenues and streets of the complex are, like those of the city, the domain of communality, where the individual

> 'Two themes, both fundamental to Italian culture, are equally basic to the project. The first is that of the family Max Mara is a family enterprise, a "family" in itself, moreover of closely associated but distinct companies, working together under the same roof. The second theme is that of the city. The project builds on the civic and urbanistic ideals which have typified Italian architecture and flexible sense of purpose and hierarchy to a diverse range of activities. From these themes the scheme has evolved a new and radical approach to the design of the workplace.'
>
> *Andrew Hapgood*

meets the community and where the community meets the outside world. In its balance of private and public space, Max Mara is nothing less than a city in miniature, a place with a collective life of its own but equally one where individuals can flourish. The desire was for connectivity, and the final landscape design achieves a penetration of the geometry of the fields through the buildings and out the other side. The penetration is achieved with insistent rows of poplar trees which, in fact, become a site element as powerful as the buildings themselves.'

REDEVELOPMENT OF PETER JONES – BRINGING THE FOUNDER'S VISION UP TO DATE

I am very anxious that our shop shall make an impression of cheerfulness, gaiety, modesty and good-fellowship.

Spedan Lewis (1934)

The entire philosophy and culture of the John Lewis Partnership, of which Peter Jones is part, was formed by Spedan Lewis who took over the direction of his father's company in 1914. And even though Spedan died in 1963, Beverley Bolton, Managing Director of Peter Jones comments, 'It is staggering how John Spedan Lewis influences what we are doing today.'

The powerful concept he introduced was that of partnership. In 1920 his staff became officially known as 'partners' – but not only in name. He also handed an interest in the company over to his employees by giving them shares. To this day, the company is run on the principle of co-ownership, and all partners in the business also share in the decision-making process. An attempt to float the company in the mid-1990s was overwhelmingly rejected by partners. Beverley comments on the advantages of being a privately held company, 'Not being publicly listed means that we can take a much longer view which is a huge advantage. For example, we are spending over £100 million on the refurbishment of Peter Jones. It is not likely that this would have gone past shareholders. Not having shareholders also enables us to take history and culture into account to a much higher degree. The notion of the partnership was born here at Peter Jones and it is seen to be very important to retain this site even though we would probably have been able to build a new department store for around £25 m. But it is quite unthinkable not to trade here any longer.'

The Peter Jones department store in London goes back 1871 when Peter Jones leased two adjoining shops in London. He moved to Sloane Square, in the affluent Chelsea district, in 1877. A year after Peter Jones' death in 1905 the business was bought by John Lewis who hands it over to his son Spedan in 1914.

Peter Jones holds a special place within the John Lewis Partnership, as it was here that Spedan first translated his vision into physical reality with a new building revealed to the public in 1936. It was to provide a pleasant and light environment for both shopper and staff. The building, which featured the first glass curtain wall in Europe, was highly acclaimed in the press, but in the end did not provide the bright work environment Spedan had envisaged as shop fittings were put in front of the windows. He is quoted as saying, 'It has the elegance of a hippopotamus where it should have been a Persian cat.'

The redevelopment of the site had been under discussion for quite some time, not least because it consisted of a number of separate buildings and access between the parts was cumbersome and difficult – Spedan's original plans had been halted by the Second World War and the last phase was finished only in 1960. In Beverley's words, 'What we have inherited is a Modernist architect's view of a modern building that did not quite get finished. In a way we are finishing what architects Crabtree and Riley started in the 30s.' However, she also points out, 'If it had been a purely commercial decision we would probably have closed the building down.' But closing down would have been completely against her principal purpose, which is 'to secure the fairest possible sharing by all its members of the advantages of co-ownership, gain knowledge and power, that is to say, their happiness in the broadest sense.'

Normally a refurbishment project would have been taken on by John Lewis' in-house team. But getting planning permission for alterations to the Grade II listed building proved very difficult and the planning authorities had suggested that John Lewis commission a limited competition and bring in experts. Beverley commented on the appointment of McAslan & Partners, 'We choose McAslan because of their track record in working with listed buildings and their experience in working with the local authority' and Peter Jeffree, the department store's Chief Architect commented, 'John McAslan & Partners were approached in the spring of 1997, together with two other established practices. From the first telephone call John McAslan showed great interest in the proposed project. The interviewing team were impressed by his pragmatic approach to meeting our retailing needs. He appeared to offer a balance between the committed Modernist and the reverent academic and I sensed that he understood our objectives. John has made a strong personal contribution and has very effectively managed his client.'

Scott Lawrie lead architect for John McAslan comments on working with Peter Jones, 'Whereas normally we would

'The (Royal Fine Art Commission) strongly supports this proposal. It believes the John Lewis Partnership and the architects are to be congratulated for putting together a scheme which respects the integrity of the Peter Jones Building whilst adapting it so that it can trade more effectively as a department store.'

Royal Fine Art Commission letter, 3rd August 1998

'English Heritage warmly supports the principle of refurbishing the listed building to ensure its continued life as a major department store.'

English Heritage letter, 13th August 1998

'The (Twentieth Century Society) does not object to the renovation and upgrading of the store, as its continued commercial success was considered to be paramount for protecting the long-term interests of this important listed building.'

Twentieth Century Society letter, 3rd August 1998

primarily be in contact with management of an organization, here we get input from all levels of our client. This means we are getting direct feedback from the end user, how they would use the space, what they want, and so on. As everyone has his or her personal perspective on design issues this means that we get continually challenged.' While there may be a danger of watering down a design solution, Beverley comments, 'Generally we are working together on finding a solution that is acceptable to everyone, but if it comes to something really important Scott is also known to dig in his heels – and rightly so.' She also felt that bringing in an outsider was beneficial in another way, 'In the same way, we often challenged their suggestions they also challenged what we did – and by doing so helped to create 20% more floor space.'

While it was not possible to change too much on the outside, inside they wanted their culture to be reflected as much as possible. They had started in 1995 with very broad design guidelines developed by the company's Chairman and their design consultant Douglas Cooper. Amongst the words they had come up with were 'elegant and self-effacing'. In 1999 they set about translating the vision into reality, developing guidelines for specifics projects including: assortments, shop fittings, signage, corporate identity etc. For example, the guideline 'clean lines on interior' were reflected in the use of glass and brass rather than, say, wood. In a third step the guidelines were translated into drawings addressing each aspect of the interior, e.g. all doors were to be all flush with the surface of the wall so they disappear, rather than having architraves.

The partners' needs were an important consideration from the outset. Beverley emphasizes, 'While the commercial side is always on my mind, I am here to make sure that the work environment is guided by the partnership concept and my principal objectives (i.e. ensuring the happiness of Partners and continuing to serve the community).'

Many organizations write 'people are our most important asset' into their annual reports and value statements, but not many put their money where their mouth is. Peter Jones does. Whereas you would normally expect about 80–90% of floor space in a department store to be dedicated to selling, in the new layout of Peter Jones they will have 50–60%, the rest will be dedicated to partners. Beverley explains, 'We will have light offices, rest rooms, dining facilities, internet café – you have to keep up with the times – a social club and a bar. The partners' rest room will be on the 7th floor with two sides in glass, giving you fantastic views over London.'

QUESTIONS

1. Think about the work environment you are currently working in/last worked in. How would you describe it and what kind of behaviours and values does it support?

2. If you are keen to develop a work environment that is supportive of innovation, what aspects may you want to include into the architect's brief?

APPENDIX I: MAIN PLAYERS INVOLVED IN THE DESIGN AND BUILD OF YAPI KREDI BANK

Client:	Yapi ve Kredi Bankasi AS
Architect:	John McAslan & Partners
Associate architect:	Metex Design Group, Istanbul
Engineering design:	Arup Mühendislik ve Müsavirlik Ltd
Space design and office furniture:	DEGW International Consulting Ltd
Interior design:	Tabanioglu Architects, Istanbul
Landscape advisor:	Peter Walker, San Francisco
Electrical engineering advisor:	Dr Turhut Tüfekci, Istanbul
Mechanical engineering advisor:	Atakat Ltd, Istanbul
Security:	Videf Security Management Ltd, Staffordshire
Catering:	Deneyim Ltd, Istanbul
Main contractor:	Baytur Constructing Inc, Istanbul

APPENDIX II: DEVELOPMENT OF THE JOHN LEWIS PARTNERSHIP

1871

Peter Jones sets up his own business, eventually leasing two small stores in what is now Draycott Avenue.

1877–1884

The shop moves to Sloane Square, an affluent district of Chelsea, and turnover increases fourfold.

1900

Peter Jones is floated as a public company. Peter Jones himself is appointed Chairman and his two sons become Board Directors.

1906

Self-made businessman John Lewis buys Peter Jones and becomes Chairman. His son Spedan is appointed Director at 21.

1914

John Lewis hands the business to Spedan. His approach heralds the birth of the John Lewis Partnership.

1920

Staff at Peter Jones become known as 'partners' and the company as 'The Partnership'.

1936

The new look Peter Jones building is unveiled. It is the first London example of a 'curtain wall' and is critically acclaimed by the architectural world.

1968

Peter Jones becomes one of the first 'modern' buildings to achieve listed status.

1985

Peter Jones extends its opening hours to six days a week.

1991

The first planning application is made to renovate Peter Jones.

1999

After a decade of planning applications, Peter Jones at last gets planning permission to renovate the Grade II listed building.

2000

Renovation work begins, PJ2 opened on 2nd May.

External walkways opened in August.

Centre of the shop completely closed from September.

NOTES ON CHAPTER 26

[1] Published by Thames & Hudson in 1999.

27 Company Culture and Architecture

A major theme from my own work is that the daily environment provided by a firm is the single most important determinant of innovative thinking among its personnel. An effective intervention in that environment is far more productive than efforts to intervene in the individual manager's thinking.

Gerald Zaltman (quoted in Grant 2000)

The McAslan case study has illustrated through three different stories what managers might seek to achieve through the built work environment – such as helping to support the establishment of new working practices (Yapi Bank), creating a platform for unifying disparate companies and cultures (Max Mara) and preserving and enforcing a specific company culture (Peter Jones). However, this does unfortunately not mean that all building projects are informed by ambitions that go beyond the purely functional. Many organizations seem to focus on the functionality, neglecting additional benefits that can be gained by considering how the building should feel and what it should communicate. This chapter will explore how the physical work environment can support company culture and help facilitate creativity and innovation. We also take a brief look at how the office environment is changing. As there has very little research been undertaken into the effect of the physical work environment, this chapter relies to a large extent on anecdotal evidence.

PUTTING YOUR WORK ENVIRONMENT TO WORK

Why, in the context of innovation, design and creativity, should we talk about the physical work environment? If you go to people's homes you will be able to find out what they value and like, and you will be able to deduce certain things about their behaviours. Someone who values good food, and good company, will probably have an open-plan kitchen/living room area. In a friendly home where members of a family enjoy being together you will see open doors, and an emphasis on shared space. Walking into a company you can make similar observations. Closed doors, senior management on the top floor guarded by fierce personal assistants send a message about the culture in the organization. A common room that is in the corner of the basement sends a different message to one that occupies a light and airy space in the centre of the building, providing comfortable seating.

Architect Ralph Buschow[1] has identified another reason why the office and the office environment have become more important: companies seem to become more and more virtual, which means that the office, the physical manifestation of the organization, becomes the focal point for the organization's culture. He states, 'In a way, a virtual organization needs a much stronger culture than a real organization. The office can help people to identify with their organization. It can show employees what the organization stands for, what values it holds – and thereby it becomes the embodiment of that organization's culture. And the architecture used to convey this culture should be implicit, not explicit – that's where post-modernism got it wrong, they were trying to be too explicit and descriptive.'

A recently conducted survey of over 1000 people in the UK (Titteron 2001) found that two-thirds of the British workforce believe that they would be more productive and would in fact work harder if their work environment was better – less crowded, better air conditioning, better lighting. But not only do the physical conditions matter; respondents also commented on the importance of the degree of 'friendliness'. Titteron reported that 'Having good people and good conversation around them as crucial to creating a positive atmosphere.' A view shared by Lynn Frost, Vice President of Product Innovation with FranklinCovey, who explains,[2] 'To me environment is everything. I think people are more productive, more creative, when their environment is beautiful and relaxed. It opens up all those channels of the best ideas inside of them. I think every human being deserves to have the environmental support. It feeds the spiritual needs of the human; it feeds the mental needs, the emotional needs and it definitely comforts the physical needs.'

We have already talked in Chapter 13 about the importance of internal collaboration for innovation. The work environment is something that can encourage and facilitate collaboration and exchange. But changing the work environment for the better has a positive impact on employee productivity for another reason. Titteron also quotes research from the US which found that *any* change in the work environment actually improves performance, because employees feel that managers care. However, there are a few more specific things that managers can do that will make a difference, particularly for innovation and creativity and we will come back to that later in this chapter.

In the context of innovation, there are three things that your work environment can do for you:

- Send signals about a company's culture
- Encourage certain behaviours
- Help to communicate change

Below we will take a look at the example of a company where management has used the physical work environment deliberately to communicate and reinforce its company culture.

SUPPORTING THE CREATION OF A CULTURE

You can use the environment to underline and accentuate certain behaviour, to underlie values, to encourage and discourage certain behaviours.

David Magliano, Marketing Director, Go-Fly[3]

When setting up business the low cost airline Go-Fly decided to take a very deliberate approach in the design of its office environment, making sure it would reflect characteristics and values of the new company's desired culture. In addition to being low cost, reflecting the company's positioning, Go-Fly's marketing Director David Magliano explained that they wanted to ensure that their work environment would reflect the company's key values, which he described as,[4]

1.   *Being open and honest* – which refers primarily to the way we communicate

2.   *Being respectful* – which involves being tolerant and accepting differences

3.   *Doing what you said you would do* – honour your commitments

4.   *Being yourself in the sense* – for example, we encourage our cabin crew to be themselves on the plane, we do not have a clone model with a 'painted face', and we do not expect a standard set of behaviours

5.   *Being part of one team* – we have a collaborative working environment

6.   *Getting involved* – we want people to take responsibility for making a difference

The Go-Fly management believe in using the physical work environment to provide employees with clues that project and enact their values. David commented, 'For example, low fares depend on low cost, so we need things to be low cost. If you have a look around you will find that the office looks a bit scruffy, a bit messy – informal. All sorts of notes are cellotaped to the doors – and I don't have a problem with that. That is a clue that we are low cost. We do not have expensive oak-framed noticeboards, nor do things have to be high gloss and look like marble. We are just not that kind of company. I think it reflects that we are busy and democratic.' He continues, 'We use our environment to communicate values and culture.'

It was also interesting to note that they lived in the office space before they started modifying it to meet their needs – and support the culture they aimed to create. During this initial phase, management identified needs and desired aspects of company culture. Before they changed the layout, the space reflected a traditional office layout with straight corridors and small offices, which made communication difficult and left people isolated. David commented on the change, 'Now, because you can see what is going on, communication is much better. It is all much more informal and people just approach someone they see walking past to have a chat or ask some questions – communications has become a sort of spontaneous by-product.'

However, Go was a start-up situation and David admitted that deliberately creating a company culture is much harder for an established company to achieve. 'We had an advantage because we were able to do three things. First, we talked about how we managed and how that should be reflected in all aspects, including our work environment. Secondly, we started with a blank piece of paper regarding the people, and thirdly, we were able to choose who we recruited. I also believe that it was also helped a lot by the fact that our core team had a clear and shared vision about the kind of company we wanted to create. I don't think there are many established companies that operate under such conditions. It is not that I think it is impossible for an established company to change, but it is much harder, much more like trying to steer a super-tanker – whereas we can behave like a little yacht.'

Many managers aim to make their organizations more innovative, and this tends to require a change in culture. Some aspects of change were discussed in Chapter 6, particularly relevant here is the fact that most change will have to overcome some resistance. There are several aspects where the physical work environment can support managers in their change efforts. First, making changes in the physical work environment indicates that this change initiative is serious and that management put their money where their mouth is. Secondly, the planning of changes in the built environment allows the involvement and engagement of employees in the change, increasing the likelihood of buy-in not only into the physical changes, but also in the drivers of the change. Finally, the way office space is laid out can stimulate certain behaviours. If every employee has to enter the office through a wide open space with coffee tables, newspapers and ample seating, the likelihood of chance encounters and informal networking is much higher than if you walk straight past a receptionist into the lift, and along a narrow corridor into the office.

Of course, senior management needs to lead the way in making sure people understand that having a chat with colleagues over a cup of coffee is accepted behaviour, and not seen as a waste of time. One CEO I interviewed mentioned that he was encouraging people to have lunch in the nearby park to refresh their minds. When asked whether he actually did so himself he commented, 'No, I think that is a bit of a waste of time.' Not surprising, then, that his employees did not go either. Most employees are too intelligent to fall for the 'do as I say, don't do as I do'. But besides providing employees with spaces that facilitate change encounters, there are more things managers can do to encourage and facilitate creativity and innovation through the work environment.

CHARACTERISTICS OF WORK ENVIRONMENTS THAT SUPPORT CREATIVITY AND INNOVATION

The following aspects associated with the work environment will help managers create an atmosphere where creativity and innovation flourish:

- Meeting and recreational space
- A variety of different work spaces
- How you arrange departments
- Space dedicated to project teams
- Spaces dedicated to innovation and creativity

MEETING AND RECREATIONAL SPACE

David Magliano already alluded to the value that lies in spontaneous encounters and informal networking. Both are important facilitators of innovation. So for managers who are seeking ways to improve the innovation performance of their company, providing space where people can casually meet and just 'bump into each other' is one possible lever.

Architect Ralph Buschow has observed a change in attitude towards spaces that in architectural speak used to be called 'functional area' – kitchens, corridors, restrooms, etc. The aim used to be to keep such spaces to a minimum as they were seen as a necessary evil to allow people to get from A to B, or pick up a cup of coffee – in many organizations not something that managers wanted to encourage. However, this has changed. Ralph comments, 'In the work environment the kitchen, for example, is a very important element. It used to be in the corner, in the basement – somewhere out of the way. Today we have come to change our view on this: the kitchen is a meeting point, people bump into each other, exchange ideas, this is where networking happens – this is where things generally just happen. Questions which in old days may have been saved up for the weekly meeting are now discussed in the corridor, in between meetings. Views are collected and decisions are made on a much more continuous and spontaneous basis than before.'

A VARIETY OF DIFFERENT WORK SPACES

Until fairly recently, office space was either one or the other: open plan or separate offices. Ralph Buschow argues that this is no longer enough. 'It is clear that there is no one right environment that suits everyone. It would be naïve to think that we are all the same and have the same needs. Even splitting people into extrovert and introvert is too simplistic. We all tend to be a bit of both. So you cannot say, this person is introverted so he or she gets a separate office, and this person is extroverted so they will prefer an open-plan situation with continuous stimulation. You have to offer both. The employee then decides what he or she needs, and when. Most are happy to use shared spaces, get away from their own little area – be right in the middle of things – at times. We believe that people should be allowed to make the choice which environment they prefer – not just once but basically every day.'

Jon Leach, partner of the advertising company HHCL, agrees and believes in providing employees with a choice of working spaces and meeting rooms.[5] He commented, 'We do have a certain number of different size meeting rooms. They vary not only in terms of size but also in terms of their atmosphere, some have a very quiet ambience, there are some with nice views, others where you can't look out at all. These meeting rooms are scattered throughout the place – for private conversations, rooms without chairs for brief meetings, there is a café area, and so on. So we try to offer a variety of meeting spaces to cover all sorts of needs and different kinds of human interaction.'

HOW YOU ARRANGE DEPARTMENTS

Another trick to encourage cross-departmental communication, that coincidentally also enhances mutual understanding and respect, which in turn makes collaboration easier, is to mix departments up, or arrange their locations in such a way that maximizes traffic. David Magliano explained, 'While we have avoided functional silos as such, there are certain more or less dedicated areas such as the rooms for the cabin crews to meet. On the other hand,

> 'Because these project teams expand and contract and interact with lots of other people throughout the course of a project, we have not isolated any of the support functions, such as finance. These are not located in some far away corner but scattered in between.'
>
> *Jon Leach, HHCL*

we have deliberately put two groups which have to talk to each other a lot in separate corners of the building so that there has to be a lot of traffic across the office space between those groups. So we try to force movement.'

SPACE DEDICATED TO PROJECT TEAMS

Linking from the previous point is to provide dedicated space for project teams. Jon Leach commented, 'Rather than having distinct departments we are organized around disciplines, and as a consequence there is no strong departmental ethos. With looking at job functions and sharing clients, the organizing principal for us is the project team. This tends to be a 5–6 person unit, consisting of an account manager, a planner, a creative team, maybe a publicist, maybe a producer – whatever is needed on that particular project. So basically it means that a small team works together on the project from beginning to end. We find that this way of working produces better ideas and higher levels of customer, as well as employee, satisfaction, which, at least theoretically, also leads to higher profits. Our architecture is designed to support this particular structure, i.e. project teams, not departments; it is designed to support groups of people working together.'

Additional benefits were highlighted by the innovation agency IDEO. During a workshop run for the Innovation Exchange, a company representative explained that they dedicate space to project teams. Such space would be decorated with drawings, notes from brainstorming sessions, prototypes and other items. As such, project space tends to be part of the open-plan structure; it is easy for other members of the organization to see what is going on, to drop in, and thereby contribute to that particular project and provide their insight and expertise.

ADDITIONAL STIMULI

Not explicitly part of the physical work environment, but somehow related, is the benefit of providing a wide range of stimuli – be it in the office space itself, in meeting rooms, or other parts of the office. Such stimuli can books, materials, prototypes, objects that people value or find particularly innovative, competitor products, and so on. IDEO provide an additional source of inspiration: their materials library. In each of the eight offices around the world the company maintains a set of drawers full of interesting, curious, and strange materials and products which are suggested by employees, and entered into a database. Into this database are entered comments, benefits, problems, uses and application providing a rich source of information.

SPACES DEDICATED TO INNOVATION AND CREATIVITY

Finally, many companies have come to provide their employees with dedicated innovation spaces. Such spaces are designed to encourage creativity, and take people away from their everyday job and everyday environment. Snead and Wycoff refer to such spaces as collaboration rooms, and emphasize the need to distinguish them from meeting or conference rooms. They explain, 'It's important to keep in mind that most meeting and conference rooms are designed for presentations, not collaboration. The standard conference room set-up is a long table surrounded by chairs, perhaps a small whiteboard at one end of the room, an overhead projector and a video system. These rooms are designed primarily for information presentation. One person sits or stands at the front of the room and presents information, using the whiteboard, the overhead projector, or the video monitor. Participants are focused on the front of the room and the information being presented. Discussion may or may not be encouraged, but participants are seldom invited to take control of the pen or the overhead or video monitor. There is no real co-creation of understanding or plans. There is, however, order and control. Collaboration rooms are very different in that they invite a flow of ideas and energy with little concern for either order or control. Imagine a room surrounded with floor-to-ceiling whiteboards well stocked with coloured markers. There are moveable easel pads and an abundance of sticky notes of various colours. Tables and chairs are smaller... or non-existent, allowing more space to move around, cluster around engaging ideas, or back off for contemplation.' The characteristics they believe innovation centres should have are listed in Box 27.1.

> ### BOX 27.1   Characteristics of Innovation Centres (Snead and Wycoff 1996) (reproduced by permission of Wycoff, J.)
>
> *Interaction* – Collaborative spaces invite interaction and movement, allowing people to move around, grouping and regrouping as ideas and energies shift. Small tables for 4–5 people are generally better than large conference tables.
>
> *Visual thinking* – Ideas and thoughts gather power and energy when they can be seen and interacted with. No collaboration room is complete without generous whiteboard space, large sheets of paper, boxes of coloured markers and a large supply of Post-it™ notes.
>
> *Beauty* – Beauty operates at a deep level, opening up the imagination and the heart. Lynn Frost, Vice President of Product Innovation with FranklinCovey (see inset box) states, 'I believe in Goethe's quote that every day you should read some poetry, see a beautiful picture, get into nature so that we don't lose the sense of the beautiful that's in all of us.' You can make your space visually pleasing by using plants, water fountains, windows that let in natural light and beautiful scenes, colours, and a variety of textures.
>
> *Fun* – Play is an important part of creativity and collaboration. Fun breaks down barriers and frees us from the inhibitions that keep us 'in the box'. Bean bag chairs, toys, bright graphics, crayons and silly hats all help create an atmosphere of fun.
>
> *Abundance* – An atmosphere of abundance sets up a mindset of generosity and sharing which promotes collaboration and idea generation. A feeling of abundance can be created by having large bowls of fruit,

▶

candy or snacks available (chocolate is always a winner), keeping a refrigerator well stocked with bottled water and soft drinks, making sure there's always markers, writing pads and sticky notes available.

Tools – The purpose of collaboration rooms is to work together more effectively. It's very important to have the right tools immediately available in the room. This will vary for different organizations but generally includes a phone with a fast modem for connection to the internet, a good computer system complete with mindmapping and project management software, a printer, an overhead projector and VCR.

CHANGES IN WORKING PRACTICES AND THE OFFICE ENVIRONMENT

This section could as well have been called, 'new ways of working', or perhaps equally appropriate, 'how information technology changes the way we work', as it is IT that has triggered significant changes in working practice. One change is the increasing number of people who are working from home. This has been facilitated by increasingly powerful computers, modems and mobile phones. What does working from home – or, for that matter, any place outside the office – mean? What are implications for innovation, design management and product development?

According to the 1997 Olsten Forum on Managing Workplace Technology (http:www.Olsten.com), 51% of North American companies now permit employees to telecommute through pilot and ongoing schemes, with 74% expecting their use of telecommuting to increase.

Matathia and Salzman (1999)

IT has a fundamental impact on how we communicate. There used to be two constraints to communication: location and time. People had to be in the same place at the same time for communication to take place. Telephone has removed the former and now email and internet chat-rooms have removed the latter. More and more people rely on email – rather than phone calls or face-to-face interaction to communicate with their colleagues. Several aspects about emails are worth noting. It takes no time at all to write and send an email – which on the one hand is a good thing, it speeds up communication, independent of the location of the sender and recipient. On the other hand, because it is so easy emails tend to be much more informal. The fact that emails are so easy to produce, and that it is so easy to copy as many people in as one likes, also means that people are getting inundated with emails. And finally, because they are more informal, they are written in a hurry, without greeting and closure, often in a language that is casual and likely to be less precise than language used in a memo or letter.

But what is the purpose of communication? It is to transfer information. If we are imprecise, the information might not be conveyed properly, if too many emails are received, people get selective with the ones they read. This can lead to important information getting lost. In fact, some organizations have introduced rules that emails are not allowed if people work in the same building, people have to pick up the phone or go and seek a direct conversations with the person in question. There are several reasons why face-to-face communication is so important, particular if a difficult or new subject is broached. In a face-to-face conversation we have the opportunity to see the person's reaction. We can read their body language and facial expression and we can hear their tone of voice. This gives us an idea whether or not the message has been received and at least an indication of whether it has been received correctly (one of the reasons that video conferencing has become so popular). Over the phone we have at least the voice to help. But when sending an email we do not have any opportunity to judge whether our message has been received correctly or not.

Imprecise communication can cause problems for innovation and product development. Successful development of a new product depends upon all members of the team sharing an understanding of what the aim of the project is and how they are going to achieve it. Without the possibility to ask and explain immediately, there is a greater risk of misunderstanding and misinterpretation. This does not mean that project teams should not communicate remotely, but it does mean that greater care has to be taken to ensure a shared understanding. By the way, the fact that different departments, let alone companies, tend to speak 'different languages' does not make this task any easier – see Figure 3.2 in Chapter 3.

On the other hand, IT enables sharing of information, irrespective of time and location, which can have great advantages for new product development. People working in different organizations, on different continents – wherever – can work on the same project either together at the same time or, if on different continents, during their respective working hours. Ford Motor Company is an example of a company where project teams in several different locations and time zones work together on one project, accelerating development time significantly.

In the interview conducted with architect Ralph Buschow of Buschow Henley, he commented on about the changes in working practice he was observing during his work. He too commented on the impact of information technology: 'A number of things affect the way we work, technology being one. Not necessarily technology itself but the effects it has. Today's technology allows consideration of a subject while being physically removed. It also enables much faster decision making than ever before. Previously the boss in his (!) corner office used to sign off a number of letters or proposals at the end of the day. Today, with hierarchies much flatter, more people are involved in decision making, all over the organization. This has increased complexity. Another contributor to complexity is the fact that companies tend to be involved in a wide range of activities. There are lots of specialist around – which cannot be managed top down any more. Because of their special expertise they need to be involved in the decision-making process, which means that decisions are often made by teams. Not that there weren't any specialists before, but they tended to write lengthy reports that were then used by their bosses as basis for decision making. In today's fast moving environment, this process is far too cumbersome and time consuming.' As a consequence, he reasons, the previously static work environment has to become much more flexible and needs to offer both flexibility and continuity.

He reasons that spending money on the work environment makes sense. For most companies, particular in the service industry, salaries are the largest expenditure. This naturally means that it should in the interest of an organization's to get the best out of their people – and the best way to achieve that it to make them want to come to work, to make them happy at work. He comments, 'A one percent increase in productivity will pay for all sorts of things!'

However, Ralph also points out that one cannot change a work environment *for* employees, one has to do it *with* them, 'We generally start by looking at how people in the client organization work, what they need, what their history is – in short, we undertake a cultural analysis to ensure that the solution we proposes fits with their culture and ambition.'

Jon Leach of HHCL agrees, 'The important thing is not to get too hung up about the principle but to develop ways to tolerate different views and different needs. You have to watch that you develop things in a way that takes all – or at least most – people with it. I believe it worked for us because we had good communication throughout and good people working on it, rather than seeing it as a facilities exercise. We put together a team of people together who could talk to architects and planners but also talked to people who were interested in the human psyche and human behaviour patterns. It had to be right for everyone and so we did not have that many casualties.'

And in addition it is important to understand about the work environment – as with everything to do with innovation – that it is essential to remain open and to continue experimenting. To quote Jon again, 'It never finishes: we find that there are some parts of the blueprint we wrote 18 months ago where we ask ourselves today, why did we want one of those? For example, we have one room upstairs with very expensive revolving doors which no one really uses. Probably because it feels very unpleasant – but it still seems to have been too expensive to change. So we are continuously reviewing what we have and how we can improve it.'

CHANGE THE WORK ENVIRONMENT – BUT FOR THE RIGHT REASONS

Design represents a minute proportion of the lifetime cost of a building – less than 1% – but done well it has a disproportionate impact on how well the building, and its surroundings, perform.

Stuart Lipton, Chairman, Commission for Architecture and the Built Environment, The Independent *8*[th] *February 2001*

Finally, a comment on the motivation behind changes to the work environment. Managers in many companies are motivated to review the work space arrangement out of financial and cost considerations. However, employees will be well aware as to whether changes in the work environment are suggested to save cost, or improve working conditions. Jon Leach comments, 'One of the key aspect of our space planning is that it was not about "how much can we save". It so happened that our density has increased. It is about 70 square foot per person, which is pretty low – it was about 110 before. But increasing density was not where we were starting from; our starting point was, we are in the people communication business, which is to do with innovation and collaboration, how can we create an office space that encourages that? It was rather nice to discover that because of the way the people work, we did not need quite as much space as we did with the previous model but it was a side effect, not the reason for doing it.'

READING SUGGESTIONS

Olmsted, Barney and Smith, Suzanne (1994) *Creating a Flexible Workplace*. New York: Amacom

Comment: This book presents alternative work arrangements, including flexitime, compressed workweek, flexplace and part-time alternatives such as regular part-time employment, job sharing, phased and partial retirement, voluntary reduced work time programmes, leave time and work sharing. For each option, the authors explain the origins, who uses it, where it is appropriate, what the advantages and disadvantages are, whether it might be appropriate for your organization, how to introduce the concept and what special considerations for managers and supervisors are

Turner, Gavin and Myerson, Jeremy (1998) *New Workspace New Culture – Office Design as a Catalyst for Change*. Aldershot, UK: Gower

Comment: The book provides insights into current working practices, what the barriers to change are, how these can be overcome, and what possible future work scenarios are

SOME USEFUL WEBSITES

www.theworkfoundation.com

Comment: On this website you find some insights from research into workspace-related issues

http://www.spaceforbiz.com.

Comment: Lots of articles relevant to workplace issues are summarized or referenced

NOTES ON CHAPTER 27

[1] Interview conducted by Bettina von Stamm in April 1999; for full interview see http://iexchange.london.edu/html/int_r_buschow.html.

[2] In an interview with G. Lynne Snead and Joyce Wycoff, published on the Innovation Network website (www.thinksmart.com).

[3] David Magliano in an interview conducted by Bettina von Stamm for the Innovation Exchange, May 1999; for full interview visit the Innovation Exchange website (http://iexchange.london.edu/html/int_d_magliano.html).

[4] Go-Fly is serious about its values and does not only have them written down; they are part of the induction programme every employee goes through, and either he or CEO Barbara Cassani have a session with each new employee to make sure that the values are communicated and received appropriately.

[5] Jon Leach was interviewed by Bettina von Stamm for the Innovation Exchange, June 1999; for full interview visit the Innovation Exchange website (http://iexchange.london.edu/html/int_j_leach.html).

28 Outsourcing – Designers In or out?

Although not directly addressed, the McAslan case study included some insights relevant to working with external designers, or to put it differently, to the outsourcing of design services. Architecture is probably one of the most likely candidates for outsourcing, however, there are many organizations that outsource all design activities as well as development activities. There are a number of issues to be considered in the outsourcing decision, and selection of the most appropriate designers which we will investigate in this chapter, and which will be illustrated through the case study of the Skorpion, a motorbike designed by a British design consultancy for a former East German company. There is, of course, a wider debate on outsourcing in general, and we briefly review a few insights into outsourcing in general before focusing on the outsourcing of design services.

INS AND OUTS OF OUTSOURCING

In a way outsourcing is a variation on the theme of collaboration and some of the issues addressed in Chapter 13 are applicable to the outsourcing debate, such as:

- Doing it for the right reasons – e.g. a strategic need and not a short-term cost-saving exercise

- The need for a good fit of areas of expertise

- Mutual respect and understanding of each others' needs and ways of operating

In fact, outsourcing is one end of a spectrum of possibilities of collaborating with other organizations. In their article on how to decide on whether to outsource or not, Chesbrough and Teece (1996) provide a number of useful categorizations and guidelines. Their starting point is the suggestion that outsourcing is a potentially

> 'American firms have traditionally taken a piece-meal approach to outsourcing: in deciding what to contract out, they have tended to look at short-term savings in overheads, rather than at long-term strategy. By contrast, the Japanese companies, which pioneered outsourcing, use it to improve long-term quality and efficiency rather than to cut overheads. This, paradoxically, has resulted in bigger savings. Outsourcing now accounts for more than a third of Japanese companies' total manufacturing costs, and routinely reduces those costs by over 20%.'
>
> *Anonymous,* Economist November 1st 1999

fast route to innovation. They warn that managers should consider carefully the kind of innovation they are engaged in before making the outsourcing decision. They differentiate two different types of innovation (see Figure 28.1):

- *Autonomous innovation* – something that can be developed independently of other parts or components that stands alone and does not affect/is not affected by other parts such as a turbocharger in an engine. They suggest that for such an innovation a virtual organization would be suitable

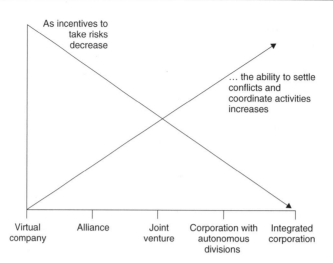

Figure 28.1 Finding the Right Degree of Centralization (Chesbrough and Teece 1996) (Reprinted by permission of Harvard Business Review. From 'When is virtual virtuous? Organizing for innovation' by Chesbrough, H.W. and Teece, D.J. Januray–February, 1996. Copyright 1996 by the Harvard Business School Publishing Corporation; all rights reserved)

- *Systemic innovation* – something that makes sense only in conjunction with other innovations such as instant photography where both camera and film are needed. For such innovation an integrated corporation would be more suitable

So the first three questions managers should ask are (1) what is the possible pay-off (and hence the incentive to take risks), (2) how important is the ability to settle conflicts and coordinate activities, and (3) what kind of innovation are we seeking. A fourth question is whether capabilities are readily available or whether they have to be developed. This is probably a tough question to answer at the outset of a development – not least, habits and assumptions can get in the way of realistic assessment of a development task (see also Chapter 25). However, depending on what kind of innovation – autonomous or systemic – and availability of capabilities – existing or need to develop – the authors suggest to chose from a spectrum between going virtual or bringing everything in-house (see Figure 28.2).

Figure 28.2 Matching Organization to Innovation (Chesbrough and Teece 1996) (Reprinted by permission of Harvard Business Review. From 'When is virtual virtuous? Organizing for innovation' by Chesbrough, H.W. and Teece, D.J. Januray–February, 1996. Copyright 1996 by the Harvard Business School Publishing Corporation; all rights reserved)

According to the Outsourcing Institute in America, managers have come to realize that outsourcing only adds value beyond the short term if a strategic approach is taken. In their Fifth Annual Outsourcing Index,[1] in which they report the latest outsourcing trends and challenges, the Institute comments on 'The diminishing role that cost saving plays when deciding to outsource. The majority of participants (55%) gave "improving their company's focus" as their main reason for outsourcing with "reducing and controlling operating costs" holding the second place (54%).' The numbers becomes more significant when realizing that in the previous year's survey improving focus was identified by only 40% of participants as the main driver of outsourcing, whereas 48% declared the cost issue to be the main reason. The authors of the report consider this insight particularly relevant as they would not have expected focus to take precedence over cost in times of economic downturn. However, in my view is conflicting with the above is the finding that 65% of participants determine whom they are outsourcing to based on price with quality taking only second place (51%).[2] However, this varied with size of company whereby larger companies placed almost equal value on quality. Still, it seems that intentions and knowing what it should be are ahead of reality.

A white paper produced by the company Wind River considers the following to be strategic benefits of outsourcing:

- *Time to profitability* – outsourcing is seen to decrease time to market

- *Product robustness and reliability* – due to brought-in expertise that may not all be available in-house

- *Product features set* – linked to the above, the additional expertise is considered to lead to improved product features

- *Controlled costs* – due to contractual agreements cost are agreed upfront, no need to train and invest in expertise, infrastructure and organizational structures

- *Optimal use of resources* – only the people, technology, space required for the project are paid for; gives company optimum level of flexibility

Across different company sizes, the three main factors seen to underlie a successful outsourcing relationship were:

- Finding the right vendor (63%)
- Managing the relationship (rated higher by larger companies than by small and medium-sized ones)
- Structuring the contact properly (ranked number two for medium-sized companies (500–999 employees)

These, interestingly, were seen to be more important than understanding the firm's goals and objectives.

As to problems encountered with outsourcing, participants ranked issues around time and expertise as number one problem (44%) followed by budget issues (33%), bandwidth (20%) and problems in identifying service providers (15%). Wind River have identified the following reasons for outsourcing failure:

- Teaming up with the wrong partner; which is often due to insufficient care and time being spent during the selection process

- Start looking too late in the process; companies might progress their products too far in-house before involving the outsourcing partner

- Wrong expectations; generally due to unclear specifications or brief or changes in programme after the project has started

- Treating a strategic partner like a 'body shop'; problems can arise when the outsourcing company tries to interfere with the outsourcing partners structures and systems

- Poor supervision; a lack of monitoring and management of the relationship

- Internal barriers; resentment and resistance in the outsourcing company
- Bad contracts; contracts should include:
  — clarity about billing
  — indemnification for patent infringement
  — non-complete clauses
  — split risks (bonuses for exceeding targets etc)
  — project halts (what to do if a project is aborted)

To maximize the chances of success, the authors recommend the following process:

1. *Identify your needs* – what does success and failure mean in the context of your organization (see also Chapter 25); what is it the company you are outsourcing to should deliver; how should the relationship be structured?

2. *Develop a request for proposal* – the authors suggest that whether you want to invite one or more companies to submit proposals will depend on how many companies could realistically provide the services you are seeking

3. *Evaluation process* – ensure that you are only considering proposals that meet *all* your needs before you look at costs, and make sure you evaluate against your success criteria

4. *Selection process* – the authors suggest that you take the finalists through the 'best and final offer' process, ensuring that they have the skills and resources to deliver what you need. One interviewee suggested that cost/price should account for around 30% of the decision. However, it will also depend upon the key success drivers, and the authors give the example of selecting a neurosurgeon where you would want to go for the technically best rather than the cheapest, however much cheaper he or she might be

5. *Contract execution* – signing the deal

6. *Administrative functions* – this includes regular reporting, the authors suggest asking for reports on a monthly basis, to make sure the project says on track

7. *Close out* – after completion of the contract, a final report should be requested that provides a review of the contract and its fulfilment, any changes to the original plan and why they have occurred as well as measurement against the set success and performance criteria

DESIGNERS – IN OR OUT?

After a more general view on outsourcing, this section turns to the specific issue of outsourcing design. In 1997 about £10 billion or 2.6% of annual manufacturing turnover in the UK was spent on product development and design both in-house and bought in (Sentance and Clark 1997).[3] The two critical questions managers should ask are (a) should we design in-house or should we buy in outside expertise, and (b) if we decide to involve external designers, how should the relationship be structured? Interestingly, the trend towards outsourcing reported in the above mentioned report by the Outsourcing Institute has been observed in the specific area of design and new product development (Cooper and Press 1995; Anonymous 1996). In the following, we look at the different options an organization has regarding the location of design, as well as the advantages and disadvantages for each choice. The decision on whether designers are employed internally or not will also vary with the type of design in question (see Table II.1 in Appendix II).

Managers have three basic options when considering the location of design:

- Develop the design in-house
- Employ an external designer or design consultancy to develop the design
- Use a combination of in-house and external design.

If the in-house option is chosen there are several possible locations for design:

- *With marketing* – a choice quite popular with fast moving consumer goods

- *Within the technical domain (either R&D or production)* – most likely to be found in engineering or technology-based organizations

- *An independent design department*

- *A combination of the above*

- *An organization might decide not to have any explicit design expertise at all*

Not using designers, be they located in-house or externally, does not mean that companies do not undertake design. In their research Walsh *et al.* (1992) found that design activities are often undertaken by someone without any particular design-related qualification. Then there is also the issue of 'silent designers' (see also Chapter 1), i.e. people whose decisions have a critical impact on design and development of a product, but who would not consider themselves designers nor perceive themselves to be actually making design decisions.[4]

The importance of design for a company's competitive position and the MD's attitude towards design are company-specific factors that are likely to influence the treatment of design within an organization, as will the level of design consciousness that prevails within an organization (see Figure 1.3, Chapter 1). How frequently an organization engages in the design and development of new products will also influence the decision. A company being continuously engaged in the design and development of new products is more likely to develop an in-house expertise than an organization where development efforts are only undertaken sporadically.

A discussion with members of small and medium-sized organizations in the UK identified the following as factors that may influence the decision about the treatment of design:[5]

- *Company size* – a small company may not have the resources to entertain an in-house designer or design team

- *Radical or incremental* – some companies might engage external designers to help develop radical new product concepts

- *Market segment* – how important is design to the customer. If design is not considered to be important organizations might consider it unimportant, rightly or wrongly, to spend money on design

- *Innovator or a follower* – participants felt that a company might be quite successful copying what other companies develop, without the help of any designer, though I would argue this is not a sustainable position long term

- *Commodity or customized* – several factors might influence the perspective on design:
  - Is the purchase a one-off or a repeat purchase?
  - Can specific features make a difference to the purchasing decision?
  - Does the purchase depend on reputation?
  - Is it the product or the packaging which distinguishes one product from the other?

The views brought forward by participants of the discussion allow two conclusions. First, many organizations, SMEs in particular, seem to hold the view that involving designers in the product development process is a luxury that 'one can get by without'. Secondly, the discussion with members of SMEs confirms views presented in the literature (Sparrow 1987; Pilditch 1989) that the major driver behind the decision on whether or not to outsource design is the need for, and degree of, creativity and new ideas. Based on a study of the UK textile industry, Coles et al. (1997) described the trade-off between internal and external design activities as one between greater control and design protection on the one hand, versus access to a wider range of ideas on the other. Drawing on the insights from the discussion and the literature, Table 28.1 lists the arguments for and against each choice.

As usual, there is no one right solution, and as Sparrow (1987) points out, each company needs to make the decision about whether or not to outsource the design.

A study into the relationship between external designer and commissioning organization, conducted on behalf of Business Link London City Partners in 1997 sheds some light on barriers to using external designers, the benefits of using external designers and how business tends to find the designer.[6] Interestingly, half of the participating companies that had not used external designers declared to have an in-house design team, and about one-third declared that they did not have a need for design services.

The majority of organizations used external designer for their company logo (82%, or 32 organizations) and company stationery (77%, or 30 organizations). Table 28.2 lists for which tasks and how frequently external designers are used by business organizations.

Survey Responses – Industries (von Stamm 1997)	
Area of business	% of resp. (n = 51)
Printing/publishing	8
Clothing industry	21
Professional services	6
City/financial services	21
IT companies	34
Other	10

The most frequently noted barrier to the use of external designers (about two-thirds) was the cost – reflecting the view that design is a luxury, followed by difficulties in finding the designer or design consultancy most appropriate for the company's need (see Table 28.3). There was generally a concern that design companies did not understand business concerns – a criticism that filters through to the debate on design education today and the call for increased commercial awareness and education of designers. The 'Media and Creative Industries Skills Dialogue' (DfES 2002) reported that one of the concerns of business recruiting designers was their lack of business awareness.[7] The three barriers very much reflect the commonly held preconception about the design profession.

The barriers identified in the Business Link research show some overlap with barriers identified by the Design Council (1998) – at least with the main obstacle to using external designers, finances. The three barriers identified by the Design Council are:

- The financial barrier – design is seen as cost rather than investment; there is also still a problem of acknowledging and evaluating the benefits of design from the investor side

- The right barrier – it can be difficult, costly and time consuming to obtain and protect intellectual property rights

- The size barrier – particularly small businesses do often not have the time, experience or finance to employ the services of a designer

By far the greatest benefit from using designers was seen to be an increase in the company's recognition. This was followed by increases in brand awareness and employee satisfaction. It is interesting to note that nearly 30%

Table 28.1   Advantages and Disadvantages of Internal and External Design (von Stamm 1997)

	Advantage	Disadvantage
In-house	• Cost efficiency • Accessibility • Easier coordination with other in-house departments • Company retains control • Designer develops intimate understanding of company	• Lack of creativity/new ideas • Keeping the design team busy, e.g. ongoing development work • Losing touch with external developments
External	• New inspiration • Access to specialists' expertise • Relieves workload • Accessibility of additional skills/staff • Speed • Options of changing and exploring different options	• Lack of understanding of company specific issues • Problems of ready accessibility • Problems in the coordination with in-house design and/or other departments • Potential lack of confidentiality • Company needs skills to evaluate the design work • Not-invented-here syndrome • Problems with industrializing the externally developed design • Loss of control • Credibility gap if design is too far removed from company's own style

Table 28.2   Tasks for External Designers (von Stamm 1997)

Project	% of respondents (n = 39)
Company logo	82
Company stationery	77
Company brochure	59
Product literature	33
Forms	23
Advertising	23
External signage	21
Exhibition design	21
Interior design	15
Packaging	13
Fashion design	13
Textile design	8
Industrial design	3
Workflow design	3

Table 28.3 Barriers to Using External Designers (von Stamm 1997)

Barrier	% of resp. (n = 52)
Too expensive	65
To difficult to identify the design organization with the right skills	35
Might not understand business concerns	29
To difficult to know where to start looking for a design organization	19
Would not understand specific needs	15
Problems with on-time delivery	13
We have all skills in-house	12

Table 28.4 Benefits from Using External Designers (von Stamm 1997)

Benefit	% of resp. (n = 26)
Increase in company recognition	88
Increase in brand awareness	46
Increase in employee satisfaction	38
Increase in turnover	35
Increase in customer satisfaction	27
Increase in market share	23
Increased efficiency (cost)	23
Increased press exposure	15
Increase in profit	12
Other – professionalism	8
Increase efficiency (materials)	4

of organizations felt that as a consequence of using external designers, their turnover had increased, whereas only just over ten felt that it had increased their profit. Table 28.4 lists the benefits suggested and the frequency with which business organizations agreed. Interestingly, those organizations that experienced benefits from using external designers saw more then one benefit, e.g. those that found that the use of external designers had increased turnover also felt that it had increased company recognition and employee satisfaction.

A survey conducted by the Design Council in 2002 shows a very different picture, though it has to be noted that the use of design – rather than external designers – had been the issue of concern. Depending on company size, up to 82% of respondents felt that the use of design had increased their competitiveness (see Table 28.5).

According to the Design Council survey, companies that experienced rapid growth in 2001/2002 were amongst those that said that design was an integral part or a significant part of their strategy (71%), as opposed to the overall national average of 41%, and only 9% of rapidly growing companies declared that design had no part to play, compared with 42% of all participating companies. To top this, the Design Council also reports that UK companies recognized for their positive use of design, as indicated by design awareness, outperformed the stock market by 25%.

Table 28.5 Percentage of all Companies (by Employment Size) Saying Design has Contributed at Least to some Extent, to the following (Design Council National Survey 2002) (reproduced by permission of Design Council)

	0–19	20–49	50–249	250+
Increased competitiveness	25	75	82	80
Increased profits	22	79	78	76
Better communications with customers	26	80	83	87
Reduced costs	6	62	64	54
Improved quality of products and services	26	69	87	78
Increase market share	16	70	83	83

Once the decision to outsource design has been made, managers need to address two questions. First, how to find the most appropriate designer or design consultancy; and secondly, how to manage the relationship (Oakley 1990). The second part of the study for the Business Link London involved questioning design consultancies on their relationship with clients. Design consultancies reported that most frequently the contact had been initiated through a third party recommendation, followed by repeat business (see Table 28.6). Considering that businesses mentioned difficulties in finding the most appropriate designer or design consultancies as one of the main barriers to using outside consultants, it seems that there is a need to provide 'matchmaking' services, trusted by both designers and businesses, to bring companies and designers together. One attempt at filling this gap has been undertaken by the Design Council through setting up a website (www.designdirectory.org) which provides companies with some help on how to find the right designer/design consultancy and how to brief a designer.

The problems in finding the right partner might also suggest nurturing the relationship once it has been successfully established. In addition, developing a long-term relationship can also help to overcome issues such as the perceived lack of understanding of business-specific issues or the 'not invented here' syndrome. However, research indicates that 'In-house product development and design activities have a much more positive impact on business growth prospects than bought-in design' (Sentance and Clark 1997), and that one reason underlying the failure of projects which involved external design consultants was the actual management of this relationship (Roy and Potter 1990).

Table 28.6 How do Designers and Business Get Together? (von Stamm 1997)

Initiation of contact	% of resp. (n = 244)
Third party recommendation	32
Existing client (repeat business)	20
Competitive and credentials pitch	11
Personal contact	10
Cold call and telesales	9
By client directly	6
Direct mail (by design consultancy)	6
Reputation	3
Roster	3
From a design directory/yellow pages	1

Hence, careful attention needs to be paid to the management of that relationship. This should lead managers to reconsider their position on the outsourcing of design.

This section has contemplated theoretical issues around the location of design and selected aspects of the relationship between designer and business organization. The following section provides a 'real-life' example of cooperation between company and external designer.

THE CASE STUDY OF THE MUZ SKORPION[8]

The Skorpion is a motorbike produced by the former East German company MuZ. The motorbike, designed by a British design consultancy, was first presented to the public in December 1992 at a major motor show in the UK.

BACKGROUND TO THE PROJECT

The commissioning company was a producer of motorbikes founded at the beginning of the 20th century. Before the Second World War it was one of the leading manufacturers of motorbikes in the world, innovative and creative. Located in what was the Eastern Bloc and, hence, with company policy set by central government, the formerly innovative company lost its leading edge and became known for cheap, simple and badly designed, if robust motorbikes. In Eastern Bloc countries the company continued to be a market leader, producing 80,000 motorbikes per year. To put this figure in perspective, total sales of motorbikes in the UK in 1988 was just under 62,000, in Germany about 93,000; while Japan produced 5.8 million bikes the same year.

Its success in the Eastern Bloc was due not least to the fact that people had to wait up to 16 years to get even the most basic car. A motorbike was *the* alternative means of transport. The company was neither aware of its actual cost structure, nor did it have any responsibility for marketing its products or finding customers. A cost analysis undertaken by the government institution charged with privatizing the state-owned enterprises after the collapse of communism, revealed a loss of an equivalent of £267 per bike.[9]

With the collapse of most communist regimes, caused not least by liquidity problems, the company's export markets in Eastern Europe folded and 2500 of the company's 3500 employees were made redundant. Finding investors proved difficult. In July 1992 the assets of the company were bought by private investors. Only in July 1993, having been threatened by closure several times, did the company finally manage to secure a government guarantee and with its access to new financial resources.[10] By this time total staff was down to about 200 employees.

When the new managing director – who had initially been brought in to help with privatizing the company but then decided to buy the company himself – took over in June 1992, he continued what had been initiated by one of the company's European importers: the development of a new motorbike.

DEVELOPMENT OF THE NEW BIKE

According to the Managing Director, the selection of a foreign design consultancy was influenced by the consultancy's reputation in designing motorbikes and its in-depth knowledge of the motorbike market. The briefing for the new bike was simple, 'Here is a four-stroke engine, the one we use for all our other four-stroke models, develop a prototype that will help us to survive. There is hardly any money and the bike has to be ready for a big motor show in six months' time.' For a similar job the design consultancy would normally have scheduled 18 months.

But the design consultancy was delighted to accept this job, as one of the partners put it, 'This motorbike producer was the one company that all bike designers would want to work for and they approached us with the absolute dream brief, please help us, what should we do?' The concept was agreed upon later in July 1992, and it was not until 30th November 1992, with only a few hours to the opening of the Birmingham Motorshow, that the MD saw the new bike for the first time.

The working prototype of the motorbike had been developed almost exclusively by the design consultancy. For some critical technical issues, industry specialists were involved, for example for the development of the frame, for which the designer brought in a renowned bike specialist. He also knew that the well informed motorbike market would know that when this person got involved, the result would be a light and therefore fast machine.

The outstanding success at the motor show came as a surprise, and a journalist commented, 'The idea that a new motorbike by this company could be the star of a major international motorcycle show in the 1990s might seem as unlikely as a Trabant outshining a Ferrari, but by common consensus the improbable became reality at this event.'

The acclaimed design of the motorbike and the attention it had received at the show played an important when the local government granted the company a guarantee which secured the company's medium-term financial survival.

THE MOTORBIKE AND ITS PREDECESSORS

The prototype of the new product was a major deviation from the motorbikes the company had produced previously:

- The frame was glued (not welded) together with adhesives normally used in the aircraft industry

- Some parts of the bike had dual functions (structural and functional), such as

    - the chassis which also contained the tank

    - the battery box which structurally supported the steering head

- It had some 30% fewer parts than conventional bikes

- It weighed only 134 kg[11]

Some of the changes were not only new to the company, but had not been generally used in the industry before.

The designer commented, 'When the Japanese came on the motorcycle scene in the late 1960s they hijacked the concept of the motorcycle as a simple, economical form of transport and slowly turned it into the technically complex, expensive piece of leisure equipment we know today. This motorbike doesn't need a high-tech factory because it's simple to manufacture and assemble.'

During the reorganization of the company, and driven by the aims to reduce cost and control stock, it was decided to increase outsourcing from just under 5% under the communist regime to up to 85% under the new management.[12] In addition to the introduction of new products, new production processes and outsourcing, the organization underwent several changes in management and organizational structure, while at the same time fighting for economic survival. The financial difficulties were also acting as a barrier to bringing in more highly qualified staff or developing staff dedicated to new product development internally.

THE PROTOTYPE

At the outset of the project, the design consultancy decided to base the new bike on what they perceived as the old values of the innovative and creative company of the early part of the century. Said the designer, 'Our guiding principles in designing the bike as a focal point for the company's resurgence were the three qualities which the company have traditionally pursued – the three Ss, as we call them: simplicity, sustainability and (common) sense. By applying these principles, which governed the company's product development for decades, yet are an entirely appropriate proposition for the 1990s, it is possible to produce high-quality, low-cost motorcycles which represent an attractive alternative to the over-complicated, overweight machines currently on offer elsewhere.'

Even though the technologies used to assemble the bike were chosen for their simplicity and ease, the technological concepts which had worked well for the prototype and had helped to create a simple but elegant looking product, proved difficult in the production of the 'real' product, primarily because the necessary skills were not available in-house. Several changes to the specification were required which took time, increased cost and ultimately changed and diluted the original design concept.

REALIZATION OF THE DESIGN CONCEPT

Resistance, not to the externally developed bike itself but to the production methods, came from the workforce. There had been resistance to using an increasing number of parts from a Japanese motorbike manufacturer (with whom the design consultancy had a longstanding working relationship). The aim had been to position the company as a local producer, not least because of the high levels of unemployment in the area. Whereas the use of Japanese parts could not be avoided, the company's engineers succeeded in vetoing the manufacturing technique. Instead of using the novel, for the motorbike industry, gluing technique they reverted to traditional welding. This had the advantage that the workforce did not have to acquire new skills, while the disadvantages were that it was more expensive and time consuming to produce, and that it diluted the original design.

The reasons for changes were manifold:

- As stated above, due to company internal objections the suggested manufacturing technique (gluing) had to make way for conventional welding

- The exhaust needed to be changed to adjust to environmental regulations (noise emission)

- A tank for the oil reserve had to be added as the original idea, to use the frame for the oil reserve, would only have worked in winter, i.e. there was a cooling problem

- Despite objections by the company's marketers, who tried to establish the motorbike as a nationally made motorbike, a Japanese engine was used (it was the only one that would fit into the constrained space available for the engine)[13]

All these changes led to over three months' delay for the first delivery, and to a much lower than anticipated production output. Industry experts felt that due to this delay the company lost out on the 'spring rush' characteristic of the motorbike industry. Exports to the US had to be delayed even further because additional adjustments were required to meet stricter US noise and emission standards.

Despite the bike's big success at the motor show, and the fact that it had won several design awards in both the UK and the US, the company continued to struggle, and filed for liquidation in July 1996.[14]

LESSONS FROM THE CASE STUDY

This case study clearly represents an extreme situation and not a company's everyday experience of developing new products. Both parties acted under severe constraints: the design consultancy was given only six months to develop a working prototype and the MD of the commissioning organization (a) had to spend most of his time fighting for the financial survival of the company, (b) had not lead a manufacturing organization before. Furthermore financial resources were extremely restricted. However, similar, if less drastic, problems can arise in any client–consultant relationship.

One of the major problems concerning the design of the new motorbike was that while industry specialists and journalists praised the simplicity of the bike – and the designer had emphasized that the bike was 'simple to manufacture and assemble' – this was not how it presented itself to the manufacturing organization. The motorbike required manufacturing techniques with which the company was not familiar. There was a significant mismatch between the company's capabilities and the manufacturing demands arising from the new motorbike.

Even if the end result was perceived to be simple, (a) the way to achieve the result may not be simple, particularly taking into account that the skills required to achieve the result were not readily available within the firm, and (b) how complex a product is within a company's context depends on the degree of newness *to the company*, and only to a certain degree on the newness to the industry. In short, the manufacture of the motorbike was by no means simple for the people who had to actually do it.[15]

The development challenge and the scope of complexities of transferring the project back into the commissioning organization need to be understood at the outset. Applying the Complexity Framework introduced in Chapter 25 would have helped identify the gaps between existing and the new motorbikes, and might have helped if not prevent the problems so at least minimize their negative impact. Figure 28.3 summarizes and compares the conditions under which previous products (⬤) and the new product (★) were developed and produced.

From this comparison, it becomes clear that conditions and demands of the new bike were significantly different. While it is not suggested that the required changes were impossible to achieve, the company would have needed to (a) be aware of the differences, (b) take actions to initiate and facilitate the changes (training, acquisition of new skills, change in company culture), (c) provide sufficient resources (time and money), and (d) ensure close communication between designer and company to enable it. Instead, and as a consequence of the persistent financial constraints, compromises were made: the design was diluted and the market entry delayed. But rather than being an educated decision and conscious trade-off, it was reactive fire fighting.

IN-HOUSE VERSUS EXTERNAL DESIGNER

The successful development of a new product was seen to be critical to repositioning the company and achieving a turnaround. Management was aware that the skills necessary to develop a radically new design were not available

Figure 28.3   Development Conditions New Motorbike – Predecessors (von Stamm 1997)

in-house, and hence decided to use a design consultancy. In addition, even if a new product could have been developed in-house the company would have had difficulties convincing the motorbike community that this new product would be of higher quality than its predecessors. To employ a designer experienced in the industry – the design consultancy had worked with other motorbike manufacturers before – also had the advantage of bringing in market expertise and awareness of trends in consumer taste.

AUTHORITY OF THE DESIGNER

Because management was preoccupied with securing the financial survival of the firm – and trusted the designer explicitly – they did not get involved in the development of the new product, and nor did anyone else from the company. As the MD put it, 'He is the designer he knows what he is doing.' The result of this development process was a product that attracted unexpected attention at an important international motor show and won several design awards, but which was also seen to be very different from everything else the company had developed before.

There were concerns whether the company might have overstretched its brand, and there was a debate as to whether the bike would actually be associated with the company – or rather with the designer. This meant that the company had to convince dealers and bikers that it was capable of building the new product to the high standards set by the designers. The fact that the design was diluted and that the product reached the market with a significant delay did not help to defuse the concerns.

COMMUNICATION AND EXPECTATIONS

Many of the problems could have been avoided not only by an increased awareness of actual levels of complexity, but also by better communication. Better communication and closer cooperation between designer and commissioning company could have highlighted potential problem areas in advance while time was still available for either training the workforce or adjusting the motorbike design to the skills available within the company.

CONCLUSIONS

It is not suggested that the company should not have taken on the new design, or should have designed a motorbike entirely within its existing capabilities. However, it should have become clear during the design and development of the prototype that the product would be far beyond the company's capabilities, and there are a number of lessons which can be learned from this experience:

1. *Outsourcing decision*

Given the starting point of the motorbike manufacturer, with a reputation for low-quality bikes, a workforce that was used to being punished for taking initiative, and the company's desperate need to come up with a new, creative and imaginative bike, the decision to employ an external designer was the only way forward. The choice of design consultancy, an organization renowned for its knowledge of and expertise in the motorbike industry, was sensible and appropriate – as the success at the motor show proved. The decision promised all the benefits the employment of an external designer can bring: new inspiration, access to specialists' expertise and additional skills, and speed of development.

However, downsides of outsourcing, such as problems with the coordination of external designer and in-house team, the not-invented-here syndrome, problems with industrializing the externally developed design, and the credibility gap, meant that the commissioning organization was unable to profit from the significant benefits the relationship could have offered.

2. *Managing the relationship*

The main problem lay in the management, not necessarily of the relationship between the designer and the managing director, but the management of the transfer of the externally developed design into the manufacturing organization. Both the designer and the MD should have been aware that this new bike needed special attention and preparation within the organization to accommodate the unusual production methods, being so different not only from what the organization had produced previously, but also from the industry standard in general.

Actions would have been required to address the deficit in skills and to prepare the organization for the manufacture of the new product. This should have taken place in parallel with the development of the prototype, not once full production was supposed to start. Instead of enabling staff to build this new bike through training or bringing in adequately skilled staff, the company chose to change the design to make it manufacturable with the skills readily available within the organization. Had in-house staff been involved in the design and development of the new product, it is likely that potential problems would have been noticed earlier, and might have led to a more successful transition from prototype to manufactured product.

CONCLUDING REMARKS

The involvement of external designers is frequently motivated by a lack of the necessary expertise in-house – be it creativity or any particular technical or other knowledge. However, involving external experts can only benefit a product's design and development process when these experts become an integral part of the development team and apply their expertise with an awareness of the organization's context, its capabilities and constraints.

The bike was a huge success at the motor show in Birmingham – but many people felt that the bike would be associated with the design consultancy that had developed the bike, rather than the manufacturing company. Because the bike was sleek, exciting and well designed, people doubted that MuZ, known for its rather basic, out-of-date if cheap bikes, would be capable of producing the new bike to the quality and aesthetic standards required. The gap between the company's perceived capabilities and the positioning of the new bike caused dealers and end-users to be cautious, resulting in slower than anticipated sales, which in turn contributed to the liquidity problems for the company, and eventually liquidation. Hence, a company should consider carefully whether by outsourcing new product development and design management activities it reduces its core capabilities, and with it what the company stands for.

Hence, when employing an external designer to develop a new product, it is important that in-house staff take part in the development – and the further the new design departs from existing products, the more important close cooperation and integration becomes. Participation of and exchange with in-house staff is important not only to allow staff to 'own' the product once responsibility is passed over to the manufacturing organization, but also to allow designer and commissioning company to notice – and address – constraints and problems as early as possible.

READING SUGGESTIONS

Greaver, Maurice (1999) *Strategic Outsourcing: Risk Management, Methods and Benefits*. New York: Amacom

Comment: An amazon.com reviewer wrote, 'Maurice Greaver has written a comprehensive and practical guide for any senior executive considering or currently undertaking an outsourcing initiative within their organization'

Heywood, J. Brian (2001) *The Outsourcing Dilemma: the Search for Competitiveness*. London: Financial Times/Prentice Hall

Comment: The book addresses questions such as, why outsource, what are the benefits of outsourcing, which functions should an organization should consider outsourcing, what are the alternatives to full outsourcing and how does an organization choose an outsourcing service provider?

SOME USEFUL WEBSITES

http://www.outsourcing.com/

Comment: The Outsourcing Institute (OI) is the only neutral professional association dedicated solely to outsourcing. Recognized worldwide for its intellectual capital, outsourcing practice expertise, and unbiased thought leadership, OI tracks and forecasts the rapid evolution of outsourcing while providing new services and programs to assist buyers of outsourcing services. To get access to most of their information you need to register – but it's free

www.designdirectory.org

Comment: A website recently set up by the Design Council to help companies find and brief designers and design consultancies

NOTES ON CHAPTER 28

[1] The Index is based on survey data collected from 1110 outsourcing buyers in 2002. 69% of responses came from US-based companies.

[2] The third most common reported factor in selecting an outsourcing vendor is flexible contract terms (39%), followed by reference/reputation (34%) and scope of resources (28%).

[3] Much of this section is based on the article 'Whose design is it? The use of external designers' by von Stamm (1997).

[4] For a discussion on 'silent design', refer to Gorb and Dumas' (1987) article on this subject.

[5] The workshops took place at the Design Museum, London, in autumn 1993.

[6] The results are based on questionnaires returned by about 70 businesses and design consultancies. In each category 20 companies were interviewed either in person, or over the telephone. The questionnaires suggested possible answers, additional space was provided for respondent's personal comments. Focus group discussions were used to devise the suggested answers. The 70 participating business organizations came from five industries: printing/publishing, clothing, professional services, City/financial services, and information technology; over 85% of the respondents had fewer than 50 employees.

[7] In *Facts and Figures on Design in Britain 2002–03*, a publication by the Design Council (www.designcouncil.org.uk).

[8] The data for the case study was collected by the author post-event, in three phases between autumn 1993 and spring 1997. Interviews were conducted with the senior management of the manufacturing company, the lead designer, as well as other organizations such as the government institution charged with the privatization of the company, the lending bank, and industry experts. The interviews were supplemented with documentation available in the public domain.

[9] Calculated at exchange rate at the time.

[10] No bank would have been willing to lend capital to the company without a government guarantee underwriting it.

[11] A bike of comparable power, such as the Kawasaki 500cc bike, would weigh around 180 kg.

[12] Up to 85% of the parts for the new motorbike were outsourced, around 60% for old models.

[13] This meant that the only specification given in the design brief was disregarded.

[14] In late spring 1997, the remains of the company were bought by an Asian conglomerate, which named the company's new product development capacity as a major motivator behind the purchase (Anonymous 1997).

[15] However, the gluing technique was also new to the industry.

29

Putting All the Pieces into Place

CASE STUDY 10: THE TECHNOLOGY PARTNERSHIP

The Technology Partnership is infuriatingly difficult to define. At one level, it is a research organisation, with an almost academic interest in knowledge for its own sake; at another, it trades brains for cash, finding solutions to industrial problems.

Financial Times *15th January 2001*

A NEW DIRECTION?

In late 1999, Anne Miller went to Gerald Avison, Managing Director of TTP Group, to say she was ready for a change. Anne had a background in mechanical engineering and innovation with 30–40 patents under her belt. She had joined PA Technology in 1981 and left to become a founder member of TTP, a company set up under Gerald's direction in 1988. She explained, 'In joining Gerald, I wanted to be part of the culture he creates which is participative, not dictatorial.'

At TTP she had built up and led the Innovative Engineering Sector of TTP's business and had invented a diverse range of products, ranging from power tools for Bosch to the manufacturing system for the Femidom (the 'female' condom). In 1999 she knew that she wanted to explore new avenues, though initially not sure exactly what she wanted to do. Gerald suggested she go out and talk about innovation to people that TTP would not normally contact because 'something interesting will come of it, and in any case it will be good PR'. She soon realized that many companies were struggling with infusing innovation into their organization, and were very interested in how TTP had come to be so successful at it. Training and coaching was not an area that TTP had yet had much involvement in, although innovation was something Anne and TTP knew something about: it was the lifeblood of everything they did. So Anne asked herself, 'How are we doing it? Is there something in understanding the way we operate that would help other organizations to improve their own innovativeness?'

The seeds for a training arm of TTP were sown in Anne's mind – but how would the board react to such an idea that was far removed from the technology focus that had driven the company for 12 years?

HOW IT ALL STARTED

The seeds for The Technology Partnership (TTP), or TTP Group as the company is known today, were sown over 40 years ago when a small group of academics left Cambridge University to form Cambridge Consulting.[1] Originally their aim was to provide technology development services to industry, which they did. They also developed their own products, the Cambridge Audio Amplifier being a technical success, albeit commercially suspect.

> The Cambridge Amplifier was very popular at the time. During its development the group learned a lot about manufacturing, not least because the amplifier with its brushed aluminium front was expensive to manufacture and maintain blemish free.

In 1969, seeking a fresh challenge, a group of about five people led by Gordon Edge approached PA Consulting, assuring them that PA desperately needed a technology business. PA bought into the idea and left it to Gordon and his team to set up and run what was then called Patscentre (short for PA Technology and Science Centre), and which later became PA Technology. Under Gordon's leadership the division thrived and become a major contributor to PA's profitability. By 1986 PA Technology was a global business under Gordon's overall authority, and had laboratory operations in Melbourn, Herts, Princeton, NJ, Melbourne, Australia and Brussels, as well as industrial design studios in London and Sydney. Overall the Group accounted for over 20% of PA's turnover, and a rather higher proportion of the profit. The growth was entirely organic, with overseas operations being set up by a small team relocating from the UK and then recruiting locally.

In 1985 the arrival of a new CEO to the PA Consulting Group resulted in a structural reorganization and a significant reduction in Gordon's sphere of influence. Not happy with how things were developing, Gordon made alternative plans, which eventually lead, in autumn 1986 to him leaving with a number of other staff to form Scientific Generics (now the Generics Group). As a consequence, the CEO of PA called a meeting of PAT's 15 most senior people declaring, 'If any of you want to leave as Gordon

> In September 1987 PA sued three people they regarded as the ring leaders for breach of contract; they also sued the Australian and the new company; PA Technology's remaining 22 people were sent off to gardening leave and forbidden to take up new work. Around January 1988 PA had to release all those who wanted to join TTP. The legal battle was finally settled out of court in February 1990.

did, just go, we are not standing in your way.' Over the next six months about 15 PA Technology staff joined the Generics Group. Three months after Gordon Edge left, the Melbourne Australia Laboratory of PA Technology, then employing about 65 staff, successfully negotiated with PA a management buy-out of the company. The new company was called Invetech. A number of years later Invetech reversed into a quoted Australian company, Vision Systems.

Over the following nine months the changes being introduced by the new PA CEO gathered pace, and many of the PA Technology staff felt that this was not the company that they had originally joined. In September 1987 this culminated in the simultaneous resignation of about 25 (85%) of the senior managers at the Melbourn Cambridge Laboratory and the formation of The Technology Partnership, with the financial support of Invetech and an Australian VC.

COMPANY GROWTH AND DEVELOPMENT

To finance the new venture a mixture of internal and external investment was sought. Staff were – and still are – encouraged to own shares in the company. The company's management went to Lloyds and Barclays to negotiate preferable conditions for loans their employees could take out to buy a stake in the business. The arrangements eventually negotiated were that the banks would lend employees up to £25k, with no security, at an interest rate of 2.5% over base, with a three-year repayment holiday, and ten-year pay-back.[2] By this means the founders raised over £700,000 of their own money to invest in the business. Staff, of whatever seniority, were allowed to invest as much or as little as they could afford. As a consequence the shareholding was very evenly spread, with no one individual holding more than 4%.

TTP is a Private Company Operating an Employee Share Ownership Programme (ESOP)

TTP has set up a scheme under which shares are allocated to employees on a bi-annual basis, funded out of a share of the profits. Everybody gets the same allocation; no new shares are issued, and the pool is fed by shares bought by the ESOP in the internal market from former and existing employees. Shares allocated by the ESOP have to be A shares.

There are four classes of TTP shares

1. A shares: may be held by anyone. If offered for sale they must be offered in turn to B, C and D holders and only then to anyone else. The price for A shares has to be approved by the directors. This type was held by the Australian VC and the Australian Lab

2. B shares: can only be bought and owned by current employees of TTP and its subsidiaries; by employees' spouses, adult children and family trusts; and by the ESOP. When B shares are sold it tends to be more like an auction

3. C shares: can only be held by the VC backer, originally CINVen, but now 3i. The price for C shares has to be approved by the directors

4. D shares: are what B shares become when the employee leaves or retires and are non-voting. They can only be sold back into the company and become B shares again when bought

---

Additional money came, as noted, from the backer of the Invetech management buy-out, and, eventually, CINVen, the venture capital arm of the Coal Board and British Rail Pension Fund.

CINVen had a mixture of ordinary shares and convertible, redeemable shares and preference shares. The last had a coupon of 7% and were redeemable over years three to five. A proportion of these could be converted into normal shares if the cumulative profit over the first three years was less than £1.89 m on a linear sliding scale down to £1.13 m. At £1.13 m profit, CINVen's share of the equity would be increased by 70% from about 13% to 22%. But, as Gerald Avison recalls, 'In our third year we were firing on all eight cylinders, so our financial results were very good, and we made it.'

Part of the agreement with CINVen was that no dividends should be paid during the first five years, any profit was to be ploughed back into the business. After the five years, 50% of post-tax profit were to be paid out as dividends. Future flotation was raised as a possibility though TTP's management, who privately agreed that they would rather keep the company private, made no firm commitment. In 1988, 60% of the company shares were owned by TTP staff[3] and the remaining 40% by institutions (CINVen, Vision Systems, and the Australian venture capitalist).

The five units with which TTP started in 1988 were formed around the founding members' key skills and interests. The units, with 2–5 people each, were: scientific products, product engineering, computers and communications, tactical technology and automation. In 1989, with a turnover of £4.5 million, the company grew to 50 people, including five more from PA who set up a control group, and a person from Deloittes who contacted the company after seeing a newspaper article and who joined to set up a strategy consulting arm. The following years saw continuous growth and expansion, and by 1999 the turnover had grown to £41.1 m, resulting in operating profits of £6.8 m (more details can be found in Appendix III). Milestones in the company's development are shown in Box 29.1.

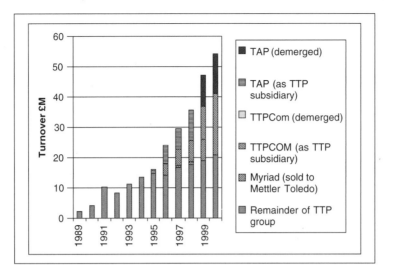

TTP Clients

- BA
- Bayer
- BOC
- Bosch
- Braun
- Burmah Castrol
- Compaq
- Esselte
- Fuji
- GlaxoWellcome
- ICI
- Merck
- NEC
- NCR
- Norton
- Philips
- Rhode and Schwarz
- Smith and Nephew
- Sony
- Sulzer
- Tetrapak
- Zeneca

BOX 29.1   Milestones in TTP's Development

1989   Consulting assignment for the consortium that became Orange to help them secure a first generation digital communications spectrum licence. TTP's first involvement with GSM technology

1990   Commence design of first GSM chip
Australian VC sells his 15% stake, which are picked up by 3i (80%) and TTP employees (20%), including an ESOP set up to involve new employees in share ownership

1991   Development of first pharmaceutical automation product
Early studies of ink-jet printing market and first involvement with Research Labs of Australia (RLA)

1992   Undertake major automation supply contract for Merck in the US

1993   Computers and communications division starts partnership with Analog Devices Inc. to make GSM chips
Set up ToneJet, a 50/50 joint venture with RLA in non-contact digital printing
Set up Wavedriver, a 50/50 JV with PowerGen on electric vehicle drives

1994	Automation division takes on a pharmaceutical focus
	Tactical technology division is renamed manufacturing technology. It has a mainly consulting function
1995	Acquired Signal Computing, a software company based in Guilford which had been working primarily for the defence sector, from ITN
	Set up automation unit as a wholly owned subsidiary The Automation Partnership
1996	Exit from Wavedriver, the joint venture with PowerGen, as timing for introduction of electric vehicles in California was delayed
	Established silent software division to provide complex software development service to the group
	Computers and communications division achieves first type approval of a mobile phone containing its chip designs and GSM software
	CINVen sells its shares to: TTP for its ESOP (50%), the Vision Systems (25%), and 3i (25%), changing the ownership structure to 75% TTP staff and 25% institutional. All shares except the ones purchase by 3i were converted from C to B shares
1997	Change in group holding structure. TTP Group created as a holding company, with TTP, Signal Computing and The Automation Partnership as wholly owned subsidiaries.
1998	Full statutory de-merger of The Automation Partnership
	Sale of the rights to the Myriad product range of synthesizers for combinatorial chemistry, as well as the transfer of seven staff to Mettler-Toledo to form Mettler-Toledo Myriad
	Computers and communications division set up as separate business called TTP Communications
	TTP Venture Managers set up as wholly owned subsidiary and TTP venture fund started
	TTP Group increased investment in life sciences
1999	Set up Libris, a joint venture with Dextra Laboratories to develop and sell carbohydrate compound libraries
	Set up Apocyte, a joint venture with the University of Nottingham in the field of cell apoptosis
	Set up IP. Access to use and develop TTPCom's intellectual property to provide mobile phone network basestations
2000	De-merged and floated TTP Communications (including IP.Access)
	Acquisition of Melbourn Science Park enabling continued joint location of TTP business
	Set up Odem, a joint venture with Bespak (UK) and Pari (German) (1/3, 1/3, 1/3) for the development of drug inhaler products
	Set up Ashes Investments, 50/50 joint venture with RLA for electrographic printing
2001	Set up TTP Labtech (instrumentation) and Acumen Bioscience (high throughput screening) as wholly owned subsidiaries

Gerald Avison is serious when he comments, 'I would rather we made 200 people relatively well off than a handful of us very rich.' 15% of company profits are redistributed to employees through a bonus. Two-thirds of it is handed out as a percentage of salary, whereby the percentage is the same for everyone; the other one-third is given in shares, whereby each person receives the same number of shares. This is about to change as a consequence of the replacement of the old ESOP rules by the new SIP. The balance is likely to shift towards equality.

Salary distribution is one of Gerald's responsibilities. He agrees with the board how much the company can spend on salaries. After setting aside about 10% of the budgeted amount to retain some flexibility, he does a dummy run on who is getting how much. This is used as a basis for advising each head of departments how much they have to spend and asking them how they wish to distribute this. Once they come back to him he looks at peer groups and makes sure that all is fair, part of which involves making suggestions for moving people up or down a bit and using the sum set aside earlier to balance where necessary. The ownership structure for 2000 is shown in this graph.

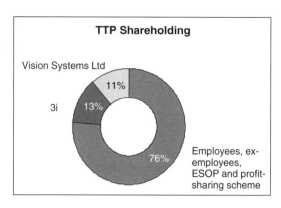

YOU ARE WHO YOU HIRE

As well as its work with mobile phones and industrial automation, the group is also involved in the printing and pharmaceutical sectors. It is currently investing in electrographic techniques, which could one day replace web offset printing. In pharma it is working on ways to screen chemicals for biological activity, and can spot cancer cells 'needle in a haystack' fashion.

Cambridge Evening News *Tuesday 20th March 2001*

Gerald Avison comments: 'Since inception our purpose has been to innovate. Our core values are "partnership", "we deliver what we say we will" and "have fun and make money".' The last is certainly true considering that someone who had invested £1 in the company in 1987 would have seen it grow to £600 by the end of 2000. But the fun bit is taken seriously, too. Again, Gerald says, 'We

> 'While we enjoy joint ventures, growth through acquisition does somehow not feel right for TTP. Organic growth allows people to grow with business. People get the chance to grow knowledge and responsibilities over time, within the business.'
>
> *Gerald Avison*

do things because they look interesting and we don't do things if we think they are boring. When everyone jumped onto the bandwagon of the Millennium Bug, where lots of money was to be made, we did not do it because we were just not interested. For us there has always to be the curiosity factor. For example, we floated TTPCom partly because we had not done that before – of course, there were other reasons too, but that was an important one. If someone says, things have to be done this way, we tend to do just the opposite – we very much avoid the message that there is a standard way of doing things.' There are no fixed office hours, people can more or less come as they please, as long as they work the contractually agreed hours – and as most employees are enthusiastic about their work, delivery of content has never been a problem, in fact they probably work between 45–50 hours on average.

From the outset management was aware that the kind of organization they had in mind would only work with the right kind of people. Gerald commented, 'During a conference I heard someone from an IT service business of about 2000 staff talk about the scientific approach they take to recruitment. He explained that they were using 50

> 'You need cultural fit at a personal level but not at the professional level. We go for individuals and move people between groups to ensure good cultural fit between individuals and groups.'
>
> *Gerald Avison*

criteria on which they assessed and selected their staff and the speaker was very proud to announce that they had a staff turnover of only 20%. A second speaker of another company described a quite different approach, he just said, "We hire nice people and are nice to them, and our staff turnover is 6%".' Staff turnover at TTP runs between 4–5%.

'We seek talented, experienced people who not only have bright ideas, but who can create innovative solutions to make their ideas work. We invest heavily in core technologies, facilities and training. I believe that we have established a working environment in which every individual has a voice and the chance to develop and grow. We know there's more to life than work, so we also try to make it fun!' So states Gerald Avison in TTP's recruitment brochure. Gerald explains that each successful candidate will be interviewed at least twice, the first time they will meet two to three people from their prospective peer group. After some consultation and comparing notes, those who come the second time will meet the MD of the operating subsidiary and Gerald. The meeting with Gerald has three objectives: first, to ensure the applicant understands what the business as a whole is about; second, for TTP to find out about the applicants, what they are good at and what they are like as a person; and third, to give some space to ask any questions the applicant may not have had a chance to ask earlier. Every candidate is also encouraged to talk to anyone in the organization and ask any questions they want, off the record.

> After years of downsizing and concentrating on the short term, many companies have lost the ability to innovate and are asking TTP to carry out the whole product development process or to assist them in becoming more creative. But as one of the TTP founders Chas Sims says, this is a lot easier to talk about than to achieve. Stressing that TTP tends to take on staff who have had some experience in the real world of manufacturing, he says that the company succeeds because staff are given freedom and responsibility. The front end of product development 'Is not about monkeys and typewriters,' he adds. 'It comes down to people, how you stimulate them and how you let them react to each other.'
>
> *Independent on Sunday, 27th July 1997*

Elaborating on the company's recruitment process, Gerald explains, 'Until I became Group MD and handed over recruitment recently to the MD of TTP, I made sure to meet every single person we recruited. I still try to do that but we make sure that, as a minimum, the MD of the operating subsidiary meets every person who will join their company. We believe strongly that business is about people, and that it is therefore essential that the person running the business knows every person working for them.' Heads of business units have the responsibility to make sure that there is a fit between the people and the environment. In addition, all prospects meet the top so they understand the tone and culture of the company as well as the wider picture of the organization. 'Our HR function is there to support recruitment, to run the salary system, benefits and keeping records – the administrative side but selection and management of people is the responsibility of management,' Gerald emphasizes. Once people have joined they attend an induction course that Gerald runs every six weeks. They are also encouraged to meet as many of their colleagues as possible. To quote Gerald again, 'If you want to find out about who knows what you go and talk to people. We have a comprehensive intranet, but we do not have a database in which we store information about people – people should talk to each other. Face-to-face meetings are important – that's why we have lots of free drinks machines. We believe that if people want to find someone with a particular expertise they should find him or her within three conversations and about ten minutes.'

Personnel reviews are held by managers on an annual basis. But, as Gerald points out, 'It is not an annual criticizing event. I strongly believe that positive as well as negative feedback should be given right away and not be saved for an annual conversation. The reviews are about establishing development plans, where a person is going next, what

> 'I can meet people who are far more experienced than me. I'm surrounded by people who are incredible intelligent, and I have the opportunity to pick their brains.'
>
> *From TTP's recruitment brochure*

the responsibilities are and should be, what training is required in the coming year and so on. A lot of the learning takes place on the job and through conversations.' Preparation for management roles is part of the menu. Gerald, who keeps an eye on people's development, strongly believes that, 'Professionals should be led by professionals and not by administrators. There is no one management style – but who ever is in a management role better make sure he or she is open and fair. And if something seems to go wrong the management team gets involved to help sort it out. For example, in the early 1990s, one group was disbanded and the staff distributed amongst other groups because of limitations in the managers capability.' He also points out that no one is forced into a management role. When he handed over responsibility for the Group's largest operating subsidiary to the then head of scientific products division, that division was split in two. One of the people who were approached was not too sure whether he really wanted to move into management. Conversations and discussions continued over two months, and while management were very confident that he was the right person for the job they made sure not to push him. In the end he accepted the job, but there was no inducement or pressure.

Twice a year meetings are held to report the company's half year and full year results. In addition, informal meetings with drinks and snacks are held late afternoon every Friday. The responsibility for organizing these events, which last about one hour and to which 25–30% of employees turn up, rotates between the different groups of the organization. During these sessions the director summarizes important events and developments of the week gone – and anything else that might be of interest to everyone in the organization. In addition, the group arranging the event nominates one of their people to talk about a subject of their choice – and this does not have to be work related. For example, past presentations included talks about Chinese cooking, scuba diving, radio telescopes and the activities of GCHQ in the last war. 'Presenting in front of a bunch of bright and curious people can be quite a daunting prospect,' Gerald acknowledges, 'So to encourage less experienced speakers to get involved we have an agreement that questions should be aligned to the speakers experience and confidence.'

THE PATHS WE CHOOSE

Curiosity and people's personal interests play an important role in determining the areas in which the company operates. When the company started off business units were set up around people's expertise. Gerald describes their approach as 'planned opportunism' and uses the story of how they got involved in GSM technology as an example.

'Senior people do not have the copyright on ideas – nor on benefits. All benefits – pension, health insurance, etc. – are the same throughout the company, and we do not have a company car policy.'

Gerald Avison

In 1990 Maggie Gray, wife of a TTP employee, and a man from British Aerospace (BAe) met over coffee while doing their part-time MBA at Cranfield. The BAe man was concerned about a recommendation that they had received from a consulting company regarding the communication standard that should be adopted for a satellite linked telephone system that BAe were planning to develop for deployment in under-developed locations. Maggie suggested that they should get a second opinion from TTP's communications consultants. They commissioned a study, which recommended the newly emerging GSM standard, rather than the out-of-date CT2 standard proposed by the first report. BAe concurred with this, and invited TTP to develop GSM technology for them. During the early stages of the development, it became clear to TTP that not only was the GSM standard based on IP owned by companies such as Nokia, Motorola and Ericsson, but that these companies also had a monopoly on some of the silicon needed. Moreover, they were not interested in selling these components to potential competitors. By now hooked on the idea, this obstacle did not deter TTP, and they decided to invest in creating their own intellectual property in GSM purchasing suitable computers and software and hiring a team of chip designers.

When BAe subsequently decided to dispose of their satellite communications business to the French company, Matra, the project was stopped. This decision naturally had an adverse effect on TTP's financial performance that year. However management at TTP decided to keep the team together, and when in the following year TTP met Analog Devices (AD), they entered into an agreement to

> 'Teamwork is essential, it is part of the development process; you are always likely to encounter problems that have been impossible to anticipate; you want people who are interested in sorting out problems, not allocating blame.'
>
> *Gerald Avison*

design a new generation of GSM chipset which would be sold and fabricated by AD, in return for royalties. This was the starting point for the TTP Communications plc. In the three and a half years following the agreement, TTP invested 250 man-years in the development of the technology. It was mid-1996 before the first handset designed around TTP's IP gained type approval, and six months after this that the royalty stream began to flow and TTP started to get a return on the investment.

Through normal prospection activity, which involves a lot of travelling and securing meetings with companies that have been chosen as potential customers or partners, TTP established contact with Hitachi in 1994. Hitachi was market leader in GSM Radio Frequency (RF) power amplifiers, had developed good silicon-processing technology and was looking for a partner who could provide them with the technology for their next generation GSM RF chip. TTP's computers and communications division had extensive expertise in radio engineering, and was looking for an opportunity to add an RF offering to the digital baseband GSM chip technology embodied in the Analog Devices agreement, as well their own

> Pure development projects are always risky and a key issue for TTP is how to manage this risk. Projects are structured in phases to ensure that risk is contained and TTP uses its experience in development to estimate the development costs. Inevitably some developments prove more difficult and more expensive than anticipated. Where the benefits to the customer are clearly substantial, the terms of business allow TTP to pass these costs on to the customer. In other cases, TTP may absorb the overspend, particularly if it is judged that the problems should have been foreseen.

suite of software. This would mean they would be in a position to supply all the technology necessary to make a GSM mobile phone. The two companies decided to collaborate on a development, which eventually led to a range of GSM radio chips, which became known as the BRIGHT radio chips. Without countless lawyers being involved, it was agreed that the collaboration would be royalty based, that intellectual property would be owned jointly, and that rather that spelling out each party's tasks in detail, broad areas of responsibility would be allocated under which TTP Communications were responsible for the overall system architecture and design, and Hitachi were responsible for the detailed silicon circuit layout, fabrication, sales and distribution. To kick off collaboration, Hitachi engineers spent four weeks in the UK, working alongside their TTP counterparts. The relationships were sustained through six face-to-face meetings annually, as well as frequent video conference calls.

Despite the fact that the first product gained limited acceptance in the market and was not commercially successful for either partner, the relationship continued. The partners were thus well positioned to take advantage of the shift towards dual band technology in 1997, which required a phone to operate either at a frequency of 900 MHz, as used in the UK or 1800 MHz as used in much of the rest of Europe. The second product achieved a significant success, and the partners are now onto the development of the fourth generation triple band product, which will work also at the 1900 MHz frequency used in the USA.

By 1998, TTP's computers and communications division had developed considerable expertise in GSM software and associated chipsets, and the business around had grown sufficiently to make it appropriate to set it up as a separate wholly owned subsidiary business, called TTP Communications (TTPCom).[4] In 1999, when TTP Group and TTPCom established IP.Access, shares were offered to staff who raised about £250,000, the equivalent of 12.5% of the equity.[5]

> 'The first of its [TTP's] offspring to make a stock market debut, TTP Communications, which designs the insides of mobile phones, was subscribed nine times when it went public four months ago. Its shares, although closing on Friday at 217'1/2 p below the 245 p offer, price, have held up well compared with the devastation in the technology sector, suggesting TTP is in the business of producing golden eggs rather than the turkeys which resulted from dotcom mania.'
>
> Financial Times *15*[th] *January 2001*

LEND A HELPING HAND

It came to prominence last year as an incubator, an organisation which nurtures small companies with big ideas until they are ready for the stock market. Rather than fostering separate companies, however, TPP cultivates its own specialist divisions.

Financial Times *15*[th] *January 2001*

Many good ideas fail to gain the support of venture capitalists because the technologies involved are difficult to understand. TTP knows this. To quote the *Financial Times*, 'What Mr Avison realizes is that the market has difficulty understanding what TTP does – and might not like it if it did. "We can do more while privately held than as a public company," he says. "Some of the risks we have taken would be hard to justify to institutional shareholders." He points, for example, to the investment of 250 man-years of effort – equivalent, say, to £38 m – in establishing TTPCom as a market leader in its field.' Because it nurtures business ideas internally, by the time TTP's offspring are spun out they have customers, products, a management structure and an accounting system. But, as TTP knows, these things do not happen overnight.

Being aware that many good ideas die because they are not understood by the financial markets, a couple of people within TTP felt very strongly that TTP should set up its own venture capital fund. They felt that the edge they would have over other VC firms was that they had the technical knowledge necessary to assess proposals. David Connell TTP Ventures' chief executive declares. 'Our ability to understand and add value to science and technology-based investment propositions is proving highly attractive to both entrepreneurs and investors. We are only interested in those technologies and industries we are able to assess.' He lists telecoms, electronics and IT equipment, instrumentation, hi-tech engineering, medical equipment and drug discovery technology, materials and chemicals as potential investment targets, and continues: 'The businesses which we would be interested to invest in would have to have a highly differentiated offering, based on science or engineering. There would have to prove that they have a strong management team – or the potential to create one.' So rather than investing exclusively in their own ideas, the venture fund allows investing in external ideas. Gerald comments, 'You will generally find that the more mature the investment fund, the more protectionist and complicated the structures tend to get. People are always trying to insure against the exception rather than provide for the rule. Our fund, on the other hand, is rather straightforward – not least because the two people who set it up did not have any preconceptions of venture capital, but had a lot of experience of being close to and involved in growing business around technology!' The fund, which was set up as a separate entity called TTP Ventures and had £35 million at its disposal, received much attention from the press when it was set up in 1998 (see Appendix IV). TTP's track record for technical expertise and profit attracted a number of high-profile backers, including NPM Capital, the largest independent fund in the Netherlands, Boeing, Siemens, two undisclosed UK pension funds, and Abbey National.

THE WORK ENVIRONMENT

The physical work environment at TTP has received special attention too. As reported in the *Cambridge Evening News* of 5th September 2001, 'TTP Group has bought the Melbourn Science Park for an undisclosed sum from AXA Sunlife Pensions. The park is over 17 acres.' Gerald is quoted as saying: 'Ownership of the park enables us to accommodate our continuing growth and allows us to maintain our commitment to being based in Melbourn and supporting the local community. One of the most attractive features of the park is the planning permission that already exists for further development. This will give us the flexibility we need to shape the future of our business.'

But it is not only flexibility, it is also variety. Acknowledging different views and needs, TTP has taken this approach to its nine conference rooms. To achieve this, three interior designers with quite different styles were selected to design three rooms each. The aim was to create environments for meetings that did not intrude on the business of the day, but were at the same time memorable.

Since its inception the company has received many awards. To name a few:

- 1994 National winner of the *Sunday Times* 'Quest for Growth' award, awarded to the company judged most likely to demonstrate sustained growth

- Spring 2001: Business Investment Award, sponsored by Barclays

- May 2000: nominated one of the UK's most successful companies in profits growth in the *Sunday Times* and PricewaterhouseCoopers' survey

- Feb 2001 TTP listed in the Vision 100 index, which recognizes organizations with unique and exceptional vision

- In 1999 TTP received Queen's Award for Technological Achievement

QUESTIONS

1. How and why is this organization different? What are aspects of the company that encourage and foster innovation?

2. Is the learning transferable to other organizations, and if so how?

3. If you were in the position of Gerald Avison and his board, would you give Anne Miller the go-ahead? Arguing from the company's perspective, why or why not?

APPENDIX I: MAJOR DEVELOPMENTS IN THE TTP GROUP SINCE 1990

1990

- Settled dispute with PA

- Company grows to 100 staff

- Cooperation with British Aerospace on the development of GSM/satellite-based telephony

- Commence design of first GSM chip

1991

- Turnover dropped, because of recession and investment in GSM (part way through the year the contract with BAe stopped; BAe sold the space systems division to Matra in France)

- Automation division started work on the first pharmaceutical automation product

- Researched and sold a market report on emerging technologies and developments in digital printing, including ink-jet printing. The aim was as much to get into the market and network with companies, as to generate consultancy work

- Through the above study, first contact with the Research Labs of Australia (RLA) whose expertise was in toner (printers, copiers) and were behind Canon's move into electrographic printing

1992

- Work on electric drive for electric vehicles leading to JV with PowerGen, called Wavedriver

- Search for means of capitalizing on GSM expertise, including unsuccessful discussions with venture capitalists about a new company to finish and commercialize the development half completed for BAe

- Period of general consolidation as the economic climate picked up

1993

- The computers and communications GSM team met Analog Devices in US who wished to make a first generation digital chipset for GSM; Analog Devices would fabricate and sell the chip while TTP undertook the chip development, receiving royalties in return

- Meetings with RLA led to the companies setting a 50/50 joint venture (ToneJet) in which TTP would develop printhead technology and RLA would provide toner and ink formulation

- A further joint venture called Wavedriver, this time with PowerGen, was set up to develop technology for electric cars. TTP provided the IP and PowerGen the money

- Total number of employees of the TTP Group is up to 160

- Turnover up again

1994

- The automation division focuses on automation products for the pharma industry

- Tactical technology (TT) division is renamed manufacturing technology (MT)

1995

- TTP acquires the software company Signal Computing. When Signal's parent ITN was seeking for a purchaser of the software company, Signal approached TTP. Initially TTP left the company, which had primarily dealt with the defence sector, to its own devices, but when the business did not shown any signs of significant growth after several years, TTP brought in its own manager. An attempt to move the business into m-commerce in 2000 was unsuccessful and the business was closed in 2001

- The automation division becomes The Automation Partnership (TAP), a wholly owned subsidiary of TTP, marking the completion of a four-year transition process to an accounting system and management structure appropriate for a manufacturing company

1996

- TTP establishes a software division to undertake complex software system developments in support of hardware across the entire group. This was particularly valuable for the ink-jet printing development, automated equipment and instrumentation. The division was set up by a former colleague from PA. Because software could often not be seen but was essential to making much of the projects work the division was called Silent Software (SS) – an abbreviation that made the company's marketing man in Germany uneasy

- TTP sold its 50% stake in Wavedriver to PowerGen when it became clear that electric vehicles would not happen as quickly as originally anticipated – legislation in California had changed

- The first mobile phone handset incorporating the Analog Devices chipset and TTP Communications software secures type approval and goes on sale

1997

- TTP's new group structure:

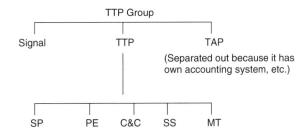

ToneJet is a separate business, which owns patents belonging to the joint venture but has no staff; the work is done by people in SP, SS, and RLA

1998

- The computers and communications division is set up as a separate, wholly owned business called TTP Communications (TTPCom)

- Full statutory de-merger of TAP

- MT division is renamed to PID (process and instrumentation division); because of the focus on life sciences it begins hiring chemists and biochemists

- Development of Myriad, a machine for synthesizing new chemical entities, completed for consortium of seven pharmaceutical companies; TTP started selling the machine

- Swiss company Mettler-Toledo buys the rights to the Myriad product range and sets up a UK subsidiary, Mettler-Toledo Myriad under Richard Gray who transferred from TTP

- PID's ChemScan machine is awarded the status of a millennium product

- TTP Venture Managers is set up as a wholly owned subsidiary and the first TTP venture fund started

1999

- Libris, a joint venture for carbohydrate compound libraries, with Dextra Labs, a company specializing in carbohydrate chemistry (Reading in UK) is set-up. The Myriad prototypes and the right to use them were kept and exploited through Libris. (Background: pharmaceuticals buy libraries of chemical compounds hoping that there is something in them they can use; Dextra Labs develop compounds, the Myriad machine is used to synthesize variations on these compounds to build large compound libraries. The compounds are sold to various pharma companies)

- Apocyte, a joint venture with the University of Nottingham, is set up to work in the field of apoptosis (cell death) with the aim of discovering drug targets for a range of clinically important conditions such as cancer and wasting diseases

- IP.Access is formed from within TTPCom to exploit wireless GSM technology and the potential of the internet protocol to transport voice and data. IP.Access' mini basestations enable the use of mobile phones in areas of poor coverage as well as extending their functionality so that they can be used as internal phones

- TTP Venture's first venture capital fund is closed at £35 million

2000

- TTPCom is separated through a partial statutory de-merger floated on the LSE (10% still held by TTP Group) with a market capitalization of £540 million. TTPCom acquired IP.Access as part of the de-merger. After flotation the company was 55% owned by staff and ex-staff; 45% owned by institutions (3i, RLA and new investors). In the flotation £30 m was raised by the selling shareholders and £40 m by TTP Communications

- TTP Group has about 300 staff after the TTPCom de-merger

- Odem, a joint venture with one-third each for TTP, Bespak and Pari (a private company based in Munich, Germany) is set-up. TTP provided electronic aerosol technology, Pari provided high-value nebulizors (about £30–40/unit) used for respiratory conditions; Bespak provided high-volume, low-cost inhalers (£1–2/unit, about 10 m units/year)

- Ashes Investments set up as a joint venture with RLA in electrographic printing (high-speed and high-quality web-based printing, for long and short print runs)

- Tagtec set up by a local entrepreneur with an idea for a radio tagging product. TTTP developed technology and registered two patents in return for one-third of the equity. Now the company has secured external funding and TTP is working under contract to develop the product

- Melbourn Science Park Ltd is set up to run the newly acquired science park

2001

- Establish wholly owned high throughput screening subsidiary

- Establish wholly owned instrumentation development and manufacturing business

APPENDIX II: GROUP STRUCTURE

APPENDIX III: FINANCIAL PERFORMANCE (FROM ANNUAL REPORT 2000)

FIVE-YEAR FINANCIAL SUMMARY

Extracts from the consolidated profit and loss accounts of the group for the five years ended 31 March 2000 are set out below:

	1996 £000	1997 £000	1998 £000	1999 £000	2000 £000
Turnover	24,353	29,687	35,697	36,883	41,067
Cost of sales	(16,863)	(19,687)	(22,959)	(24,547)	(23,279)
Gross profit	7,490	10,000	12,738	12,336	17,788
Other operating expenses	(5,882)	(6,339)	(8,516)	(8,054)	(12,395)
Profit on sale of Myriad activities	—	—	—	5,581	—
Operating profit	1,608	3,661	4,222	9,863	5,393
(Provision for)/release of provision for investment in associates	(541)	541	—	—	—
Profits/(losses) from interests in joint ventures	(7)	(15)	36	(59)	9
Profits/(losses) from interests in associates	(4)	45	(61)	(4)	(6)
Profit on disposal of fixed asset investments	—	—	—	—	1,154
Income from investments	—	27	61	105	164
Interest receivable and similar income	118	154	296	342	266
Provision for reduction in value of investments	—	—	—	(427)	—
Interest payable and similar charges	(19)	(56)	(37)	(23)	(179)
Profit on ordinary activities before taxation	1,155	4,357	4,517	9,797	6,801
Tax on profit on ordinary activities	(380)	(1,318)	(1,461)	(1,775)	(1,943)
Minority interests	—	—	—	—	162
Dividends	(388)	(1,519)	(1,529)	(4,008)	(2,505)
Retained profit for the year	387	1,520	1,527	4,014	2,515
Statistics					
Earnings per share before exceptional items	£1.69	£2.16	£2.65	£2.46	£3.33
Earnings per share	£0.67	£2.63	£2.65	£7.06	£4.37
Diluted earnings per share before exceptional items	£1.69	£2.16	£2.65	£2.46	£3.25
Diluted earnings per share	£0.67	£2.63	£2.65	£7.05	£4.26
Dividends per ordinary share	£0.33	£1.29	£1.30	£3.40	£2.12
Group operating margin (%)	6.6	12.3	11.8	26.7	13.1

APPENDIX IV: THE VENTURE FUND – ARTICLE FROM *FINANCIAL NEWS*

Financial News July 2000

Abbey pumps £5 m into TTP, CAROLINE SWIFT

The well-documented profits growth of the TTP Group is enough of a pointer to see why Abbey National has just announced the commitment of £5 m (E8m) to its early stage technology fund, TTP Venture Fund.

The £35 m fund was launched by new venture capital firm TTP Ventures, a subsidiary of the technology development company which took the laurels as one of the UK's most successful companies in profits growth in the *Sunday Times* and PricewaterhouseCoopers' survey in May.

The fund is focused on early stage investments in technologies and industries in Western Europe in which its parent company has expertise. It is this ability to draw on TTP's skills, which has seen it acquire the backing of NPM Capital, the largest independent fund in the Netherlands as its cornerstone investor. Other investors include Boeing and Siemens and two undisclosed UK pension funds – a blue chip private sector pension fund and a local authority pension fund

David Connell, TTP Ventures' chief executive, puts the ability to assess opportunities in science and technology as a key to investments, which so far have been made in three UK companies. 'Our ability to understand and add value to science and technology-based investment propositions is proving highly attractive to both entrepreneurs and investors,' he says.

The privately held TTP Group, formerly known as The Technology Partnership, a strong cash generator, has a non-discretionary co-investment in all investments. The 400-strong organization is involved in product innovation with leading manufacturers such as Siemens, NCR, Hitachi, Gillette and GlaxoWellcome; in business strategy consulting with ICI, Shell, IBM and British Airways, and in product innovation and development contracts with companies ranging from Cadburys to Unilever.

'We are only interested in those technologies and industries we are able to assess,' says Connell, who confines the fund to those with potential for superior financial returns He lists telecoms, electronics and IT equipment, instrumentation, hi-tech engineering, medical equipment and drug discovery technology, materials and chemicals.

'The businesses which we invest in must have a highly differentiated offering, based on science or engineering. There must be a strong management team or the potential to create one,' says Connell, who has no minimum investment policy.

Typical investments fall between £500,000 and £2.5 m per company with initial shareholdings of 15% to 40%.

The funds chairman is serial entrepreneur Tony Davies, the Chairman and Managing Director of Bowman Power. Other directors include Nigel Hamway, a director of Charterhouse Development Capital, John King, Chairman of telecoms analysts Analysys, who is a former main board director of British Telecom, and Dr Gerald Avison, Managing Director of the TTP Group.

Investments by the 10-years limited-life fund include $1m invested as part of a $13 m first funding round by Element-14, a business formed as a buy-out from Acorn Computers, the incubator of successful UK chip maker ARM, £500,000 in Visual Thinking International, a Glasgow-based supplier of decision management software, and the fund has led a small syndicate investing in Ashby BioSystems, a company based on patented 'opencell' material for cell culture support, with applications in biotech processing and medical implants.

In the telecoms area, the venture fund draws on the expertise of TTP Communications, the telecoms subsidiary of the TTP Group and a leading provider of GSM technology to mobile phone manufacturers.

'For a fund of this kind we have to deliver very significant returns towards the top end of the VC spectrum,' says Connell. 'We look at highly differentiated business opportunities with the potential to deliver real value. What we have not done is limit ourselves to sectors that currently happen to be fashionable. We look at what a sector is going to deliver over the next few years and aim to beat that significantly. We are certainly looking for upper quartile performance.'

NOTES ON CHAPTER 29

[1] Today Cambridge Consultants is owned by Arthur D. Little.

[2] When employees approached their own banks, most were happy to match these conditions.

[3] With no one individual owning more than about 4%.

[4] When the business was de-merged and floated on the LSE in 2000 it was valued at £540 m.

[5] When TTPCom was de-merged and floated on the LSE in October 2000, it acquired IP. Access from TTP Group in return for shares in TTP Communications plc. Staff who had invested in IP Access nine months previously secured a return of about a factor of about 15 on their money.

30 The Innovative Organization

Uncertainty and mystery are energies of life. Don't let them scare you unduly, for they keep boredom at bay and spark creativity.

R. I. Fitzhenry (Innovation Network email 11ᵗʰ November 2002)

In the case study of The Technology Partnership, almost all aspects of best practice for innovation, design and creativity best practice are represented. Every aspect of the organization is aligned to support the culture, to support the company's ambition. Systems, processes, leadership style and culture all enforce one another, and we find illustrations of best practice discussed in previous chapters, such as an emergent strategy, strong emphasis on internal and external collaboration, conscious use of the physical work environment and a learning culture.

Two aspects that have played their part in each of the ten case studies and are paramount for creating a successful organization but have not yet discussed are the main subjects of this last chapter: leadership style and culture.

LEADERSHIP – THE MOST CRITICAL INGREDIENT

Those who have changed the universe have never done it by changing officials, but always by inspiring the people.

Napoleon Bonaparte

If there is one single factor that is critical to innovation success, it is committed and supportive leadership, and in the literature there is far-reaching consensus about the importance of top management support in enabling successful new product development and innovation. Without clear senior management approval and encouragement, innovation activities will lack a sense of importance and urgency – and as a consequence, attention and commitment by participating individuals and functions. So clear signals from the top are key. But there is also the issue of leadership which is different from senior management support.

Leadership can take place at any level within the organization, and whereas 'management' is about directing people, about efficiency, structuring and organizing, leadership is about motivating people and about inspiring them to go the extra mile – something that is often required in innovative projects – 'Leadership is about inspiring individuals to higher levels of performance,' as Professor Rob Goffee, London Business School, puts it. In the Black & Decker case study it was the inspirational and supportive leadership from the top through Stephen Bird, Marketing Director Europe and Lawrie Cunningham, Director of Innovation, providing a balance between encouragement and freedom, that facilitated the creation of an innovative power tool. In the case study of Dumfries Recycling, the licence to innovate and explore around the creation of products made from recycled material came from the very top of the organization, from Cameron McLatchie, Chairman and CEO of bpi, the parent company. In a way, top management commitment is a qualifier, something that allows innovative projects to be initiated and approved, but what makes projects happen is generally the leadership at the project level. In fact, sometimes the leadership and determination at the project level can push projects through despite resistance at higher levels.[1] The BBC case study is an example of strong leadership at the project level. It was Tim's ability to enthuse his collaboration partners (FrameStore), secure funding and manage the interface with senior management within the BBC, thereby ensuring that the project team could get on with their work.

Whatever the level, what makes good leadership? Research commissioned by the DTI and CBI in 1995 identified the following six traits as characteristics of good leaders:

- Enthusiasm
- Championing change
- Communicating
- Leading by example
- Tolerating risk
- Being open (approachable, willing to listen)

While it is not quite clear what 'good' meant in the context of the survey, it seems that a person with such characteristics would also make a good innovation champion.

Findings from interviews conducted with members of the Innovation Exchange certainly identified the ability to inspire people as one of the key characteristics of successful innovation leaders (von Stamm 2001). Insights into what it actually means to be an inspirational leader are provided by Goffee and Jones (2000). In their work they have identified four traits of inspirational leaders, all of which seem to be about being oneself, about empathy and sincerity, and about confidence:

- They selectively show their weaknesses. By exposing some vulnerability, they reveal their approachability and humanity.

- They rely heavily on intuition to gauge the appropriate timing and course of their actions. Their ability to collect and interpret soft data helps them to know just when and how to act.

- They manage employees with something we call tough empathy. Inspirational leaders empathize passion-ately – and realistically – with people, and they care intensely about the work employees do.

- They reveal their differences. They capitalize on what's unique about themselves.

For leaders to inspire people to innovate, they themselves have to be open towards change and experimentation. Someone with a low score on Kirton's adaptor-innovator scale (see Chapter 10) might be a good leader, but not a great champion for innovation, as his or her preference will be to improve things incrementally rather than encourage and implement step-changes. A person who likes to drive change has a different profile form a person who is good at optimizing things and making sure they run smoothly. While most senior managers nowadays seem to buy into the argument that innovation is important to their organization's long-term success, their personal preference may be one for incremental changes. In that case they will not be the most appropriate person to lead an organization's change initiative or to improve innovation performance (see Figure 30.1). This may account for some of the discrepancies between what is said in annual reports and public statements – 'We believe that innovation is a

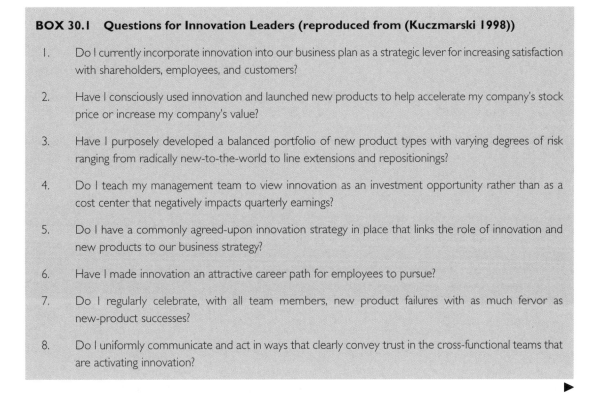

Figure 30.1 Finding the Right Leader (reproduced from (Prather 2002))

major contributor to our organization's growth' – and everyday reality, where radical ideas are adjusted and changed until they seem less threatening and more conform with what is tried and tested.

Kirton's questionnaire might be a good starting point for identifying people who would make good change and innovation leaders. There are also a number of check lists and lists with suggestions on how to improve the climate for innovation within an organization. In Box 30.1 you will find Thomas Kuczmarski's (1998) 20 questions for leaders who want to find out whether they are actually creating the right conditions for innovation to flourish.

BOX 30.1   Questions for Innovation Leaders (reproduced from (Kuczmarski 1998))

1. Do I currently incorporate innovation into our business plan as a strategic lever for increasing satisfaction with shareholders, employees, and customers?

2. Have I consciously used innovation and launched new products to help accelerate my company's stock price or increase my company's value?

3. Have I purposely developed a balanced portfolio of new product types with varying degrees of risk ranging from radically new-to-the-world to line extensions and repositionings?

4. Do I teach my management team to view innovation as an investment opportunity rather than as a cost center that negatively impacts quarterly earnings?

5. Do I have a commonly agreed-upon innovation strategy in place that links the role of innovation and new products to our business strategy?

6. Have I made innovation an attractive career path for employees to pursue?

7. Do I regularly celebrate, with all team members, new product failures with as much fervor as new-product successes?

8. Do I uniformly communicate and act in ways that clearly convey trust in the cross-functional teams that are activating innovation?

▶

9.   Do I stimulate an entrepreneurial environment by having a performance-based compensation system in place for new product participants?

10. Do I measure and communicate throughout the organization the return on innovation for our company?

11. Do I really know how much innovation costs, and do I set realistic return expectations for innovation?

12. Do I provide 'ceilingless' and motivating compensation rewards to new-product participants and allow them to invest in the new products they are developing?

13. Do I select the best people within the company (for example, those I feel I can't afford to remove from the existing business) to activate the new-product process?

14. Do I make sure we conduct consumer research prior to idea generation to identify problems and needs?

15. Do I ensure that idea generation is a problem-solving endeavor aimed at generating potential solutions to address consumer needs?

16. Do I maintain funding and resource allocation for innovation at a consistent level rather than pulling the plug after a 'down' quarter?

17. Do I truly accept that 40 to 50% of our future new-product launches will fail?

18. Do all R&D people get at least 15% 'free time' (unassigned to any specific project) to give them room to breathe and freedom to explore their own ideas?

19. Do I have a well-articulated technology strategy that defines technology platforms and areas of needed technical expertise to help support the innovation initiatives?

20. Do I hear others throughout the organization talk about my positive, enthusiastic, supportive, and 'can-do' attitude toward innovation?

The second is from Rosabeth Moss Kanter's (1983) book *The Change Masters*, first published over 20 years ago. She suggested five ways in which managers can improve an organization's environment for innovation:

- *Encouragement of a culture of pride* – highlight the achievements of the company's own people through visible awards, through applying an innovation from one area to the problems of another, and letting the experienced innovators serve as 'consultants'.

- *Enlarge access to power tools for innovative problem solving* – provide vehicles (a council? an R&D committee? direct access to the steering committees?) for supporting proposals for experiments and innovations – especially for those involving teams or collaborators across areas.

- *Improvement of lateral communications* – bring departments together; encourage cross-fertilization through exchange of people, mobility across areas; create cross-functional links, and perhaps even overlaps; bring together teams of people from different areas who share responsibility for some aspects of the same end product.

- *Reduction of unnecessary layers of hierarchy* – eliminate barriers to resource access; make it possible for people to go directly after what they need; push decisional authority downward; create 'diagonal' slices cutting across the hierarchy to share information, provide quick intelligence about external and internal affairs.

- *Increased, and earlier, information about company plans* – where possible reduce secretiveness; avoid surprises; increase security by making future plans known in advance, making it possible, in turn, for those below to make their plans; give people at lower levels a chance to contribute to the shape of change before decisions are made at the top; empower and involve them at an earlier point, e.g. through task forces and problem-solving groups or through more open-ended, change-oriented assignments, with more room left for the person to define that approach.

Her list really summarizes what still is the essence of innovation best practice, covering all aspects from leadership to strategy and vision, to the work environment and culture. Interestingly, she does not mentioned processes as such. But the two lists above also reinforce that the single most influential factor in facilitating – or hindering – the right climate for innovation and design to flourish is a company's leaders. Aspects of a culture that support innovation, creativity and design, and other relevant issues around culture will be explored further in the following section.

THE ROLE OF COMPANY CULTURE

Culture consists of patterns, explicit and implicit of and for behaviour acquired and transmitted by symbols, constituting the distinctive achievement of human groups, including their embodiment in artefacts; the essential core of culture consists of traditional (i.e. historically derived and selected) ideas and especially their attached values; culture systems may, on the one hand, be considered as products of action, on the other, as conditioning elements of future action.

Kroeber and Kluckhohn (1952)

So what are key issues around creating a culture for design, creativity and innovation? First, we have just established that creating the right culture is key to innovation, and that the most influential person in establishing culture is a company's leader. Secondly, it is important to note that when trying to change a culture towards increased innovativeness many companies encounter resistance. There is a general reluctance to change that seems to be part of human nature, as well as some specific reasons to object changes such as a loss of power or autonomy. To expand on this, research by the Innovation Exchange (von Stamm 2001) indicates that many companies move towards stronger centralization to coordination innovation activities and better harness the benefits (see also Chapter 4). However, as many organizations used to have decentralized structures with far-reaching autonomy of the regions, the shift towards centralization means that they would have to give up their power and coordinate more strongly with the centre.

Thirdly, there may also be aspects of a company's heritage that go against the grain of what innovation is about. Again, to give an example from the Innovation Exchange research, a scientist-based company commented on the fact that collaboration – a central aspect of innovation – tends to be seen as a weakness by scientists. It is therefore important to uncover and understand any aspects of an organization's cultural and heritage that might get in the way of changing towards greater innovativeness.

Finally, there are certain characteristics that are typically found in an innovation culture – most of which are implicit in the two lists above. The arguably most important ones will be discussed briefly below.

EXPERIMENTATION AND TERMINATION

One of the key characteristics of innovative organizations is their willingness to *experiment*. Coming up with a range of feasible starting points for experimentation also includes the *challenging* of the status quo. One reason stated by

Gerald Avison to float TTP Com was that they had not done this before. However, if you experiment and play around you cannot expect every attempt to succeed. For example, TTP did not hesitate to pull out of the hydro car venture when it turned out that legislation and resulting time frames would delay progress significantly.

Three further characteristics of an innovation culture follow from that. First, an essential part of the experimentation culture is the *acceptance of failure*. Secondly, if you start with many different options, exploring a number of different avenues, you also have to have the ability and willingness to terminate projects. The art lies in starting as broad as possible and narrowing down as quickly as is feasible. Finally, innovative companies are not only good at killing projects at an early stage, they are also good at analyzing projects, particularly ones that have failed or been discontinued at a late stage, to see what can be learnt from why and how they went wrong.

A further characteristic of an innovation culture related to the habit of experimentation is the 'can-do' approach. It is best encapsulated in the typical 3M line of 'it is better to ask for forgiveness than permission'. People in innovative organizations feel at liberty to try things out and experiment, often without asking explicit permission from anyone before doing so. The following example is from product design and innovation firm IDEO. An employee, usually travelling to the office on his bicycle, never quite knew where to put it upon arrival. He started hoisting it up into the beams of the roof construction. No one complained, no one needed to be asked for permission, and soon others copied the idea.

This displays a degree of ownership and feeling at home that many organizations lack. If people feel comfortable to experiment and explore, they are more likely to bring forward some 'ridiculous' idea they have – and of course there is the saying that if an idea does not seem ridiculous at first it is probably not worth pursuing. Another example of what can happen if people feel free to bring themselves to work is again described by Hargadon and Sutton (2000). One of IDEO's designers, Dennis Boyle, was in the habit of bringing samples of his vast collection of things – toy cars, robots, prototypes from previous projects and other assorted objects – to brainstorming sessions and other occasions in the office. He describes the items as 'a congealed process-three-dimensional snapshots of the ideas from previous projects.' It was his collector's habit that seeded the idea for the materials libraries, cabinets with over 400 materials and products, that can now be found in each of the eight IDEO offices around the world (also referred to in Chapter 27).

COLLABORATION AND COMPETITION

The importance of collaboration to innovation has already been elaborated upon in Chapter 13. Innovative companies engage in collaboration, be it internally through cross-functional teams, or externally through joint ventures, alliances, or less structured forms of networking. But many innovative organizations also believe in the value of internal and external competition, though this does not tend to be cut-throat competition with high levels of secrecy or fierce and negative politics. It has more to do with setting up competing project teams that spur each other to higher performance where when the best teams the 'losers' are happy to support the winners on their way forward. In a company with a positive competitive culture, to lose is not equal to losing face or missing out on the next potential promotion. In companies that believe in collaboration, people cannot help but to collaborate, as Hargadon and Sutton (2000) report from a visit at IDEO:

> IDEO's studios are also laid out so that everyone sees and hears everyone else's design problems. We witnessed hundreds of unplanned interactions in which designers overheard nearby conversations, realized that they could help, and stopped whatever they were doing to make suggestions. One day we were sitting with engineers Larry Shubert and Roby Stancel, who were designing a device for an electric razor that would

vacuum up cut hair. We were meeting at a table in front of Rickson Sun's workstation. He soon shut his sliding door to muffle the noise from our meeting, but he could still hear us. He emerged a few minutes later to say he'd once worked on a similar design problem: a vacuum system for carrying away fumes from a hot scalpel that cauterized skin during surgery. Sun brought out samples of tubing that might be used in the new design and a report he had written about the kinds of plastic tubing available from vendors. The encounter shows how having the right attitude drives people to help each other solve problems. Shubert commented, 'Once Rickson realized he could help us, he had to do it or he wouldn't be a good IDEO designer.'

FUN AND FOCUS

A third trait is a combination of fun and focus. Fun, exploration and play are all aspects that prepare a fertile ground for innovation. A humour-filled atmosphere encourages ideas and suggestions, makes 'failure' more bearable, and allows the exploration of seemingly silly ideas. But at the same time, successful innovation cultures are result oriented – as reflected in TTP's vision statement that reads 'Have fun and make money'.

It is actually a myth that innovation is strangled through focus or constraints. Max de Pree writes, 'Creative persons, like the rest of us, need constraints. The famous industrial designer Charles Eames once called restraints "liberating." And I doubt that Rembrandt ever began a painting on an unlimited canvas. One of the most striking characteristics of the creative persons I know is their ability to renew themselves through constraints.' The widely held view that 3M allows its scientists 15% of their time to explore their own ideas means total and utter freedom is not quite true. Scientists at 3M are well aware of the core technologies and areas of business on which the company focuses, and most of their innovations are within and between what the core of the company is about. Providing no framework at all for innovation can lead to the development of concepts and ideas that do not have anything whatsoever to do with the company, resulting in wastage of valuable company resources.

On the other hand, innovative companies show a remarkable degree of flexibility as to their company's direction. 3M has started as a mining company and has been involved in a number of different industries during its existence. Pearson is another example of a company that has morphed and changed throughout its existence. Having started out as a construction company in 1844, Pearson moved into media in 1920, and says today about itself, 'Today, Pearson is all about education. We help teachers teach, students learn, train professionals and enrich minds.' So many innovative organizations are characterized by an ability to shift and change their focus, letting go of areas that used to be the core of their expertise. So it is 'letting go' of things not only at the project level as indicated above, it is also the ability to let go of 'projects' at the business level.

ALIGNMENT OF SYSTEMS AND PROCESSES

A fourth characteristic of an innovative organization is that all systems and processes, particularly concerning those related to human resource management, are set out to support an innovation culture. The TTP case study provides some good examples of this.

Human resource policy, including recruitment, and remuneration are particularly critical factors, as they determine how things are done and what is valued within an organization. They should reinforce company strategy and support the culture. If a culture of teamwork and cooperation is desired, but rewards and remuneration of employees are based on their individual achievements, people will be reluctant to cooperate and share. If people are recruited based on their technical qualification alone, rather than being also assessing on their 'cultural' fit with the organization, managers will at best end up with the sum or the parts. The more important teamwork and cooperation are for a company's success, the more emphasis should be placed on the right 'soft' skills. It might also be worth considering what kind of person is required; no organization can survive with 'innovators' or 'adaptors' alone: a good mix of different skills and strengths is required to come up with great ideas, *and* realize them in the marketplace.

It starts with their recruitment and the signals they are sending through their website to potential applicants (see Box 30.2 for the recruitment text from their website www.ttp.com). Once an applicant has entered the process, he or she has the opportunity to talk to current employees, as well as to the CEO. All this also reflects the open and flat-hierarchy culture. Once an employee has joined, he or she might even get the opportunity to influence the company's direction, as two people who suggested the setting up of an investment fund, or Anne Miller, who suggested the establishment of a subsidiary to provide creativity and innovation training services. When she had the idea she did not spend days or weeks on developing elaborate business plans, but took her idea straight to the CEO who, as she knew, would be open and willing to listen. Of course, once the idea was discussed a business plan was developed with all necessary details and diligence. The commitment to its employees is also reflected in a subsidized canteen and support of sports activities.

BOX 30.2   Recruitment Text from TTP's Website

Mavericks. Non-conformists. Revolutionaries.

In other words, our kind of people.

TTP provides solutions to problems that in many cases the industry is not yet aware exist. We identify situations where new technology is able to satisfy a market need. We then develop the product.

Smart, fresh thinking is critical to our growth and ongoing success. We recruit outstanding minds. We want to hear from enthusiastic, energetic people who can identify market opportunities and come up with fresh, effective, ingenious solutions to problems ahead of deadlines.

The facilities, core technologies and training are of a jaw-dropping quality at TTP. And not only is the work environment first class, but everybody has a voice in the way we conduct our business too.

We're here to have fun and make money. It's our mission statement. What's yours?

Communication processes also play an important part in TTP. The informal presentation meetings on Friday afternoons provide employees with a platform to test their presentation skills, allow them to bring themselves into the organization, and foster informal networks between members from different parts of the organization. Further ways of fostering informality, familiarity and networking as the policy of keeping individual business units below 200 people, working through multiple overlapping project teams and dynamic desks which mean that people get mixed up on a regular basis.

True to its mission of 'Having fun and making money', the company has also the tendency to devolve businesses. As Anne Miller commented in a presentation to members of the Innovation Exchange in May 2001, 'We believe that continually devolving power and businesses supports innovation and growth and is good for our existing shareholders and employees. However, this strategy might not be right for everyone as it makes the business difficult to value, and is bad for the MD's ego.'

The human resource function can in itself become a source of innovation, as the example from an insurance company illustrates. There was an increasing concern that the senior management was too much out of touch with technology development, primarily the advance of the internet. A conversation between the manager of the e-commerce section and the HR people led to the development of a scheme through which board members would be matched up with young high flyers, familiar with the internet and world wide web.

CULTURE AND DESIGN

To create a strong company culture, reflecting what the company stands for, the values and beliefs ought to be reflected in everything it does and produces. Management, leadership and the human resource function can establish the values and facilitate and encourage the right behaviours. Design and design management can facilitate the accurate visual representation of the beliefs and values and ensure consistency in the physical appearance and representation of the organization, including products, any form of company literature, and the physical work environment (see also Chapter 27). In companies such as BMW, that have placed design at the core of their strategy, it is the role of design management at the strategic level to ensure visual consistency and the alignment of the company's interfaces (products, services, other forms of communication such as promotional literature, advertising, etc.) with company strategy and company culture. The role of a strategic design manager is also to ensure that an awareness for the value and contribution of design in the organization is maintained, as Blaich and Blaich (1993) point out in their book *Product Design and Corporate Strategy*.

COMMITMENT TO INNOVATION

Finally, innovative companies are committed to the course of innovation; they do not change policies, dissolve innovation teams or cancel projects because economic times are getting a bit more difficult. A survey conducted by the Innovation Exchange Spring 2002[2] revealed that companies that consider themselves to have a positive attitude towards innovation tend to spend more, not less, on innovation when times get difficult. And interestingly, but not surprisingly, those companies who indicated a positive attitude towards innovation in general seemed to have fared better than companies who cut back on innovation (see Box 30.3). This was reflected in increased market share and/or profitability, in comparison with the industry, as well as increased profitability in the current year.

> **BOX 30.3   Benefits from Being an Innovator (von Stamm and Riley 2002)**
>
> - Seventy percent (70%) of organizations with a positive attitude towards innovation declared that they are outperforming their competitors (an additional 17% felt their performance was at least level with their competitors).
>
> - Those companies that have seen an increase in profits over past years all possess a positive attitude towards innovation.
>
> - These companies also tend to have larger market shares than their closest competitors.

According to the survey, companies that subscribe to innovation are also more likely to engage in radical innovation, and are successful at it. Those organizations that were successful in the past indicated that in future they are planning (a) innovation in additional areas (e.g. strategic, operational and/or organizational), and (b) more radical innovation than in the past. Success seems to increase companies' willingness to take risks, creating a positive momentum for innovation.

I would like to finish with two quotes:

If most of us are ashamed of shabby clothes and shoddy furniture, let us be more ashamed of shabby ideas and shoddy philosophies.

Albert Einstein

Don't worry about people stealing an idea. If it's original, you will have to ram it down their throats.

Howard Aiken

READING SUGGESTIONS

Goffee, Rob and Jones, Gareth (1998) *The Character of a Corporation, How your Company's Culture can Make or Break your Business.* London: HarperCollins

Comment: Building on their earlier *Harvard Business Review* article, they expand and develop their framework. Full of case studies and examples

Clegg, Brian (1999) *Creativity and Innovation for Managers.* Oxford: Butterworth-Heinemann

Comment: Useful and easy to read book on innovation; useful stuff including mechanisms for innovation, training, rewards and remuneration for innovation, etc.

Kuczmarski, Thomas (1996) *Innovation – Leadership Strategies for the Competitive Edge.* Chicago: NTC Business Books

Comment: This book, equally relevant for the leadership section, provides some good insights about how to lead innovation from the top; it has got a few check lists and questionnaires that might help determine how you or your CEO (as an innovation leader) fair – Kuczmarski's questionnaire on the innovation mindset can also be found on the Innovation Exchange website (library)

NOTES ON CHAPTER 30

[1] For characteristics of successful project leaders, see Chapter 3.

[2] The survey was conducted in between April/May 2002 by Dr Bettina von Stamm for the Innovation Exchange, in collaboration with the InnovationNetwork (www.thinksmart.com) and the Design Management Institute (www.dmi.org).

Appendix I How to Use the Case Studies

The cases can be used individually in traditional MBA courses (see Table I.1), to infuse innovation into traditional subjects, or as a set, forming the foundation for a course dedicated to innovation, as has been done at London Business School. The latter might challenge current business school and university structures, as it is not likely to fit neatly into any existing department. As creating an innovative organization is heavily dependent on leadership, and is about creating an appropriate culture, organizational behaviour departments might be best suited to accommodate such a course. While it is strongly recommended that the overall coordination of the course remains with one or a maximum of two people to ensure consistency and continuity, the course would benefit tremendously if additional expertise from other faculty areas, as well as from 'the real world' could be integrated.

Table I.2 shows in which traditional faculty areas the case studies might be used.

Table I.1 By Discipline

	BBC	ihavemoved	Black & Decker	Lotus Elise	Dumfries	Roche	GKN	Bank of Scotland	John McAslan & Partners	TTP Group
Strategic management	—	×	—	×	×	×	×	×	×	×
Operations management/ manufacturing	—	—	×	×	×	×	×	—	—	—
Marketing incl. branding and market research	×	×	×	×	×	—	—	×	—	—
Organizational behaviour	×	—	×	×	—	×	×	—	—	×
Finance/ entrepreneurship	—	×	—	×	×	—	×	×	—	×
Economics	—	—	—	—	×	×	—	—	—	—

Table I.2 Exploring Issues Relevant to Innovation

	BBC *Walking with Dinosaurs*	ihavemoved	Black & Decker Quattro	Lotus Elise	Dumfries Recycling	Roche Saquinavir	GKN	Bank of Scotland	John McAslan & Partners	TTP Group
Wider context	—	—	—	—	X	X	—	X	—	—
Timing	—	X	—	—	X	—	X	X	—	—
Green issues	—	—	—	(X)	X	—	(X)	—	—	(X)
Patenting	—	—	X	—	—	X	(X)	—	—	—
Strategy – internet	—	X	—	—	—	—	—	—	—	—
Strategy – flexibility	—	X	—	X	—	X	—	—	—	—
Globalization	X	—	—	—	—	—	—	—	—	—
Internal investment	X	—	—	X	X	—	X	X	—	X
External investment	X	X	—	—	—	—	X	X	—	X
Levels of innovation	—	—	—	—	—	—	X	X	—	—
Def. of succ. and failure	—	—	—	—	X	—	—	X	—	—
Innovation culture	—	X	X	X	X	—	X	X	—	X
The role of individuals	X	—	X	X	X	—	X	X	—	X
Project leader	X	—	X	—	X	—	X	X	—	—
Company leaders	—	X	X	X	X	—	—	X	—	X

	1	2	3	4	5	6	7	8	9	10
Commercial awareness	X						X	X	X	X
Passion/commitment/determination	X		X	X	X		X		X	X
Communication	X				X		X	X	X	
Personal relationships		X	X		X	X		X	X	X
Defiance	X			X			X	X		
Internal networks	X			X	X		X	X		X
External collaboration		X	X	X			X	X	X	
Designers' involvement	X	X	X				X	X	X	X
Team spirit					X		X	X		
Early involvement								X		
Role of mkt. research			X				X	X		X
Prototypes							X	X		X

Appendix II Categories of Design

Here we consider the different categories of design projects one might encounter.[1] Some references to additional reading as well as case studies are provided. Some aspects of the design process may vary with project type, and I aim to point this out where appropriate. Before we take a look at individual types of design below, a brief discourse into the history of the development of 'design'.

HISTORY OF 'DESIGN'

In the traditional understanding, 'design' is often associated with a person who is involved in both the design and production of an object. This concept began to change with the outset of the Industrial Revolution, which initiated the division of work and the need for specialization. Resulting from this, two strands of design evolved, 'design as art' and 'design as engineering', each with a different meaning and different emphasis in education. Part and consequence of the development into specialization was the separation of industrial and engineering design, about which Ivor Owen (1990), a former director of the Design Council, says, 'I strongly believe that the schism between engineering design and industrial design has been one of the most damaging issues in manufacturing industry imaginable.' Sir William Barlow (1988), a former chairman of the Design Council, asserts this by pointing out that almost every product requires an appropriate balance of both. A similar view is presented in the earlier Corfield Report (1979), which states that product design includes both industrial and engineering design. While the Bauhaus attempted to reconcile these two strands, with Gropius promoting the 'marriage between design and machine', the split between the two aspects of design remained. In recent years, the shift towards working in multidisciplinary teams has brought the different strands back together, if not in one person at least in a closely operating team.

The closer cooperation between different functions has also brought out cultural and language differences between departments, and highlighted the need to develop tools and methods to overcome these differences and allow the development of a shared understanding. Here metaphors, suggested by, for example, Black (1962), Kendall and Kendall (1994), McWilliam and Dumas (1995) and Walsham (1991), and prototypes, suggested by Leonard-Barton (1991) or Rettig (1994), are frequently mentioned as tools that can help to achieve this aim (see also Chapter 12). The further specialization went, the wider the range of activities associated with the term 'design'. Walker (1989) devised what he calls the 'Design Family Tree' (see Figure II.1), which shows the different types of specialization associated with design, while at the same time giving a feeling for their historical development. There does seem to be some overlap between categories, whichever way one tries to cut them, i.e. each category of design project is likely to involve a range of different types of design activity. Table II.1 links Walker's five categories with the categories suggested here.

Any one project is likely to involve a range of different types of design, and for each project the skills mix required will be different. However, the mix will not only vary by product, but is also likely to differ at different stages of that product's life-cycle. Remember the Sony Walkman? Focus on miniaturization of the technology in the early phases, then modifying to serve the needs of different customer segments. Each of these changes required a different set of design skills: engineering design for the former, industrial and packaging design for the latter. One implication is that if a second generation of a product is developed, an organization should think carefully whether the original team is the best solution, or whether different skills are required. Another is that constraints are likely to vary.

Table II.1   Types of Design

	Environment	Product	Graphic	Fashion	Engineering
Town planning and urban design	X	X	X	—	—
Architecture and interior design	X	X	X	—	X
Garden and landscape design	X	X	X	—	—
Exhibition design	X	X	X	—	X
Product design	X	X	—	—	X
Packaging design	—	X	X	—	—
Graphic design	—	X	X	—	—
Corporate identity	X	X	X	X	—
Brands	—	X	X	—	—
IT design and multimedia	(X virtual!)	—	X	—	—
Service design*	—	—	X	—	—
Textile design	X	X	—	X	—

*Please see Chapter 24.

When thinking about different types of design projects, it might also be worth thinking about the time horizon and the number of 'units' produced. Some categories are, by nature, one-offs, whereas others are repeated frequently. For example, architectural and town planning projects tend to be one-off, whereas graphic design projects, such as annual reports or stationery, happen quite frequently. Corporate identify projects are somewhere in the middle. While I am not suggesting that it does not matter if a graphic design projects does not meet customer requirements, particular care should go into one-off projects to ensure that it meets customer needs. After all, the cost and effort involved into printing new stationery is quite different from attempting to rectify an architectural project.[2]

The design process will vary slightly for different types of design projects, and the following publications prepared by the Design Business Association for the DTI, also referred to in the relevant categories, might be useful:

- Managing corporate identity programmes (1992)
- Managing interior design projects (1992)
- Managing packaging design projects (1992)
- Managing product design projects (1992)

TOWN PLANNING AND URBAN DESIGN

Town planning and urban design projects tend to be of a large scale and, more often than not, initiated by the public rather than the private sector. They also tend to be long term in nature, and can require a lengthy negotiation process involving citizens, politicians and special interest groups. Hence, the involvement of stakeholders and the incorporation of their concerns is a major part of the development process. It can have a critical influence, particularly on the timing of the execution.

With increasing population and ever growing demand for new dwellings, environmental concerns and environmental impact analysis are becoming increasingly important. Just recently it was announced that over 900,000 new homes should be build in the south of England over a ten-year period – one wonders whether there will be any countryside

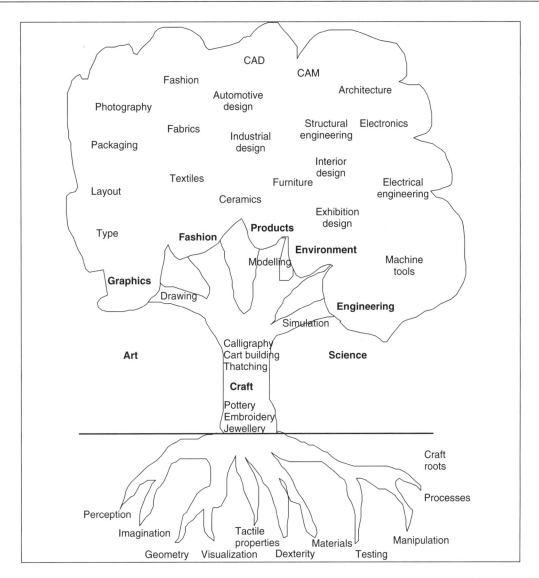

Figure II.1 Walker's Design Family Tree (reproduced from (Open University Press, 1989))

left. But at the same time, the demand opens up new opportunities: disused land, empty dwellings, sites left unused by dying industries in the centres and around the edges of towns are all calling out for imaginative reuse of what is called 'brownfields'.

ARCHITECTURE AND INTERIOR DESIGN

Much of research into the design process and decision making in design has taken place in the field of architecture – for many it is still closest associated with 'design as art'. More than most of other types of design projects, architecture and interior design projects are centred around an individual – rather than a group or a company name. Many of the big architectural practices are known by their founders' name(s), and his or her personality is often the main selling point.

But it is also the architects you probably find wondering into 'foreign' territory most frequently. Think of le Courbusier, Mies van der Rohe, or Behrens, who has not only designed the buildings for AEG but also their logo and lots of products (electric irons, heaters, kettles, fans, etc.). Even though it might not have been called that at the time, the AEG story is an early example of a holistic approach to corporate identity. It seems to me that today organizations are becoming more aware of the importance of architecture and interior design in supporting and shaping a company's image. I believe the importance will continue to increase, not least because of an increasing need for organizations to have a strong culture. Why? Because in a time where people work away from the office and outside the cultural atmosphere of the organization more and more, the organization needs to take greater care in communicating its culture, and the work environment is one way this can be done. So, the built environment can support an organization's culture – or work against it.

Thinking about retailing, interior design is probably even closer associated with branding and image. Particularly with franchised businesses, the 'product concept' and design language are essential.

Architecture is also a field where environmental considerations can have a significant impact: on heating, 'green' climate control, reuse of water, use of environmentally friendly/recycled building material, and so on. It is a field where much is possible – but little is done at present.

GARDEN AND LANDSCAPE DESIGN

This is a type of design project where planning and execution are often undertaken by the same person. It is probably also a category of design that does not come immediately to mind when talking about 'design' in the context of this course – and it is an area where designers from other areas hardly ever venture. It is also an area where you are less likely to find a formalized design process and the team that develops and executes the design is generally quite small. As design manager you are probably most likely to come across it as part of larger architectural projects.

EXHIBITION DESIGN

Exhibition design is an interesting one: it is extremely short term in two ways: (a) it is generally only for the duration of the exhibition, and (b) developed and delivered in quite a short time span. It is generally offered by highly specialized companies. I believe it basically breaks down into two markets: one is for standardized exhibition products such as poster stands, etc.; the other is for specialist, custom-made solutions. Think about the big motor shows, where car manufacturers tend to invest heavily in spectacular stands.

While the past has seen exhibition design that was, more often than not, removed from the company's identity, I believe that in future companies should use their exhibition stands to make a statement about their organization, about their personality. They should use the opportunity to communicate their values and what they stand for.

PRODUCT DESIGN

This category is what probably comes to mind first when talking about design in the business context. While all products are designed – if design (as activity) is defined as 'generating information from which a required product can become reality' – by no means all products are developed with the involvement of an industrial designer. It seems that product design may be undertaken by engineers, marketers, other technical staff, the manager – just about everyone. As we know, these designing 'non-designers' are called 'silent designers' (Gorb and Dumas 1987).

In many cases, the industrial design is used only for the 'styling', and only at the end of the development process. In my view, this is a big mistake as design can contribute significantly beyond the aesthetic aspects of a product.

Whether a design consultant or internal resources are used varies from company to company (see Chapter 28 for a discussion of advantages and disadvantages of each option). But I believe that are also trends at industry and country level. For example, hi-fi products are more likely to be developed with the involvement of designers than, say, microwaves and washing machines. I believe that there are some differences at national level. For example, German companies are more likely to have in-house design facilities than in the UK. However, I think that this type of design is generally the one most likely to be undertaken in-house. Most of the literature on the design process concerns this category.[3]

PACKAGING DESIGN

Packaging design is probably most important for FMCGs (fast moving consumer goods). Repackaging has sometimes brought a brand back into customer's favour, and it is here that communicating the right values messages is very important. Think about all the fancy water bottles you can get today – sold at a premium. Generally, with food products packaging is particularly important as it often contains important information about use and preparation – and is a major factor of differentiation. But increasingly, packaging design goes beyond 'around the product', it becomes part of the product itself, and is often source for innovation. Think about aerosol cans, 'blown-up' packaging for crisps, elaborate perfume bottles, and so on. On the other hand, for electronic consumer goods, being displayed without packaging, the packaging is less important. This is a category where companies tend to rely on external rather than internal designers.

GRAPHIC DESIGN

Graphic design can play part in many other design projects, such as exhibition design, product design, packaging design, and of course, corporate identity projects. Typeface, layout, colour and language all carry a message and need to be selected carefully. Some typefaces convey traditional values, some look modern, elegant, technical, and so forth. Colours have messages too – red for danger, green for environment, blue is generally perceived as cool – but beware, the meaning of colours can vary from country to country. Graphic design is of particular importance for the front-end of service products, where visual clarity and ease of access are critical.

CORPORATE IDENTITY

For me corporate identity encompasses everything an organization stands for, and this should be reflected in every encounter with the organization, be it with a person or product, reception, shop floor, cloakroom, or director's office. Designers are responsible for translating what a company stands for into a visual image, into the appropriate symbols, colours and typefaces. BP and Shell are examples of corporate identities that have been changed and adapted over time. The core ingredients are still the same, but the visualization has been updated in keeping with the time.

Managing the corporate identity is often the main task for a company internal design manager. While many companies restrict the responsibility to managing company literature and logo, I believe that it should go further and include products – tangible and intangible – and environments.

Visual representation is more powerful than many people realize. I always liked an exercise used by Dr Angela Dumas to illustrate this: she shows pictures of three abstract paintings (the ones shown in Box II.1 are not exactly the ones she has used, but I hope close enough to make her point).

She then asks two questions. The first is, if these paintings represented organizations, which one would you like to work for? The answer depends on preferences for structure and freedom, and so on. She then asks, and if these paintings represented airlines, which one would you like to fly with? She generally does not need to say any more to convince people of the power of visual images. It is interesting though that the answers shift over time – since Virgin Airlines have entered the market people are not quite as worried any more about flying with 'A'. There are also cultural differences. I found it interesting that most Westerners assumed that Japanese would prefer to work in organization B – but in fact, the fast majority of Japanese see themselves working for company A. So visual metaphors and tools can also be extremely helpful in uncovering hidden assumptions.

BOX II.1   Which Airline would you Fly with? (reproduced from www.art.com)

A Wassily Kandinsky

'Yellow, Red Blue'

From : www.art.com

B Mondrian

'Composition 1921'

www.xycharts.com/ mondrian.html

C Kurt Freundlinger

'Sunshine Country II'

www.art.com

BRANDS

Brand design and corporate identity are closely related – both are concerned with communicating a certain set of values, and both have a stronger strategic component than other categories of design. One could say that corporate identity deals with branding issues at the company level, brand issues concern the product level.

IT DESIGN AND MULTIMEDIA

IT and multimedia design are probably the youngest member in the design category family. And, particularly for web design, this is a field where technical and design skills have to be matched. Technical possibilities are probably ahead of customer requirements and conscious needs and development cycles are often extremely short. Developments in IT have changed the way we work, where we work, and how we interact. Whether an interaction is a pleasurable or unpleasurable experience depends very much on user friendliness and design.

(For the use of metaphors in the development of information systems, read Kendall and Kendall (1994) 'Metaphors and their meaning for information systems development'.)

TEXTILE AND FASHION DESIGN

Textile design is another category of design you are probably less likely to encounter, unless of course you work in the fashion or textile industry. Branding plays an important role, certainly at the top end of the market; fashion is certainly one area where people are paying a premium to be associated with a certain brand, and the lifestyle associated with it. While custom-made clothes have been a privilege of the rich and famous, mass customization techniques allow more and more people to walk into a shop and have their, for example, jeans made to order to their particular shape and figure. Interior design is probably the other design field most likely to incorporate some aspects of textile design.

FURNITURE DESIGN

Finally, there is furniture design. As above, it tends to happen in dedicated companies, though many architects also try their hand in furniture design. It seems that furniture design seems to take on more and more characteristics of fashion design, with parallels in custom-made items and mass-produced goods.

SUMMARY

Table II.2 summarizes some aspects for the different design categories; it does not aim to be comprehensive, but provides some food for thought.

Table II.2 Different Types of Design

	Link with other design activities	Time horizon/ 'life expectancy'	Frequency	Tends to be associated with	More likely to be located
Town and urban	Graphic	Long term	One-off	Organization	External
Architecture and interior	Graphic Textile Landscape Furniture	Long term Medium term	One-off Sporadic	Individual Organization	External External
Garden and landscape	Architecture	Medium term	Sporadic	Organization	External
Exhibition	Graphic Interior Architecture IT and multimedia	Short term Medium term	Sporadic/regular	Organization	External
Product (industrial and engineering)	Packaging Graphic Branding	Depending on product, short to long term	Depending on product, sporadic to ongoing	Organization Individual	Internal

Table II.2 (*continued*)

	Link with other design activities	Time horizon/ 'life expectancy'	Frequency	Tends to be associated with	More likely to be located
Packaging	Graphic Product Brands	Medium term	Sporadic	Organization	External
Graphic	Most other categories	Short to medium term	Sporadic	Organization	External
Corporate identity	Architecture Interior Branding Graphic IT and multimedia	Should be long term	Sporadic	Organization	External
Brands	Product Graphic Packaging	Should be long term	Sporadic	Organization	Internal
IT and multimedia	Graphic Product	Short to medium term	Sporadic	Organization	External
Service*	Graphic Architecture Interior IT and multimedia	Medium term	Depending on product, sporadic to ongoing	Organization	Internal
Textile and fashion	Branding Graphic	Seasonal	Depending on product, sporadic to ongoing	Individual Organization	Internal/ external
Furniture	Textile	Medium	Sporadic/ongoing	Individual Organization	—

*Please see Chapter 24.

READING SUGGESTIONS

Buying into Design (1998) The Design Council, London

Comment: Booklet with case studies illustrating how to purchase design, as well as the positive implications from using design; published by the Design Council

Managing. . . Series (1992) prepared by the Design Business Association for the DTI

Comment: Useful booklets on process and management of a number of different design projects including, corporate identity, interior design, packaging design, product design

Thackara, John (1997) *European Design Prize Winners! How Today's Successful Companies Innovate by Design.* Aldershot, UK: Gower

Comment: The book not only presents case studies of the winners of the European Design Prize 1997, but also provides much useful information, statistics and trends that are relevant to design and innovation

Olins, Wally (1996) *The Guide to Identity: How to Create and Sustain Change Through Managing Identity*. London: Gower

Comment: Wally Olins, co-founder of probably the first corporate identify consultancy to take the subject to a strategic level, provides a comprehensive guide to corporate identity, explaining what it is and how it can be used to full effect

Mackenzie, D. (1991) *Green Design, Design for the Environment*. London: Laurence King Publishing

Comment: Offers an environmental perspective on different types of design, providing a number of case studies

Lyle, John T. (1999) *Designs for Human Ecosystems, Landscape, Land Use, and Natural Resources*. New York: Island Press

Comment: Providing a number of examples and case studies, the author explores methods of designing landscapes which function like natural ecosystems

Allinson, Kenneth (1995) *The Wild Card of Design – A Perspective on Architecture in a Project Management Environment*. Oxford: Butterworth Heineman

Comment: The book provides an architectural perspective on the design process

SOME USEFUL WEBSITES

- For a debate on the potential of brownfield developments in England, conducted by the Royal Agricultural Society England on 2nd April 1998, have a look at http://www.rase.org.uk/communications/greenfield.html
- www.ArchitectsWorldwide.com is the portal site for international architects' websites
- http://www.riba.org is the website of the Royal Institute of British Architects and on http://store.yahoo.com/riba-links/ you find more than 500 architecture-related websites
- www.aiaonline.com/ is the website of the American Institute of Architecture
- www.BuildItWorldwide.com is the portal site for international construction websites
- www.AecWW.comi is the portal site for international design websites
- www.DesignersWorldwide.com is the portal site for international designer websites
- www.EngineersWorldwide.com is the portal site for international engineering websites
- www.cfsd.org.uk/ Centre for Sustainable Design. A European centre of excellence focusing on the implications of sustainable on the design of products. Facilitates discussion and research about the effects of the 'triple bottom line' on design: environmental, social and economic needs
- http://www.csfi.demon.co.uk/ is the website of the Centre for the Study of Financial Innovation; the CSFI is an independent London-based think-tank, funded by the world's top banks. It explores the future of the financial services industry. They have an active agenda of meetings, seminars and research projects which are of wide interest to all who work in, or use, the financial markets. 18 Curzon Street, London W1Y 7AD, United Kingdom, Tel: +44(0)171 493 0173, Fax: +44 (0)171 493 0190
- http://www.ozemail.com.au/~caveman/Creative/index.html Charles Cave's extensive collection of creativity information

- http://www.edwdebono.com Edward de Bono's website – an extensive catalogue of items related to Edward de Bono from around the world, including training centres, seminar schedules, books, and games
- http://www.micaworld.com/MICA Management is a Toronto-based training and consulting organization, specializing in creativity and innovation, leadership development, and personal and organizational effectiveness. MICA distributes the Serious Creativity CD in Canada and North America
- http://www.creativesparks.org/NCCI is the website for The National Center for Creativity, a non-profit organization established to help facilitate the growing interest in the field of creativity and innovation, NCCI provides educational opportunities through seminars, training courses and a specialty bookstore, the NCCI Resource Mart

NOTES ON APPENDIX II

[1] This is but one way that design categories may be cut differently and other categories added.

[2] Having said that, even buildings that are disfunctional are being pulled down (many of which were built in the 1960s and 1970s).

[3] And to be even more specific, a lot of it originates from research into the automotive industry.

References

Aaker, D. (1991) *Managing brand equity: capitalising on the value of a brand name*. New York: Free Press.

Abernathy, W.J. and Clark, K.B. (1985) Innovation: mapping the winds of creative destruction. *Research Policy*, **14**, 3–22.

Adler, N. (1986) *International dimensions of organizational behaviour*. Boston, MA: PWS-Kent Publishing Company.

Adler, P.S. (1992) Managing DFM: learning to co-ordinate product and process design. In: Susman, G.I. *Integrating design and manufacturing for competitive advantage*. New York: Oxford University Press.

Allen, D. (2000) Living the brand. *Design Management Journal*, winter, 35–40.

Allinson, K. (1995) *The wild card of design – a perspective on architecture in a project management environment*. Oxford: Butterworth-Heinemann.

Amabile, T.M. (1998) How to kill creativity. *Harvard Business Review*, September–October 77–87.

Amabile, T.M. (1988) A model of creativity and innovation in organisations. In: Staw, B.M. and Cummings, L.L. *Research in organisational behaviour*. Greenwich, CT: JAI Press, 123–167.

Amabile, T.M., Conti, R., Coon, H., Lazenby, J. and Herron, M. (1996) Assessing the work environment for creativity. *Academy of Management Journal*, **39**, 5, 1154–1184.

Ambler, T. (2002) Brand and innovation. Presentation given at the London Business School as part of the course 'Managing Innovation, Design and Creativity'.

Ambler, T. (1997) Do brands benefit consumers? *International Journal of Advertising*, **16**, 3, 167–197.

Ancona, D.G. and Caldwell, D. (1990) Improving the performance of new product teams. *Research-Technology Management*, **33**, 2, 25–29.

Anonymous (2002) Brands and the economy. http://www.aim.be/brand/brand_economy.html.

Anonymous (2002) The British Brands Group. http://www.britishbrandsgroup.com.

Anonymous (2002) Consumer products – branding. http://www.sgs.co.uk/consulting/industries/consumer/branding.htm.

Anonymous (2001) *A question of culture? Collaborative innovation in UK business*. London: CBI.

Anonymous (2001) Innov8 – Brands and the innovation imperative. The Brands Conference 2001. Conference summary.

Anonymous (1999) Achieving new product success in highly innovative versus incremental new industrial services.

Anonymous (1997) Bei MuZ brummt der Motor wieder. *Kieler Nachrichten*, 10th May.

Anonymous (1997) Not designed here? Decision making over design sources of UK textile firms.

Anonymous (1997) Sharing knowledge through BP's virtual team network. *Harvard Business Review*, **75**, 5, 152–153.

Anonymous (1996) Outsourcing product development. *Supervision*, **57**, 10, 10–12.

Anonymous (1995) The outing of outsourcing. *The Economist*, 1st November, 99.

Anonymous (1987) The organization of design: an interdisciplinary approach to the study of people, process and contexts.

Anonymous (n.d.) *A guide to brand X*. London: British Brands Group.

Anonymous (n.d.) Strategic outsourcing of design and development. Wind River White Paper. www.windriver.com/whitepapers/strategic-outsourcing.pdf.

Ash, R. (1996) *The top ten of everything*. London: Dorling Kindersley.

Balachandra, R. and Friar, J.H. (1997) Factors for success in R&D projects and new product innovation: a contextual framework. *IEEE Transactions on Engineering Management*, **44**, 3, 276–287.

Balmer, J. (1999) Increasing sensitivity to corporate branding and identity. Speech given by Prof. John Balmer, Director of International Corporate Branding. 1st Summer Symposium for the ICCIS.

Barclay, I. and Lunt, P.J. (1987) Successful management of the introduction of new technology. In: Rothwell, R. and Bessant, J. *Innovation, adaptation and growth*. Amsterdam: Elsevier, 81–91.

Barkan, P. and Iansiti, M. (1993) Prototyping: a tool for rapid learning in product development. *Concurrent Engineering Research and Applications*, **1**, 125–134.

Barkema, H.J., Bell, J. and Pennings, J. (1996) Foreign entry, cultural barriers and learning. *Strategic Management Journal*, **17**, 151–166.

Barlow, W. (1988) The importance of design. In: Gorb, P. (ed.) *Design Talks!* London: Design Council.

Barnholt, E.W. (1997) Fostering business growth with breakthrough innovation. *Research Technology Management*, **40**, 2, 12.

Baxter, M. (1995) *Product design – practical methods for the systematic development of new products*. London: Chapman & Hall.

Belbin, M. (1991) Design innovation and the team. *Design Management Journal*, winter, 38–42.

Berner, K.M. (1997) Is your prototype yours? *Design News*, **52**, 9, 200.

Bernstein, D. (1986) *Company image and reality*. Eastbourne, UK: Holt, Rinehart and Winston.

Black, A. (1990) Traits of creative people. http://creativeideas.org.uk.

Blaich, R. and Blaich, J. (1993) *Product design and corporate strategy – managing the connection for competitive advantage*. New York: McGraw-Hill.

Blumberg, D. (1989) The Consultant Forum, 5, 1.

Blumberg, D.F. (1987) Developing service as a line of business. *Management Review*, **76**, 2, 58.

Bobrow, E.E. (1997) *The complete idiot's guide to new product development*. New York: Alpha Books.

Bohm, D. and Peat, F.D. (1991) Science, order and creativity: In: Henry, J. *Creative management*. London: Sage Publications in association with The Open University, vol. 1, 24–33.

Booz Allen Hamilton (1982) *New product development in the 1980*. New York: Booz, Allen, Hamilton.

Bower, J.L. and Hout, T.M. (1988) Fast-cycle capability for competitive power. *Harvard Business Review*, November–December 110–118.

Boze, B.V. and Patton, C.R. (1995) The future of consumer branding as seen from the picture today. *The Journal of Consumer Marketing*, **12**, 4.

Branscomb, L.M., Florida, R., Hart, D., Keller, J. and Boville, D. (1999) *Investing in innovation*. Cambridge, MA: MIT Press.

Brenner, M.S. (1994) Practical R&D project priorisation. *Research-Technology Management*, **37**, 5, 38–42.

Bruce, M. and Cooper, R. (1997) *Marketing and design management*. London: International Thomson Business Press.

Bruce, M. and Morris, B. (1995) Approaches to design management in the product development process. In: Bruce, M. and Morris, B. *Product development, meeting the challenge of the design-marketing interface*. Chichester, UK: John Wiley & Sons, 99–116.

Bruce, M., Biemans, W.G., Bruce, M. and Biemans, W.G. (eds) (1995) *Product development: meeting the challenge of the design–marketing interface*. Chichester: John Wiley & Sons Ltd.

Bryan, L., Fraser, J., Oppenheim J. and Rall., W. (1999) *Race for the world*. Boston, MA: Harvard Business School Press.

Bullmore, J. (2002) Posh Spice & Persil, the brands lecture 2001. London: The British Brands Group.

Burall, P. (1996) *Product development and the environment*. London: Gower.

Burall, P. (1992) How to be green. *Design*. August.

Calantone, R.J., Schmidt, J.B. and Di Benedetto, C.A. (1997) New product activities and performance: the moderating role of environmental hostility. *Journal of Product Innovation Management*, **14**, 179–189.

Carter, C.F. and Williams, B.R. (1957) *Industrial and technical progress*. London: Oxford University Press.

Chryssochoidi, G.M. and Wong, V. (2000) Service innovation multi-country launch: causes of delays. *European Journal of Innovation Management*, **3**, 1, 35ff.

Clark, K.B. and Wheelwright, S.C. (1993) *Managing new product and process development, text and cases*. New York: Free Press.

Claxton, G. (1997) *Hare brain tortoise mind, why intelligence increases when you think less*. London: Fourth Estate.

Cleland, R.S. (2000) Building successful brands on the internet. MBA dissertation at the Judge Institute of Management Studies, Cambridge University.

Cohen, M.A., Eliashberg, J. and Ho, T.-H. (1996) New product development: the performance and time-to-market tradeoffs. *Management Science*, February, 173–186.

Cohen, S.H. (1996) Tools for quantitative market research. In: Rosenau, M.D.J., Griffin, A., Castellion, G. and Anschuetz, N. *The PDMA handbook of new product development*. New York: John Wiley & Sons, 253–267.

Coles, A.-M., Dickson, K. and Woods, A. (1997) Not designed here? Decision making over design sources of UK textile firms. Academy of Management Annual Conference.

Cooper, R.G. (1994) Third-generation new product processes. *Journal of Product Innovation Management*, **11**, 3–14.

Cooper, R.G. (1988) The new product process: a decision guide for management. *Journal of Marketing Management*, **3**, 3, 238–255.

Cooper, R.G. (1986) *Winning at new products*. London: Kogan Page.

Cooper, R.G. and Kleinschmidt Elko J. (2001) Stage gate process for new product success. *Innovation Management*.

Cooper, R.G. and Kleinschmidt, E.J. (1996) Winning business in product development: the critical success factors. *Research-Technology Management*, **39**, 4, 18–29.

Cooper, R. and Press, M. (1995) *The design agenda, a guide to successful design management*. Chichester: John Wiley & Sons.

Craig, A. and Hart, S. (1992) Where to now in new product development research. *European Journal of Marketing*, **26**, 11, 1–49.

Crawford, C.M. (1994) *New Product Management*. Reading, MA: Addison-Wesley.

Cross, N. (1993) Science and design methodology: a review. *Research in Engineering Design*, **5**, 63–69.

Davies, H. and Hom, H. (1993) The impact of competitive structure abd technological environment on design management: a case study of the UK touring caravan industry. *Design Studies*, **14**, 4, 365–378.

Davis, R.E. (1996) Market analysis and segmentation issues for new consumer products. In: Rosenau, M.D.J., Griffin, A., Castellion, G. and Anschuetz, N. *The PDMA handbook of new product development*. New York: John Wiley & Sons, 35–49.

Davis, R.E. (1993) From experience: the role of market research in the development of new consumer products. *Journal of Product Innovation Management*, **10**, 309–317.

de Brentani, U. (2001) Innovative versus incremental new business services: different keys for achieving success. *Journal of Product Innovation Management*, **18**, 169–187.

de Brentani, U. (1996) Success factors in developing new business services. In: Hart, S. *New product development, a rereader.* London: The Dryden Press, 401–427.

de Brentani, U. (1989) Success and failure in new industrial services. *Journal of Product Innovation Management*, **6**, 239–258.

de Pree, M. (2001) Creative leadership. *Leader to Leader*, 20.

Dermody, J. and Hammer-Lloyd, S. (1995) Developing environmentally responsible new products: the challenge for the 1990s. In: Bruce, M. and Biemans, W.G. *Product development: meeting the challenge of the design-marketing interface.* Chichester, UK: John Wiley & Sons Ltd.

Design Council (2002) *Facts and figures on design in Britain 2002–03.* London: Design Council.

Dixon, J.R. and Duffey, M.R. (1990) The neglect of engineering design. *California Management Review*, **32**, winter, 9–22.

Dollinger, M.J. (1999) *Entrepreneurship strategy and resources.* Eaglewood Cliffs, NJ: Prentice Hall.

Donnellan, E. (1995) Changing perspectives on research methodology in marketing. *Irish Marketing Review-Dublin*, **8**, 81–90.

Dormer, P. (1993) *Design Since 1945.* London: Thames & Hudson.

Dougherty, D. and Bowman, E. (1995) The effects of organizational downsizing on product innovation. *California Management Review*, **37**, 4, 28–44.

Dumas, A. (1994) Building totems: metaphor-making in product development. *Design Management Journal*, winter, 71–82.

Dumas, A. and Mintzberg, H. (1991) Managing the form, function and fit of design. *Design Management Journal*, **2**, 3, 26–31.

Espey, J. (1991) When global markets get tough. *Chief Executive*, 71, 44ff.

Evamy, M. (1994) The train that lost its way. *Design*, May, 16–19.

Fairhead, J. (1988) *Design for corporate culture: how to build a design and innovation culture.* National Economic Development Office.

Faust, W. (1993) Cross-functional teams in design: a case study of the thermos thermal electric grill. *Design Management Journal*, fall, 28–33.

FitzGerald, N. Life and death in the world of brand. XXX Unilever magazine.

France, G., Kohen, S. and Mahieddine, Y. (2001) *Pulling together: making alliances work.* Ernst & Young.

Friedman, T.L. (2000) *The lexus and the olive tree.* New York: Anchor Books/Doubleday.

Fujimoto, T. (1991) Product integrity and the role of designer-as-integrator. *Design Management Journal,* spring, 29–34.

Fujimoto, T., Iansiti, M. and Clark, K.B. (1991) *External integration in product development.* Boston, MA: Harvard Business School Press.

Fuller-Love, N. and Cooper, Joan (2000) Deliberate versus emergent strategies: A case study of information technology in the Post Office. *International Journal of Information Management,* **2**, 3, 209–224.

Gaddis, P.O. (1959) The project manager. *Harvard Business Review,* May–June, 89–97.

Gadrey, J.F., Gallouj, S.L. and Weinstein, O. (1994) Innovation et R-D dans les services: des modalites originales, qui peuvent enrichir les conceptions industrielles. *Management of Services: A Multidisciplinary Approach.* Proceedings of the 3rd International Research Seminar in Service Management, Aix-en-Provence, France.

Gause, D.C. and Weinberg, G.M. (1989) *Exploring requirements, quality before design.* New York: Dorset House Publishing.

Goel, V. and Pirolli, P. (1992) The structure of design problem spaces. *Cognitive Science,* **16**, 395–429.

Goffee, R.J.G. (1996) What holds the modern company together? *Harvard Business Review,* November–October, 133–148.

Goffee, R. and Jones, G. (2000) Why should anyone be led by you? *Harvard Business Review,* September–October, 62–70.

Goffee, R. and Jones, G. (1998) *The character of a corporation, how your company's culture can make or break your business.* New York: HarperCollins.

Gorb, P. and Dumas, A. (1987) Silent design. *Design Studies,* **8**, 3, 150–156.

Grant, J. (2000) Goodbye, pork-pie hat. *Financial Times Weekend Magazine,* 25th November, 38–41.

Grant, R.M. (1991) *Contemporary strategy analysis: concepts, techniques, applications.* Cambridge, MA: Basil Blackwell.

Gray, R. (2001) Modifying NPD for a shrinking world. *Marketing,* 19th April, 39–40.

Griffin, A. and Hauser, J.R. (1996) Integrating R&D and marketing: a review and analysis of the literature. *Journal of Product Innovation Management,* **13**, 191–215.

Gurteen, D. (1998) Knowledge, creativity and innovation. *Journal of Knowledge Management,* **2**, 1, 5–13.

Haigh, D. (1996) *A review of current practice in brand valuation.* London: Institute of Practitioners in Advertising.

Hales, C. (1986) *Analysis of the engineering design process in an industrial context.* Cambridge: Cambridge University Press.

Hall, D. (2001) *Jump starting your business brain – win more, lose less and make money.* Cincinnati, OH: Brain Brew Books.

Hargadon, A. and Sutton, R.I. (2000) Building an innovation factory. *Harvard Business Review,* **78**, 3, 157–166.

Hart, S.J. and Service, L.M. (1988) The effects of managerial attitudes to design on company performance. *Journal of Marketing Management,* **4**, 2, 217–229.

Hart, S.J., Service, L.M. and Baker, M.J. (1989) Design orientation and market success. *Design Studies,* **10**, 2, 103–111.

Hatch, M.J. (1997) *Organization theory, modern symbolic and postmodern perspectives.* Oxford: Oxford University Press.

Hatch, M.J. (1993) The dynamics of organizational culture. *The Academy of Management Review,* **18**, 4, 657.

Hay, M. and Williamson, P. (1997) Good strategy: the view from below. *Long Range Planning,* **30**, 5, 651–664.

Hay, M. and Williamson, P. (1991) Strategic staircase: planning the capabilities required for success. *Long Range Planning,* **24**, 4, 36.

Heany, D.F. (1983) Degrees of product innovation. *Journal of Business Strategy,* spring, 3–14.

Heiss, B. and Fraser, E. (2000) Is your company ready to go global? *Communication World,* **17**, 6, 29–32.

Hem, L., de Chernatony, L. and Iversen, N.M. (2001) Factors influencing successful brand extension. Unpublished paper on www.interbrand.com.

Henke, J.W., Krachenberg, A.R. and Lyons, T.F. (1993) Cross-functional teams: good concept, poor implementation! *Journal of Product Innovation Management,* **10**, 216–229.

Henry, J. (1991) *Creative management.* London: Sage.

Henry, J. (1991) Making sense of creativity. In: Henry, J. *Creative management.* London: Sage, 3–11.

Higgins, J.M. (1996) A plan for innovation. *R&D Innovator,* **5**, 8.

Hipple, J., Harde, D., Wilson, S.A. and Michalski, J. (2001) Can corporate innovation champions survive? *Chemical Innovation,* November, 14–22.

Hofstede, G. (1991) *Cultures and organizations: the software of the mind.* New York: McGraw-Hill.

Hofstede, G. (1980) *Culture's consequences: international differences in workrelated values.* London: Sage.

Hollins, G. and Hollins, B. (1991) *Total design, managing the design process in the service sector.* London: Pitman.

Holt, K. (1987) *Innovation: a challenge to the engineer.* Amsterdam: Elsevier.

Hultink, E.J. and Robben, H.S.J. (1996) Measuring product development success and failure. In: Rosenau, M.D.J., Griffin, A., Castellion, G. and Anschuetz, N. *The PDMA handbook of new product development.* New York: John Wiley & Sons, 455–461.

Idenburg, P.J. (1993) Four styles of strategy development. *Long Range Planning,* **26**, 6, 123.

Johne, A. and Storey, C. (1998) New service development: a review of the literature and annotated bibliography. *European Journal of Marketing,* **32**, 314, 184–251.

Johne, F.A. and Harborne, P. (1985) How large commercial banks manage product innovation. *International Journal of Bank Marketing,* **3**, 1, 54–70.

Jones, T. (1997) *New product development, an introduction to a multifunctional process.* Oxford: Butterworth-Heinemann.

Judge, P. (2001) In my opinion. *Management Today,* August, 14.

Justice, L. (2001) Predicting the success of your web site. *Design Management Journal,* summer, 63–69.

Kapferer, J.-N. (1997) *Strategic Brand Management.* London: Kogan Page.

Kaplan, R.S. and Norton, D.P. (1992) The balanced scorecard: measures that drive performance. *Harvard Business Review,* **70**, 1, 71–79.

Kaplan, S.M. (1999) Discontinuous innovation and the growth paradox. *Strategy & Leadership,* **27**, 2, 16–21.

Karger, D. (1960) *The new product.* New York: Industrial Press.

Kelley, T. (2001) Prototyping is the shorthand of innovation. *Design Management Journal,* summer, 35–42.

Kemp, R. (1993) *The European high speed rail network.* Manchester: GEC Alsthom Transport.

Kemp, R. (1993) *The Eurostar project,* Manchester: GEC Alsthom Transport.

Kennedy, M. (2001) Building a service innovation engine. *Telecommunications Americas,* **35**, 6, 24.

Khurana, A. and Rosenthal, S.R. (1997) Integrating the fuzzy front end of new product development. *Sloan Management Review,* winter, 103–120.

Kim, C.W. and Mauborgne, R. (2000) Knowing a winning business idea when you see one. *Harvard Business Review,* September–October, 129–137.

Kirton, M.J. (1980) The way people approach problems. *Planned Innovation,* **3**, 51–54.

Klein, N. (2001) *No logo.* London: Flamingo.

Kleinschmidt, E.J. and Cooper, R.G. (1988) The performance impact of an international orientation on product innovation. *European Journal of Marketing*, **22**, 10, 56ff.

Kotler, P. and Rath, A. (1984) Design: a powerful but neglected strategic tool. *Journal of Business Strategy*, **5**, 2, 16–21.

Kroeber, A.L. and Kluckhohn, F. (1952) *Culture: a critical review of concepts and definitions*. Peabody Museum Papers, **47**, 181.

Kuczmarski, T.D. (2001) Five fatal flaws of innovation metrics. *Marketing Management*; **10**, 1, 34–39.

Kuczmarski, T. (1998) Tools@work: The CEO innovation mindset test. *Journal for Quality and Participation*, **21**, 6, 48–49.

Kuczmarski, T.D. (1988) *Managing New Products*. Englewood Cliffs, NJ: Prentice Hall.

Kuczmarski & Associates Inc (1995) *Winning new products and services for the 1990s*. Chicago: Kuczmarski & Associates Inc.

Lane Keller, K., Sternthal, B. and Tybout, A. (2002) The questions you need to ask about your brand. *Harvard Business Review*, September, 3–8.

Leifer, R., McDermott, C.M., Colarelli O'Conner, G., Peters, L.S., Rice, M. and Veryzer, R.W. (2000) *Radical innovation – how mature companies can outsmart upstarts*. Boston, MA: Harvard Business School Press.

Leonard-Barton, D. (1992) Core capabilities and core rigidities: a paradox in managing new product development. *Strategic Management Journal*, **13**, 111–125.

Leonard-Barton, D. (1991) Inanimate integrators: a block of wood speaks. *Design Management Journal*, summer, 61–67.

Leonard, D. and Rayport, J.F. (1997) Spark innovation through empathic design. *Harvard Business Review*, **75**, 6, 102–108.

Lewis, H., Gertsakis, J., Grant, T., Morelli, N. and Sweatman, A. (2001) *design + environment – a global guide to designing greener goods*. Sheffield, UK: Greenleaf Publishing.

Littler, D., Leverick, F. and Bruce, M. (1995) Factors affecting the process of collaborative product development: a study of UK manufacturers of information and communications technology products. *Journal of Product Innovation Management*, **12**, 1.

Lookwood, T. (2000) Designing automobiles for global value: ten market trends. *Design Management Journal*, fall.

Lord, M.D., Mandel, S.W. and Wager, J.D. (2002) Spinning out a star. *Harvard Business Review*, June, 5–11.

Lorenz, C. (1990) *The design dimension*. Oxford: Basil Blackwell.

Lovins, A.B., Lovins, L.t. and Hawken, P. (2001) *A road map for natural capitalism*. In: Henry, J. (ed.) *Creative management*. London: Sage, vol. 2.

Machlis, S. (1996) Rapid prototyping weeds out bad designs early. *Design News*, August, 70–74.

Mackenzie, D. (1997) *Green design, design for the environment*. London: Laurence King.

MacKenzie, G. (1996) *Orbiting the giant hairball*. OpusPocus Publishing.

Mahajan, V. and Wind, J. (1992) New product models: practice, shortcomings and desired improvements. *Journal of Product Innovation Management*, **9**, 128–139.

Mainemelis, C. (2001) When the muse takes it all: a model for the experience of timelessness in organisations. *Academy of Management Review*, **26**, 4, 548–565.

Markides, C. (1999) *All the right moves*. Boston, MA: Harvard Business School Press.

Martin, C.R.J. and Horne, D.A. (1995) Level of success inputs for service innovations in the same firm. *International Journal of Service Industry Management*, **6**, 4.

Martin, J. (1995) Ignore your customers. *Fortune*, 1st May, 83–89.

Matathia, I. and Salzman, M. (1999) *Next? A vision of our lives in the future*. London: HarperCollins.

Maylor, H. (1996) *Project management*. London: Pitman.

McGrath, M.E. (1996) *Setting the PACE in product development*. Newton, MA: Butterworth-Heinemann.

Mintzberg, H. (1990) The design school: reconsidering the basic premises of strategic management. *Strategic Management Journal*, **11**, 171–195.

Monge, P. and Fulk, J. (1999) Communication technology for global network organizations. In: DeSanctis, G. and Fulk, J. (eds) *Shaping organization form: communication, connection, and community*. London: Sage, 71–100.

Morris, P.W.G. (1994) *The management of projects*. London: Thomas Telford.

Moss Kanter, R. (1989) *When giants learn to dance*. New York: Simon & Schuster.

Moss Kanter, R. (1985) *The change masters*. Carmichael: Touchstone Books.

Nadler, G. (1991) Design teams: breakthrough for effectiveness. *Design Management Journal*, spring, 10–19.

Naslund, B. (1986) Financial innovations. A comparison with R&D in physical products. EFI research paper/report, Stockholm.

Nonaka, I. (1991) The knowledge-creating company. *Harvard Business Review*, **69**, 6, 96–1044.

Norman, D.A. (1988) *The psychology of everyday things*. New York: Basic Books.

Oakley, M. (1990) Assembling and managing a design team. In: Oakley, M. (ed.) *Design management, a handbook of issues and methods*. Oxford: Blackwell Reference.

Oakley, M. (1990) Policies, objectives and standards. In: Oakley, M. (ed.) *Design management, a handbook of issues and methods.* Oxford: Blackwell Reference.

Oakley, M. (1984) *Managing product design.* London: Weidenfeld & Nicolson.

Olson, E.M., Cooper, R. and Slater, S.F. (1998) Design strategy and competitive advantage. *Business Horizons*, **41**, 2, 55–61.

Olson, E.M., Walker, O.C. and Ruekert, R.W. (1995) Organizing for effective new product development: the moderating role of product innovativeness. *Journal of Marketing*, **59**, January, 48–62.

Owen, I. (1990) Industry and design. In: Gorb, P. (ed.) *Design management.* London: Architectural Design and Technology Press.

Papanek, V. (1991) *Design for the real world.* London: Thames & Hudson.

Pavitt, J. (2000) brand.new. London: V&A Publishing.

Perry, T.S. (1995) Designing a culture for creativity. *Research-Technology Management*, March–April, 14–16.

Peters, T. (1995) Design is. . .. *Design Management Journal*, winter, 29–33.

Peters, T. (1994) Uncork a grand design. *Independent on Sunday*, 29th May.

Peters, T. and Waterman, R.H. (1982) *In search of excellence.* New York: Harper & Row.

Petroski, H. (1997) Designed to fail. *American Scientist*, **85**, 5, 412–416.

Pilditch, J. (1989) *Winning ways.* London: Mercury Business Books.

Pilditch, J. (1987) What makes a winning company. In: Walker, D. and Henry, J. (eds) *Managing innovation.* London: Sage.

Plant, R. (2000) *ecommerce: formulation of strategy.* London: Financial Times/Prentice Hall.

Plant, R. and Willcocks, L. (2000) E-branding: leadership strategies. http://www.brandchannel.com/papers_review.asp?sp_id=58 (abstract).

Plsek, Paul E. The creativity process from. 96. http://www.directed creativity.com/pages/WPModels.html

Polanyi, M. (1983) *The tacit dimension.* Gloucester, MA: Peter Smith.

Porter, M.E. (1980) *Competitive strategy, techniques for analyzing industries and competitors.* New York: Free Press.

Prather, C.W. and Gundry, L.K. (1995) *Blueprints for innovation.* New York: American Management Association.

Prather, C.W. and Turrell, M.C. (2002) Involve everyone in the innovation process. *Research-Technology Management*, September–October, 13–16.

Pringle, H. and Thompson, M. (1999) *Brand spirit: how cause related marketing builds brands*. New York: John Wiley & Sons.

Prokesch, S.E. (1997) Unleashing the power of learning: an interview with British petroleum's John Browne. *Harvard Business Review*, **75**, 5, 146–168.

Purcell, J. Raising finance. *Innovation Business*, **28**, 13.

Quintas, P., Lefrere, P. and Jones, G. (1997) Knowledge management: a strategic agenda. *Long Range Planning*, **30**, 3, 385–391.

Repenning, N.P. (2002) A simulation-based approach to understanding the dynamics of innovation implementation. *Organization Science*, **13**, 2, 109–127.

Rettig, M. (1994) Prototyping for tiny fingers. *Communications of the ACM*, **37**, 4, 21–27.

Robinson, A.G. and Stern, S. (1997) *Corporate creativity – how innovation and improvement actually happen*. San Francisco: Berrett-Koehler.

Rock, A. (1992) Strategies versus tactics from a venture capitalist. In: Schulman, W.A. and Stevenson, H. *The entrepreneurial venture*. Boston, MA: Harvard Business School Press, 215–221.

Roellig, L. (2001) Designing global brands: critical lessons. *Design Management Journal*, fall.

Ross Ashby, W. (1964) *An introduction to cybernetic*. London: Chapman & Hall.

Rothwell, R. (1992) Successful industrial innovation: critical factors for the 1990s. *R&D Management*, **22**, 3, 221–239.

Rugman, A. (2000) *The end of globalization*. London: Random House.

Rugman, A. and Hodgetts, R. (2001) The end of global strategy. *European Management Journal*, **19**, 4, 333–334.

Rumizen, M.C. (1998) Report on the second comparative study of knowledge creation conference. *Journal of Knowledge Management*, **2**, 1, 77–81.

Sanchez, R. and Sudharshan, D. (1993) Real-time market research. *Marketing Intelligence & Planning*, **11**, 7, 29–38.

Schein, E.H. (1992) *Organisational culture and leadership*. San Francisco: Jossey-Bass.

Schrage, M. (2000) *Serious play – how the world's best companies simulate to innovate*. Boston, MA: Harvard Business School Press.

Schrage, M. (1993) The culture(s) of prototyping. *Design Management Journal*, winter, 55–65.

Schumpeter, J.A. (1976) *Capitalism, socialism, and democracy*. London: Routledge.

Seltzer, K. and Bentley, T. (1999) *The creative age*. London: Demos.

Sentance, A. and Clark, J. (1997) *The contribution of design to the UK economy*. London: Design Council.

Service, L., Hart, S.J. and Baker, M.J. (1989) *Scotland*. Edinburgh: Design Council Scotland.

Simon, H.A. (1992) *Sciences of the artificial*. Cambridge, MA: MIT Press.

Sisodia, R. (1992) Competitive advantage through design. *Journal of Business Strategy*, **13**, 6, 33–40.

Slevin, D.P and Covin, J.G. (1997) Strategy formation patterns, performance and the significance of context. *Journal of Management*, **23**, 2, 189–209.

Sloan, A.P. (1963) *My years with General Motors*. London: Sedgwick & Jackson.

Slusher, A.E. and Ebert, R.J. (1992) Prototyping for managing engineering design process. In: Susman, P. (ed.) *Integrating design and manufacturing for competitive advantage*. Oxford: Oxford University Press, 123–139.

Smith, M. (2001) Sorry, that's too interesting . . .. *Financial Times*, 18th December, 15.

Smith, P.G. and Reinertsen, D.G. (1995) *Developing products in half the time*. New York: Van Nostrand Reinhold.

Snead, G.L. and Wycoff, J. (2001) Stimulating innovation with collaboration rooms. www.thinksmart.com

Snead, G.L. and Wycoff, J. (1996) *To do, doing, done! A creative approach to managing projects and effectively finishing what matters most*. New York: Simon & Schuster.

Sowrey, T. (1987) *The generation of ideas for new products*. London: Kogan Page.

Sparrow, S. (1987) Design: in-house or agency. *Industrial Marketing Digest*, **12**, 2, 35–39.

Storey, C. and Kelly, D. (2001) Measuring the performance of new service development activities. *The Service Industries Journal*, April.

Sundbo, J. (1997) Management of innovation in services. *The Service Industries Journal*, **17**, 3, 432–455.

Takeuchi, H. and Nonaka, I. (1986) The new product development game. *Harvard Business Review*, January–February, 137–146.

Temple, P. and von Stamm, B. (1996) *Design and ISO 9000*. Preliminary report to the Design Council.

Terrill, C.A. and Middlebrooks, A.G. (1996) Service development. In: Rosenau, M.D.J., Griffin, A., Castellion, G. and Anschuetz, N. *The PDMA handbook of new product development*. New York: John Wiley & Sons, 315–331.

Tether, C.S. (2002) Who co-operates for innovation and why – an empirical analysis. *Research Policy*, **31**, 947–967.

Thackara, J. (1997) *European design prize winners! How today's successful companies innovate by design*. Aldershot, UK: Gower.

Tidd, J. (1993) Technological innovation, organizational linkages and strategic degrees of freedom. *Technology Analysis & Strategic Management*, **5**, 3, 273–283.

Tidd, J., Bessant, J. and Pavitt, K. (1997) *Managing innovation; integrating technological, market and organisational change.* Chichester, UK: John Wiley & Sons. (Also 2nd edn, 2001.)

Titteron, D. (2001) Spotlight on workplace atmosphere. Sunday Times Enterprise Network (STEN) website. www.sunday-times.co.uk/enterprisenetwork

Turner, R. (2000) Design and business: who calls the shots? *Design Management Journal*, fall, 42–47.

Tushman, M.L. and Anderson, P. (1986) Technological discontinuities and organisational environments. *Administrative Science Quarterly*, **31**, 439–465.

Ulijn, J.O.D., Weggeman, M., Ledlow, G. and Hall, H.T. (2000) Innovation, corporate strategy, and cultural context: What is the mission for international business communication? *Journal of Business Communication*, **37**, 3, 293–316.

Ulrich, K.T. and Eppinger, S.D. (1995) *Product design and development.* Singapore: McGraw-Hill.

Upshaw, L.B. (2001) Building a brand.com. *Design Management Journal*, winter, 34–39.

Upshaw, L.B. and Taylor, E. (2000) *The masterbrand mandate.* Chichester: John Wiley & Sons.

Urban, G.L. and Hauser, J.R. (1993) *Design and marketing of new products.* Eaglewood Cliffs, NJ: Prentice Hall.

Utterback, J.M. (1994) *Mastering the dynamics of innovation: how companies can seize opportunities in the face of technological change.* Cambridge, MA: Harvard Business School Press.

Vishwanath, V. and Mark, J. (1997) Your brand's best strategy. *Harvard Business Review*, May–June, 123–129.

von Stamm, B. (2002) *Innovation in turbulent times.* London: Innovation Exchange, London Business School.

von Stamm, B. (2001) Innovation best practice and future challenges, a study into innovation best practice in Innovation Exchange member companies and the literature. Innovation Exchange, London Business School.

von Stamm, B. (1999) Creativity is an individual act. Interview with John Hunt conducted for the Innovation Exchange, London Business School.

von Stamm, B. (1999) The effects of context and complexity in new product development. Doctoral thesis, London Business School.

von Stamm, B. (1999) Interview with Jon Leach conducted for the Innovation Exchange, London Business School.

von Stamm, B. (1999) Interview with Ralph Buschow conducted for the Innovation Exchange, London Business School.

von Stamm, B. (1997) Whose design is it? The use of external designers. *Design Journal*, **1**, 1, 41–53.

von Stamm, B. and Riley, D. (2002) Innovation in turbulent times. Unpublished report to members of the Innovation Exchange.

Voss, C., Johnston, R.J., Silvestro, R., Fitzgerald, L. and Brignall, T. (1992) Measurement of innovation and design performance in services. *Design Management Journal*, winter, 40–6.

Walker, D. (1990) Managers and designers: two tribes at war? In: Oakley, M. (ed.) *Design management, a handbook of issues and methods*. Oxford: Blackwell Reference.

Wallas, G. (1926) *The art of thought*. New York: Harcourt Brace-Jovanovich.

Walsh, V., Roy, R., Bruce, M. and Potter, S. (1992) *Winning by design, technology, product design and international competitiveness*. Oxford: Blackwell.

Weick, K.E. (1979) *The social psychology of organizing*. Reading, MA: Addison-Wesley.

Weisburg, R.W. (1986) *Creativity, genius and other myths*. New York: Freeman.

Wheelwright, S.C. and Clark, K.B. (1993) *Leading product development, the senior manager's guide to creating and shaping the enterprise*. New York: Free Press.

Williams, G. (2000) *Branded? Products and their personalities*. London: V&A Publications.

Williamson, M. (1994) Becoming a world power. *CIO*, **7**, 16, 40ff.

Wood, B.D. (2000–2001) The globalization question. *Europe*, 402, 12–14.

Wright, I. (1998) *Design methods in engineering and product design*. London: McGraw-Hill.

Zien, K.A. and Buckler, S.A. (1997) From experience: dreams to market: crafting a culture of innovation. *Journal of Product Innovation Management*, **14**, 4, 274–287.

Zuckerman, A. (2001) Managing global logistics operations. *Transportation & Distribution*, **42**, 6, GL4–GL9.

Index